THE YELLOW FARMHOUSE COOKBOOK

ALSO BY CHRISTOPHER KIMBALL

THE COOK'S BIBLE

THE
YELLOW
FARMHOUSE
COOKBOOK

Christopher Kimball

1837

LITTLE, BROWN AND COMPANY

BOSTON NEW YORK LONDON

First Edition

Recipe for Dewey Buns from *The Breakfast Book* by Marion Cunningham.
Copyright © 1987 by Marion Cunningham.
Reprinted by permission of Alfred A. Knopf, Inc.
Pillsbury Bake-Off® Contest recipes for Southern Pecan Bars and Blueberry Boy-Bait
used with permission of The Pillsbury Company.
Bake-Off® is a registered trademark of The Pillsbury Company.

Library of Congress Cataloging-in-Publication Data
Kimball, Christopher.
The yellow farmhouse cookbook / Christopher Kimball. — 1st ed.
p.   cm.
Includes index.
ISBN 0-316-49699-5
1. Cookery, American.   2. Low budget cookery.   I. Title.
TX715.K449   1998
641.5973 — dc21   98-17545

10   9   8   7   6   5   4   3

MV-NY

Book design by Julia Sedykh

Scratchboard illustrations by Doug Rugh
Line drawings by John Burgoyne

Printed in the United States of America

For Marie Briggs, Floyd Bentley,

and Charles Bentley, Jr.

Quit not certainty for hope.

— ALDACE W. NEWTON

Clarendon, Vermont

Contents

Acknowledgments

THIS COOKBOOK is a group effort, one that involved the goodwill and hard work of many people. First and foremost, my wife, Adrienne, has cooked virtually all of the recipes in this book as part of the recipe testing process. She is an excellent cook and also a perceptive editor. Her insights have been both apt and welcome. My test cook, Jeanne Maguire, evolved into a full partner on this project, reworking and contributing recipes that she developed on her own. I could not have completed this book without her. A particular note of thanks to Jean Eisenhart, from our small town in Vermont, who shared many family recipes with me, especially her Aunt Nellie Newton's cream pie, which I have been trying to acquire for over a decade. A very special thanks to Junior Bentley, the farmer I worked for as a boy, who was kind enough to share many stories from our town as well as recipes from Marie Briggs, our town baker. He also introduced me to farm life, teaching me to milk a cow, use a corn knife, change the clutch on a Farmall, and throw a bale of hay. My mother, Mary Alice, has also been a great help, sharing both stories from her childhood on a farm in Virginia and her extensive knowledge of country living.

Clifford McKee, a neighbor, lent me a family diary that spanned ten years during the mid-nineteenth century. This was helpful in getting a feel for old-fashioned farmhouse life. Bill Haggerty was good enough to share a videotape made by his brother Steve that recorded many of the stories told by some of our town old-timers, some of whom have since passed away. Jim Link was good enough to put down on paper some of his favorite town anecdotes and share his collection of town photographs. Others, including Susie and Valerie de Peyster, Dave Trachte, Sonny Skidmore, Tom and Nancy Bochiochi, Susan Knapp from Hick's Orchard, Darryl Brown, and Dean Bishop also shared their stories. In addition, Joe Speiser was a great help in searching out cookware to be tested for this book.

My colleagues at *Cook's Illustrated* have been a source of both help and inspiration, from the best method for making cornbread to testing various methods for prebaking pie crusts. A special thanks to John Willoughby for his assistance and friendship, especially for sharing his research and extensive culinary knowledge. Thanks also to Pam Anderson, Mark Bittman, Eva Katz, Jack Bishop, Adam Reid, Mary Ellen Driscoll, Stephanie Lyness, Susan Logozzo, Annie Yamanaka, and Dawn Yanagihara. Shirley Corriher has been generous with her time and knowledge of kitchen science. My agent, Angela Miller, has been invaluable. My editor at Little Brown, Jennifer Josephy, has been both a treasured critic and cheerful supporter; many thanks to the book's designer, Julia Sedykh, for bringing the spirit of the manuscript to life. I also owe a great debt of gratitude to Amy Klee, my art director at *Cook's Illustrated,* and her husband, Greg, for design assistance. Many thanks to Kelley Caslin for her help in the kitchen.

Finally, a very special thanks to Marion Cunningham for sharing her recipes, her friendship, and her limitless enthusiasm for American home cooking.

About the Recipes

I MAKE NO CLAIMS of authenticity for these recipes, since old farmhouse "receipts" need a great deal of updating and reworking for the modern kitchen. I have taken the liberty of including ingredients, olive oil in particular, which were never used in a farmhouse kitchen. Most, however, are in the spirit of farmhouse cooking, using simple ingredients simply prepared. That being said, many recipes were culled from neighbors and also from local cookbooks and other materials available at our town library. In addition, I did much research on European cooking, primarily the cuisines of Germany, Eastern Europe, and Britain, in an effort to explore the origins of many farmhouse dishes such as dumplings, puddings, stews, and the like.

As in the pages of *Cook's Illustrated* and also in my first book, *The Cook's Bible,* my approach is to find the best method for preparing a particular dish. With some recipes, baking and roasting for example, this requires a great deal of testing and I have provided my test results in the recipe introductions. Other recipes, however, are simpler and more a matter of taste than technique and thus are less heavily annotated. I have also included equipment ratings and food tastings where appropriate.

In *The Cook's Bible,* I called for kosher salt, which is my salt of choice. However, for this book I used regular table salt, since that is more common and is in keeping with farmhouse cooking. If you prefer to use kosher salt, use about 50 percent more salt than called for in the recipe. Also note that for many dishes, baking being an obvious exception, salt levels are only approximate. Please taste the dish before serving to check for salt level as well as for the proper amounts of other seasonings. In my opinion, insufficient use of salt is perhaps the single greatest mistake by home cooks.

Also be aware that cooking times are approximate since each stovetop, oven, skillet, or saucepan is different. When cooking with a heavy cast iron Dutch oven, for example, the heat retention is vastly different than with a thin gauge stainless steel pan. When baking, start checking the dish halfway through the specified oven time to check on its progress and to see if it needs to be turned in the oven for even browning. Also remember to use plenty of heat when sautéing. Home cooks are afraid of getting skillets really hot, a necessary requirement when browning meats. Restaurant cooks have no such reservations.

I have assumed that most farmhouse kitchens are rather modest and therefore no expensive equipment is necessary to make the recipes in this book. You do not need a food processor or an expensive standing mixer but you will need an electric hand-held mixer, a blender, and a hand-turned food mill. (I list recipe variations for both food processors and standing mixers where appropriate.) I strongly recommend that you purchase a large cast iron Dutch oven, the most used and best piece of cookware in my kitchen, and also a 9- or 10-inch cast iron skillet. For a complete list of kitchen equipment, see pages 28 to 33.

Finally, these recipes are family food, not designed for extravagant entertaining. In the long tradition of farmhouse cookery, they are modest, practical fare but, I hope, also delicious.

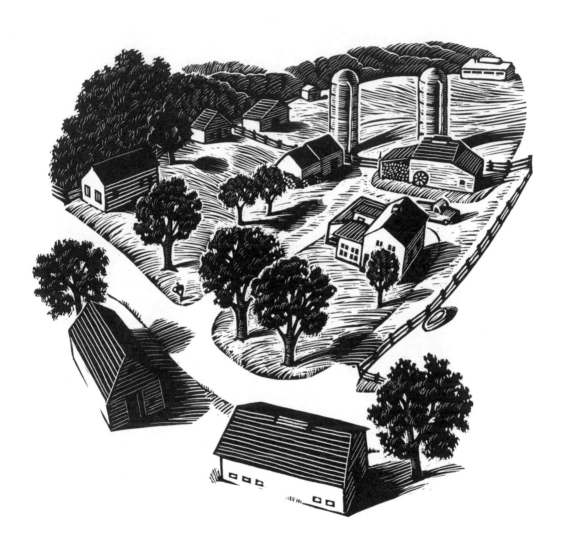

About the Yellow Farmhouse

THE SMALL YELLOW FARMHOUSE described in this book still exists, located just off the main road in a small town in Vermont. It was part of a large working farm originally owned by Fred Bentley, with three large barns, a corn crib, a sap house, an outhouse, a pigsty, and a small yellow shed which was used through the 1950s and '60s as housing for the farmhands. Although the shed now abandoned, there are still faded green workshirts hanging from pegs, curtains on the windows, an old stove, and mattresses stacked by one wall. It's as if the occupants went out one morning expecting to come back to wash up before supper and never did.

In 1955, our family built a small cabin on a 20-acre piece of side hill that was part of the old Ford farm. It started as a summer and weekend retreat, but a few years later we purchased the Lomberg farm and raised pigs and Black Angus with the help of a local couple, Bernie and Lucy Squires, who occupied the small farmhouse and did the chores when we weren't there. Since the farm included good bottom land running down to the Green River, my mother named our enterprise Green River Farm, the brand name we used when selling our sausage to local restaurants. We named it Whole Hog sausage, since we used even the prime parts of the pig to make our links.

During summers, when I wasn't doing chores on our farm, I worked for Junior Bentley, who leased a long red barn where we milked about 25 head twice each day, all Holsteins, but spent most of our time haying, fixing equipment, or feeding the many horses that were pastured around town. However, the yellow farmhouse was the center of this activity, since it was the home of Marie Briggs, the de facto town baker, and her common-law husband, Floyd Bentley, as well as Junior, who was Floyd's first cousin. Dinner was served promptly at noon each day, all the farmhands crowding around the table for a roast, baking powder biscuits, milk gravy, potatoes, boiled greens, homemade anadama bread, and a good dessert: pound cake, molasses cookies, or once in a great while, a fruit pie.

If you were to visit the old yellow farmhouse today, you would see that the original front door of the house has gone out of service. A side entrance, which is closer to the back barn, was in use during my years on the farm, but has also lost favor, the entrance now being a door cut into the back pantry. The old green Kalamazoo wood stove is still in the front room, although no longer connected to the chimney. It's still in good shape, with a working foot pedal that pops open the oven door, a water reservoir, and four burners. The parlor seems smaller today than it did back in the 1950s. The faded green sofa where old Floyd used to hunker down with a cigarette hanging from his lower lip is gone, as is the sink with the hand pump (the well is just outside by the porch) and the dining table covered with red and white checkered oilcloth, which was in use all day either for eating, knead-

ing bread, or preparing dinner. It was a busy room, never empty of visitors at any hour, really the town center for many decades. It is quiet now, although I remember the stories told in the small parlor, tales that filled the room with a special cadence, a flash of wit, a drawn-out adjective that spoke to the uncertainties of country living. Perhaps I remember most fondly the smell of that small parlor, the ripe scent of yeast, molasses, fresh bread, green wood, maple syrup, wood smoke, and pickled meats, a heady perfume that seeped into the wallpaper and floorboards and that remains today. It was a dark, still room, even in summer, since the closed windows were often steamed from the simmering water on the stove. It was a world submersed in half light, visitors appearing suddenly from the outside without warning, the sun at their backs, their approach having gone unnoticed.

Marie Briggs was a short woman but sturdy, of good Vermont stock, with graying hair always turned in a bun, thick black-frame glasses, and sturdy black shoes. Like a well-conditioned athlete, she kept a steady pace all day, taking only two breaks, one for noon dinner and the other at four o'clock for tea, served with warm slabs of just-baked country bread spread with a thick layer of rich yellow butter. The farmhands included Herbie, a large bull of a man who could flick a bale of hay up on the back of a pickup and then grin, his gap-tooth smile a familiar trademark. But Herbie also liked to cut corners. He was known to sit in front of that old Kalamazoo with the fuel door open, a log sticking halfway out, and as it burned down, shove it a little farther in until the door could be closed. Others would come and go over the years, including farmhands such as the gangly Onie, or Junior's half sister Louise King, who helped Marie with the baking, and Wally, who was always in a hurry when he spoke, spewing words carelessly as if they had no meaning. But the two dogs were there every day, the overweight mongrel Bonnie and Dixie, the skittish collie. Of course, guests came and went by the dozen, people checking in on their way in or out of town.

About twelve years ago, my wife and I bought the old Tikander farm over on the west side of town (the Green River Farm was sold in the 1970s) and built a small yellow farmhouse of our own. We keep bees and grow both hay and corn. Our four children spend the summers there, much the way I did back in the 1950s and '60s. We explore old cellar holes and caves, go swimming in the Baptist hole in the Green River, take a walk through the Moravian cemetery after dinner, or spend the afternoon up at the pond hunting frogs. I'm glad to say that the town hasn't changed much, although both Floyd and Marie have passed on, Junior Bentley being the one surviving member of that extended family. He fills the barns every year with hay and keeps horses and cattle. He now lives about a mile up the road at his father's place, not too far down from the gravel pit. I would guess that he is in his seventies, but he can outwork most people I know. He is not a big man, but wiry and with plenty of staying power. He likes a good meal, and my wife and I invite him over to the house when we can, especially Sunday evenings in the summer. Then he tells some of the old stories, although, like most Vermonters, he is not forthcoming about the past. He misses the kitchen hops and church socials, I think, when you could grab a girl and hold her tight and get something good to eat. But I would bet that on many nights he dreams of cows coming down off the mountain for the afternoon milking, the dull clank of the bells, and the sound of the generator starting up in the milk house. While he shares a story, many of which are recorded in this book, I bake a loaf of Marie's anadama bread or a dozen of her buttermilk doughnuts. We each have our work to do and we know how to do it. It has always been that way on farms. Nobody stops to say "good job" or to slap you on the back. When Marie's bread came out just right or her baked custard was light and tender, it was simply eaten along with the rest of the meal and quietly appreciated. This is the unwritten code of the farmhouse: an expectation of hard work and a reliance on others to do their jobs tempered by modesty and an interest in the well-being of the community. In hard times, these were necessary traits for survival, but now that times have changed, I think that we could do worse than to take a moment to stop by the yellow farmhouse, take a seat at the table, backs warmed by the old green Kalamazoo, and share the food and the stories. Marie and Floyd and Junior wouldn't have thanked you for stopping by but they would have nonetheless been glad of your company.

THE YELLOW FARMHOUSE COOKBOOK

The Country Kitchen

IN 1938, MY MOTHER spent a summer in a Quaker work camp near
Dayton, Tennessee, an area that was still hard hit by the Depression. She
became friendly with two local girls who invited her back to their parents'
home, a board shack with snakes under the front porch and holes in the floorboards. The father worked for the TVA, barely making a living, and his wife
looked poorly, but she baked a cake for my mother; they dressed up in their
best, and were proud to have her over. It was a white cake and my mother still
remembers the small red ants that covered the icing like jimmies on an ice
cream cone. She smiled, took a great big bite, and, as she often told me when
I was a kid, "The ants were small, so they didn't taste like much." But she was
touched by their kindness, and in many ways it was the best piece of cake she
ever had. It is her fondest memory, a house of memories in rural Tennessee.

For me, the memory house in our town sits right up by the old dirt road,
heading up to an almost impassable track over the mountain where, on a
cold morning, the old-timers claim they could see "forty smokes." Today there
are just a few houses remaining, the rest surviving only as overgrown cellar
holes. The house is now owned by Junior Bentley as it was by his father before
him. It has a new dull red metal roof with freshly painted white clapboards

although the milk-paint green window trim is chipped and flaking and the roofline sags a bit, hinting of the sap house next door, which has dropped down into the undergrowth. It sits just off the road, weeds growing up around the foundation, a laundry line and burn barrel just out back and a small open-faced garage set twenty feet to one side, old license plates — yellow, brown, and black — nailed to one side going back to 1927. The garage also contains the usual odds and ends, including tension springs, an old sign announcing a school budget vote at 7:30 P.M., five-gallon plastic buckets of Hydra Tranz transmission fluid, disconnected lawnmower handles with a metal pipe running between the ends of the fork to hold up a reel of barbed wire, a large galvanized tub, an eight-ton hydraulic jack, and a faded sign nailed just under the eaves that advertises Vermont Mutual Fire Insurance.

Like most old-time Vermont homes, this one is entered through a porch since the original front door is abandoned, hanging at a broken angle in its frame and covered over with a large spray of stinging nettles. The unheated entryway is filled with a wide freezer, a wooden cupboard painted white, an old leather halter, a brown and yellow floral print easy chair, three ears of dried corn nailed to the wall, and one horseshoe, hung facing downward. Through the screen door and then the back door, you wend your way back through the kitchen, down a short hallway, and then back into a dark living room, where Junior sits in an old green armchair, surrounded by a calendar from the local lumber company, the obligatory mounted buck, and a large print of a red

barn in the early morning with a pair of horses being groomed outside.

One afternoon last summer, I stopped by with my older daughter, Whitney, and we found ourselves in the back room of that farmhouse facing its owner. At first, we didn't say much. Vermont conversations have a way of stopping and starting, since old-timers only speak when they have something to say. They don't feel obliged to fill in the long awkward silences as most city folk do. When he finally looked up he said, "Do you want to see the museum?" Now I had heard that he had a small room off the kitchen where he had assembled an odd collection of old farm implements and cookware over the years.

The first thing I noticed was a photo of Duke and Dan, the legendary team of horses that old Floyd Bentley used for mowing and raking hay as well as for horse draws. Just below the old photo there was a second-prize ribbon from the 1961 Bondville Fair in the 2,800-pound class. Some of Dan's white mane was trimmed off and is now kept in an envelope by the photograph. There were turkey bells that were tied onto the necks of domesticated birds to find their nests, a homemade piece of cast iron that was used to pull metal from fenceposts, two pieces of wood harnessed together with a chain, used to flail oats, a broadax for trimming logs into boards, a corn knife and a corn stabber for planting seed in the furrows, a hay knife for grabbing loose hay in a barn, a muzzle used to keep farm animals from eating hay while working, and the bell from the Number One schoolhouse, which was given to the kids one year for keeping up the town road so well. There were also Colic Drops, Numbers 1 and 2; a few old issues of *Hoard's Dairyman;* and a Jack Jumper for skiing (a seat on a post attached to one ski). A few kitchen implements also survived, including a tin dough machine (put the ingredients in, crank the handle a few times, and let the dough rise) and a small wooden finger-mounted peg used to husk a large pile of corn.

As we started to leave, Junior showed me a dusty black-and-white photo of Dixie, the high-strung collie that used to stand beside him in his old green Ford pickup. I instantly remembered summer evenings when I was just a kid, Junior and I driving back from the barn after milking, with Dixie, one leg on my thigh, nervously dripping saliva onto the dark green seat, the smell of manure on my boots, the baling twine, pliers, and can of Bag Balm sitting up on the dashboard. I was ten years old again, Dixie's hot breath in my ear, sitting high up in the cab of an old pickup. It is this simple memory, the window rolled down, the day's work done, looking forward to supper, that will grow in time, like my mom's piece of cake in a board shack in 1938. I like to imagine our children when they are grown, stopping to take a bite of a just-baked biscuit and remembering a warm summer afternoon, work done, heading home to our supper table. Then I smile, hopeful that my wife and I have filled each of them with enough homemade biscuits to nourish them long after the two of us are just a young couple in an old photograph on the wall of their memory house.

I PREFER kitchen tools like the well-worn farm implements in Junior Bentley's museum: ones that are simple and well made and that perform their task well. That doesn't always mean that I buy the cheapest model or refuse to consider the latest technological advances. I am motivated instead by what really works — and that may be a $42 instant-read thermometer or a simple $12 cast iron pan. I am not prone, however, to gadgets that clutter up kitchen drawers or to electric machines that take up more space than they are worth.

In writing this book, however, I made some ground rules about what a country cook is likely to have in the kitchen. After surveying what my Vermont neighbors have available, I decided to write recipes that did not require the use of an electric food processor or a mixer. I do call for an electric blender, however, for certain soups and sauces, since a food mill doesn't always do the trick. I have chosen cast iron for the basic cookware; it's cheap and since it retains heat so well, it is ideal for most cooking applications. After a year of constant cooking in cast iron, I now prefer it to any of the expensive cookware for any sort of sautéing, browning, or stewing. I also discovered that a well-seasoned cast iron pan will not react with acidic foods.

What follows is a discussion and comparison of the major cookware choices from saucepans to Dutch ovens to knives to thermometers. At the end of this chapter, however, I also provide a shopping list of items that you will need to make the recipes in this book, which is, by the way, a good back-to-basics inventory for any home kitchen.

Cast Iron

I recently stopped by my favorite cookware shop in Vermont and spent a half hour walking down the aisles, checking out new merchandise, and chatting with the owner, Joe, who not only knows a lot about pots and pans but is my local guide to the best pick-your-own orchards from sour cherries to blueberries, apples, strawberries, and raspberries. Unlike most kitchen shops, his carries a complete line of cast iron, up to ten different pieces; but he also carries the French Le Creuset pots as well. (These are made from enameled cast iron. Since a well-seasoned cast iron pot is nonreactive, I see no benefit in purchasing enameled cast iron, which sells for a whopping $120, while a five-quart cast iron Dutch oven from Lodge is just $28.) Without a doubt, cast iron cookware is the best bargain going and, for most applications, it is also the best choice.

The two most important features of any piece of cookware are heat conductivity and heat retention. Cast iron excels in both categories. Once a piece of cast iron is up to temperature, it retains heat well because of the properties of cast iron as well as the sheer weight and mass of the pan. An eight-inch cast iron pan weighs just over four pounds, yet a stainless steel skillet with an aluminum bottom weighs half as much, a bit over two pounds. This weight has an added benefit. Cast iron cookware never warps, unlike most of the thinner-gauge cookware available today. All of my stainless steel or anodized aluminum Dutch ovens and stockpots have warped bottoms, a serious problem when sautéing foods in butter or oil; the fat simply runs to the sides of the pan since the

center is higher. In addition, a cast iron pan heats evenly; there are no hot spots. The only drawback to cast iron is that since it is so good at retaining heat, the pan will not adjust rapidly to changes in temperature. However, since cast iron is not used for saucepans, just for skillets and Dutch ovens, this is not relevant. When making a custard in a saucepan, for example, a quick change of temperature is desirable if the mixture is overheating. But when sautéing or stewing, maintaining a constant temperature is more important. When browning meat for a stew, for instance, a cast iron Dutch oven is outstanding, since the pan will not cool off easily, providing plenty of heat for the browning process. Many pans will lose heat rapidly, and the meat is stewed rather than browned.

For country cooks, cast iron skillets and Dutch ovens are staples. Two hundred years ago, of course, there wasn't much else available. Cast iron was plentiful and cheap. That being said, good pots were highly regarded. Mary Washington, the mother of George Washington, regarded the disposition of her "iron kitchen furniture" after her death as worthy of serious consideration. Her will specified which pieces would go to which grandson or granddaughter. Part of her admiration for cast iron must have been that it was also durable, nonstick, and good for long slow cooking, since it retained heat and was not apt to burn food. If aluminum pans were available to a chuck wagon cook (cast aluminum cooking utensils were introduced around 1889), it is unlikely they would have curried much favor since timing would have been tricky, the pan being very sensitive to the heat of the fire or coals. For many country cooks, cast iron was the original Crock-Pot. While the adults, men and women, were outside all day working in the fields, dinner would cook slowly in a Dutch oven heated by coals. There were two ways to do this. One could start a fire in a pit, create a good bed of coals, place a Dutch oven full of beans or stew onto the coals, shovel coals and then dirt on top and let the food cook underground. About one third of the coals were placed under the oven and two thirds on the lid. A hole, often lined with rocks, was usually dug just a few feet from the fire so that the coals could be easily transferred. The other method was to simply place the Dutch oven on top of a bed of coals sitting on top of the ground and then add coals to the lid. But the pit helped retain heat, a useful technique for all-day cookery. (The top of these ovens had flat, rimmed lids, which held the coals in place and could do double duty as a griddle; they were turned upside down, placed on a few supports over a bed of hot coals, and then used to fry eggs or pancakes. Other models, however, including most of the Dutch ovens sold today, have domed lids. On the underside are concentric circles which force moisture to drip back onto the foods, a form of self-basting. These models are designed to be used in an oven.)

A "Dutch" oven is nothing more than a wide, deep pot, usually with a wire handle; it was originally manufactured with "ears" on the side (small, round tabs used to pick up the pot) and a top that had a lip around the edge. The latter design element was important in keeping the coals placed on the lid from falling off. One could bake biscuits, cobblers, stews,

beans, just about anything with this method. Some cooks also used it for baking bread and pies; others used it to braise steaks and roasts or cook rice, hominy, and oatmeal. It was, in the full sense of the word, an oven. It was also a key feature of chuck wagons, the mobile kitchens invented in 1866 by Charles Goodnight, who customized a government wagon. Photographs from the latter half of the nineteenth century show four or five huge Dutch ovens in use around a campfire, each one cooking a different dish.

I have read that, originally, the best cast iron came from Holland and the cast iron pots are therefore referred to as Dutch ovens. (However, there are plenty of other theories, one being that the Pennsylvania Dutch popularized the term.) These early pots were thick-walled and heavy, cast in dry sand molds. In the early eighteenth century, an Englishman, Abraham Darby, traveled to Holland to inspect the process and then developed a superior sand-casting technique, which yielded more refined pots. By the 1700s, his pots were being exported to the colonies. You can tell the difference between a pot made before 1750 and one after. The earlier models had a round projection, or seam, on the bottom of the pot (from the casting process), whereas later models had a thinner, less noticeable seam.

Of course, some of the cast iron pots were huge and were used indoors, hung from a brace attached to the fireplace and swung out over the fire for cooking. These models were different from the "bake ovens" and "camp Dutch ovens" described above, since they had no legs and no rimmed lid to hold coals for baking.

Other than weight, the only real drawback of cast iron is that it is considered "reactive" — that is, acidic foods can react with the metal, causing changes in flavor and color. When manufacturers were queried on this topic, they claimed that a well-seasoned cast iron pan is nonreactive. To test this theory, I simmered 28-ounce cans of crushed tomatoes for twenty minutes in three different pans: an old, well-seasoned cast iron skillet, a new but seasoned cast iron skillet, and a stainless steel skillet. I could detect no difference in flavor or color. I then added one third of a cup of white wine to each pan of tomatoes and simmered them for an additional ten minutes. Again, there were no off colors or flavors. However, it is a good idea to reseason a cast iron pan after exposing it to acidic ingredients, and I also suggest that you use a nonreactive skillet or pan when preparing a recipe very high in acid content such as pickled beets.

HOW TO SEASON CAST IRON COOKWARE

Most folks have an aversion to cast iron because it rusts easily, but more important, most home cooks have had little luck seasoning it. This is because the directions supplied by the manufacturer don't work. I just purchased two large skillets from Lodge, and their instructions state that the pan should be warmed, coated with shortening, placed in a 300 to 350 degree oven for 30 to 60 minutes, and then wiped with a paper towel. As anyone who has tried this method knows, this is a nonstarter. Half the time, the pan ends up sticky and there isn't much of a coating. A vastly better method is to place the pan over high heat for four to five minutes, move it off the burner, coat it with veg-

etable oil or hydrogenated vegetable shortening, and then wipe it clean with paper towels. The theory is that the intense heat opens up the "pores" of the metal, allowing the oil to penetrate more deeply. I have also found that the best way to strip down the surface of a badly treated cast iron pan is to place it on a bed of coals (a fireplace works well) for a couple of hours. (Over time, if a cast iron pan is not properly maintained, the interior will develop an uneven finish created by a buildup of leftover food. At this point, the skillet or Dutch oven is no longer nonstick.) This will remove every bit of finish from the pan, bringing it back down to the cast iron. Of course, the pan then needs to go through reseasoning. Here is my recipe.

How to Season a Cast Iron Pan

| 1 | cast iron skillet or Dutch oven |
| 1–2 | tablespoons vegetable oil depending on size of pan |

1. Place pan over high heat for 4 to 5 minutes or until you cannot leave your outstretched hand 1 inch above the bottom surface of the pan for more than 2 seconds. Meanwhile, tear off 6 sheets of paper toweling in 2-sheet bunches. Wearing heavy oven mitts over both hands, remove pan from heat and pour in oil. Holding the handle in one hand, rub oil into pan with first batch of towels. Repeat with second and third sets of paper towels. If this is a new pan, repeat twice.
2. After each use, scour the pan gently with a stiff brush and soapy water, rinse, dry,

HOW TO BUY CAST IRON COOKWARE

Selling at a fraction of the cost of more modern cookware, cast iron is the ultimate bargain and is great for browning or sautéing meat.

PAN SIZE	LODGE	WAGNER	BENJAMIN and MEDWIN
Skillets			
6½ inches	$5.21	$7.50	$4.99
8	7.39	9.00	6.99
10	10.06	NA	NA
10½	10.56	14.00	9.99
11¼	16.46	NA	12.99
12	17.52	17.00	NA
13¼	29.14	26.00	NA
15¼	35.23	NA	NA
Dutch Ovens			
2-quart	27.82	10.83	NA
5-quart	27.98	28.00	19.99
7-quart	51.50	NA	NA
10-quart	59.78	NA	NA

WHAT TO BUY: Although the Benjamin and Medwin line is limited, their Quantum Supercast Non-Stick cast iron cookware does perform as advertised. I suggest purchasing the 10½- and 11¼-inch skillets. For a Dutch oven, however, I would go for the 5- and 10-quart sizes. Lodge is the only manufacturer who makes a 10-quart and I would opt for the Quantum Supercast for the 5-quart. You can call Benjamin and Medwin at 212-686-0060 (230 Fifth Avenue, New York, NY 10001) and Lodge can be reached at 423-837- 7181. Most skillets can be purchased with either glass or iron covers.

and then repeat process above. Once the pan acquires a smooth, nonstick finish, repeat this process every second or third use.

One manufacturer, Wagner, makes a line of cast iron cookware that is much smoother than the traditional rough-surface skillets. I tested them and found that although they were smoother at first, after proper seasoning and a couple of weeks of use, both the traditional pans and these newer, smoother pans per- formed about the same. (I fried an egg in both types of pan to measure how much it would stick.) Another manufacturer, Benjamin and Medwin, makes a line of cast iron called Quantum which is billed as nonstick cookware. I tested their 11¼-inch skillet using the same method I employed in *The Cook's Bible*. I fried an egg in it using no fat whatsoever. To my surprise, the egg did not stick. Since these pans are a fraction of the cost of All-Clad

HOW TO BUY SAUCEPANS

To test the heat conductivity of these saucepans, I sautéed onions in butter and also sprinkled a bit of flour on the dry pan and heated it to see if it browned the flour evenly. I also measured how long it took to boil one quart of water and then measured the temperature of the water 5 minutes after it came to a boil and was removed from the heat. Items are listed in order of price.

BRAND	PRICE	CAPACITY	BROWNING	BOILING	TEMP 5 MINS
All-Clad Stainless	$75	2 quarts	even	5½ minutes	186 degrees
Cuisinart Everyday Collection	50	3¾ quarts	very uneven	7 minutes	177 degrees
Tramontina	48	3 quarts	even	5½ minutes	180 degrees
Cuisine Cookware Classic 200	40	3 quarts	uneven	7½ minutes	169 degrees
Revere Solutions	30	3 quarts	very uneven	8 minutes	165 degrees
Chef's Pride Series 3000	25	2 quarts	very uneven	7 minutes	180 degrees

WHAT TO BUY: The best pan on the market is the All-Clad, although the 4-quart model will run you a whopping $142 (you can probably find it cheaper on sale). Note that All-Clad also makes a somewhat less expensive series called Master Chef, which runs about 15 percent less. They are also wonderful pans. However, the Tramontina, imported from South America, is a good bet; it performs well and is relatively inexpensive. They make a whole line of cookware and sell sets that are very affordable. To find out more about them, call 713-827-7809.

or Calphalon nonstick pans, I highly recommend them.

The chart on page 9 lists the sizes and prices of both skillets and Dutch ovens from three different manufacturers.

SAUCEPANS

Every kitchen needs a 2- and a 4-quart saucepan. The problem is that the vast majority of saucepans are no good. They are not heavy enough to brown foods evenly (sautéing onions for example), which means that you have to watch the cooking food carefully to avoid disaster. In *The Cook's Bible,* I tested a variety of pans, most of them over $50. For this book, I wanted to test pans that cost under $50, but I also included my top choice from previous testing, the All-Clad Stainless, which is, in my opinion, the best saucepan on the market. Virtually all of these saucepans are made of stainless steel with a plate on the base fashioned from aluminum. Aluminum is an excellent conductor of heat and stainless steel is nonreactive. Other than the All-Clad, the only saucepan worth purchasing is the Tramontina, which sells for just under $50.

STOCKPOTS

There is really only one choice to make when purchasing a stockpot. Do you wish to purchase one with a plate in the bottom or not? The plate simply gives the bottom of the pot more heft, which moderates temperatures thus making it more difficult to scorch foods during cooking. This is not a problem if all you are doing is making stocks, which are mostly water. Tall and narrow, stockpots are designed

To sharpen a knife using a sharpening stone, start with the heel end of the blade (the wide portion near the handle) on the stone. The blade should be at a relatively flat 15 to 20 degree angle to the stone. Wet the stone first with a small amount of water or vegetable oil. If your stone does not have a nonslip bottom, place it on a damp kitchen towel.

Draw the blade across the stone while moving the knife toward you as you work.

When you reach the end of the stone, the tip of the knife should be in contact with the sharpening surface. Do this on both sides of the knife until sharp. Many stones are two-sided, having a medium grind on one side and a fine grind on the other. Start with the medium grind and then finish off with the finer side. It will take about ten minutes to properly sharpen a knife.

specifically for simmering bones, meat, and vegetables in large quantities of water. They are not well suited to sautéing foods, because the high sides make it difficult to get at the food and the small diameter can't hold large quantities. I therefore recommend that a Dutch oven be used for this purpose and stockpots be relegated to making stock or for cooking pasta, lobsters, and the like. The expensive stockpots, those with aluminum or, in some cases, copper plates in the bottom, can cost well over $100, which is no bargain. The most common stockpot, however, is sold under a variety of names such as Metro, and is stainless steel with a colored enamel finish. These are cheap, running only $13 for an eight-quart model and a

HOW TO BUY A CHEF'S KNIFE FOR UNDER $50

I assembled a group of inexpensive chef's knives and used them to perform light kitchen tasks such as chopping onions. I also weighed each knife for comparison. The bolster referred to in the chart is the ridge of metal which separates the blade from the handle. Items listed in order of price.

BRAND	PRICE	WEIGHT	COMMENTS
Commercial Sabatier Cuisine de France	$49.99	8⅞ ounces	bolster; handle a bit awkward; good knife
Hoffritz Signature	49.99	10⅝ ounces	bolster; heavy handle and well balanced; good knife
J. A. Henckels	34.99	8 ounces	bolster; handle a bit smooth; well balanced
Dexter Russell	27.95	5⅜ ounces	no bolster; white molded plastic handle; excellent balance between handle and blade; preferred knife for lighter cutting jobs
Zwilling J. A. Henckels	19.95	5⅞ ounces	no bolster; smooth plastic handle; good hand feel
Stanton	19.95	8 ounces	no bolster; stainless steel; wood handle; very awkward since handle is so light and blade is so large
Farberware Professional	11.99	8 ounces	no bolster; handle a bit light; excellent knife for the price

WHAT TO BUY: The Farberware at $11.99 is an almost unbelievable bargain. I also like the Dexter Russell knife; it is well balanced and you feel as if you have terrific control over the blade. The problem with these knives is that they are very light and aren't going to be much good for cutting through an acorn squash or a chicken bone. However, an inexpensive Chinese cleaver works well for these sorts of tasks.

modest $20 for the twenty-quart pot. Since stockpots are just for boiling water, I would purchase an inexpensive twelve-quart stockpot with a plate, which adds just a few dollars to the price. The two most commonly found brands were Progressive International and Tools of the Trade Grand Prix (from Macy's), both of which have bottom plates. They run in price from $15 to $25 depending on size.

KNIVES UNDER $50

There are plenty of high-quality knives for over $50, the best of which, in my opinion, is the Wüsthof Trident Grand Prix. Henckels and Chef's Choice are also serious contenders. The problem is that an eight-inch chef's knife (chef's knives have recessed handles, which allow one to chop food without hitting one's knuckles on the cutting surface) can cost upwards of $85.

HOW TO BUY HAND-HELD ELECTRIC MIXERS

I tested whipping egg whites and heavy cream and made batches of cookie dough. All hand-held mixers are not equal in the cleaning department. Some are inexplicably designed with openings and grooves that attract batter like flies to sugar. Others are well-sealed to make cleanup a breeze. Items are listed in order of price.

BRAND	PRICE	SPEEDS	EGG WHITES	WHIPPING CREAM	COOKIE DOUGH	CLEANING
KitchenAid KHM9PHW	$89	9	excellent	excellent	excellent	excellent
KitchenAid KHM&TWH	82	7	excellent	excellent	excellent	excellent
KitchenAid KHM5TB	65	5	excellent	excellent	excellent	excellent
Cuisinart HTM-5	40	5	good	good	good/fair	excellent
Braun Multi Mix	30	3	fair	good	fair	good
Sunbeam Mixmaster 2485	25	6	good	good	fair	fair
Hamilton Beach	25	5	fair	good	fair	fair

WHAT TO BUY: The 5-speed KitchenAid KHM5TB is the best buy at a reasonable $65. Don't bother with any of the less expensive models; they just won't perform up to speed. The KitchenAid also has a nice range of speeds. The 7- and 9-speed models have a slow setting of just 350 rpm with a high setting of 1300 rpm. They also have enough horsepower to work a thick cookie dough, the acid test for any hand-held mixer.

For this book, I decided to investigate chef's knives that are more modestly priced.

After extensive testing, it became clear that inexpensive knives are actually well suited to most kitchen tasks, except for heavy-duty jobs such as cutting through an acorn squash. Although many models are very light, the cheapest knife, the Farberware Professional, which sells for an unbelievable $11.99, weighs in at a respectable eight ounces. (Expensive knives run eight to ten ounces.) In addition, some of the lightweight models such as the Dexter Russell were actually well balanced and particularly good for precision cutting, such as mincing garlic or a small onion. However, when it came to handling a big job, I did miss my $85 Wüsthof Trident. It boils down to the difference between a fun-to-drive Volkswagen versus a serious, well-engineered driving machine such as a Mercedes. For most home cooks the inexpensive knives are fine. In fact, I now reach for the Dexter Russell for most cutting and slicing tasks. It's precise and fun to use.

HAND-HELD ELECTRIC MIXERS

Many cookbook authors assume that readers have $250 standing mixers for making cookie dough or whipping egg whites. Although I do have one and use it frequently, this is not a common kitchen appliance among country cooks. For this reason, I have tested hand-held electric mixers to see which models are worth the money. I tested by whipping egg whites, whipping cream, and making cookie dough, and I also checked out how difficult it was to clean. The difference in performance was substantial. Some mixers have slow speed settings that are much too fast; I ended up with a face full of flour. Others just don't have enough horsepower to blend cookie dough. Some models were neat; they did their job without splattering the kitchen and the cook. Others sent gobs of dough and cream whipping around the room, splattering everything within three feet. I also looked for mixers without grooves or openings in the housing that make cleanup more difficult. I did find that manufacturers such as Braun also offer lower-priced mixers, which are essentially the same machine as the more expensive models, but without all of the extra attachments. As with most appliances, we find attachments to be not worth the money. They usually get left in the back of a drawer and forgotten.

INSTANT-READ THERMOMETERS

One of the greatest and least expensive secrets of a well-stocked kitchen is the instant-read thermometer. Most cost under $20 and will quickly determine the temperature of a roast, a loaf of bread, a steak in a pan. Instead of guessing when your roast chicken is properly cooked or even when to take a loaf of bread out of the oven, you can know within 10 seconds, with an instant-read thermometer, exactly what is going on inside the food.

There are two basic models: the traditional analog dials and the newer digital models. For years I used the former, which are cheap (under $20), but relatively inaccurate, since the small dials must cover 200 to 300 degrees. One can purchase models with larger dials but it is still difficult to get an accurate reading within 10 or 15 degrees. They are fine, however, for roasting meats or baking breads, which can tolerate less exacting measurements. Over the years, however, I have decided that the more expensive digital models are truly superior and worth the investment. They move from room temperature to over 200 degrees in just seconds and the readings are extra-ordinarily accurate. When I tested an "instant-read" candy thermometer against a digital model when making jam, I found that the former took well over one minute to reach the ambient temperature of the mixture and the dial made it difficult to get within 5 degrees of accuracy. This is a disaster, since the mixture must reach 218 to 220 degrees for the fruit to set up properly when canned. When choosing a digital instant-read, you should also consider the style of the probe. It should not be too

HOW TO BUY AN INSTANT-READ THERMOMETER

I tested these thermometers in boiling water to see if they were properly calibrated and then in a slurry of ice and water. (They were all fine.) I then tried them in meat loaf and in a loaf of bread. Items listed in order of price.

BRAND	PRICE	TEMP RANGE	EASE OF USE	PROBE	TYPE
Owen Thermapen	$60	−50 to 550 degrees	excellent	4.2 inches	digital
Component Design	42	−40 to 300 degrees	good	2.65 inches	digital
Taylor Bi Therm	32.50	50 to 550 degrees	fair	8 inches	dial
Maverick Ready	29.99	32 to 239 degrees	fair	3⅛ inches	dial
Taylor Candy	19.95	20 to 400 degrees	good	no probe	dial
Taylor Digital	19.95	−58 to 302 degrees	excellent	4¾ inches	digital
Taylor Instant	14.95	20 to 220 degrees	good	4¾ inches	dial
Taylor Roast	11.95	105 to 185 degrees	fair	2¾ inches	dial

WHAT TO BUY: The Taylor Digital is the best for the money since it is easy to read. The Taylor Bi Therm, for example, is virtually impossible to read since it crams 500 degrees of readings onto one small dial. The Maverick has a thick probe, which made huge holes in the bread. The best of the lot is the Owen Thermapen (this is the model I use) but it is expensive. It has a probe which folds back into the housing, the digital display is very large and easy to read, and it is very accurate. The Component Design is an attractive thermometer, it fits into its own black plastic case, but the on/off button is tiny, making it hard to use, and the probe is well under 3 inches long, too short for most applications.

short and it should also not be too thick. Short models (I have seen small digital instant-reads, which have probes under 3 inches long) are not long enough to get to the center of a ham or large roast, and thick probes punch gaping holes in the food, which either look unattractive (in a loaf of bread, for example) or provide sizable conduits for the juices to run out into the pan. Look for probes that are at least 4 inches long, 6 inches being preferable.

The Polder company produces an unusual instant-read thermometer which has many advantages but two serious drawbacks. It has a long metal wire running out of the case which ends in a long metal probe. It is designed so that the probe can be inserted into the food during cooking and the thermometer can be set to a particular internal temperature. (You can stick the probe in a roast and then run the wire out of the oven, closing the oven door on it.) Once the preset temperature is reached, the timer goes off. This is a nifty feature, but I often don't have a convenient spot to leave the thermometer during roasting. To take a reading without leaving the probe in all the time is also problematic, since one either has to hold both the probe and the timer or find a non-greasy flat spot to place it while taking the reading. Finally, there is no on/off switch — the timer is always on, which tends to run down the battery quickly. (It should be noted that I have had mine for eight months and the battery is still working.) However, it is well designed and the ability to preset the internal temperature can be a big plus. (To purchase one, call either the Chef's Catalogue at 800-338-3232 or the King Arthur Flour Baker's Catalogue at 800-827-6836.)

It is important to check a thermometer's accuracy from time to time, especially with less expensive models. Simply place the probe in boiling water and make sure that it reads 212 degrees (that is, if you are at sea level).

HOW TO BUY MANUAL GRATERS

I tested four different styles of graters: 4-sided box graters, large flat, small flat, and the rotary models. I used hard cheese, medium cheese, soft cheese, and chocolate for my testing. Ease of cleanup was also considered.

TYPE	HARD CHEESE	MEDIUM CHEESE	SOFT CHEESE	CHOCOLATE	CLEANING
4-sided box	great	great	great	great	good
Flat large	great	great	great	great	great
Flat small	good	fair	fair	fair	great
Rotary	great	good	bad	bad	fair

WHAT TO BUY: The large flat graters are best since they are easy to clean. They also take up less storage space.

MANUAL GRATERS

There are four basic types of nonelectric graters: the classic four-sided box grater, the newer flat graters, a small hand-held grater, and the rotary grater. When purchasing a box grater, I found that the ones with plastic trim (prices range from $2.99 to $6.99) are flimsier and somewhat harder to clean. Also, be sure to purchase one that is large enough so that you can get your hand up inside it for cleaning. Williams Sonoma carries a four-sided grater that runs about $16 and is sturdy and well made, but you can purchase less expensive models for as little as $9. The larger flat graters work well since they are a breeze to clean up and they are big enough to do large jobs such as grating mozzarella, Parmesan, or chocolate. The small flat graters are fine for adding a bit of grated cheese to pasta at the table, but are not big enough to be useful as a serious kitchen tool. Finally, the rotary graters do a great job with harder cheeses such as Parmesan, Swiss, and even Cheddar but are a mess when used with softer cheeses such as mozzarella. Besides, they are hard to clean. The clear winner in this category is the large flat graters that come with a variety of surfaces to cover any grating need from fine lemon zest to larger pieces of soft cheese.

KNIFE SHARPENERS

As I pointed out in *The Cook's Bible*, most home cooks think that a sharpening steel, those swordlike instruments that often come with knife sets, actually sharpen a knife. Well, they don't. They simply tune up the edge between sharpenings. In fact,

a knife can lose its edge rather quickly, especially when used to cut up a chicken or some other edge-blunting task.

If you want sharp knives, you have four options. The first is to send your knives out to be sharpened. This is not expensive (from $1.50 to $3.50 to sharpen each knife) but adds up quickly over the life of a good knife. (To find a company that sharpens knives, simply look under "Sharpening Service" in the Yellow Pages.) In addition, knives need to be sharpened frequently, as often as every two weeks if you use them a lot, so this alternative is impractical.

The best but most expensive option is to purchase a Chef's Choice electric knife sharpener, which costs about $85 for the three-slot model and between $50 and $60 for the two-slot sharpener. Each slot is shaped like a wedge, and the knife is pulled through each side of it slowly and gently. The knife blade is held in place by magnets, which keep it at the proper angle to the spinning diamond sharpening wheel. Each slot performs a different level of grinding, from a major overhaul of the knife to a tune-up, akin to the results if you used a sharpening steel. I strongly recommend, if you wish to make the investment, the more expensive model, as it provides a serious regrinding slot which is not included on the cheaper two-slot model. I find this necessary every three or four months and would otherwise have to send out my knives two or three times per year. I have tested electric sharpeners extensively and the *Cook's Illustrated* test kitchen has also performed a series of tests. We both have found the Chef's Choice to be superior. It grinds a sharp edge and removes the minimum of metal during the process. Some other models take off too much steel and grind too deep which, over time, can do serious damage to a knife.

That being said, many folks don't want to spend $85 on a knife sharpener. In that case, the cheapest option is to purchase two whetstones, one for grinding and the other for finishing. (Whetstones come with different finishes. Some are coarse for major reshaping of a knife edge and others are harder and smoother, good for tuning up an edge. Some models have one finish on one side and another on the back.) For example, you can buy two six-inch Arkansas whetstones for $15 each. Smaller stones, say four inches long, are too short for an eight-inch chef's knife, so avoid these models. I would also steer clear of the really expensive models such as Diamond Machine Technology stones, which run $50 for a six-inch model and a whopping $78 for the eight-inch. For that money, you are better off with the Chef's Choice electric sharpener. Another choice is the Norton India Stones, which price out at $19.95 for the six-inch and $22.50 for the eight-inch models. They have a medium grit on one side and a coarse grit on the other.

The problem with whetstones is that they take a long time to get a good edge, at least ten minutes per knife, and it is hard to do well. The blade must be kept at a 15 to 20 degree angle to the stone, and it must be moved across the length of the stone while it is also drawn from heel to tip across the surface. (See illustrations page 11.) Most stones require that you use either honing oil or water on the surface of the whetstone to assist in the

sharpening process, although you can use the expensive Diamond Technology stones dry. If you take the time to learn how to use a stone and you don't have a dozen different knives to sharpen, they are your best, most economical choice. Be warned, however, that most home cooks will never master the technique.

Finally, there are many small hand sharpeners on the market. Some look like yo-yos; the knife is rolled back and forth between two wheels. Others are simply sharpening slots with handles. Whatever the design, I find these devices imperfect at best, unable to deliver a really sharp knife and certainly unable to recover a really dull knife. Any sharpener with only one grind is, in the long run, worthless. Eventually, the edge will become dull and the knife will have to be sent out for sharpening.

Of course there is one other alternative. Folks with a grinding wheel in their barn or garage can sharpen just about anything. You won't catch a Vermont farmer with an $80 electric knife sharpener. However, you probably won't catch him with a sharp cooking knife either.

WHISKS

Whisks should be stainless steel with a smooth, rounded handle, which is sealed to prevent moisture from penetrating. (Wire handles are fine for small whisks but a good sturdy wooden or metal handle is best for serious whisking.) Prices range from $5 to $12 for 6-inch to 12-inch models. If most of your mixing and beating is to be done with an electric mixer, you will only need a small to medium-size whisk for blending dry ingredients or whisking a few eggs together or making a salad dressing. However, if you intend to do serious whipping by hand, a larger balloon whisk is advisable. I also find that a flat L-shaped whisk is excellent for whisking in saucepans when it is important to make good contact with the bottom and sides of the pot. The traditional whisk shape is poorly designed for this application.

WOODEN SPOONS

There are three types of wooden spoons: beech wood are the cheapest, running $1 to $5; next are olive wood, priced between $5 and $10; and the most expensive are boxwood, which run $10 to $15. The more expensive spoons are less likely to absorb flavors, but I buy the inexpensive models, using at least two medium spoons, one for savory and one for sweet foods. I also suggest purchasing two very large spoons for working with large amounts of batter or dough.

THE NO-MELT SPATULA

These are relatively recent inventions and are a must if you are using a nonstick skillet. You can stir foods in a very hot pan and the spatulas won't melt. Pyrex makes an inexpensive model for $1.99, but the handle is on the short side, a problem when sautéing hot foods. Also, after just a month of testing, the Pyrex spatula looked a bit worn. A better choice is a Rubbermaid spatula, which comes in two sizes. The smaller one is $8.99 and the larger one is $10.99. They have red handles,

which is helpful since you can pick them out of a nest of kitchen tools in a second. I have used one for three years and it still looks like new.

RUBBER SPATULAS

Every kitchen needs to have two of these: one medium and one extra-large. They are essential for folding together ingredients, mixing pie dough, blending batters, and the like. A wooden spoon has a much smaller head and the oval shape is not well suited for the classic French folding motion, which homogenizes ingredients quickly without overworking batters.

DOUGH SCRAPER

These are rectangular metal blades with either metal, wood, or plastic handles and are used to move dough, scrape up debris from a counter, move chopped vegetables, etc. They have a million uses around the kitchen and are well worth the modest $8 price tag. You can also buy plastic scrapers (these run under $2), which are excellent for any task for which a bit of flexibility is important such as cleaning rolling pins or scraping out a bowl. Some are kidney-shaped, which makes them perfectly contoured to the inside of any round pan or bowl.

MIXING BOWLS

You have four choices here: earthenware, stainless steel, tempered glass, and plastic. Although I am partial to my huge ochre-colored earthenware mixing bowls, they are not recommended if you are using a hand-held electric mixer since they will take a beating over time. Earthenware is also more expensive. For a lot less money, you can purchase a five-piece set of stainless steel bowls from Creative Home for just $15.99 (1½-quart to 8-quart), while Pyrex offers 2-, 3-, and 4-quart bowls from $2.99, $3.99, and $4.99 respectively. A set of eleven glass mixing bowls runs just $30 from Williams Sonoma. White plastic bowls are also available and many models come with a gasket around the bottom of the bowl to prevent slippage on the work surface. A set of three (1½-quart to 5-quart) is $20.

You also need to think about sizes. I love huge bowls for mixing. You have more room to work, less flour ends up on the counter and floor, and mixing is a lot easier. So go out and buy at least one huge bowl, one that holds at least six quarts. You also want bowls that are stable, with a bottom wide enough to handle the weight and height of the bowl.

MEASURING CUPS AND SPOONS

Stay clear of plastic measuring cups and spoons. The handles break off, they crack, and the ring that holds the spoons together inevitably disappears, leaving the lesser sizes to fend for themselves, obscured by the hundred other things you stuff into your catchall drawer. I also have found that there are two types of metal measuring spoons. One is cheap and uses thin-gauge metal. (They run around $3 per set.) These are terrific for seeding cucumbers, peppers, and even peeling kiwis! (For that last trick, see *The Cook's Bible*.) The metal is so thin that the edges are somewhat sharp, a big plus when scoop-

ing out foods. The more expensive stainless measuring spoons run close to $10 and are recommended for actual measuring, since they will never get dented. The model I have also has very deep bowls, which makes measuring more precise. The shallow-bowl models are less accurate, since the difference between filling a wide bowl almost to the top versus actually filling it can be substantial. That is one reason I like very narrow glass measuring cups over the wider models. They are more accurate.

CUTTING BOARDS

I suggest that you purchase two boards. One should be thick, made of wood, and quite large. Leave this one on your kitchen counter permanently and use it for chopping and other daily tasks. Also purchase a small, thin, polyethylene board, one that is small enough to go into the dishwasher. Use this for both high-risk foods such as meat, fish, and chicken as well as for pungent ingredients such as onions and garlic. A small 14 × 11-inch board runs about $8 and a 17 × 11-inch board will run $10.

ROLLING PINS

As usual, I have strong opinions about rolling pins, but also as usual, it does depend on the cook. I find thinner straight or tapered pins to be best since they enable me to get a good feel for the dough. The maple pins with ball bearings attached to the handles are fine, and many people prefer them because it gives them added leverage. These pins are heavier, which can be important for a short cook who is not towering over his or her kitchen counter, able to use a bit of upper body weight to press down. I don't think that marble pins are worth the money. Pins that adjust to produce different thicknesses of dough do work. (By turning the adjusters next to the handles, the pin itself will end up at any one of six or so different heights from the work surface.) Two words of advice. Make sure that you have a large enough work area to accommodate the length of your rolling pin. You need a surprising amount of room free from cookie jars, utensil holders, drainboards, and the like to work with even an average-size pin. Second, nonsealed pins should not be washed with water. The surface of the wood can become tacky over time, sticking to the dough. Just scrape off any remaining dough and flour with a dough scraper and wipe clean with a damp sponge.

HOW TO BUY A BAKING SHEET

Chocolate chip cookies, each cookie using 2 tablespoons of batter, were baked on 8 different makes of baking sheets, each of which had been sprayed with Pam. Items are listed in order of price.

MODEL	TYPE	COOKIE SIZE	COLOR	PRICE
Calphalon	heavy-duty aluminum, nonstick	3 inches	golden	$23.99
Revereware	stainless steel	2½ inches	very light	16.99
Kaiser Non-Stick	thin aluminum, gray nonstick finish	2½ inches	very dark	11.99
Cushionaire	aluminum with cushion "sandwich" inside	3 inches	golden	9.99
Chicago Metallic	aluminum with Silverstone finish	2½ inches	dark	8.99
Ekco	aluminum with shiny gray, nonstick finish	2½ inches	dark	7.99
Kaiser	thin aluminum sheet	just under 3 inches	golden	6.99
Roshko	aluminum with black nonstick finish	2½ inches	dark	3.99

WHAT TO BUY: The Calphalon overall did produce the best cookie but not that much better than either the Cushionaire or the Kaiser, the latter being only $6.99, which is therefore the best buy. If you use parchment paper on your baking sheets, a nonstick surface is not necessary. It was interesting to note that the Kaiser Non-Stick baking sheet was the worst of the bunch yet the simple, thin aluminum model from Kaiser did fine.

Pie Plates

To determine the best pie plate, I baked my pie pastry recipe blind (without filling) in four different types of pans: tinned steel, aluminum, pottery, and glass. I set the glass and pottery pans directly onto a pizza stone on the floor of the oven; the metal pans were placed on a rack in the lower third of the oven. Although all four types of pans worked well — that is, the crust came out nicely browned — I did find that glass tends to work best, since it conducts heat so well. The metal pans are fine, although somewhat slower to brown, and the pottery models provide the least even crust of all. Glass plates have two other advantages. One can see the color of the crust as it bakes, and since glass is nonreactive, it can be used for fruit cobblers and crisps as well. A 9-inch Pyrex (glass) pie plate runs only $3; metal plates run $4 to $5 for a set of two. You should also look at the rim of the plate. It should be wide enough to support a fluted edge. Some porcelain pie plates in particular have narrow rims. I also prefer pie plates with two small tabs or "ears" on the side of the rim. This makes it easier to pick them up and move them.

HOW TO BUY A MUFFIN TIN

I baked lemon corn muffins in each of 6 different muffin tins and then compared the shape and color of the muffins. In terms of shape, I was looking for a traditional tall muffin, neither too wide nor too short. Items listed in order of price.

MODEL	TYPE	QUANTITY	SHAPE	COLOR	PRICE
Calphalon nonstick	heavy-duty aluminum	12	very good	golden	$24.99
Revereware	stainless steel	6	squat	very light	16.99
Cushionaire	aluminum with cushion "sandwich"	6	squat	light	13.99
Kaiser Non-Stick	lightweight aluminum, nonstick coating	12	short	very dark	13.99
Chicago Metallic	aluminum with Silverstone nonstick coating	12	very good	golden	13.99
Village Baker	heavy aluminum	12	very good	golden	9.99

WHAT TO BUY: The two best muffin tins are made by Village Baker and Chicago Metallic. The latter has a nonstick surface and sells for $13.99. The Village Baker needs greasing since it is not nonstick.

Baking Sheets

A home cook can spend from $3.99 to a whopping $23.99 to purchase a simple baking sheet. Does the color of the surface, the thickness of the gauge, or the type of finish (nonstick or not) really matter? To answer this question, I baked chocolate chip cookies on eight different baking sheets to see what would happen. I lightly greased them first with Pam, and each cookie was made with 2 tablespoons of dough. The only consistent result was that the darker-colored sheets seemed to set up the cookie quickly, producing a higher cookie and one that was more browned than the flatter varieties produced by lighter-colored sheets. The big surprise, however, was that price did not seem to be a determining factor. The thin aluminum Kaiser sheet ($6.99) did about as well as the $24 Calphalon model. As far as nonstick goes, I prefer to use parchment paper on my baking sheets, since a freshly baked batch of cookies can simply be whisked off the hot pan and a new batch whisked on and into the oven.

Muffin Tins

The right muffin tin does make a difference. Some pans cook too quickly, over-browning the outside of the muffin before the inside is thoroughly cooked. Others produce squat muffins with rounded edges on the bottom. Of the six models I tested, five were made of aluminum and one was stainless steel. The latter produced the lightest-colored muffins, since stainless steel is a rather poor conductor compared to aluminum. As with the baking sheets, the Calphalon model

---

HOW TO BUY A LOAF PAN

Four separate types of pans were tested with two recipes: the Johnnycake on page 215 and a basic French bread recipe from Julia Child. The flimsy, cheap aluminum pan did just fine. A basic loaf pan measures approximately 5 x 9 inches. Items are listed in order of price.

DESCRIPTION	COMMENTS	PRICE
Aluminum with nonstick Silverstone finish	very good; can scratch finish; easy to clean	$9.99
Tinned heavy-duty steel	very good; can scratch finish; must dry thoroughly to prevent rust	7.00
Glass	bread hard to remove; excellent height with French bread	4.99
Thin aluminum	very good; not very durable; not easy to clean	2.99

WHAT TO BUY: The best pan of the bunch is the aluminum Silverstone with a nonstick finish since it is well made and easy to clean, and the baking results were fine. However, for a mere $2.99 you can purchase a thin aluminum loaf pan that works fine in the oven, but it is harder to clean up and is likely to become bent and creased over the years.

---

is overpriced, coming in at a whopping $24.99 for a twelve-cup tin, whereas the Village Baker, one of our top-ranked models, sells for a more modest $9.99. The nonstick finish is not necessary, but be sure to thoroughly grease the inside of the muffin cup and along the top of the pan (so the caps don't stick). All in all, the Village Baker was a good buy at just $9.99 and the Chicago

Metallic, which has a nonstick finish, is also worth the price for slightly more money.

Loaf Pans

I have been a big fan of heavy-duty loaf pans, assuming that they browned more evenly and produced a better rise. But being a slave to objective testing, I chose

---

HOW TO BUY A ROASTING PAN

As with most bakeware, pans are made of stainless steel, aluminum, and glass, as well as porcelain and steel covered with either enamel or a ceramic coating. Potatoes were roasted in each pan for comparison. Cleanup was an important factor since many of these pans were close to impossible to clean. Items are listed in order of price.

BRAND	TYPE/SIZE	TEXTURE	COLOR	CLEANING	PRICE
Farberware	heavy-duty stainless 15 x 11 inches	very good	golden	easy/ dishwasher	$39.99
Various	porcelain finish	very good	light brown	easy/ dishwasher	20.00 up
Progressive	thin stainless steel 15 x 11	slightly dry	dark	impossible	19.99
Roshko	ceramic on steel 17 x 22	dry	very dark	impossible	19.99
General Housewares	enamel on steel 18 x 12	dry	very dark	difficult	9.99
Wilton	very thin aluminum 13 x 9	slightly dry	very dark	difficult	7.69
Various	glass	very good	golden	easy/ dishwasher	6.99 up

WHAT TO BUY: Glass is cheap and easy to clean. It also has excellent cooking characteristics. Stay away from steel pans coated with enamel or a ceramic finish, since they are nearly impossible to clean up. The thin aluminum and stainless steel pans were also difficult in this regard. The Farberware is a wonderful pan, but it is pricey.

---

four different types of pans and subjected them to two different tests. The pans were made from heavy-duty tinned steel, aluminum with a Silverstone finish, glass, and cheap, thin aluminum. First, I made a standard cornbread recipe and the results were surprising. They all baked in the same amount of time with the same height and texture! The only slight difference was that the Silverstone pan's was slightly darker, although not burnt, on the bottom. We also found that it was hard to get the cornbread out of the glass pan and the outside of the bread was grainier than with the other pans. I then followed a recipe from Julia Child for basic French bread and this time the glass pan produced the most height and also baked up five minutes faster than the loaves in the other pans. But, again, it took some doing to get the bread out of the pan. The Sil-verstone once again produced a slightly darker crust. The big surprise is that the flimsy, cheap $2.99 aluminum pan did just fine in the testing, although it is less likely to withstand years of use. If you are an occasional baker, however, these pans are fine.

Roasting Pans

Roasting pans can cost upward of $100, yet cheaper models run under $10. Some are light and others are so heavy that using them qualifies as aerobic exercise. Some are made from aluminum, others from stainless steel, and others are steel coated with either an enamel or ceramic finish. After roasting potatoes in seven different models, I found some very big differences.

The steel pans finished with enamel or

HOW TO BUY A FOOD MILL

If you don't have a food processor, a food mill comes in handy for puréeing or breaking down cooked fruits and vegetables. For example, it can purée beans in a bean soup, make a sauce out of cooked tomatoes, or make applesauce out of cooked apples. Two of the models can be placed directly into a dishwasher, a big plus. Items are listed in order of price.

BRAND	APPLES	TOMATOES	SOUPS	POTATOES	CLEANING	PRICE
Macina Legumi	great	great	great	good	dishwasher	$32.00
ACEA	great	great	fair	fair	good	24.00
Foley Food Mill stainless steel	great	good	difficult	gluelike	dishwasher	20.00
Foley Food Mill tinned steel	great	good	difficult	gluelike	dry by hand	20.00

WHAT TO BUY: The Macina Legumi is the most expensive but the best. It even did a good job with the potatoes, which usually become starchy and gluey after being run through a food mill or food processor. It can also be thrown into the dishwasher, which is a big plus.

a ceramic coating tested the worst. The potatoes tended to be drier inside and too brown. They also have a big drawback when it comes to cleaning. They are either impossible or nearly impossible to wash up. Food sticks to the outer coating like glue. The heavy stainless is the best of the bunch but it runs close to $40, way out of the ballpark in terms of pricing. Basic porcelain or glass models worked just fine, the latter being very cheap, starting as low as $6.99. The thin metal varieties, such as the Progressive, brown too quickly and are also a bear to clean. Stick to glass. It's cheap, it works just fine, and it cleans up easily.

Food Mills

Since this is a country cookbook, I have assumed that many readers do not have a food processor. This is certainly true in Vermont, where I am accused of being elitist whenever I publish a recipe in *Cook's Illustrated* that calls for this appliance without providing instructions for completing the task by hand. The simple fact of the matter is that, contrary to what New York food writers like to think, most home kitchens do not have a food processor. Although I rarely use mine, it is terrific for making pie pastry, biscuits, and the like. It is also good for some puréeing and chopping tasks. That brings us to the food mill, which is a must for puréeing soft foods such as apples for applesauce, tomatoes, potatoes, and soups. I found four reasonably priced models and tested each one with each of the four foods. Features that were important were capacity, the size of the holes (if the holes are too small you cannot get a nice chunky sauce), and whether it can be run

through the dishwasher, not a minor consideration. There was a clear winner, the Macina Legumi, which was the most expensive ($32) but worth every cent. I did, in passing, note one model that retails for $300, but since that cost three times more than my first car (a 1961 Volkswagen Beetle), I thought I'd pass.

Apple Peeler/ Slicer/Corers

Everyone has seen these gadgets. They clamp onto the side of a kitchen counter and an apple is impaled on a long metal prong, which is then turned. As the apple moves slowly down to the business end of the contraption, a blade peels it, a sharp hollow cylinder cores it, and another blade slices it into rounds. Either the peeling or slicing is optional; the machine can simply core, core and peel, or core and slice. The question is, do they really work?

After coring and peeling two dozen apples with the Apple-Mate 3 from Norpro, I can confidently recommend using one, but only for big jobs. The major drawback is that the peeling blade must be very carefully adjusted to remove just the right amount of skin and flesh. This takes time and precision. Once you are up and running, however, each apple can be done in 10 seconds, a big savings over the hand method. So for one pie, six to eight apples, I do it by hand, but for bigger jobs, I dig out the peeler/corer/slicer. By the way, this contraption works best with fairly uniform apples. Specimens with uneven outer surfaces — bumps or hollows — will be peeled unevenly.

CHERRY PITTERS

Up until last summer, when their trees were killed by disease, our family used to pick six to eight quarts of sour cherries at a local orchard in Granville, New York. This meant that I had to pit thousands of cherries in one afternoon so that they could be combined with sugar and ascorbic acid and frozen. I purchased a variety of cherry pitters and found that only one model worked well, a yellow plastic contraption made by Norpro. It has a small tray that holds about 25 cherries. One cherry at a time falls down into a small depression at which point a plunger with a small sharp four-part prong is depressed, which pits the cherry, the pit falling down into a small plastic container. The pitted cherry rolls out of a small chute into a waiting bowl. I was able to pit about thirty cherries per minute with this device. The small plastic hand-held pitters, which look like hole punches, are worthless for more than a small handful of fruit. They also tended to mash the cherries more than the Norpro, which pitted them without mangling the fruit.

THE BEST STRAINER

Beekeepers use a nine-inch-diameter, two-part strainer that fits on top of a five-gallon plastic bucket. The honey, once it is removed from the combs, is poured into this double filter and then it drips down into the collection bucket. I find that this set of strainers is terrific for the home cook as well. They fit over large bowls (there are three two-inch plastic tabs that will fit nicely over the rim of a bowl) and are excellent for straining custard or other foods. You can purchase a set by calling Dadant Beekeeper's Supply Catalogue at 217-847-3324.

CAKE TESTERS

In my experience, cake testers are pretty much worthless, especially the metal ones. (Very little sticks to metal, even a wet, partially cooked batter.) If you are going to use a cake tester, straw from a broom is the best choice. (Use the end closest to the handle. It is clean and intact, unlike the end used for sweeping.) However, a good home cook will press down on the top of a cake to see if it is firm and then watch to see if it springs back when released. (It should.) You can also do this with the flat side of a fork to avoid burning your fingers. Another sometimes false clue is whether or not the cake is pulling away from the sides of the pan. This can be a good indication but is not always reliable; the cake sometimes pulls back after it is removed from the oven.

HOW TO CALIBRATE AN OVEN

One of the biggest problems for home cooks is that their oven may be improperly calibrated, running 25 to 50 degrees hotter or colder than the setting. I recently had this problem with a new oven and even went to the expense of purchasing three different oven thermometers, placing all of them at once in the oven to gauge the temperature. They consistently showed that the oven was running 25 to 40 degrees cool. I soon found out, however, when a service man came to call, that all of them were inaccurate when measured against his expensive measuring device, which showed a markedly smaller margin of error.

He then offered some advice, which I have found invaluable and which prevents having to purchase expensive thermometers. Purchase two cans of biscuits sold in cardboard cylinders in the refrigerator section of your supermarket. Follow the directions exactly and then bake the first batch. Since this recipe has been tested a thousand times, the timing will be perfect if your oven is properly calibrated. If not, adjust your oven up or down, give it time to adjust, and then bake the second batch. You should now have an accurate reading of how far off your oven is.

How to Organize Food Preparation

Many home cooks work in a very unorganized environment, with ingredients all over the counter. I find that a bit of organization will make food preparation go a great deal faster. First, place a cutting board directly in front of you. I prefer one that is perfectly flat, without gutters for juices. (This makes it easier to sweep small ingredients off the board onto the counter.) If you are right-handed, place the food that requires chopping to the right of the board. To the left of the board, place a number of small, inexpensive metal bowls, to be used to hold the chopped ingredients. (Check the recipe first to see how many bowls you will need. If all of the ingredients are to be added at once, say onion, carrots, and garlic, then one will do. However, most recipes call for adding vegetables in batches so you will probably need more than one.) When you work, take the first item that needs chop-

ping from the foods at the right, chop it, and then, using a dough scraper in your right hand and pushing with your left, scoop up the prepared food and place it in one of the bowls to the left. Use the scraper to remove the unwanted debris away from you, off the board and onto the counter. Continue until done.

The Country Kitchen

Here is an illustrated list of what I consider to be a good basic kitchen for country cooks. The choice of cookware is important, yet one needs a relatively modest number of items.

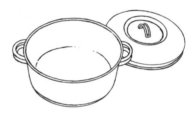

NONREACTIVE DUTCH OVENS are usually made from stainless steel with an aluminum core. This model is a Tramontina and is less than half the price of most similar Dutch ovens.

3-QUART SAUCEPANS are a workhorse pan for any kitchen. Buy a good heavy model such as this All-Clad Master Chef.

2-QUART SAUCEPANS are also a must for any kitchen. I prefer this narrow design from All-Clad since it simmers gently without burning and can handle lesser quantities due to its small diameter.

A CAST IRON DUTCH OVEN is my most prized kitchen tool. It is excellent for stews, braising, browning, and frying since thick-guage iron retains heat better than any other cookware material. They are easy to season and are both nonstick and nonre-active for almost all culinary tasks. They are also cheap, running $40 or less.

A CAMPING DUTCH OVEN, such as this model, has a raised lip on the lid which is designed to hold coals. Coals are put both below and on top of a Dutch oven when it is used for baking. These models are still available from the Lodge Company for those who wish to camp outdoors.

STOCKPOTS are relatively tall with a narrow diameter. This is a good place to save money by purchasing an inexpensive (under $30) model.

CAST IRON SKILLETS can be used for many of the recipes in this book. A 9-inch skillet is the most useful.

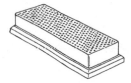

SHARPENING STONES are inexpensive but relatively hard to use for many home cooks. The Chef's Choice electric knife sharpener, which retails for $85, is an eas-ier, foolproof method for sharpening knives at home.

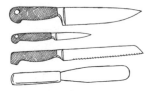

A SET OF KITCHEN KNIVES does not have to include a dozen different styles and a $500 investment. All you really need is an 8-inch chef's knife (top), a paring knife, a bread knife, and a metal spatula to use for frosting cakes.

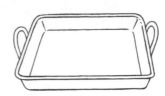

STANDING MIXERS usually come with three types of beaters: a whisk (top), a dough hook (left), and a paddle (bottom). The whisk is used for most applications, the dough hook is used for kneading bread dough, and the paddle is good for the initial mixing of bread doughs or batters which require only moderate mixing. Although a good standing mixer is a useful kitchen appliance, the recipes in this book require only the use of an inexpensive hand-held mixer.

LARGE, HEAVY-DUTY ROASTING PANS are a must for large turkeys as well as for roasting vegetables. Large, stationary handles are better than small wire handles which can be hard to grab when using oven mitts. I like heavy pans, although one should take into account the total weight of a heavy roasting pan loaded with a 20-pound turkey. It can be awkward to move, especially when hot.

HAND-HELD MIXERS were tested extensively for this chapter and I prefer the five-speed KitchenAid KHM5TB, which costs a reasonable $65.

PYREX PIE PLATES that have "ears" — small round handles — are best. The crust will bake up a bit crisper and the ears make it easier to pick up a hot pie.

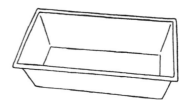

FOOD MILLS may seem old-fashioned but they do a better job than a food processor for some tasks when you do not want a purée. The Macina Legumi, which costs $32, is the top-rated model.

LOAF PANS are used not only for yeast breads but also for quick breads. Cheap, thin aluminum pans work as well as the more expensive, heavy-duty models.

9 X 9-INCH BAKING PANS are very useful for fruit crisps, brownies, bar cookies, etc.

ELECTRONIC TIMERS are vastly more accurate than the old-fashioned spring-driven models. Be sure to purchase one that can time more than one event at a time. Large buttons are also important. This model is made by WestBend.

MEASURING SPOONS come in two styles. The one at the left is made from a thin metal which produces a sharp edge, good for seeding cucumbers and other minor kitchen tasks. The model at right is more durable, since it is made from thicker metal, but cannot be used for anything but measuring.

THE POLDER THERMOMETER/TIMER is a wonderful kitchen tool. In addition to timing, this unit can measure the internal temperature of foods using its unique metal probe. The temperature can be pre-set, the probe inserted (into a chicken, for example), and the timer will beep when the pre-set temperate has been reached. The long metal wire can be run from the timer into the oven with the door closed during cooking.

INSTANT-READ THERMOMETERS come in either digital or analog models. The digital models are more accurate and a lot easier to read.

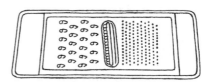

FLAT GRATERS are easier to clean than box graters and can be placed across the top of a bowl.

A DOUGH SCRAPER OR BENCH KNIFE has many uses including cleaning a work surface, lifting pie, bread, and pizza dough, and cutting bar cookies and brownies.

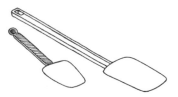

RUBBER SPATULAS are indispensable. Have at least two on hand; a small one for little jobs and a large one for mixing or folding together large amounts of batter or dough.

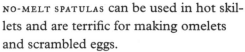

NO-MELT SPATULAS can be used in hot skillets and are terrific for making omelets and scrambled eggs.

POULTRY SHEARS are a must buy for removing the backbone from a chicken, a necessary step for cutting a chicken into parts. Fiskars, the model shown here, makes a very good pair for about $10.

BISCUIT CUTTERS come in many sizes but, in a pinch, one can use the top of a glass or jar.

PLASTIC FLOUR BUCKETS are essential for anyone who likes to bake. This model holds 10 pounds of flour and measuring cups can be dipped right into the flour, a vast improvement over working with a small bag of flour. On a farm, plastic buckets are readily available. Others may purchase their buckets through the King Arthur Flour Baker's Catalogue, a mail order company located in Norwich, Vermont.

FAT SEPARATORS OR GRAVY STRAINERS are useful when trying to defat a sauce or gravy. Simply pour in the sauce, let it sit a few minutes, and the fat will rise to the top. Since the pouring spout is attached the bottom of the pitcher, you can pour off the defatted sauce, leaving the top layer of fat behind.

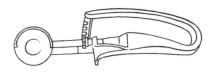

ICE CREAM SCOOPS come in many sizes. Smaller models are excellent for measuring out batter for muffins or cookies.

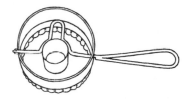

DOUGHNUT CUTTERS are simple but essential for making doughnuts. The other side is designed as a biscuit cutter.

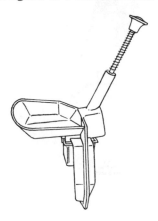

THE NORPRO CHERRY PITTER is the best model I have found. It can pit 30 cherries per minute, a vast improvement over the smaller, hand-held pitters.

You will also need:

THREE MIXING BOWLS The largest should be huge and hold 6 quarts, the medium bowl should hold 3 quarts, and a small bowl is good for mixing salad dressing.

TWO PYREX MEASURING CUPS Purchase the 4- and 2-cup models.

WHISK Only one simple whisk is necessary, mostly for whisking together flour mixtures or eggs for a batter. If you do not have an electric mixer, a large balloon whisk is necessary for beating egg whites.

WOODEN SPOONS You need two sets of these: one for savory foods and one for sweets. Be sure you have a couple of larger spoons with flat blades, which are good for scraping the bottom of a skillet.

CUTTING BOARD I use two boards: one for garlic, meats, etc., and one for all other foods. You don't want to chop chocolate on a board that smells of garlic or that is used for cutting raw chicken. A thin, polypropylene board is light and easy to store.

ROLLING PINS Just about any model is fine. I prefer thinner pins for better control.

BAKING SHEET Any cheap supermarket model will perform as well or better than the expensive models. You will need two.

MUFFIN TIN Village Baker and Chicago Metallic make the best muffin tins. They are nonstick and retail for about $14.

LOAF PAN A $3 aluminum loaf pan works just fine. Buy two.

ROASTING PAN Glass actually works quite well for a roasting pan. For a metal pan, the Farberware heavy-duty stainless pan (15 × 11 inches) is a good buy. Roasting pans also double as casseroles.

CASSEROLE One large round dish with a cover and one large shallow baking dish are essential. The latter is good for cobblers and other fruit desserts.

The Soup Pot

OUR TOWN HAS THREE main roads: one is the main road up to Beartown, another veers off to the west, through the notch (a narrow mountain pass), and down into the valley where we have our farm, and the third goes pretty much east, up over a four-wheel-drive track, down into the next village. The smaller roads are named after old town families such as Wilcox or Woodcock, winding through the hollows or around Swearing Hill and Minister Hill, which face each other across the valley, or Red, Moffitt, and Bear Mountains, which rise to just over 3,000 feet. Our town is also blessed with many small streams, most of which feed into the Green River, including Terry Brook, Chunks Creek, and Baldwin Brook over on the west side and Pruddy Brook, Hopper Brook, and Tidd Brook in the main part of town. I used to live near Tidd Brook as a child, catching small crayfish and trout under the barn-red wooden bridge. The sound of the cars rattling the old timbers, one at a time, echoed off the side hills of our small hollow, but today they are just a memory now that the bridge has been replaced by a cheaper and quieter culvert. Back then, there weren't many cars on our roads and they moved slowly, old Charlie Bentley Sr. hunched over the large steering wheel of a black 1950 Ford, or Fred Woodcock Sr. driving down to the row of mailboxes, anxious for his Social Security check. In bed at the end of a long summer day as the light was just fading to twilight, I would stare out my window at the side hill of thistle and timothy and wait for the sound of a crossing, a promise of a chance visit to break the silence of the house.

Of all the roads in our town, it is the dirt road that passes by our farm that I love the most. During the long days of summer, we put the dishes to soak after dinner and take a walk down the road in the twilight. During the day, I can smell sweet fern as I bush-hog over a wet corner of the meadow, the hot scent of wild sage, the occasional whiff of spearmint. I feel the blast of heat from the tractor and see the wind turning the leaves a milky silver, the birds swooping down over the mowed grass, an ocean of yellow and orange Indian paintbrushes against waves of large bright purple clover, overstuffed bumblebees as big as a thumb, and I hear the rhythm of the engine and the mower, the hum of pistons, gears, axles, and whirring blades. But now, in the still of the evening, I walk down our road and witness hundreds of fireflies sparking over a field of knee-high sunflowers, a goat perched halfway up a small tree by a neighbor's barn, two large chestnut mares standing stock still in a lower field with a doe and two fawns grazing just behind them, a sky that is tinged with pink clouds that turn into a swath of copper and peach as the broad strokes are painted just above our small valley, a handsome bowl of trees and pasture and old Vermont houses that is hidden quietly in the mountain valley. I crouch next to one of our hives, listening to the warm buzzing of 40,000 bees, the wooden frames alive with newly minted

workers, happy I suppose to be at the end of another long day. I can hear our voices clear and soft drifting up over the valley on a slight breeze that stirs up out of the west. We walk slowly back home along the lazy S of the dusty country road to our small farmhouse, the last swath of sun lighting up the top of the ridges with deep ochres and golds. The children run ahead, thinking of great bowls of homemade vanilla ice cream with sweet stewed rhubarb. They carry a small railroad lantern which swings back and forth as they race ahead down our dirt driveway by the old apple trees that need pruning, and the young cornfield, and the groundhog who sits atop his hole watching it grow, patient and hungry. On these evenings, I stand and watch our three children, standing quietly for a moment by the side of a meadow, enchanted by a glimpse of the unknown in a thousand blinking lights moving across a field blanketed by twilight.

OTHER THAN the country store, the gas station is our town's hub, the one place you can meet neighbors, farmers from over in New York State, or even complete strangers. When I was a boy, it was run by Carl Hess, but now it is owned by a local boy, Doug Wright, who is no less a character. The station consists of a small room to the right with a cash register, boxes of candy bars, packets of Pearlized Crappie Jigs, a faded reproduction of Norman Rockwell's "Town Meeting," and an old black and white sign stating "Carl Hess, Proprietor." To the left is the garage itself, just as greasy and unorganized as it was thirty years ago when Carl ran it.

There is a large compressor for tires, a pit for changing oil, a sign reading "Santa Please Stop Here," a Sir Walter Raleigh tobacco can filled with nuts and bolts, the same can I remember from the 1960s, Barb-Liner Hose, Gates Self-Eze Gaskets, tire patches, fan belts, tires, inner tubes for rental to weekenders at $5 apiece for floating down the river, and a soda machine out front, a green beacon that glows in the twilight as you drive down out of the mountains and through the cornfields toward the main road.

Doug is a smart operator, as are most Vermonters, so when a good-looking young girl moves into town, he tries to hire her to pump gas. A few summers back, he hired a good-looker staying with her aunt for the summer. She pumped gas in shorts and a brief halter top and I remember seeing a pack of pickups stopped by the old gas station at all times of the day, the new employee surrounded by animated, awkward locals. One day she came up to Doug and said, "I guess Vermonters sure are cheap." Doug asked what she meant and she answered, "Well, they keep coming by and getting only fifty cents' worth of gas at a time."

Doug has a short-cropped beard and pumps gas in shorts and sandals in the summer. His face is rough, showing lines etched from squinting at the constant glare of the sun, the bright blue of his eyes startling when he gets up close to the car window and fully opens them, like driving up to an old gray weathered farmhouse and then looking up to see a beautiful woman staring at you from a bedroom window. Unlike old Carl, who had emphysema and moved slowly from the dinner table to the pumps if you happened to stop by at suppertime (the white clapboard house is right next door), Doug is quick, darting out of the small office always in mid-story, delivering the punchline over his shoulder to the small, ever-changing crowd still seated in the half-light of the office.

LIKE THE CROWD down at Doug's place, soups are a grab bag of ingredients, made up of whatever you happen to have on hand. (The most unusual and simplest soup I have come across was published in a local Vermont cookbook in 1939. It was called Peanut Butter Soup and was made from one pint of heated milk to which are added two tablespoons of peanut butter and one scant tablespoon of flour.) In fact, I find that soups are less about vegetables than they are about stock. Although some recipes (many authentic Italian recipes for minestrone, for example) call for just water as a foundation, this is largely unsatisfactory unless the ingredients are just-picked and bursting with flavor. Canned stock will do in a pinch, if one purchases the correct brand (see page 38), but homemade chicken stock makes a world of difference. I offer a simple chicken broth recipe on page 39 in which a whole chicken is simmered for forty minutes in water with a few vegetables. When it is removed, the meat can be used for salads or sandwiches, and the broth is then simmered an additional twenty minutes. It's simple and fast, and does not require the use of bones or carcasses, which are hard to find and hard to store in a small freezer.

But this is a country cookbook and many of the farmers I know eat a whole

HOW TO BUY CHICKEN STOCK

Thirteen different commercial stocks were heated and tasted side by side. Although most of the canned stocks listed chicken broth as the first ingredient, all brands had at least five other ingredients and some up to fourteen including MSG. Brands are listed alphabetically.

Campbell's Chicken Broth	flatter, somewhat harsher flavor than College Inn; has dull aftertaste
Campbell's Healthy Request Chicken Broth	good chicken flavor; tied for first place in tasting
Campbell's Low Sodium Chicken Broth	flat, tasteless dishwater; awful
College Inn Chicken Broth	simple, natural flavor but salty; watery aftertaste
College Inn No Fat Chicken Broth	no fat means no flavor; tastes like water
College Inn Lower Sodium Chicken Broth	very mild chicken flavor but free from chemical and other off flavors; watery
Herb Ox Chicken Bouillon Cubes	salty, celery flavor; only uses chicken fat, which is the fifth ingredient, salt being the first
Herb Ox Chicken Bouillon Packets	bright yellow with no chicken taste whatsoever; tastes like onion powder, which is the third ingredient
Stop & Shop Chicken Broth	salty, chemical flavor
Swanson Chicken Broth	good chicken flavor; tied for first place with Campbell's Healthy Request Chicken Broth
Swanson Natural Goodness Chicken Broth	although the ingredient list is simple, this broth has an unpleasant aftertaste; still, better than most
Swanson 99% Fat Free Chicken Broth	decent chicken flavor but a bit salty; unpleasant aftertaste
Wyler's Chicken Flavor Bouillon	not even a hint of chicken; truly awful (chicken is the fifth ingredient on the label)

WHAT TO BUY: Campbell's Healthy Request Chicken Broth and Swanson Chicken Broth are the winners with good chicken flavor and some depth. College Inn has the cleanest, purest flavor of the lot but the regular brand is very salty. The low-sodium version is good but very weak in flavor. Note that Swanson has fifteen different ingredients and College Inn has only seven. Swanson builds a complex flavor profile using a host of additives. This is not a case of simply using more chicken.

lot of Campbell's soup. Few admit it, but a canned stock is used in even the most respectable kitchens, so I conducted an informal taste test of the major brands.

Note that in this book the terms *broth* and *stock* are used interchangeably.

I have discovered a few other useful techniques when testing soup recipes. A blender works better than a food processor or a food mill for puréeing soups. The blender provides superior texture; a food processor often leaks when filled more than halfway with hot soup (the hot liquid manages to seep out around the shaft of the motor, which fits up into the blade), and a food mill does a lousy job with fibrous ingredients such as asparagus or artichoke hearts. To thicken a soup, potatoes and rice work nicely if you do not wish to use heavy cream. You can also purée a small portion of the solid ingredients and add them back to the soup just before serving. I often add just a bit of heavy cream (say ½ to ¾ cup) to many soup recipes when I want a silkier texture without losing the bright flavor of the ingredients. Cream complements root vegetables better than fresh green vegetables. Bean soups are vastly better when prepared with ham hocks or a ham bone. Although these are listed as optional ingredients in many recipes, beans need a great deal of flavoring, and without a bit of meat or bone, the resulting soup is bland.

40-*Minute Chicken Stock*

Most classic chicken stock recipes call for long, slow simmering using bones and vegetables. That's fine if you have the bones and the time but I prefer to use a cut-up chicken and simply simmer it for 40 minutes. I used to remove the chicken and continue simmering the stock for another 20 minutes, adding celery and parsley. Although this does add some flavor, I often don't bother when I am running short on time. The most important rule about this stock is to add only 2 quarts of cold water. If you use 3 or 4 quarts, you will have a hard time tasting the chicken.

1   (3½- to 4-pound) chicken
1   large onion, coarsely chopped
1   medium carrot, coarsely chopped
1   bay leaf
6   whole cloves

1. Cut chicken into 9 pieces (legs, thighs, breast halves, wings, and the backbone). Use the neck, if available, but reserve the liver for another use.
2. Combine all the ingredients plus 2 quarts water in a large pot (an 8-quart pot is best) and bring to a boil. Simmer for 40 minutes. Don't bother skimming the fat and foam as it rises to the surface — the stock will be strained after cooking. Remove chicken pieces and use with another recipe. Remove stock from heat and taste; it should have a nice chicken flavor as well as a nice color. Strain (use a quadruple thickness of cheesecloth). Salt very lightly as the stock may be reduced for another recipe which would render it oversalted. The broth can now be used or immediately refrigerated. If the latter, it is best to cool it quickly by placing it in a bowl, preferably metal, which is placed inside a larger bowl half filled with ice. Stir occasionally until it reaches room temperature and then refrigerate. Remove

the congealed fat layer on top of the broth before reheating. Stock can also be frozen.

MAKES A SCANT 2 QUARTS CHICKEN STOCK

BROWN STOCK VARIATION

Browning the chicken first is a bit more work but dramatically improves the color and flavor of the stock. Most folks have a stockpot with a thin bottom; therefore I suggest that you use a cast iron pan for browning the chicken. If you have a high-quality stockpot, simply brown the chicken in the same pot in which you prepare the stock.

Rinse chicken and pat dry with paper towels. Season liberally with salt and freshly ground black pepper. Heat 2 tablespoons of olive oil in a large cast iron skillet. Brown chicken in batches until golden on all sides and then add to stockpot as stated in step 2 of the master recipe. Pour off fat from skillet, place over high heat, and add 1 cup of water. Scrape the bottom of the pan with a wooden spoon; when all of the browned bits and pieces have been loosened, pour the contents of the skillet into the stockpot. Proceed with master recipe.

MAKES 2 QUARTS

Beef Stock with Meat and Roasted Bones

In *The Cook's Bible,* I indicated that browning the bones was an optional, although important, step. After additional testing, I have concluded that browning is essential, the flavor and color of the final stock being dramatically improved. Mixing bones does work — you can even use chicken carcasses, and I highly recommend oxtail. Although not always available, they are cheap and add plenty of meaty flavor. Ask your butcher to cut up the beef bones for you — if you are using leftover bones and don't have a large cleaver, you can skip this step. Note that I also use beef as well as bones, which, thanks to some research done by Pam Anderson at *Cook's Illustrated,* dramatically improves the quality of the stock.

A large meat cleaver is a useful kitchen tool, since a regular chef's knife was not designed to chop bones. There are two types of cleavers available: one is for cutting meat and bone — it has a blunt, rather dull edge — and the other is a vegetable cleaver, which is more delicate. Once you start using cleavers, you'll find them addictive and easy to use.

5	pounds beef bones cut into 4-inch pieces
2	carrots, cut into 2-inch pieces (do not peel)
2	large onions, quartered
3	quarts cold water, approximately
2	pounds inexpensive beef on the bone (oxtail, shank, or any cheap beef cut into chunks)
2	tomatoes, fresh or canned, coarsely chopped
2	cloves garlic, crushed
1	teaspoon black peppercorns
2	bay leaves
2	celery stalks, coarsely chopped
½	cup chopped parsley

1. Heat oven to 450 degrees. Place bones in a roasting pan and add half the carrots.

Roast for about 20 minutes, turn the bones over, and then add half the onions. Roast an additional 30 minutes or until bones are well browned but not burned. Watch the onions carefully — they have a tendency to burn if touching the bottom of the roasting pan. (Try to place them on top of the carrots and bones.) Transfer bones from pan to a large (at least 8-quart) pot. Pour off any excess fat and place roasting pan on the stovetop over medium-high heat. Add 2 cups of the water and bring to a boil. Cook for 3 minutes, scraping up browned bits from the bottom of the pan.

2. Pour contents of the roasting pan into a stockpot along with other ingredients except celery and parsley (there should be just enough water to cover). Bring to a boil and reduce heat to a slow simmer. Don't bother removing the scum as it rises to the surface — it will be strained out after cooking. Simmer uncovered for 2½ hours. Add celery and parsley and simmer an additional 30 minutes. Ladle as much stock as possible into a sieve lined with a quadruple thickness of cheesecloth. Remove and discard solids and let settle for 10 minutes. Carefully pour the remaining liquid into the sieve. Taste — if stock is too weak, put it in a cleaned stockpot and simmer until flavor is increased. (You may simmer up to 2 additional hours if you have time.)

3. Add a modest amount of salt to taste since it may be reduced (boiled down) in another recipe. It is best to cool stock quickly by placing it in a bowl, preferably metal, which is placed inside a larger bowl half filled with ice. Stir occasionally until it reaches room temperature and then re-frigerate. Remove the congealed fat layer on top of the broth before reheating. Stock can also be frozen.

MAKES ABOUT 2 TO 3 QUARTS STOCK

Quick and Easy Beef Stock

I tried a number of methods for producing a quick and easy beef stock, and this method was the best. I also tried using ground meat, which was a disaster; it simply tasted like ground beef simmered in water.

1   tablespoon olive oil
1   pound beef with bone, cut into pieces (shank makes excellent stock)
1   quart chicken stock, preferably homemade
1   tablespoon brandy

In a Dutch oven or large skillet, heat the olive oil over medium-high heat and add the cut-up beef. Thoroughly brown on all sides, 12 to 15 minutes total. Over high heat, add 1 cup of the chicken stock and scrape down the bottom of the pan with a wooden spoon. When all of the browned bits are loosened, add the remaining 3 cups of stock and the brandy. Bring to a boil, then lower heat and simmer for 5 minutes. Use immediately as is or strain through cheesecloth and refrigerate or freeze.

MAKES 1 QUART

Chicken Noodle Soup

I don't know why more home cooks don't make their own chicken noodle soup.

It contains two of America's favorite foods and it is easy to make. The best part of the recipe is that it makes its own chicken stock while the chicken cooks. The meat is then used in the final soup.

1   (3- to 4-pound) chicken or the same
    amount of parts
    Salt and freshly ground black pepper
    to taste
3   tablespoons butter
1   large onion, quartered
3   medium carrots, coarsely chopped
2   bay leaves
12 whole cloves
3   medium celery stalks, coarsely
    chopped
½   cup finely chopped onion
½   cup finely chopped carrot
4   ounces egg noodles
1   cup frozen peas
2   tablespoons finely chopped flat-leaf
    parsley

1. Cut chicken into 10 pieces, cutting each breast half in half again. (You should have 4 breast pieces, 2 legs, 2 thighs, and 2 wings.) Rinse and pat dry with paper towels. Season liberally with salt and pepper.
2. In a 6- to 8-quart stockpot or large cast iron Dutch oven, heat butter over medium-high heat until foam subsides. Brown chicken parts on both sides in 2 batches, about 10 to 15 minutes for each batch. Pour off excess fat, leaving no more than 2 tablespoons. Return all parts to the pot, add 2½ quarts cold water along with the next 5 ingredients and bring to a boil. Reduce heat to a simmer and cook uncovered until the chicken is cooked through and the broth is nicely colored and flavored, about 45 minutes.

3. Remove chicken and reserve. Strain the soup through a double layer of cheesecloth into a bowl and then return to the pot. Taste and add salt and pepper if needed. Bring back to a simmer. Add the chopped onion and carrot and cook until carrots are barely tender, about 3 to 4 minutes. Meanwhile, chop chicken into bite-size pieces, discarding skin and bones. Add the noodles, the peas, and the chicken and simmer until noodles are cooked, about 5 to 7 minutes. Stir in parsley and serve. (If some of the soup is to be served the next day as leftovers, cook the pasta separately, place into individual serving bowls, and top with soup. Otherwise, the noodles will swell overnight, absorbing much of the broth.)

SERVES 4 TO 6

Master Recipe for Vegetable Soup with Meat

I picked up this idea from Julia Della Croce, who cooks meat in some of her tomato sauces to add flavor and then, when cooked, removes it and serves the sliced meat along with the dish. Here, I use a chop or steak to flavor the soup, creating its own stock. If you have a choice, I prefer veal or pork to beef and I make sure that the meat is no more than ¾ inch thick; otherwise it will not fully cook. This soup is rich and cloudy, not like the clear, bright stock of the basic vegetable soup, but there is plenty of flavor. This is an excellent way to make 1 chop serve 4.

1   veal or pork chop, with bone, no
    thicker than ¾ inch, or chuck steak
    with bone

Salt and freshly ground black pepper to taste

1 tablespoon olive oil
1 large onion, coarsely chopped
3 cloves garlic, minced
¼ cup white wine
1½ pounds root vegetables such as potatoes, sweet potatoes, carrots, turnips, or parsnips, coarsely chopped
½ pound tender vegetables such as corn kernels, peas, or coarsely chopped green beans or summer squash
6 cups homemade chicken stock or canned low-sodium chicken stock
1 teaspoon dried herbs or 1 tablespoon fresh (thyme and basil are the most frequently used herbs for vegetable soups)
Pinch of sugar
½ pound spinach or Swiss chard or kale, stemmed and coarsely chopped (optional)
¼ cup sour cream, heavy cream, or yogurt (optional)
Freshly grated Parmesan cheese (optional)

1. Season the meat with salt and pepper and brown it in a 6-quart cast iron Dutch oven. When thoroughly brown on both sides, remove from pan and pour off all but 1 tablespoon of fat. (There may be very little rendered fat in the pan depending on the leanness of the meat.)

2. Put olive oil in pan and heat over medium-high heat for 2 minutes. Add onion and sauté over medium heat until softened, about 8 minutes. Add garlic and cook for 1 minute — be careful not to burn. Add wine and scrape up any browned bits from bottom of pan with a wooden spoon.

3. Return browned meat to pan and add vegetables, chicken stock, and herbs, if using dried. Bring to a boil, cover, and simmer for 15 minutes. Add a pinch of sugar plus salt to taste.

4. Replace cover and continue to simmer for 30 minutes. Remove chop or steak, cut away meat, chop it into bite-size pieces, and return it to the pot with the bone. Add herbs, if using fresh, and optional spinach, and cook for 10 minutes. Remove and discard bone.

5. If you like, stir in ¼ cup of sour cream, heavy cream, or yogurt and sprinkle the soup with Parmesan cheese. Serve with thick slices of crusty peasant or French bread slightly toasted.

SERVES 4 TO 6

Master Recipe for Bean Soup

The ham bone or ham hocks are optional, although they do add lots of flavor as well as bits of meat. However, a good smoky bacon will also help. If you do use a ham bone, simmer the soup for a good 2 hours (up to 3 or 4 hours if you have the time) to extract the full flavor of the bone.

½ pound (1 cup) dried beans (black, Great Northern, navy, red, chick-peas, etc.)
1 quart chicken stock
4 slices thick-cut smoked bacon
2 tablespoons olive oil
1 tablespoon butter
2 medium onions, chopped
3 cloves garlic, crushed
1 stalk celery, chopped
1 leek (white part only), chopped

1	bay leaf
1	teaspoon salt, less if using a ham bone
	Ham bone or 2 ham hocks, optional
	but recommended
¼	cup dry sherry
	Freshly ground black pepper to taste

1. Rinse and pick over the beans and soak overnight in cold water. Drain and cover beans with 1½ quarts of fresh water and 1 quart of chicken stock (per the chart on page 38). Set aside.
2. Cook the bacon in a skillet and drain on paper towels. Remove all but 1 tablespoon of bacon fat from skillet and add the olive oil and butter. Over medium heat, cook until foam subsides, then add the next 4 ingredients (onions through leek) and cook, stirring frequently, for about 8 minutes or until lightly browned. Add 2 cups of liquid from the beans and stir. Bring to a boil. Pour mixture into the pot with the beans and add the next 3 ingredients (the ham bone is optional). Simmer uncovered for 1 hour (or 2 hours if using the bones).
3. Remove the bay leaf and bones, if any. Pour the soup through a large sieve or colander over a large bowl. Purée the solids with some of the liquid in a blender, food processor, or food mill. Return puréed solids to the pot with the liquid and stir to combine. Add the sherry, reheat soup, and add freshly ground black pepper to taste. Simmer for 5 minutes. Crumble bacon and sprinkle on individual servings.

SERVES 6 TO 8

Split Pea Soup

This is a good soup to serve in the dead of winter since it is hearty, warming, a good "pantry" soup, and the sort of meal that would be served in Vermont when it was cold. Although this is an easy, straightforward recipe, be sure to use the ham hock or ham bone. I have tested this soup without it and find that without the bone it is not really worth making.

4	slices thick-cut smoked bacon
2	tablespoons olive oil
1	tablespoon butter
2	medium onions, finely chopped
3	cloves garlic, crushed
1	stalk celery, chopped
2	carrots, peeled and finely chopped
3	bay leaves
2½	quarts low-sodium canned chicken stock or 1½ quarts regular canned chicken stock plus 1 cup water
1	smoked ham hock (about 1 pound) or bone from a cooked ham (with some meat still attached)
1	pound (2 cups) dried split peas, rinsed and picked over
	Salt and freshly ground black pepper to taste

1. Cook the bacon in 6-quart stockpot or Dutch oven and drain on paper towels. Pour off all but 1 tablespoon of bacon fat, then add the olive oil and butter. Over medium heat, cook until foam subsides. Add the onions and cook over medium-low heat, stirring frequently, for 15 to 20 minutes, until onions are dark brown and have caramelized.
2. Add the next 3 ingredients and cook,

stirring frequently, for 5 minutes or until carrots have softened. Add the remaining ingredients, except the salt and pepper, and bring to a simmer over high heat. Reduce heat to low, cover, and simmer gently for about 1½ hours, until peas fall apart and soup is thick.

3. Remove and discard the bay leaf. Remove the ham bones; trim off any meat, chop coarsely, and return the meat to the pot, discarding the bones. Whisk soup until smooth. Taste and adjust seasonings. (The ham is salty and therefore it is unlikely you will need to add salt.) Crumble bacon and sprinkle on individual servings.

SERVES 6 TO 8

Lentil Soup with Tomatoes, Spinach, and Rice

This is nothing fancy, but it's a good, cheap, hearty soup perfect for a farmhouse supper. Be sure to adjust the salt level carefully. Undersalting this soup produces a dull dish indeed.

2	tablespoons butter
2	tablespoons olive oil
1	large onion, chopped
2	carrots, chopped
1	rib celery, chopped
2	cloves garlic, minced
1	cup lentils, rinsed and picked over
5	cups chicken stock, homemade preferred
5	cups water
2	cups canned or fresh tomatoes, chopped, with their juice
½	teaspoon salt or to taste
	Freshly ground black pepper to taste
¼	cup uncooked rice

½	pound fresh spinach, rinsed and stemmed
	Grated Parmesan cheese for garnish (optional)

1. Place a heavy-duty stockpot or soup kettle over medium heat. Add butter and olive oil. When butter stops foaming, add onion, carrots, and celery, and sauté until the vegetables soften, about 8 to 10 minutes. Add garlic and cook another 2 minutes. Add lentils, chicken stock, water, and tomatoes. Cover and simmer for 45 minutes to 1 hour or until lentils are very soft.

2. Add salt and pepper and rice. Cover and cook for another 15 minutes. The soup will have thickened a bit and the rice should be tender. Check the seasonings and add more salt if necessary. Stir in the spinach, cover, and cook another 2 to 3 minutes or until spinach is fully cooked. Adjust seasonings.

3. Ladle into bowls and serve with a bit of grated Parmesan cheese and hunks of country bread.

SERVES 8

Carrot Soup with Cashew Milk

I found a version of this recipe in *A Mountain Harvest Cookbook* by Roberta Sickler. I tested it using both roasted and raw cashews and found that the latter are vastly preferable. When tested with roasted nuts, the soup was not as creamy and the roasted flavor was overpowering. Raw cashews are available either at farm stands or at health food stores.

2½ cups chicken stock
¾ cup raw cashews
2 tablespoons olive oil
1 medium onion, peeled and finely
  chopped
1 cup peeled and coarsely grated
  carrots
2 whole cloves
1 clove garlic, minced
1 teaspoon grated orange zest
½ cup half-and-half

1. Bring the chicken stock to a boil in a large saucepan. In a blender or food processor, grind the cashews fine and then slowly add the hot chicken stock with the motor running. Blend until smooth. Set aside.

2. Heat the olive oil in the same saucepan. Add the onion and sauté over medium-low heat for 5 minutes. Do not let onion brown. Add the carrots and cook over medium-low heat, stirring frequently, until carrots are tender, about 8 to 10 minutes. Add cloves, garlic, orange zest, and reserved cashew mixture. Stir over medium heat until hot.

3. Remove and discard the cloves. Transfer soup to blender or food processor. Purée until smooth and return to saucepan. Stir in half-and-half, heat through, and serve.

SERVES 2 AS A MAIN COURSE

Master Recipe for Potato Soup

I find that the more subtle herbs seem to work best here, including tarragon, chervil, and marjoram. You can purée this soup if you like after cooking.

2 tablespoons butter
1 tablespoon olive oil
1 medium onion, chopped
1 cup chopped leeks (white part only)
1½ pounds potatoes, peeled and cut into
  ½-inch dice
½ teaspoon sugar
3 cups chicken stock
¾ cup heavy cream
1 tablespoon fresh herbs, minced (basil,
  tarragon, chervil, thyme, mint, or
  marjoram)
½ teaspoon salt or to taste
  Freshly ground black pepper to taste
¼ cup minced parsley or chives,
  for garnish

Heat the butter and olive oil in a large pot. Add the onion and leeks and cook covered over low heat for 15 minutes — do not let onion and leeks brown. Add the potatoes, sugar, and chicken stock, bring to a simmer, and cook until the potatoes are just tender, about 25 minutes. Add the heavy cream and herbs and cook 5 minutes longer. Season with salt and pepper to taste. Garnish each serving with parsley or chives.

SERVES 4

Green Pea and Watercress Soup

Across the dirt road from our farmhouse, there is a small stream that runs down from an upper pasture on its way to Baldwin Brook. In the summer, great patches of watercress can be found right in the middle of the stream, fed by a slow trickle of water which gently feeds the crop. I often take the kids over just before dinner armed with a basket and scissors and we harvest just enough to add to a salad or to use in a fresh spring soup. I have made this recipe with a variety of other ingredients including orange zest, white wine, and sour cream as a garnish. However, the soup has a wonderful fresh flavor and these embellishments just muck it up. This is one soup that should be simply made.

4	cups frozen or shelled fresh green peas
4	cups watercress leaves, lightly packed
4	tablespoons (½ stick) butter
¼	cup minced onion
1½	tablespoons flour
2	teaspoons minced fresh thyme or 1 teaspoon dried
½	cup mint sprigs, lightly packed
4	cups high-quality chicken stock
	Salt and freshly ground black pepper to taste

1. Cook only 2 cups of the peas in boiling water: 7 minutes for fresh and just 2 minutes for frozen. Add watercress and cook for 1 minute longer. Pour into a colander and rinse under cold water. Let drain in sink.
2. In a 4-quart Dutch oven or large saucepan, melt the butter over medium heat; when foam subsides, add the onion and sauté for 5 minutes or until softened. Whisk in the flour and cook over medium-low heat for 2 minutes, stirring constantly. Add the thyme, mint, and cooked peas/watercress mixture. Stir to mix.
3. Stir in 1 cup of the stock. Transfer the mixture to a food mill or food processor and purée until smooth. Return to the

saucepan and add remaining stock. Bring to a simmer and cook for 5 minutes. If using fresh peas, add the remaining 2 cups now. If using frozen, simmer for 10 minutes in a small saucepan with ¼ cup water and drain before adding. Simmer soup for an additional 5 minutes. Serve as is or with a dollop of sour cream.

SERVES 6 AS A FIRST COURSE;
4 AS A MAIN COURSE

New England Clam Chowder

My children love New England clam chowder and order it whenever they find it on a menu. What arrives at the table is most often a glutinous white porridge that tastes nothing like clams, which is exactly why my kids like it. It can be best described as a medium béchamel, cream thickened with flour and butter. In my own kitchen, I started experimenting with a variety of recipes only to find that many of them were also thick and heavy, the delicate, briny taste of the clams lost in a dairy sea.

The first issue was which type of clams to use. A series of taste tests in the test kitchen of *Cook's Illustrated* determined the larger the clam, the worse the flavor. Small littlenecks were clearly the best although expensive. Quahogs, often used for chowder, tend to have a strong mineral flavor (this is due to the contents of their large bellies) which can be extraordinarily unpleasant. You can also use cherrystones, which are medium-size clams, if you wish to be more economical.

The next issue was the liquid. Many recipes use nothing but the broth made from cooking the clams in water, plus heavy cream. I found that this makes a dull dish and preferred a chowder with a bit of white wine and half-and-half (or half cream and half milk). The wine adds a hint of acidity which balances the creamy, bland taste of the half-and-half. Chicken stock also worked well as an ingredient (as opposed to fish stock or clam juice) since it adds a nice flavor and is both economical and readily available. I also discarded the notion of thickening the chowder with flour. It disguises the fresh, lively taste of the clams, which is, in my opinion, the primary objective of this dish. I also tried thickening the chowder with cornmeal, which results in a lumpy mess. If you do wish to thicken this recipe, I suggest using white cracker crumbs (do not use heavily salted crackers), which is also traditional.

Any serious New England cook will issue a call to arms upon discovering that this recipe calls for bacon and not salt pork. (Although one might not think that clam chowder is a farmhouse recipe, it was in fact rather common in the interior of New England, such a recipe having appeared in a local guild cookbook published in a nearby town in 1939.) Since the latter is not a common kitchen staple these days, I have opted for the bacon. Purists may wish to substitute the more authentic salt pork. (Use 4 ounces, follow the recipe directions for the bacon, and discard any bits that have not rendered.) I also found it best to cut the bacon into matchstick pieces before cooking. This promotes even cooking and makes for a more attractive presentation.

I also tried celery as an ingredient, which I found both unappealing and unnecessary.

Once the half-and-half is added, it is best to simmer the chowder gently or it may curdle and ruin the recipe. Keep in mind that a sufficient quantity of salt and pepper is crucial to this dish. Do not use a light hand. Finally, remember that a clam chowder is all about the clams. Inferior clams make a second-rate chowder.

4	pounds littleneck clams, scrubbed
2	cups water
¼	cup white wine
3	tablespoons butter
3	slices thick-cut smoked bacon, cut into match sticks
1	cup finely chopped onion
2	large waxy potatoes, cut into small cubes
1	teaspoon minced fresh thyme, or ½ teaspoon dried
2	bay leaves
1	cup high-quality chicken stock
2	cups half-and-half or 1 cup milk and 1 cup heavy cream
	Salt and freshly ground black pepper to taste
¼	cup minced chives or flat-leaf parsley

1. Place clams, water, and white wine in a large (6-quart) pot. Bring to a simmer, cover, and cook until clams open, about 10 minutes. Remove from heat.
2. Discard any unopened clams. Remove meat from opened clams, chop, place in a bowl, and toss with 1 tablespoon butter. Pour liquid in pot through 2 layers of cheesecloth into a large glass measuring cup (to remove sand and bits of broken shell) and reserve.

3. Wipe pot clean and place over medium-high heat. Add bacon, and when cooked, remove from pot to paper towels and reserve. Pour off all but 2 tablespoons fat. Add remaining 2 tablespoons of butter, and after foam subsides, add onion and cook over medium heat for 10 minutes.

4. Add the reserved cooking liquid along with potatoes, thyme, bay leaves, and chicken stock. Bring to a simmer and cook until potatoes are tender, about 15 to 17 minutes.

5. Add half-and-half and bring to a very gentle simmer. Add salt and pepper to taste. Add reserved clams and heat through, about 2 minutes. Remove bay leaves. Garnish with chives or parsley and reserved bacon.

SERVES 6 AS A FIRST COURSE;
4 AS A MAIN COURSE

The Root Cellar

OUR TOWN HAS A SMALL white clapboard house that was owned for many years by Marie Briggs. Ever since I was a kid, it has been referred to as the "corner house," since it marks the corner of Southeast Corners Road and the main road leading up into town. It sits in a small stand of mature red oaks on the edge of an old hay field that was later planted with alfalfa and now with cut flowers, a business started by a local schoolteacher, Jim Link. There is a small fenced garden out back, tended and harvested by a few local women, and the town sandpile used to be located across the road until the residents finally voted in the money to purchase land for a town garage. There is a long roost of mailboxes just across from the house and the Green River runs behind it; the kids go wading in the brisk, pale green water every July Fourth following our annual Independence Day parade. After the yellow farmhouse, which served as the town center for decades, was rented out, Marie moved back up into the old Bentley place and the corner house became the place to go for potluck special events including birthdays and mud season parties when most of the town has come down with cabin fever.

One Saturday night, my wife and I showed up for such a party and the small house was packed from wall to wall. The front steps are three long pieces of fieldstone and the door itself is weathered unpainted wood, with a small lion's head knocker and a bell that is rung by turning a brass key. Once through the entrance, we found ourselves in the small, square kitchen, amidst the bustle of a country potluck supper. Folks were trying to find a spot to put down baked beans, shepherd's pie, bean and macaroni salads, and cheese-covered casseroles, kids were banging doors and running up and down the short stairs that lead to the upstairs bedroom, and one of the town's old Socialists was singing vintage Pete Seeger folk songs.

After dinner, we all packed into the side room, the old bachelors heavily seated on rundown faded blue sofas and rockers covered with worn blankets, canes leaning up against the back wall, kids up in front, and our unofficial town mayor, a woman about my age who organizes these events, started the movie. To my surprise, it was from the agricultural extension service and was on how to grow and cook rutabagas.

Over the years, I have thought a good deal about that evening. I guess that root vegetables and farmers have much in common. A turnip, parsnip, or beet is sturdy and plain, but as you become familiar with each of them, they surprise you with their sweetness and complex flavors. They are more than they seem at first, more subtle and complex. After spending a lifetime roasting beets with the skins on, for example, I discovered that roasting them already peeled was vastly better, the sweet juices caramelizing on the outside, thick and dark.

But perhaps I like root vegetables most because to walk into a root cellar in January is to step into a room full of memories; of summer, of onions drying in the sun, of parsnips dug out of the warm earth, sweet and pale, the moist earth still clinging to the parchment surface. Like old farmers, they keep well over the winter, hidden inside in small dark rooms, well preserved and full of secrets.

A MODERN ROOT CELLAR is nothing more than a partitioned section of the basement, with a window hooked up to a thermostat that opens to the cold winter air when the room gets too warm. Bins hold beets and turnips and parsnips and potatoes. Some years I grow onions, and garlic, and shallots as well, the shallots holding particularly well throughout the year. Some vegetables are best packed in large, extra-heavy black plastic garbage bags filled with peat moss; others are best hung in wire baskets with plenty of air for drying. But farmers could be extraordinarily inventive about growing fresh foods over the winter. I have read that barrels were drilled with holes through which were placed freshly dug parsley roots, the leaves and stems hanging outside. The barrel was filled with good garden soil and the barrel was kept in the basement through the winter, the fresh, growing parsley snipped off as needed.

Although not glamorous, root vegetables require attention in preparation to bring out the full range of their complex flavors. Mashed turnips on their own are bitter and watery, but when paired with potatoes have just the right amount of snap and backbone. Raw turnips can be grated for a coleslaw to which raisins are added for just a hint of sweetness. All roasted root vegetables should be cooked covered at high temperature and then the cover removed for the last 20 minutes. This yields a moist interior and crisp skin.

To explore all the possibilities, I started by boiling, steaming, and then roasting beets, carrots, parsnips, rutabaga, turnips, and butternut squash. I tried different sizes of many of these vegetables, since a large turnip cooks quite differently than a small one. Below are the results.

Beets

Beets are full of flavor and therefore, unlike potatoes, don't lend themselves to many recipe variations. Perhaps the most delicious and simplest root vegetable dish is beets roasted after having been skinned. I discovered that if you skin beets before roasting them (almost all recipes I have

BOILING ROOT VEGETABLES

Beets, carrots, parsnips, rutabaga, and turnips were cooked in plenty of boiling salted water (2 teaspoons of salt per 4 quarts of water). I have also included butternut squash, which is not a root vegetable but is similar in texture.

ROOT VEGETABLE	SIZE/PREPARATION	COOKING TIME
Beets	whole	36 minutes
	quartered	25 minutes
	½-inch slices	15 minutes
Butternut squash	1-inch chunks	15 minutes
Carrots, thin	cut in half lengthwise then in half across the width	
	thin end	15 minutes
	thick end	20 minutes
Carrots, thick	cut in half lengthwise then in half across the width	
	thin end	11 minutes
	thick end	16 minutes
Carrots, chunks	2-inch chunks	18 minutes
Parsnips	cut in half across the width, then cut thick end in half lengthwise	
	thin end	9 minutes
	thick end	12 minutes
Parsnips, chunks	2-inch chunks	12 minutes
Rutabaga	2-inch chunks	30–35 minutes
Turnips, baby	1½ inches in diameter	13 minutes
Turnips, small	2½ inches in diameter	26 minutes
Turnips, chunks	2-inch chunks	24 minutes

found suggest skinning after roasting), the sweet juices come to the surface and are caramelized. The result is spectacular.

I find that beets are apt to become woody and tasteless when picked too late; beets are best when they are small or medium-sized. I grow two crops of them; one gets started in the spring and one in August. Beet tops, when small, can be used in salad much like turnip tops. When the leaves are larger, they can be prepared like any other tough green: boiled briefly and then sautéed or served along with dried white beans which have been cooked and then dressed with plenty of olive oil, salt, and pepper. Beet tops are also wonderful when sautéed briefly, without blanching or boiling, along with roasted beets and chopped raw onion. The slightly bitter tops are a good partner to the sweet, caramelized beets.

STEAMING ROOT VEGETABLES

Beets, carrots, parsnips, rutabaga, and turnips (and a nonroot vegetable, butternut squash) were steamed. Here are the cooking times.

ROOT VEGETABLE	SIZE/PREPARATION	COOKING TIME
Beets	whole	45 minutes
	quartered	30 minutes
	½-inch slices	22 minutes
Butternut squash	1-inch chunks	20 minutes
Carrots	cut in half lengthwise then in half across the width	
	thin end	22 minutes
	thick end	30 minutes
Carrots, chunks	2-inch chunks	26 minutes
Parsnips	cut in half lengthwise then in half across the width	
	thin end	15 minutes
	thick end	30 minutes
Parsnips, chunks	2-inch chunks	12 minutes
Rutabaga	2-inch chunks	35 minutes
Turnips, baby	1½ inches in diameter	15 minutes
Turnips, small	2½ inches in diameter	32 minutes
Turnips, chunks	2-inch chunks	22 minutes

Master Recipe for Roasted Beets

I used to roast beets whole and then skin them by rubbing vigorously with paper towels. However, that requires last-minute preparation, which I would rather not do when putting dinner on the table. This method, suggested to me by Jeanne Maguire, puts all of the preparation up front. Perhaps more important, peeled beets tend to exude juices during roasting, and these juices caramelize, adding a great deal of flavor. (That being said, older beets do not fare as well with this method since they are more desiccated and can dry out during roasting.) Roasted beets are a nice accompaniment to grilled meats.

ROASTING ROOT VEGETABLES

Beets, carrots, parsnips, rutabaga, and turnips (and a nonroot vegetable, butternut squash) were roasted at 350 degrees, 400 degrees, and 450 degrees. As I discovered in other roasting tests, the higher temperature won out. (I also tested 500 degrees and found that the outside of the vegetables burned before the inside was thoroughly cooked.) However, it is best to cover the vegetables with aluminum foil for the first 20 minutes and then roast uncovered. (Peeled beets are best left covered for 35 minutes to avoid burning the very sweet juices.) This ensures that the inside of the vegetables will still be moist and creamy instead of dried out. All vegetables were tossed with olive oil, salt, and freshly ground pepper before roasting.

ROOT VEGETABLE	SIZE/PREPARATION	COOKING TIME
Beets	whole	60 minutes
	quartered	45 minutes
Butternut squash	1-inch chunks	30–35 minutes
Carrots	cut in half lengthwise then in half across the width	
	thin end	35 minutes
	thick end	40 minutes
Carrots, chunks	1-inch chunks	35 minutes
Parsnips	cut in half lengthwise then in half across the width	
	thin end	25 minutes
	thick end	32 minutes
Parsnips, chunks	1-inch chunks	32 minutes
Rutabaga	2-inch chunks	55 minutes
Turnips, baby	1½ inches in diameter	30 minutes
Turnips, small	2½ inches in diameter	50 minutes
Turnips, chunks	2-inch chunks	45 minutes

8   medium to large beets, about 2¼ inches in diameter, peeled and quartered

2   tablespoons high-quality olive oil

¼   teaspoon salt
    Freshly ground black pepper to taste

1. Heat oven to 450 degrees. Place beets in a roasting pan, toss with olive oil, salt, and pepper, and arrange in one layer. Cover with aluminum foil and roast for 35 minutes. Uncover and roast for another 10 minutes or until beets can easily be pierced with a fork.

SERVES 4 TO 6

Master Recipe for Glazed Beets

This is a simple template for finishing off roasted beets with a nice glaze of butter and vinegar. A fruity vinegar such as raspberry adds a nice touch and a beautiful color as well.

16   small beets or 8 large beets, roasted (see above)

⅔   cup chicken stock

½   cup good-quality vinegar (raspberry, red wine, white wine, flavored, etc.)

3   tablespoons unsalted butter

1   tablespoon minced fresh gingerroot (optional)

1   teaspoon sugar

¼   teaspoon salt
    Freshly ground pepper to taste

If using large beets, cut into quarters. In a large sauté pan, combine stock, vinegar, butter, optional ginger, and sugar and bring to a simmer. Lower heat and sim-

mer until slightly thickened, about 5 minutes. Add the beets and simmer for about 8 minutes, tossing the beets in the sauce. Add salt and plenty of freshly ground black pepper to taste.

SERVES 6 TO 8

Pickled Beets

Pickled beets are a classic farmhouse preparation since they keep well — a few weeks — in the refrigerator and they go well with most meats. They also pack a lot of flavor, which is helpful when serving a simple roast.

⅓   cup red wine or cider vinegar

½   cup chicken stock

2   tablespoons balsamic vinegar (optional)

⅛   teaspoon dry mustard

⅛   teaspoon ground cloves

⅛   teaspoon ground allspice

¼   teaspoon salt

4   cups boiled (see page 53) or roasted beets (see page 55)

Combine all ingredients except beets in a large nonreactive skillet. Bring to a simmer over medium-high heat, reduce heat to medium, and simmer gently for 5 minutes. Add beets, increase heat, and simmer, stirring frequently, for 8 to 10 minutes or until nicely glazed. Remove from heat and serve hot, at room temperature, or chilled. Serve with meat or poultry.

SERVES 4 AS A SMALL SIDE DISH; CAN KEEP REFRIGERATED FOR AT LEAST 2 WEEKS

Farmhouse Beet Soup

When our crop of beets is young and small, I roast and then glaze them or simply serve them with salt and pepper. However, beets tend to get woody as they grow larger and they are then best used in a soup. This is nothing like a real country borscht, which contains meat, cabbage, and other vegetables, but is a simpler recipe which highlights the flavor of the beets.

2	pounds beets
2	tablespoons olive oil
1	large onion, coarsely chopped
3	cloves garlic, minced
2	cups apple juice or cider
4	cups chicken stock
3	tablespoons lemon juice
½	teaspoon salt
1	tablespoon minced fresh dill
1	cup plain yogurt
	Freshly ground black pepper to taste
½	cup sour cream for garnish

1. Roast beets according to the master recipe (page 55). When they are cool enough to handle, grate them.
2. Heat olive oil in a large nonreactive saucepan over medium-high heat for 2 minutes. Add onion and sauté over medium heat until softened, about 8 minutes. Add garlic and cook 1 to 2 minutes. Do not burn garlic.
3. Add the grated beets to the onion/garlic mixture and add the apple juice, chicken stock, lemon juice, and salt. Bring to a boil, lower the heat, and simmer for 15 minutes. Remove from heat and whisk in the dill and yogurt. Pour into a large bowl and chill in the refrigerator. Serve with freshly ground pepper and sour cream as a garnish.

SERVES 4 TO 6

CARROTS

My favorite time of year is mid-August, when the nights are cool and crisp, a few spots of orange and yellow are showing across the road on Walnut Mountain, yet the days are still hot, the tomatoes trying desperately to ripen before the first killing frost. Each day is precious, one part of me still in the dog days of summer and the other looking forward to cider pressing, apple jelly, grouse hunting, and, best of all, my fall crop of carrots. I rototill a cool-weather bed in the garden, add a good helping of composted horse manure, and then scatter a small handful of carrot seeds on the ground. I lightly rake them into the loose soil, give them a good watering, and then wait. In late September, when the leaves are marching toward full color, I start the harvest, picking out short, stubby specimens as I need them. I stand in the garden, surrounded by withered tomato vines, wild-looking stalks of brussels sprouts, a fall crop of lettuce, and a large bed of parsnips, turnips, and what's left of the red potatoes, and slowly eat a few carrots, stock still, gazing out over our small valley, with nothing on my mind but the rich, sweet taste of a just-picked carrot and the loamy scent of a fall Vermont garden.

Thymed Carrots Glazed with Vinegar

This is a classic preparation for carrots. The vinegar, sugar, and thyme combine to make a sweet-sour glaze with some punch. Dried thyme can be substituted in a pinch.

2	pounds carrots, peeled, cut into ¼-inch rounds
1	tablespoon vegetable oil
1	tablespoon unsalted butter
1	tablespoon minced fresh thyme or 1½ teaspoons dried
3	tablespoons white wine vinegar
⅓	cup water
1	tablespoon sugar
½	teaspoon salt
	Freshly ground black pepper

1. Boil carrots for 7 minutes or until just tender. Drain.
2. Heat oil and butter in a large skillet until foam subsides. Add carrots and toss for 2 minutes. Add remaining ingredients and cook over medium-high heat for 5 minutes or until liquid is reduced to a glaze. Add a few grindings of black pepper.

SERVES 8

Braised Carrots with Orange and Lime Butter

I found that lime juice works better than lemon juice here, although you can use the juice of 1 lemon as a substitute.

8–10	medium carrots (about 1 pound), peeled, cut in half lengthwise and then into 2-inch lengths
1	teaspoon orange zest
	Juice of 1 lime
¼	cup white wine
½	cup low-sodium or homemade chicken stock or water
2	tablespoons unsalted butter
1	teaspoon sugar
½	teaspoon salt
	Freshly ground black pepper to taste

Put all ingredients into a large nonreactive skillet and bring to a simmer. Cover and simmer until carrot pieces are tender, about 25 minutes. Remove cover, increase heat to medium-high, and stir constantly for a few minutes or until carrots are coated with a thin glaze.

SERVES 4

Shredded Carrots with Lemon Juice and Olive Oil

You can make this dish without the ginger for a lemony, olive oil flavor. Do not grate the carrots fine; use the largest holes possible on your grater to produce long, relatively thick pieces.

1	tablespoon lemon juice
¼	cup high-quality olive oil
½	teaspoon salt
¼	teaspoon sugar
1	teaspoon minced fresh ginger
4	cups peeled and coarsely grated carrots
	Freshly ground black pepper to taste

Whisk together the first 5 ingredients. Toss with carrots; add pepper to taste. Adjust seasonings if necessary.

SERVES 4 TO 6

ONIONS

We have a small back porch, which gets plenty of sun since it faces south. In September, it is covered with old screens set up on two-by-fours, with a mess of dirt-caked onions and shallots spread out to dry. It takes just about three good sunny days for them to dry properly; the dirt turns to a powdery dust, I rub them briskly with a towel and then put them into storage in the basement. In the dead of winter, I like to remember those warm September days, the back porch a dumping ground for work boots, onions, shovels, socks, toys, all piled up by the kitchen door, a snapshot of the week's activities. And before dinner, the kids and I sit on the top step, snapping the second crop of beans or husking a few ears of late corn.

Roasted Onions with Balsamic Vinegar

This is a simple recipe and a good way to use up large onions. As Amelia Simmons noted about onions in *American Cookery* (which was published in 1796), "if you consult cheapness, the largest are best; if you consult taste and softness, the smallest are the most delicate." She also did not think much of garlic, noting that "Garlicks, tho' used by the French, are better adapted to the uses of medicine than cookery." In this recipe, however, large onions are just fine, since they are roasted. You can toss roasted onions with other roasted root vegetables or serve them as an accompaniment to meat, chicken, or fish. Be sure to cut through the onions pole to pole so that each piece has a bit of the root end; this will help keep them intact.

4	large onions, peeled and quartered pole to pole
2	tablespoons olive oil
2	tablespoons balsamic vinegar
½	teaspoon salt
	Freshly ground black pepper to taste

Heat oven to 450 degrees. Toss all ingredients in a roasting pan. Cover pan tightly with aluminum foil and place in oven for 20 minutes. Remove foil, toss mixture, and cook uncovered for another 10 minutes or until onions are browned but not burned.

SERVES 4 TO 6 AS A SIDE DISH

Farmhouse Onion Soup

You can use beef stock instead of chicken stock for this recipe but only if it is home-made. Canned beef stock is universally inedible. Be sure to use real bread, not the sandy-textured bread crumbs than come in a can. Inexpensive loaves of Italian bread work fine. It's best if the bread is stale. A quick way to turn fresh bread into stale is to cut it up and leave it out overnight in a large plastic storage bag that is not sealed. If this soup is left overnight or if you refrigerate leftovers, additional stock will be needed during reheating, since the bread will soak up most of the liquid.

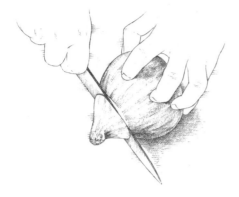

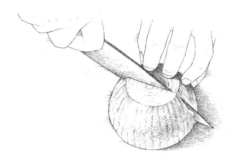

1. *To chop an onion*, start by removing the ends.

2. Now cut the onion in half pole to pole.

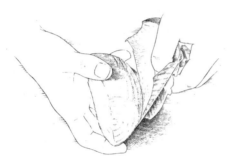

3. The outer skin will slip off easily. A whole onion is much more difficult to peel.

4. Now make a series of slices through the onion horizontally, cutting toward the darker, tougher root end. Do not cut all the way through.

5. Now make a series of vertical cuts, using the point of the knife. Do not cut through the root end.

6. Finally, chop across the onion, cutting into small diced pieces. Discard the tougher root end.

3	tablespoons olive oil
1	tablespoon butter
3	pounds onions, peeled, cut in half lengthwise, and thinly sliced
1	tablespoon sugar
½	teaspoon salt
	Freshly ground black pepper to taste
6½	cups chicken stock, homemade preferred
1½	cups dry white wine
3	tablespoons dry sherry
2	tablespoons Madeira (optional)
1	teaspoon minced fresh thyme or ½ teaspoon dried
1	(3-inch) section of rind from Parmesan cheese (optional)
3	cups stale chunks of country-style, chewy bread
	Freshly grated Parmesan cheese for topping

1. In a large saucepan or Dutch oven, heat olive oil and butter over medium heat. When hot, add onions, stir, and cover. Cook over medium-low heat for 25 minutes, stirring occasionally, until onions are soft and starting to color.
2. Uncover pot, increase heat to medium, add the sugar, salt, and pepper, and cook until onions turn a rich brown, about 30 minutes. Add 4½ cups of chicken stock, the next 5 ingredients, stir, and bring to a simmer. Cook covered for 15 minutes. Add bread and cook uncovered another 15 minutes. Stir soup occasionally. If soup is too thick, add up to 2 cups of additional stock and heat through. Remove rind, whisk soup to incorporate bread, and serve with freshly grated Parmesan cheese.

SERVES 4 TO 6 AS A MAIN COURSE

PARSNIPS

There is a bit of magic in parsnips. They are rich and sweet, the sugar increasing if they are left in the ground past the first frost. The theory is that the starches change over to sugar when subjected to cold, and I have found this to be true in our own garden. I leave them in the ground well into October and November, digging them up as I need them. They do seem sweeter than those I dig out earlier in the fall, before the cold weather moves down off our mountain and then down into the valley. Our garden sits in a field on the side of a mountain and it seems that there is more frost damage on a side hill than in the valley itself. It's as if the cold flows like water, a heavy mist that hugs the ground as it pours down off the mountaintop. Although the first frost is usually around Labor Day, on a warm year a real killing frost won't occur until late September or even early October. But that doesn't mean we don't cut our basil before the end of August to make pesto, or grab a last bunch of flat-leaf parsley, or even take as many semi-red tomatoes as we can gather up, bagging the green ones separately for ripening in the basement.

Many cookbooks claim that one can increase the sweetness of parsnips by leaving them overnight in the freezer. I tested this and found that the parsnips were no sweeter and the texture suffered terribly, becoming limp and soft. Other conventional wisdom claims that the skins can be slipped off easily after cooking. Well, this was no picnic, since the skins are a bit fibrous and it takes some pulling. The remaining flesh looked mangled. It is best to simply use a vegetable peeler before cooking. I had no serious problem with parsnips discoloring.

Purée of Steamed Parsnips with Parmesan

The addition of potatoes makes mashed parsnips smoother and the cheese adds some depth. Use chicken stock instead of half-and-half for a leaner version of this recipe. A potato ricer will not work very well with parsnips, since they are fibrous; use a masher or large fork instead.

1	pound parsnips, peeled and cut into 2-inch pieces
½	pound starchy potatoes, peeled and quartered
1	cup hot half-and-half or ½ cup hot chicken stock
½	cup grated high-quality Parmesan cheese
2	tablespoons butter, at room temperature
½	teaspoon salt
	Freshly ground black pepper to taste

1. Boil parsnips for 3 minutes in a large saucepan and then add potatoes. Cook another 15 minutes or until both are tender. Remove with a slotted spoon to a large bowl.
2. Mash the parsnips and potatoes with a potato masher or large fork. Add the half-and-half or chicken stock and beat until smooth. Add the grated cheese, butter, salt, and pepper and beat until incorporated.

SERVES 4 AS A SMALL SIDE DISH

Roasted Parsnips with Bacon and Onions

Make sure you use a smoky bacon for this recipe. Regular bacon provides only a hint of flavor, and you need a solid punch of smokehouse taste to balance the sweetness of the parsnips and onions. Parsnips can be a touch mealy and dry when roasted, although the flavor is rich and sweet, and therefore I often roast them with other vegetables such as carrots or potatoes, or I serve them with a meat that has gravy on the side.

6	slices thick-cut smoked bacon
2	pounds parsnips, peeled and cut into bite-size pieces
1	large onion, peeled and cut into wedges
1	tablespoon minced fresh thyme or 1½ teaspoons dried
	Salt and freshly ground black pepper to taste

1. Heat oven to 450 degrees. Cook bacon over medium heat until crisp and well browned. Remove to paper towels and reserve both the bacon and the fat.
2. In a large roasting pan, combine parsnips and onions and toss with 2 tablespoons of the rendered bacon fat. Cover pan tightly with aluminum foil.
3. Place pan in oven and roast for 20 minutes. Remove foil, toss vegetables, and cook uncovered another 10 minutes. Toss vegetables again and cook a final 5 minutes or until parsnips are fully cooked and sweet. Toss with crumbled bacon, thyme, salt to taste, and a few grindings of black pepper. Serve.

SERVES 4

Grated Parsnip and Carrot Salad with Citrus Dressing

Although parsnips are not that easy to grate, they work well with carrots in a simple salad. Be sure to let the dressed salad sit in the refrigerator for at least an hour before serving to allow the flavors to blend. I often double this recipe to serve 4.

⅓   pound parsnips, peeled and grated (about 1 cup)
⅓   pound carrots, peeled and grated (about 1 cup)
1   orange, juiced
½   lime, juiced
½   teaspoon sugar
¼   teaspoon salt
¼   teaspoon freshly ground black pepper

Toss all ingredients in a bowl until thoroughly mixed, cover, and place in the refrigerator for at least 1 hour before serving.

MAKES 2 CUPS OF SALAD. SERVES 2.

POTATOES

The first fact most of us learn about potatoes is that some are mealy or starchy and some are waxy. The latter are considered best for potato salads since they hold their shape well and are less apt to absorb salad dressing. The former, the starchy potato, is best for baking or for French fries since they produce a fluffy, pillowy interior. Like most easy definitions, however, this one obscures the fact that there are thousands of different types of potatoes, many of which defy simple categorization. For

example, is an all-purpose potato waxy or starchy?

ABOUT POTATOES, SWEET POTATOES, AND YAMS

For the purpose of this chapter, I refer to sweet potatoes and yams as "potatoes," although technically this is incorrect. Real yams are the large, tubular, white-fleshed root vegetables that come from Asia. However, what is labeled as a yam in an American supermarket is actually a sweet potato, a hybrid that was developed in Louisiana in the early twentieth century. It was given the name "yam" for marketing purposes to set it apart from the sweet potatoes that are grown in North Carolina, which are not as sweet, not as moist, and stringier when cooked. "Yams" also have flesh that is more orange than the yellow flesh of the regular sweet potato. In addition, sweet potatoes are not actually potatoes; they are members of the morning glory family, although they are referred to in sixteenth-century Spanish recipes as potatoes. When Columbus brought back a variety of tubers from the new world, the sweet potatoes were an instant success.

To find out which category all-purpose potatoes belong in, I followed Harold McGee's advice in *On Food and Cooking*. He states that if you create a brine solution (1 part salt to 11 parts water), you will find that waxy potatoes float while mealy potatoes sink. I assembled 13 different varieties (Russet, All-Purpose, Baking, Green Mountain, Idaho, Yukon Gold, Red Creamers, Red, Purple, Rose Gold, Red Gold, Sweet Potatoes, and Yams). With the exception of the sweet potatoes and yams, they all sank! So

A GUIDE TO 12 COMMON VARIETIES OF POTATOES, YAMS, AND SWEET POTATOES

Different varieties of potatoes have strikingly different flavors and textures. Here is a brief description of the most common varieties.

NAME	FLAVOR	TEXTURE	BEST FOR
High-Starch Potatoes (Mealy)			
Idaho	very dry; earthy	grainy; crumbly	baked; mashed
Russet	earthy; dry	dry; grainy	fries; baked
Green Mountain	earthy; dry	grainy; crumbly	baked; mashed
Medium-Starch Potatoes			
All-Purpose	light; earthy	firm; slightly dry	casseroles; roasted; thinly sliced
Yukon Gold	mild; slightly earthy	dry; firm	casseroles; mashed
Purple	mild; earthy	dry; grainy	roasted; mashed
Low-Starch Potatoes (Waxy)			
Red Creamer	mild; slightly sweet	smooth; firm	salads; boiling; whole roasted
Red	mild; slightly sweet	waxy; creamy	salads; boiling
Yellow Finn	mild; light	smooth; creamy	salads; boiling
Yams and Sweet Potatoes			
Jewel Yam	mild; sweet	soft; falls apart	mashed; baked
Garnet Yam	sweet; cloying	rich; creamy	mashed; baked
Sweet Potato	mild; sweet	moist; creamy	mashed; baked

much for science. The next step was to call the Maine Potato Board. They explained that the differences among different potatoes is the amount of solids. High-solid potatoes such as russets are mealy; low-solid potatoes such as new potatoes are waxy; and all-purpose potatoes are mealy potatoes with a lower solid content. By the way, the term "all-purpose" is pretty much a marketing term, rather than highly specific nomenclature, which applies to thousands of varieties of round white potatoes.

So where does that leave the home cook? It's fairly simple. Mealy and all-purpose potatoes have more "potato" flavor and are therefore preferred in most cases such as in recipes for baked, fried, and roasted potatoes. For potato salads, or for situations in which it is important that the potatoes do not absorb too much dressing or when you are concerned about the potatoes falling apart, use a waxy potato such as new or red potatoes. I also found in testing that all-purpose potatoes can be used in recipes that call for thinly sliced potatoes. In these situations, the all-purpose variety have the preferred taste and texture of mealy potatoes but they hold up better, which is important when sliced thin. In the following recipes I specify a particular type of potato except where I found that it simply makes no difference.

DO POTATOES TAKE ON WATER WHILE COOKING?

Many people believe that potatoes will take on lots of water during the cooking process if first cut into pieces. That's why many cookbooks suggest that potatoes be steamed or boiled whole. To test this theory, I peeled and soaked four different varieties of potatoes (Idaho, Yukon Gold, Red, and Sweet) in water for 1 hour, 2 hours, 3 hours, 4 hours, and then overnight and measured their weight before and after. Most potatoes absorbed water equal to only 5 percent of their weight when soaked overnight. In the first hour, the potatoes took on between 2 percent and 4 percent of their weight. By the way, none of the potatoes discolored at all even when soaked overnight.

Using three categories of potatoes (mealy, waxy, and sweet), I boiled the potatoes five different ways: whole with skin, whole peeled, peeled with ends cut off, peeled and quartered, and peeled cut into 1-inch dice. I measured the weight before and after cooking to determine whether or not the potato absorbed water. The unexpected result was that regardless of preparation method and type of potato, there was little water absorption. (This confirmed my results when soaking the potatoes overnight. In both cases, the potatoes took on less than 5 percent of their weight in water.) There was also no difference in flavor or texture between boiling a whole potato versus one that had been quartered or diced. So in this case, the conventional kitchen wisdom was just plain incorrect. The only significant difference was due to the skin. With the skin on, the potato had a richer, more earthy flavor, which I strongly prefer.

Below is a chart of cooking times for boiled potatoes.

Master Recipe for Boiled Potatoes

Wash and quarter potatoes. (Peeling is optional.) For 4 medium potatoes, heat 2 quarts water with 2 teaspoons salt, add potatoes, and boil gently for 15 minutes. Check with a fork. If the potato is not easily pierced through to the center, cook for another minute or two or until done. Whole potatoes take 25 to 30 minutes and potatoes cut into 1-inch dice take 10 minutes. Sweet potatoes take longer to cook: 35 minutes for whole potatoes, 17 minutes for quartered, and 12 minutes for diced. There is no difference in flavor or texture between whole, quartered, and diced potatoes.

Master Recipe for Steamed Potatoes

Steaming is really not any better than boiling but it takes less time and energy since there is much less water to heat up.

4   medium potatoes, washed and quartered (peeling is optional)

Place the potatoes on a rack above boiling water, cover, and steam for 35 to 40 minutes for whole potatoes, 15 minutes for quartered potatoes, and just 10 minutes for 1-inch dice. Check with a fork. If the potato is not easily pierced through to the center, cook for another minute or two or until done. Sweet potatoes take longer to cook: 45 minutes for whole potatoes, 16 minutes for quartered, and 12 minutes for diced. There is no difference in flavor or

HOW LONG DOES IT TAKE TO BOIL A POTATO?

Using three different categories of potatoes, I boiled each of them whole with the skin on, whole but peeled, whole with the ends cut off, quartered, and cut into 1-inch dice. Although the internal texture and flavor were the same for all preparation methods, the cooking time varied tremendously between a whole potato (about 30 minutes) and a diced potato (about 10 minutes). So for faster cooking times and no change in taste, always cut up potatoes before boiling.

PREPARATION	MEALY	WAXY	SWEET
Whole with skin	27 minutes	28 minutes	37 minutes
Whole, peeled	24 minutes	25 minutes	32 minutes
Ends removed	24 minutes	25 minutes	34 minutes
Quartered	16 minutes	15 minutes	17 minutes
Diced	10 minutes	10 minutes	12 minutes

texture between whole, quartered, and diced potatoes. Whole new potatoes or small red potatoes (2 inches in diameter) can be steamed in 10 to 12 minutes.

Boiled or Steamed Potatoes with Butter, Garlic, and Fresh Herbs

You can boil or steam waxy potatoes — either use small potatoes or cut larger ones into bite-size pieces before cooking — and then simply toss them with butter, garlic, and herbs. I tried braising them in the same mixture with a bit of chicken stock but found it quicker and easier to cook them first and then toss with the other ingredients. This recipe can be adjusted up or down and should only be made if the potatoes, parsley, and chives are really fresh. On the farm, this is how we serve just-dug new potatoes in late July and August. Be sure to use lots of salt and freshly ground black pepper.

2 pounds waxy potatoes, washed and cut into bite-size pieces, or use very small whole potatoes
3 tablespoons unsalted butter, room temperature
2 cloves garlic minced
¼ cup minced fresh parsley
¼ cup minced fresh chives
   Salt and freshly ground black pepper to taste

Boil or steam potatoes following master recipe on page 66. Toss with remaining ingredients in a large bowl and serve.

SERVES 4

Master Recipe for Baked Potatoes

A friend of mine who also grew up in our small Vermont town remembers sitting down to dinner with the farmhands one day when one of them used an unusual method for opening a hot baked potato.

HOW LONG DOES IT TAKE TO STEAM A POTATO?

Using the same categories of potatoes and preparation methods as in the previous chart, I tested measured steaming times. I could not detect any taste or texture differences between boiling and steaming. It was also interesting to note that the cooking times were dramatically higher for steam versus boiling when using whole potatoes. However, quartered or diced potatoes cooked in about the same time whether boiled or steamed. I prefer waxy potatoes, such as new or red potatoes, for steaming.

PREPARATION	MEALY	WAXY	SWEET
Whole with skin	38 minutes	34 minutes	43 minutes
Whole, peeled	36 minutes	30 minutes	38 minutes
Ends removed	36 minutes	30 minutes	38 minutes
Quartered	15 minutes	15 minutes	16 minutes
Diced	10 minutes	10 minutes	12 minutes

He simply whacked it with his fist, the potato neatly splitting apart. My friend then had a go, gave his potato a hard thump, and the contents spewed out over the table and burned his hand to boot.

Individually wrap washed but unpeeled potatoes in aluminum foil and place on a rack in a preheated 400 degree oven. After 20 minutes, remove foil and put potatoes back in oven. Allow a total cooking time of 45 minutes for starchy potatoes, 40 minutes for waxy potatoes, and 30 minutes for sweet potatoes.

DOUBLE-BAKED POTATOES

Bake 3 pounds of potatoes (about 4 large potatoes, preferably starchy) according to the master recipe (page 67). Cut a slice off the long side of each potato and scoop out the insides (creating a "boat"); place the cooked potato in a large bowl. Mash, following the instructions in the master recipe for Mashed Potatoes (page 70), leaving out the garlic, or use the roasted garlic variation and increase the amount of light cream to 2 cups. Refill potato skins and place them on a baking sheet. Put back in oven to bake for another 15 minutes.

DOUBLE-BAKED POTATOES WITH CHEESE

Follow Double-Baked Potato recipe above but grate 1 cup of cheese such as Parmesan or Cheddar and fold ¾ cup into the mashed potatoes before refilling potato skins. Top filled potatoes with remaining ¼ cup of cheese and bake an additional 15 minutes. Potatoes can also be served topped with cooked and crumbled bacon and/or minced chives.

DOUBLE-BAKED SWEET POTATOES

As noted earlier in this chapter, most yams sold in this country are actually sweet potatoes. Real yams are long and

WHAT IS THE BEST METHOD FOR BAKING POTATOES?

In *The Cook's Bible*, I determined that it was best to wrap potatoes in aluminum foil for the first half of the baking time and then unwrap them for the second half. This results in a crisp skin and a moist interior. If you don't wrap them at all, they tend to dry out during the long baking time. In this series of tests, I confirmed that this is the best method but also discovered that you can bake potatoes at any temperature between 350 and 400 degrees with good results. At lower temperatures, the baking time is unreasonably long. At higher temperatures, the potatoes tend to dry out.

TYPE	300 DEGREES	350 DEGREES	400 DEGREES	450 DEGREES
Starchy potatoes	70 minutes	55 minutes	45 minutes	40 minutes
Waxy potatoes	65 minutes	45 minutes	40 minutes	35 minutes
Sweet potatoes	40 minutes	35 minutes	31 minutes	28 minutes

tubular and have white flesh. So any orange or yellow-fleshed vegetable that is shaped somewhat like a potato is actually a sweet potato, even if the supermarket calls it a yam. I find that since sweet potato skins are very thin, double-baked yams turn out a bit misshapen. However, although they may look lopsided, they have a delicious flavor and are worth making.

4   medium sweet potatoes
4   tablespoons unsalted butter, at room temperature
4   tablespoons heavy cream
4   tablespoons maple syrup

Bake sweet potatoes according to the master recipe (page 67). Slice off the top of the long side of each potato, scoop out filling and place in a large bowl. Add remaining ingredients and mash together to desired consistency. Fill potato skins and bake for an additional 20 minutes.

SERVES 4

Master Recipe for Roasted Potatoes

Covering the roasting pan for the first 20 minutes prevents the potatoes from drying out but sacrifices none of the crispy exterior, since the potatoes finish cooking uncovered. I find that waxy potatoes are best roasted with the skin on but starchy potatoes are best roasted peeled. The skin of starchy potatoes has a strong flavor and, since it is thicker than the skin of a waxy potato, is less likely to become crispy.

2   pounds potatoes, peeled if starchy, washed but not peeled if waxy, cut into 1-inch dice
1   large onion, peeled and cut into wedges (optional)
2   tablespoons olive oil
     Salt and freshly ground pepper to taste

WHAT IS THE BEST METHOD FOR ROASTING POTATOES?

In *The Cook's Bible*, I also determined that potatoes and other root vegetables should be roasted for the first half of the cooking time in a pan covered tightly with aluminum foil. The foil is then removed for the second half. This produces moist interiors with plenty of crispy exteriors. In the tests below, I wanted to check different oven temperatures and found that 450 degrees was best. Lower temperatures provide insufficient browning and flavor development yet 500 degrees is too high; the interiors become dry. I also found that starchy potatoes are best for roasting. They come out of the oven with a nice, crispy exterior and a soft, fluffy interior. Waxy potatoes are not as crisp on the outside although the interior has a pleasant creaminess. Sweet potatoes tend to become soft, not crispy, and are a bit stringy inside. However, they are sweet and delicious.

TYPE	350 DEGREES	400 DEGREES	450 DEGREES	500 DEGREES
Starchy potatoes	40 minutes	35 minutes	35 minutes	24 minutes
Waxy potatoes	40 minutes	35 minutes	35 minutes	26 minutes
Sweet potatoes	35 minutes	30 minutes	26 minutes	22 minutes

1. Heat oven to 450 degrees. Toss potatoes and optional onion with olive oil and plenty of salt and pepper. Place in a roasting pan large enough to hold them in one layer. Cover tightly with aluminum foil.
2. Roast at 450 degrees for 20 minutes. Remove foil, toss potatoes, and continue roasting for an additional 10 minutes. Toss potatoes a second time. Roast an additional 5 to 10 minutes or until the outside of the potatoes is crispy and the inside is cooked through.

SERVES 4

Master Recipe for Mashed Potatoes

Good mashed potatoes should be mashed by hand; you can't use any sort of electric appliance to help out. If you don't have a potato masher or ricer, you can use a large fork and a very large bowl. You have to mash one potato at a time and you need room to push the others out of the way as you work. The other secret of good mashed potatoes is the proper ratio of liquid to potato. I find that each pound of potato needs ⅓ cup of liquid and 2 tablespoons of butter. I prefer light cream as the liquid of choice. You can substitute chicken stock, although you will need to reduce the quantity, as it thins out the potatoes too much.

I also tried a variety of tricks found in other recipes, including placing an onion in the cooking water, which had no effect; crushing garlic and simmering it in the cream or milk, which produced a very strong, garlicky flavor; cooking three peeled cloves of garlic in the cooking water and then adding them to the mashed potatoes, which worked very well; and finally, roasting a head of garlic and adding the contents to the potatoes, which is a wonderful variation but does take more effort. (See Roasted Garlic Variation, page 71.)

I tested using hot milk versus cold milk and the texture of the mashed potatoes was no different. (Some cooks claim that hot milk makes the potatoes fluffier.) However, it is best to use a hot liquid, since the potatoes will cool off quickly if you use cold. I also found that mashed potatoes tend to dry out quickly if not served immediately. If they cool off, place them in a saucepan over very low heat (or in a double boiler) and add an additional ¼ cup of hot liquid and an extra tablespoon of butter at the last minute to jazz up the flavor and texture.

3	pounds potatoes
2½	teaspoons salt
3	cloves garlic, peeled
6	tablespoons butter, at room temperature
1	cup hot light cream, half-and-half, or milk (see Note below)
2	tablespoons minced chives (optional) Salt and freshly ground pepper to taste

1. Fill a large pot or stockpot ⅔ full of water. Bring to a boil. Meanwhile, peel potatoes, cut into quarters, and place in a bowl of cold water to prevent discoloration. To stockpot add 2 teaspoons salt (reserve remaining ½ teaspoon), potatoes, and garlic. Cook covered until tender, 15 to 20 minutes. This will depend on the size of the potatoes and the size of the pot.

2. When potatoes are cooked, drain them, place in a large bowl, and mash potatoes and garlic with a potato masher, ricer, or fork to desired consistency. Do not use a food processor or electric mixer. Place potatoes and garlic back into the drained, still warm stockpot. Cut butter into pieces and add to potatoes along with the cream and optional chives. Mix until thoroughly combined. Taste and add additional salt if necessary and freshly ground pepper.

Note: For a healthier version of this recipe, substitute ¾ cup chicken stock for 1 cup of light cream.

SERVES 6

ROASTED GARLIC VARIATION

This version is substantially better than the master recipe above, since the garlic is roasted rather than just added to the cooking water. However it does take more time and effort and therefore I have treated it as a variation.

Instead of adding 3 cloves of garlic to the cooking water in the master recipe, cut the top off a whole head of garlic, place garlic on a small square of aluminum foil, drizzle with olive oil, and seal the package. Roast in a 350 degree oven for 40 minutes. Squeeze the contents into the cooked potatoes before mashing.

POTATO CASSEROLES

The problem with most potato casseroles was made clear after making a standard recipe. The potatoes tend to dry out and stick to the bottom of the pan.

For the first test, therefore, I precooked the sliced potatoes for 4 minutes in boiling water. This drastically reduced the cooking time to 45 minutes, which prevented the potatoes from overcooking and sticking to the bottom of the Dutch oven. I also discovered that the addition of liquid, either water or chicken stock, helped prevent the potatoes from drying out. Then I remembered a recipe for fish roasted on a bed of thinly sliced potatoes in which the potatoes created their own sauce. (The potatoes were thrown out, having leached their starch into the surrounding liquid.) So instead of precooking the potatoes, I cooked them in a skillet with 1 cup of salted water until the water thickened. This partially precooked the potatoes and also created a nice sauce to prevent their sticking and drying out. Both problems were solved.

Master Recipe for Potato Casserole

Most potato casseroles are pretty bland. Sliced raw potatoes are baked in a casserole with some sautéed onion. After seven different tests, I found that a delicious sauce could be created by starting the potatoes on top of the stove in a skillet with salted water. The starch in the potatoes leaches out into the water, thickening it. That is why this recipe calls for starchy, rather than waxy, potatoes. The mixture is then covered and finished in the oven. The folding motion referred to in the recipe is identical to the method for folding egg whites. I found that this recipe works well with sweet potatoes, too, and you can also add apples to this dish. Cooking the entire dish in a large cast iron skillet produces the best results.

4   slices thick-cut bacon
2   tablespoons olive oil
¾   pound onions, thinly sliced
¾   pound leeks, white part only, thinly
      sliced
2   pounds starchy potatoes, peeled and
      thinly sliced
1   teaspoon salt dissolved in 1 cup water
      Freshly ground black pepper to taste
2   teaspoons minced fresh thyme or
      1 teaspoon dried

1. Heat oven to 350 degrees. Cook bacon until browned in a large ovenproof skillet. Drain on paper towels and set aside. Pour off all but 2 tablespoons fat.
2. Add olive oil to pan, heat, and add onions and leeks. Sauté over medium heat, stirring occasionally, for 8 minutes. Crumble bacon and add to onion mixture. Using a large rubber spatula, fold in potatoes, salt water, pepper, and thyme. Continue folding mixture over medium heat until liquid starts to thicken.
3. Cover pan with aluminum foil and bake for 30 minutes. Uncover and bake an additional 20 to 30 minutes or until the potatoes are cooked through and the top is browned.

SERVES 6 TO 8 AS A SIDE DISH

Apple Variation

Add ¾ pound of peeled, cored, and thickly sliced apples along with potatoes.

Sweet Potato Variation

Substitute 1 pound of sweet potatoes for an equal amount of starchy potatoes.

Scalloped Potatoes

Most recipes for scalloped potatoes simply bake sliced potatoes with milk, half-and-half, or cream. This resulted in a very dull dish. Other recipes use a béchamel, a sauce made from butter, flour, and milk, but this turned out to be on the heavy side, tasting more of béchamel than potato. However, a velouté, a béchamel made with chicken stock rather than milk, was quite good; it added lots of flavor and the consistency was also preferable. A velouté is also a lot lower in fat than any of the traditional versions of this recipe. For additional flavor, add a grinding of black pepper and a touch more salt between the layers of potatoes.

5   tablespoons butter, at room
      temperature
3   tablespoons flour
1½   cups homemade or canned low-sodium
      chicken stock
½   teaspoon salt
¼   teaspoon freshly grated nutmeg
5   medium potatoes, peeled, thinly
      sliced, and covered with cold water
1   medium onion, thinly sliced
      Freshly ground black pepper to
      taste

1. Heat oven to 350 degrees. Grease a 1½-quart baking dish with 1 tablespoon of the butter.
2. Melt the remaining 4 tablespoons butter over medium heat in a medium saucepan. Whisk in the flour and continue whisking for 1 minute. Add the chicken stock, increase heat to medium-high, and whisk constantly until mixture thickens,

about 3 minutes. Whisk in the salt and nutmeg. Remove from heat.

3. Spread a layer of drained potatoes over bottom of dish. Pour some of the sauce over them, add a few slices of onion, and top with a few grindings of pepper. Continue layering potatoes, sauce, onions, and pepper until all the ingredients are used. Be frugal with the sauce, reserving enough for the final layer.

4. Bake covered for 30 minutes. Uncover and bake for an additional 30 minutes or until the potatoes can be easily pierced with a fork.

SERVES 8 AS A SIDE DISH

Potato Gratin

This is really the same type of recipe as scalloped potatoes or a potato casserole. It is simply prepared in a shallow dish. I prefer to use a mixture of chicken stock and half-and-half for a lighter but more flavorful result. Most recipes use all dairy for the liquid.

1	tablespoon unsalted butter, softened
1	cup homemade or canned low-sodium chicken stock
2	pounds starchy potatoes, peeled and thinly sliced
2	cloves garlic, minced
1	cup half-and-half
1	teaspoon salt
¼	teaspoon freshly grated nutmeg
	Freshly ground black pepper to taste

1. Heat oven to 350 degrees. Coat the inside of a shallow baking dish with the butter.

2. In a large skillet, bring the chicken stock and potatoes to a simmer over medium heat, stirring occasionally; cook for 2 minutes. Combine the remaining ingredients and add to skillet. Bring to a simmer and cook another 1 minute, stirring frequently.

3. Pour mixture into baking dish. Use a fork to distribute potatoes evenly. Bake uncovered for 75 minutes or until the potatoes are easily pierced with a fork and the top is nicely browned.

SERVES 4 TO 6

IN SEARCH OF PERFECT FRENCH FRIES
The most obvious question to ask about French fries is: Are they worth it? Should a home cook go to the trouble of heating up oil, cutting up potatoes, and then frying a batch of potatoes using the traditional two-step process? Based on my previous experience frying potatoes, my answer was an emphatic no. But when I went back to the kitchen to improve my technique, I quickly came to quite the opposite conclusion. Homemade French fries can be sublime, almost foolproof, and worth every second of effort.

The first issue was one of frying medium. Some cookbooks suggest canola oil, others peanut oil, Crisco, or lard. I tested all four, and peanut oil was the clear winner both in terms of flavor and its ability to produce a crispy fry. The lard was porky, the Crisco lacked both crispness and flavor, and the canola oil, a good second choice for those allergic to peanuts, was reasonably crisp but lacked flavor. (Modern lard is a very low quality compared to the more refined "leaf" lard used many years ago. Leaf lard comes from the area around the kidney and is very mild. Today, lard is taken from all over the pig and has a strong, unpleasant bacon flavor. This is why, in the old days, lard, with its delicate flavor, was frequently used to make pie crusts.) I also tried adding two tablespoons of rendered bacon fat to the canola oil but the taste was unwelcome.

I was also curious about which sorts of potatoes make the best fries. Dense, waxy potatoes, which are preferred for potato salads, make lousy fries since they become soggy. A long russet potato (these are referred to as "starchy," or "high-solid" potatoes) works well since it produces both a light, fluffy interior texture, a good crisp exterior, and nice long fries. All-purpose potatoes were judged to be not as good as the russets. I was pleasantly surprised to find that sweet potatoes also make good fries. Soaking cut potatoes in water preserves them until you are ready to begin frying but I did not determine, as was reported in some cookbooks, that the soaking improved the texture of the fries. However, be absolutely sure to pat the potatoes dry with paper towels before cooking. This prevents them from sticking together while frying and also keeps the oil from becoming cloudy.

I was particularly curious about why French fries require a two-step process. The fries are cooked once at 325 degrees, allowed to drain and rest, and then fried again at 375 degrees. The theory is that if cooked only once, the outside will over-cook before the inside is done. I found this not to be true when using relatively thin, ¼-inch fries. However, I did find that fries cooked in two steps were crispier and stayed that way longer. It is possible, how-ever, to use less peanut oil than you might imagine. One inch of oil in a 10-inch-wide skillet is just as good as 2 quarts of oil heated in a large Dutch oven.

I discovered a few other minor techniques along the way. First, many cooks sing the praises of brown paper bags for draining fries. I found a simple metal cooling rack works best. Set it over a jelly roll pan to catch the drippings. Second, be aware that the temperature of the oil will drop dramatically, 40 or 50 degrees, once the potatoes are added. They will continue to fry at a lower temperature than the initial setting. This is quite normal. Just keep the oil bubbling, frying over medium heat. Be sure, however, to raise the oil back up to temperature between batches.

French-Fried Potatoes

4   large, long potatoes such as russet (or sweet potatoes) peeled and cut into ¼ x ¼-inch-diameter sticks, the length of the potato (peeling is optional)
    Peanut oil for frying
    Salt

1. Rinse potatoes in a large bowl under cold running water until water turns from milky to clear. The potatoes may be prepared several hours ahead of time (even overnight) and held in cold water until ready for frying. Be sure that they are totally submerged or they will discolor.
2. Into a 10- to 12-inch skillet or 5-quart Dutch oven, cast iron preferred, pour enough peanut oil to reach a depth of 1 inch. Heat oil over medium-high heat

to 325 degrees. (Use an instant-read or candy thermometer to measure the oil temperature.)

3. Drain fries and pat dry with paper towels. Fry potatoes in batches and do not overcrowd pan. Fry for 6 to 8 minutes or until fries start to take on some spotty color. The oil temperature will drop about 60 degrees. Remove with a slotted spoon and drain on a cooling rack set over a jelly roll pan. Let oil temperature return to 325 degrees between batches. Let cooked fries sit at least 10 minutes or up to 2 hours.

4. After last batch has been fried, increase heat to 360 degrees. Repeat frying procedure, starting with the first batch of fries. Fry until the exterior is golden brown, spotty, and slightly puffy, up to 6 minutes. Drain again on a cooling rack. Season liberally with salt and serve immediately.

SERVES 4 (ONE POTATO PER PERSON)

Potato Puffs

I found this recipe in an old American country cookbook. The potato rounds puff up as they cook and are quite good as simple appetizers.

     Peanut oil for frying
2   cups boiled (see recipe page 66) and riced starchy potatoes, about 14 ounces
½   teaspoon salt
     Freshly ground black pepper to taste
2   tablespoons butter, softened
1   cup sour cream
1   cup all-purpose flour
⅛   teaspoon nutmeg, freshly grated preferred

1. Heat ½ inch of peanut oil in a large cast iron skillet over medium heat. Check the oil temperature with a candy thermometer as you prepare the dough, to make sure that it does not exceed 375 degrees.

2. In a large bowl, combine the next 5 ingredients (potatoes through sour cream). Add the flour and nutmeg and mix together until a dough is formed. If too sticky, add additional flour 1 tablespoon at a time. If too dry, add more sour cream 1 tablespoon at a time. Remove the dough from the bowl and knead by hand on a lightly floured surface for 2 minutes.

3. Roll out to a thickness of ¼ inch. Cut with a 2-inch biscuit cutter. Fry the dough in batches in 375 degree oil for 1½ minutes on one side and 1 minute on the other. Drain on brown paper bags. Sprinkle with salt and serve immediately.

MAKES 36 PUFFS

Potato Pancakes

Recipes for potato pancakes can be found in plenty of Old World cookbooks, and they most often contain flour and milk or cream along with potatoes and eggs. I started with a similar version in my testing and tried four variations: separating the eggs, beating the whites, and then folding them in; substituting sour cream for heavy cream; cooking the potatoes first; and adding 1 teaspoon of baking soda. All of these versions were disappointing — the last one actually turned the potatoes an ugly grayish-green! I then removed the flour and heavy cream and knew I was onto something. The earthy taste of potatoes came through nicely and the texture was simpler, less muddied by other ingredients. I then found that starchy potatoes were best for holding the pancakes together, although there was no advantage in flavor. I also discovered that the potatoes need to be squeezed dry after grating; otherwise the mixture is too wet. Be sure to cook the pancakes until they are well browned and crisp on both sides; otherwise the grated raw potatoes will not be cooked through. In Vermont, our family serves potato pancakes with homemade apple butter, but you can substitute store-bought applesauce. A 12-inch skillet can handle three 4-inch pancakes at one time.

3	large eggs
1½	teaspoons salt
	Freshly ground black pepper to taste
⅛	teaspoon freshly grated nutmeg
2	pounds starchy potatoes, peeled, coarsely grated, and squeezed dry
1	medium onion, grated
1	cup vegetable oil for frying

1. Lightly beat eggs with salt, pepper, and nutmeg in a large mixing bowl. Add potatoes and onion and stir to combine.
2. Put vegetable oil in a large cast iron skillet and heat until shimmering but not smoking.
3. Drop ⅓ cup of batter into the skillet at a time, flattening it into a disk with a pancake turner. Form additional pancakes until skillet is full but not crowded. (A 12-inch skillet will hold three 4-inch pancakes.)
4. Fry pancakes for 2 to 3 minutes or until browned on the bottom. Turn and cook until done, another 2 to 3 minutes. Drain on a double thickness of paper towels set on a cooling rack. Repeat with remaining batter.

MAKES TWELVE 4-INCH PANCAKES

Sweet Potatoes Georgian

This recipe was among a collection of handwritten country recipes I found in our library in Vermont. I assume that the name of the recipe refers to the state of Georgia, where this recipe may have originated. The recipe lists no ingredient amounts so I developed the version below.

1½	pounds sweet potatoes, boiled (see master recipe page 66)
2	tablespoons plus 1 teaspoon butter, softened
2	tablespoons cream
1	tablespoon sherry
2	tablespoons molasses

1. Heat oven to 350 degrees. Butter a 1½-quart baking dish.
2. In a large bowl, combine the warm potatoes with 2 tablespoons of the butter (reserve the remaining teaspoon), the cream, and the sherry. Mash and place in baking dish.
3. Melt the remaining teaspoon of butter with the molasses. Pour over the potatoes and bake uncovered for 25 minutes. Either serve as is or place under broiler for 5 additional minutes to brown the top.

SERVES 4 TO 6

Potato Salad with Chives and Mustard Dressing

This is pretty much a simple French potato salad, since it is based on a basic mustard vinaigrette. You can substitute any full-flavored mustard you like; capers also make a nice addition for a fancier salad.

2 pounds waxy or new potatoes
½ teaspoon salt
¼ cup good-quality white wine vinegar
1 tablespoon fresh lemon juice
2 teaspoons Dijon mustard
5 tablespoons high-quality olive oil
3 tablespoons minced chives
   Freshly ground black pepper
   to taste

Wash potatoes. Cut into ¼-inch-thick slices and steam until just fork tender (see recipe page 66). Whisk together the salt, 3 tablespoons of vinegar, lemon juice, mustard, and olive oil. Pour over warm potatoes in a large bowl and toss. Just before serving, toss again with the chives, pepper, and remaining 1 tablespoon of vinegar.

SERVES 4 TO 6

German Potato Salad

Being a German potato salad, this is a heavier dish than the French version above, as it includes bacon and bacon fat. However, sautéing the onion and adding a warm dressing to the potatoes makes for a fuller-flavored salad. Be sure to serve this dish immediately.

2 pounds waxy or new potatoes
4 slices thick-cut smoked bacon
1 tablespoon extra-virgin olive oil
1 cup diced onion (1 medium onion)
5 tablespoons white wine or cider
   vinegar
2 tablespoons water
½ teaspoon salt
½ teaspoon sugar
3 tablespoons minced flat-leaf parsley

¼ cup minced gherkins or other pickle
   (optional)

1. Wash potatoes. Cut into ¼-inch-thick slices and steam until just fork tender. Fry bacon in a skillet and remove to paper towels.
2. Pour off all but 1 tablespoon of fat and add olive oil. When oil is hot, add onion and sauté for 5 minutes over medium heat, stirring occasionally. Add ¼ cup of vinegar (reserving 1 tablespoon) and the water and cook, stirring, for 30 seconds. Remove from heat.
3. Place potatoes in a large bowl. Add onion mixture and toss gently. Crumble bacon and add to potatoes along with salt, sugar, parsley, and optional gherkins. Taste and adjust seasonings if necessary. Add the remaining tablespoon of vinegar. Toss gently and serve.

SERVES 4 TO 6

American Flag Potato Salad

This is the type of potato salad served at our July Fourth picnic and at most such celebrations around the country. Most American potato salads are pretty much the same. Some add chopped red bell peppers and others may add a bit of mustard to the mayonnaise, but the rule is simple — throw everything on hand into the bowl with some cooked potatoes, vinegar, and mayonnaise. This is one recipe that is not fussy.

2 pounds waxy or new potatoes, boiled,
   peeled, and cut into bite-size cubes
2 tablespoons red wine vinegar
½ teaspoon salt

Freshly ground black pepper to taste
½ cup mayonnaise
¼ cup sour cream
¼ cup diced red onion
2 hard-boiled eggs, peeled and diced
½ cup diced celery
¼ cup diced bread-and-butter pickle
3 tablespoons minced chives or scallions

Combine the just-cooked potatoes with vinegar, salt, and pepper and let sit at room temperature for 30 minutes. Add remaining ingredients and taste. Add a pinch of salt for extra flavor if you like. Serve immediately or refrigerate until serving.

SERVES 4 TO 6

RUTABAGA

It is increasingly difficult these days to find rutabaga (sometimes called yellow turnip). It is not a glamorous food, being a large, workhorse vegetable, and it doesn't have the adaptability of potatoes, since its distinctive peppery flavor doesn't meld with just anything. That being said, I am fond of rutabaga for its plainness and economy. I feel the same way about my 1983 Ford pickup, which is just good enough to go to town in but is also suited to moving beehives in the spring or hauling a load of wood or hay.

I find that pairing rutabaga with another full-flavored ingredient is best, onions and carrots being two good choices. I thought that apples would make a nice partnership as well, but a rutabaga/apple casserole filled the kitchen with an unpleasant odor during baking and the taste was equally disappointing.

You can also substitute rutabaga for no more than half the potato called for in a recipe, just to add a little more depth of flavor. Many cooks will tell you that the size of a rutabaga affects flavor, the smaller being tastier, but I have not found this to be the case. Supermarket specimens tend to be of average size, about the size of a large softball.

Mashed Rutabagas with Potatoes, Molasses, and Butter

The pairing of rutabaga with potatoes works well, since the latter improve the texture and add creaminess as well. Be sure that the vegetables are thoroughly cooked to facilitate mashing.

1 medium rutabaga (just over 1 pound), peeled and cut into 2-inch chunks
2 medium starchy potatoes (just over 1 pound), peeled and cut into 2-inch chunks
6 tablespoons butter, at room temperature
2 tablespoons molasses
½ cup half-and-half
¾ teaspoon salt
Freshly ground black pepper to taste

1. Bring a medium pot of water to a boil, add the rutabaga, and cook 5 minutes. Add the potatoes and continue cooking for another 15 minutes or until both vegetables are tender. Drain.
2. Return the cooked vegetables to the pot and add remaining ingredients. Mash with a potato masher or a fork. Serve immediately.

SERVES 6

Rutabaga and Onion Casserole

In a potato casserole, the potato starch leaches into the liquid, creating a thick, creamy sauce. In this recipe, since the rutabaga does not contain as much starch as a potato, the liquid does not thicken. However, it is absorbed during baking.

4	slices thick-cut smoked bacon
1	tablespoon olive oil
¾	pound onions, thinly sliced
1	medium rutabaga, peeled, quartered, and thinly sliced
1	teaspoon salt dissolved in 1 cup water
	Freshly ground black pepper to taste
2	teaspoons minced fresh thyme or 1 teaspoon dried

1. Heat oven to 350 degrees. Cook bacon until browned in a large cast iron skillet. Drain on paper towels and reserve. Pour off all but 1 tablespoon fat.

2. Add olive oil to skillet, heat, and add onions. Sauté over medium heat, stirring occasionally, for 8 minutes. Crumble bacon and add to onions. Stir in rutabaga, salt water, pepper, and thyme. Continue stirring over medium heat until liquid starts to thicken.

3. Cover pan with aluminum foil and bake for 20 minutes. Uncover and bake an additional 20 minutes (check after 10 minutes) or until the rutabaga is cooked through and the top is browned.

SERVES 4 TO 6 AS A SIDE DISH

Rutabaga Carrot Mash

This dish is simple to make and has a nice bright color. The sweetness of the carrots pairs well with the peppery taste of rutabaga.

1	medium rutabaga, peeled and cut into 2-inch chunks (about 12 ounces)
3	medium carrots, peeled and cut into 2-inch chunks (about 8 ounces)
¾	teaspoon salt
	Freshly ground black pepper to taste
¼	cup half-and-half or light cream
4	tablespoons (½ stick) unsalted butter, at room temperature

Following the charts on pages 53 and 54, boil or steam rutabaga and carrots until tender. Mash with a potato masher or fork along with remaining ingredients. Serve immediately.

SERVES 4 AS A SMALL SIDE DISH

TURNIPS

Unlike rutabaga, turnips come in a variety of sizes, the smaller ones being sweeter and the larger specimens possessing a stronger, more peppery flavor. The large ones are also more stringy and fibrous. I did try freezing them before cooking to see if that would add sweetness and it simply made them soggy.

Perhaps the best part of turnips, however is the tops. Last summer, I planted a good crop of Klein Bol white turnips. We had guests for lunch one day in early June and I had just thinned out the turnip bed, resulting in a large colander full of small, delicate tops narrowing down to a tiny root end, with the slightest hint of a turnip just starting to bulge. I washed them, added one head of buttercrunch lettuce, dressed them simply with white wine vinegar, extra-virgin olive oil, lemon juice, and salt, and served them with large slabs of onion pie. The Riesling was cold and fruity, the turnip tops were peppery, and the tart was rich and satisfying. A breeze blew in from the western end of our valley; the air was intensely clear, unlike the hazy days of July, as the kids, our guests, my wife, and I sat around the picnic table. The tastes of pepper and fruit, of onions and rich pie pastry, all mixed with the sounds of the valley, the soft touch of a light breeze, and the ebb and flow of just a few clouds.

Turnip Slaw with Buttermilk Dressing

The basic idea for this recipe comes from Dori Sanders, author of *Dori Sanders' Country Cooking*. The raisins add a kick of sweetness, which pairs nicely with the slightly bitter turnips.

4	medium turnips (14 ounces), peeled and grated
2	stalks celery, cut into thin pieces
¾	cup raisins
½	cup buttermilk
2	tablespoons olive oil
1	tablespoon fresh lemon juice
1	tablespoon cider vinegar
¼	teaspoon dry mustard
½	teaspoon salt
½	teaspoon sugar

Mix together first three ingredients. Whisk together the remaining ingredients and toss with vegetables.

SERVES 4

Mashed Turnips and Potatoes with Onion, Parsley, and Anchovies

This is perhaps my favorite root vegetable recipe, the big flavors of anchovy, onion, and parsley working well with the smooth, subtle flavors of the potato/turnip mixture. Don't be afraid of the anchovies; their taste is subtle, more of an accent than a fishy flavor.

2	tablespoons high-quality olive oil
4	tablespoons (½ stick) unsalted butter
2	anchovy fillets
3	medium onions, peeled and coarsely chopped
1	teaspoon salt
2	tablespoons chopped parsley
4	medium turnips, peeled and cut into 2-inch chunks
3	medium potatoes, peeled and cut into 2-inch chunks
⅓	cup heavy cream, warmed
	Freshly ground black pepper to taste

1. Heat the olive oil and 2 tablespoons of the butter in a large skillet with a top. When the foam subsides, add the anchovies and cook for 2 minutes over medium-low heat. Add the onions and ¼ teaspoon of the salt, cover pan, and cook for 20 minutes. Stir in parsley and keep warm.

2. In a separate pot, boil turnips and potatoes until tender, about 20 minutes, and drain. (Add the turnips to the boiling water first and then the potatoes 2 minutes later.) Remove to a large bowl and mash. Add remaining 2 tablespoons of butter and the warm cream. Add remaining ¾ teaspoon salt and pepper to taste. Top with onion mixture and serve.

SERVES 4

WINTER SQUASH

I tested the best method for baking both acorn and butternut squash and found that baking cut side down for the first half hour or so is vastly superior to baking cut side up. The flesh is moister and the cut surface caramelizes nicely because of the heat of the roasting pan. I also tried baking them cut side down in a roasting pan with ¼ inch of hot water (I found this method in an old cookbook) and the results were no better than baking cut side up although a bit slower.

Master Recipe for Baked Acorn Squash

Acorn squash are good for stuffing with either a bit of maple syrup or an apple/raisin mixture. They are best baked cut side down first and then turned, filled, and baked until they are done.

2   acorn squash, cut in half lengthwise and seeded
    Vegetable oil
    Salt and freshly ground black pepper to taste
2   tablespoons butter, softened

1. Heat oven to 400 degrees. Slice off just a sliver of the outside skin of each squash half so they will sit flat. Lightly grease a roasting pan with vegetable oil. Add the squash, cut side down. Bake for 35 minutes.
2. Remove pan from oven, turn squash cut side up, and fill (see variations below), or simply season with salt and pepper and add ½ tablespoon of butter to each half. Bake for an additional 10 minutes or until the flesh is fork tender all the way through.

SERVES 4

MAPLE SYRUP VARIATION

In addition to the salt, pepper, and butter called for in step 2, add 1 tablespoon of maple syrup to each half and bake as directed.

APPLE, WALNUT, AND RAISIN VARIATION

In a small bowl mix the 2 tablespoons of softened butter called for in the master recipe for Baked Acorn Squash with ½ cup chopped walnuts, 2 cups peeled, cored, and diced apples, 3 tablespoons dark brown sugar, and 2 tablespoons dark raisins. Bake squash halves as directed in step 1, remove from oven, season each half liberally with salt and pepper, fill, and bake an additional 15 minutes.

Rice and Beans

I N MID-AUGUST, one of our neighbors puts on a huge potluck supper called the Ox Roast, which is attended by almost all of the town's three hundred residents. The night before, we start a bonfire in the roasting pit, collapsible lounge chairs pulled up, thermoses of coffee and boxes of doughnuts at the ready. This is the best time of year for serious storytelling, since there isn't much to do except stoke the fire every half hour or so. Early in the morning, about 6 A.M., two of the quarters of beef are skewered with metal rods used for reinforcing concrete and then wired to the makeshift rotisserie, using sheep fencing and metal bedsprings. (We actually roast a heifer, not an ox.) All day, the meat lurches up and down, round and about, the electric motor clicking and whirring, the roast meat starting to take on color as the afternoon arrives.

During the afternoon, picnic tables are brought from all over town on pickups and decorated with bachelor's buttons, daisies, black-eyed Susans, Queen Anne's lace, and delphiniums held in large mason canning jars. Table lamps are duct-taped to the crotches of apple trees and to the top posts of the rundown tennis court, where later that night the fiddler calls the tune for the square dance. A long stretch of hay bales is used as a groaning board for the potluck salads and casseroles. Last year there were over a dozen salads, ranging from fruit, potato, macaroni, pasta, and cucumber salads to slightly more exotic fare including rice and tomato salad, creamy potato and egg salad, three-bean salad, pink cottage cheese and Jell-O salad, baked rice salad, and nacho salad. For dessert there were carrot cake squares, blondies, peach pie, apple pie, snickerdoodles, molasses cookies, blueberry cobblers, brownies, banana nut bread, date nut bread, yellow sheet cake with peaches and raspberries and whipped topping, chocolate cake, blueberry grunt, orange Jell-O, pumpkin pie baked with no crust, and orange cake. This was all chased by gallons of iced tea held in a huge metal urn. A few guests brought their own coolers of beer and sat quietly off to the side, drinking, so as not to disturb the unstated rule about no alcohol.

But the most common covered dish is baked beans, seven different casseroles of which were on display last summer. Some of the casseroles were filled with a thick purée of soft beans, more like mashed potatoes. Others were whole, firm beans, awash in a thin liquid, sweetened with molasses and a hint of spice. The ones that go first are always the darkest and thickest, indicating a liberal use of molasses, while the lighter-colored beans are usually passed over.

As people start to arrive, a makeshift stage, cobbled together with ⅝-inch plywood sheets, is set up for the cloggers. A small portable record player with 45 rpm discs is used for the music, and the women, from eighty-year-olds to one girl no older than six, rustle their red-trimmed white petticoats and pound their clogging shoes in time to the beat. About this time,

the meat is ready to be taken off. We unhook one quarter, slide one end of the metal rod out of the rotisserie, and then carry it over to the carving table, an old door rescued from the barn just behind us, where I bone and slice the huge steamship round, the cut that runs between the hip and knee. Every year, Gerald Ennis from over in New York State works his way over to the carving table equipped with his own pocketful of plastic forks, a good steak knife, and a few napkins. "Nice meat, take some, charred bits, best part . . ." he'll say and then stop a bit to eat, pulling at the blackened, crispy bits on the outside. As he spears yet another piece of charred meat he closes his eyes, chews thoughtfully, and intones, "Lovely, lovely. . . ."

When the meat is carved, it is set out on huge carving boards and ironstone platters. The crowd moves pretty quick at this point, forming a queue in seconds, hoping to get to a particular dish that has been spied earlier before it's all gone. Metal grates are set over the still red-hot fire for the soaked field corn which has been delivered in large sturdy grain sacks. The kids finish eating quickly, and then run around in threes and fours, hiding behind the berry patch or running up behind the henhouse.

When the food is done, the second-string salads finally eaten, having been ignored for more promising opportunities on the first pass, the last cakey bits of grunt scraped from the corners of the dish, we walk down to the tennis court where the makeshift band is tuning up and sorting out equipment. Groups of eight dancers form circles, the old fiddle tunes start up, played by Harry Hayden and the Kelly Stand Symphony, and the steps are called by Jimmy Wilkes. We shuck the oyster and dig the clam. We go back the other way and then on the same way. We cross under, step forward, and move back. As the couples become more experienced, the fiddler speeds up the calling, trying to mix us up, like a musical version of red light. Many of the old-timers pull up lawn chairs and watch, others get right into the thick of it, changing partners with city visitors and young kids, old farmers unexpectedly swinging their partners and doing the do-si-do.

Later that evening the crisp night air rolls down into the small hollow, the sweep of stars and sky stretches between the peaks, and I walk up into the nearby pasture. The mountains thrust upward, dwarfing the bonfire and the fiddle playing and the small house set amidst the orchard and the overgrown briars. I sit quietly and listen to Jimmy Wilkes call the dances, his voice floating up and away from the small hollow, where the cool, sharp air is scented with pine and wintergreen.

TODAY, rice and beans may sound pedestrian, but on a Vermont farm a hundred years ago, rice was rarely served and beans would only be baked, never offered, for instance, in a cold salad. The menu was, to say the least, limited and consisted primarily of boiled meat, boiled greens, and boiled potatoes. Potatoes and both wild and cultivated greens were grown locally and the meat was either an old, tough steer or perhaps a young bull, which was no good for milking. As for boiling, it is a perfectly fine method for potatoes and

greens and also recommended for tough, stringy beef that would have been inedible if roasted to medium rare. Of course, everything was slathered with milk gravy, the ubiquitous country cure-all for poor quality meat, leftovers, and yet another serving of potatoes. A poor diet was simply a fact of life for most folks in our town. One old-timer, Bernie Squires, seemed to live on nothing but coffee and canned milk, but he was proud that he could feed his family, stopping by the country store on payday and purchasing a week's worth of groceries, mostly canned goods, the fresh vegetable selection in the 1950s being restricted to a few withered carrots, a bunch of onions, and perhaps a head of celery.

RICE
New England depended upon potatoes as its starchy mainstay, since they were easily grown locally, whereas rice was grown extensively in the Carolinas, old swamps cleared to make way for rice paddies. But rice certainly made its way north, showing up in rice pudding, chicken and rice, and in any number of pilafs and other side dishes. Of course, rice and peas or beans is a classic dish both here in America and in many other cultures, often served on New Year's Eve and referred to as Hoppin' John. This chapter explores basic cooking methods and offers a few master recipes.

Over the years, I have researched and developed different methods of cooking white rice. The most interesting, and complicated, method I have found comes from Fannie Farmer's *A New Book of Cookery* and is called Parched Rice. The rice is boiled for 25 minutes, then drained, and one quart of hot water is poured over it while it is still in the colander. It is put back into the original pot and allowed to stand until cool and dry. Finally, the rice is sautéed in a frying pan with melted butter until browned. That inordinately complex method aside, I have tested at least seven different methods and find that white long-grain rice is best sautéed in a small amount of oil for just a minute, then simmered in just 1½ cups of water per cup of rice, not the 2 cups usually called for in most recipes. After 10 minutes, the rice is taken off the heat and allowed to sit for an additional 15 minutes. This makes perfect, fluffy rice with separate, smooth grains. Of course, an electric rice cooker is easiest and makes good rice, although not quite as good as the method above. I have also included in this chapter a baked rice recipe, which is easy to make and well suited for highly flavored dishes with plenty of other ingredients.

Master Recipe for Long-Grain White Rice

For years I have used an electric rice cooker, since it is so convenient. However, I recently went back to my traditional stovetop method, which I published in *The Cook's Bible*. It is substantially better, producing separate fluffy grains that have been first sautéed in a bit of olive oil and then cooked with only 1½ cups of water per cup of rice. This method is particularly good for more delicate rices such as basmati or jasmine.

1	tablespoon olive oil or butter
2	cups long-grain white rice
3	cups water or chicken stock or a combination
½	teaspoon salt

1. Heat oil over medium heat in a medium saucepan and add rice. Stir for 1 minute. Add water and salt and bring to a boil. Reduce heat to low, cover, and simmer for 10 minutes. Check after 3 or 4 minutes to make sure that the water is at a slow simmer, not at a rapid boil. Remove from heat and let stand covered for 15 minutes. Fluff with a fork and serve.

SERVES 6 TO 8

LEMON AND CHIVE VARIATION

Add half a lemon to the water along with the rice. Sprinkle chives on top of the rice after it has been removed from the heat (do not stir rice). Remove the lemon and stir chives into rice after rice stands for 15 minutes.

ONION, RED PEPPER, AND THYME

Increase the butter/olive oil to 4 teaspoons. After the oil or butter is heated, add 1 cup of diced onion (about 1 small onion), ½ cup of diced red bell pepper (about half a medium pepper), and 2 teaspoons of dried thyme. Sauté for 8 minutes or until onion is soft and translucent. Add the rice and proceed with the master recipe.

Onion and Peas Variation

Increase butter/olive oil to 2 tablespoons. Sauté 1 cup of diced onion in the butter or oil for 5 to 6 minutes until softened but not browned. Add rice and stir for 1 minute. Add 1 cup of fresh or frozen peas and proceed with the master recipe.

Onion and Mushroom Variation

Increase butter/olive oil to 3 tablespoons. Sauté 1 cup of diced onion in the butter or olive oil for 5 to 6 minutes until softened but not browned. Add 1 cup chopped mushrooms and sauté until soft. Add rice and proceed with the master recipe.

Fresh Herb Variation

Sprinkle 2 tablespoons of chopped fresh herbs on top of the rice after the cooking period but before the rice stands for 15 minutes. (Do not stir at this point.) Proceed with master recipe.

Master Recipe for Rice and Beans

On a recent trip to the Caribbean, our family shunned the four-star resorts and dined exclusively at local eateries, some at the end of potholed dirt roads, others nestled in town, by an old wharf littered with rusting lorries and backhoes. We cleaned our plates of parrot fish stewed in sweet curry sauce, freshly grilled mahi-mahi, acres of rice and peas, roasted plantains, toasted coconut slices served with rum punch made with fresh-squeezed lime juice, soursop ice cream, and a sandwich of flying fish served on thick slabs of homemade bread with freshly whisked mayonnaise and a large bowl of icy chocolate ice cream for dessert. Although these eateries were visually unappealing, they were alive with good home cooking, the soft gurgle of Carib beer being poured into glasses, the wild clatter of pans in the kitchen, and the cheerful presence of the proprietors. Most of all, the local cooks knew their rice and peas. Every dish was accompanied by this heavenly combination: the earthy, rich flavor of the beans coddled in a soft blanket of seasoned rice.

When I set out to perfect my own recipe, I found that the problem with rice and beans (peas) is the beans. With the exception of black beans, they don't have much flavor. (The next time you boil a cup of beans, taste one with your eyes closed and see if you can tell what it is.) And even when served with a sauce, the beans themselves are pedestrian at best. I started out sautéing onions, peppers, and garlic and then adding the beans and water. This helped but the beans were still dull. Finally, I resorted to a classic ingredient of American Southern cooking: ham hocks. They are available in almost all supermarkets in the frozen meat section and they pack a wallop of flavor. I found that 1 pound of hocks to 1 pound of beans worked just fine, imparting tremendous flavor to the beans along with a hint of salt.

I also determined that some cider vinegar made a nice addition to the beans just before serving. (Vinegar is soaked up by beans rather quickly and loses its flavor.)

As for the rice, you can use any flavored rice recipe — a pilaf works well — or simply serve these beans with cooked long-grain white rice. For those who prefer vegetarian beans, I have included a black bean recipe below which uses toasted spices for flavoring (cumin seed, cloves, cinnamon, and peppercorns) and omits the ham hocks. Black beans have enough flavor to get by without meat as an ingredient.

Finally, you can make this recipe without presoaking the beans. Just cook them for about two hours. The other ingredients make a nice sauce for the beans, much like baked beans.

1	pound ham hocks, scored with a knife, or 2 smoked turkey wings
2	tablespoons olive oil
2	medium yellow onions, peeled and chopped
¼	green bell pepper, chopped (about ½ cup)
2	cloves garlic, minced
1	pound dried red kidney beans, picked over and soaked for at least 4 hours in water to cover
½	teaspoon dried thyme
2	bay leaves
	Pinch of dried oregano
½	teaspoon salt
	Freshly ground black pepper to taste
¼	cup cider vinegar
3	cups cooked long-grain rice or pilaf
	A few drops Tabasco (optional)

1. In a large pot sauté the ham hock or turkey wings in oil until darkened. (If using hocks, the scores should open.) Add onions, bell pepper, and garlic and sauté until the onions are translucent, about 7

minutes. Add drained beans, thyme, bay leaves, oregano, salt, and pepper.

2. Cover with enough water to come about 1 inch above the beans. (The beans will float so estimate the level of the beans before this step.) Bring to a boil and simmer uncovered for about 1½ hours or until beans are soft. (If you did not presoak the beans, they will take about 2 hours to cook.) Add more water if necessary. If you like a thicker texture, remove 1½ cups of beans, mash them, and stir them back into the pot.

3. Just before serving, add vinegar and simmer for 5 minutes. Check seasonings. Serve over rice with a dash or two of Tabasco if desired.

SERVES 6

BLACK BEAN VARIATION

Replace red kidney beans with black beans. Place 1 tablespoon cumin seed (not ground cumin), a 3-inch cinnamon stick, 8 whole cloves, and 8 peppercorns in a nonstick skillet over medium heat. Shake pan frequently and toast until the cloves and cumin pop, about 4 minutes. Add this mixture to beans along with the onion and garlic. Omit the ham hocks, green pepper, thyme, and oregano in the master recipe. Increase the salt level to 1 teaspoon. Remove cinnamon stick before serving.

Black-Eyed Peas and Rice

This is called Hoppin' John, and my mother grew up eating it in Virginia, where her family had a small farm. This dish is often served New Year's Day, the combination of pig's feet and black-eyed peas bringing luck for the upcoming year. My mother still serves these two foods on January 1, old habits from her Southern childhood that are still very much part of the family tradition. I find that this dish can be a bit dull and therefore have added some vinegar and parsley to liven it up. According to Evan Jones in *American Food* (Random House, 1974), black-eyed peas were also referred to as field peas, cowpeas, whippoorwills, Jerusalem peas, Tonkin peas, and marble peas.

1	tablespoon olive oil
1	tablespoon unsalted butter
2	medium onions, chopped
1	large stalk celery with leaves, finely chopped
2	smoked ham hocks
2	bay leaves
¼	teaspoon crushed red pepper flakes
2	cups (1 pound) black-eyed peas, picked over and rinsed
2	cups low-sodium chicken stock
	Water to cover, about 2 cups
½	teaspoon salt
3	cups long-grain white rice, cooked according to master recipe (see page 86)
2	tablespoons cider vinegar or good quality white wine vinegar
¼	cup chopped flat-leaf parsley

1. Heat oil and butter in a large (at least 4 quarts) saucepan or Dutch oven. Add onions and celery and sauté over medium heat for 5 minutes, stirring occasionally. Add next 6 ingredients (ham hocks through water), bring to a boil, then reduce heat to a simmer.

2. Cook gently, uncovered, for 1½ hours or until black-eyed peas are very tender. Add more water if necessary. Remove meat from ham hocks, chopping it and adding to the cooked peas along with the salt. Stir to mix.

3. In a large bowl, combine and fluff together the peas, vinegar, parsley, and cooked rice and serve.

SERVES 6

BEANS

It seems that in the old days, farmers were more expressive about putting names to things. Bean varieties had many names that we don't hear of today, including clapboard beans, frost beans, six weeks beans, and lazy beans. Today we have more mundane nomenclature, including Great Northern beans, navy beans, kidney beans, and the like. Names aside, if you want to pick a fight with a cook, just start talking about the best way to cook beans. Some say that presoaking all night is essential, some use a quick presoak method, some just go right ahead and cook them in boiling water until they are done. There are also plenty of arguments about the best way to make beans digestible, from changing the soaking water frequently to boiling briefly and then soaking. There are also a host of opinions concerning the effect of salt, vinegar, and baking soda in the cooking water. How do these ingredients affect cooking time and texture? In *The Cook's Bible* I tested a variety of methods, but since that time, more arguments have ensued and more testing has been done in the kitchens at *Cook's Illustrated*. So I set out to retest all of the methods, using Great Northern beans. Here are the results:

KITCHEN TEST: TESTING DIFFERENT METHODS
OF COOKING WHITE BEANS

A variety of soaking and cooking methods were tested to determine the best method for preparing Great Northern beans. The objective was to preserve the delicate texture and flavor of the bean, to improve digestibility, and to find the most practical and easiest method. I did not find any difference in digestibility, but there were major differences in cooking time, taste, and texture. All beans were cooked uncovered in boiling water.

METHOD	TASTE	TEXTURE	COOKING TIME
Soak overnight	sweet and delicate; true bean flavor	smooth	40 minutes
Boil 2 minutes; soak overnight	sweet and delicate; true bean flavor	smooth	40 minutes
Boil 2 minutes; let soak 3 hours	good flavor	not as good as overnight soak	45 minutes
Boil 2 minutes; soak for 45 minutes	good flavor	mediocre	50 minutes
No presoaking	slightly sweet; not as good as overnight soak	soft and creamy	55 minutes
Cook with baking soda	not as sweet	beans discolored; texture not as creamy	40 minutes
Cook with ¼ cup vinegar		never fully cooked	
Cook with 1 tablespoon salt	okay	skins came off during cooking	50 minutes

THE BEST COOKING METHOD: It was clear from these tests that soaking beans overnight is usually the best method for a delicate, true bean flavor and for a creamy, soft texture. In a pinch, however, simply cooking them without any presoaking was almost as good and it would be very hard to tell the difference unless judging them side by side in a blind taste test. Never add anything acidic to beans while cooking since this will drastically increase the cooking time, and don't even think about adding baking soda since this harms the taste and discolors the beans.

Master Recipe for Cooking Dried Beans

This is a fairly simple recipe, since I wanted the beans to be delicate enough in flavor to be used for a variety of purposes such as in a salad. For stronger, punchier flavors, see the variations below or follow the master recipe for Rice and Beans (page 87). That version contains ham hocks, which add tremendous flavor, and is highly recommended if the beans are to be eaten on their own, not as an ingredient in one of the recipes that follow. (The rice is optional.) Note that the salt and vinegar are added after the beans have cooked to prevent the skins from coming off and to avoid lengthening the cooking time. That being said, many people prefer to cook their beans in salted water regardless of the effect on the skins. I tested this and found that, in fact, the beans do taste a bit better since the salt has more time to be absorbed. However, my testing also

KITCHEN TEST: COOKING TIMES FOR BEANS, PRESOAKED AND NOT PRESOAKED

This chart appeared in *The Cook's Bible*, but I wanted to retest the cooking times, since I felt that they were a bit on the short side. Unfortunately, the freshness of the beans makes a big difference in cooking times; older beans taking significantly longer to cook. Allow 6 cups of water for each cup of dried beans. One cup of dried beans produces about 4 cups of cooked beans. The chart below indicates cooking time when soaked overnight, cooking time when not presoaked, and the yield per cup of dried beans.

BEAN TYPE	COOKING TIME (SOAKED)	COOKING TIME (NO SOAK)	YIELD (PER 1 CUP)	COMMENTS
Black beans	30 minutes	45 minutes	2 cups	better soaked
Black-eyed peas	30 minutes	45 minutes	2½ cups	better soaked
Cannellini	40 minutes	60 minutes	2½ cups	better soaked
Chick-peas	45 minutes	90 minutes	2½ cups	no difference
Great Northern beans	40 minutes	55 minutes	2½ cups	slightly better soaked
Kidney beans	40 minutes	65 minutes	2½ cups	better soaked
Large limas	30 minutes	50 minutes	2¼ cups	better soaked
Lentils	15 minutes	23 minutes	3½ cups soaked 2½ cups not soaked	little difference
Split peas	25 minutes	45 minutes	3 cups soaked 2½ cups not soaked	little difference

demonstrated that the skins will become loose and fall off. If you care only about taste, salt the water before cooking. If you prefer to serve the beans intact, salt the water later, as indicated in the recipe below.

2	cups (1 pound) dried beans
6	cups water or chicken stock or a combination
1	onion pierced with 8 whole cloves
1	bay leaf
2	cloves garlic, smashed
1	sprig thyme, sage, or rosemary, optional
2	sprigs flat leaf parsley, optional
1	teaspoon salt
	Freshly ground black pepper to taste
¼	cup flat-leaf parsley, finely chopped (optional)
2	tablespoons high quality white wine vinegar, red wine vinegar, or cider vinegar

1. Soak beans overnight in plenty of water to cover. Drain and rinse under plenty of cold water. Or, if you do not have time to soak the beans, simply proceed to the next step.

2. Add the first seven ingredients (beans through parsley sprigs) to a large saucepan and bring to a boil. Reduce heat to a simmer and cook uncovered 20 minutes to 1 hour (see chart page 91) or until tender. Add salt and pepper and simmer for 3 more minutes. Remove whole onion, bay leaves, and herb sprig. Add parsley and vinegar, check seasonings, and serve.

SERVES 6

Beans with Tomato, Cloves, and Cinnamon

Add a 3-inch piece of cinnamon stick to the pot with the beans. Add 1 cup chopped and seeded tomato along with the salt and simmer for an additional 5 minutes. Omit the herb and vinegar.

Beans with Greens

Trim 2 pounds of kale, mustard greens, collard greens, beet greens, or broccoli rabe, removing thick stems and wilted leaves. Wash and coarsely chop. Cook in a large pot of boiling salted water for 5 minutes. Drain. Place in a kitchen towel and squeeze dry. When the beans are cooked, stir in greens along with the vinegar (or substitute an equal amount of lemon juice for the vinegar). Omit parsley.

Spicy Beans with Chili Powder, Chiles, and Garlic

Dice 1 carrot, 1 onion, and 1 rib of celery. Sauté in a large saucepan in 1 tablespoon of oil for 7 minutes over medium heat until the onion becomes translucent. Add the beans and water or chicken stock along with 1 tablespoon chili powder, 1 tablespoon chopped mild chile pepper, and 2 teaspoons ground cumin. Omit herb and vinegar. When beans are cooked, add the salt and black pepper, and substitute ¼ cup chopped cilantro for the parsley.

Savory Dried Beans with Chicken

Cooking the chicken with skin and bones left on enriches the flavor of this hearty dish.

1	whole chicken breast, with skin and bones, split, *or* 2 whole chicken legs
	Salt and freshly ground black pepper
1	tablespoon olive oil
1	onion, peeled and diced
1	carrot, peeled and diced
1	rib celery, diced
2	cups (1 pound) dried beans, soaked overnight and drained
6	cups water or chicken stock
1	onion pierced with 8 whole cloves
1	bay leaf
2	cloves garlic, smashed
1	sprig thyme or rosemary (optional)
2	tablespoons tomato paste
¼	cup chopped flat-leaf parsley
2	tablespoons vinegar

1. Season chicken with salt and pepper. Sauté in the olive oil in a large saucepan until well browned on both sides. Remove and reserve.
2. Pour off all but 1 tablespoon of fat and sauté diced onion, carrot, and celery until soft, about 7 minutes. Return chicken to the pot and add beans, water or chicken stock, whole onion, bay leaf, garlic, herb, and tomato paste. Bring to a boil, lower heat, and simmer covered for 40 minutes.
3. Remove and reserve chicken; continue simmering beans. When beans are fully cooked, remove the chicken from the bone and cut it into bite-size pieces, adding it back to the beans. Remove the whole onion, bay leaf, and herb sprig.

Add salt to taste and cook beans for 3 more minutes. Add parsley and vinegar, stir to mix, and serve.

SERVES 6

Master Recipe for Baked Beans

This is one recipe that has changed dramatically over time. Originally, baked beans were not sweet, and I find that the current preference for a thick, sweet sauce totally obscures the flavor of the beans themselves. That being said, I find that I do enjoy the taste of molasses with my beans and have included it here. Based on my testing reported earlier in this chapter, I have added the salt and vinegar to the recipe after the beans have cooked for 3 hours to keep the skins intact and to avoid prolonging the cooking time. Baked beans with a good amount of vinegar can take 8 hours to cook rather than 5. Although I could probably write an entire book on baked beans, I find that this version is my favorite workhorse recipe, the one I bring to the annual ox roast or to potluck suppers around town. A more traditional Vermont recipe might use maple syrup instead of molasses (see first variation) or cook the beans in apple juice instead of chicken stock.

Of course, bean cookery was not only important in colonial times but was also to be taken seriously. I was particularly taken by a quote from a Maine newspaper as reported by Evan Jones in *American Food*, which stated that every bean in a Maine bean pot "should be treated like a voter in an election. You must understand each bean to bake a collection of them."

1   pound (2 cups) navy beans
1   tablespoon cumin seeds
5   strips smoked bacon, cut into ½-inch
     pieces
1   tablespoon olive oil
1   large onion, diced
1   carrot, diced
2   cloves garlic, minced
¼   cup molasses
1   cup chopped tomato
1   tablespoon dry mustard or Dijon
     mustard
5   cups water or chicken stock or
     a combination
2   bay leaves
4   sprigs thyme
¼   cup cider vinegar
1   teaspoon salt
½   teaspoon freshly ground
     black pepper

1. Put beans in plenty of water to cover and soak overnight. Drain and rinse thoroughly with cold water.
2. Toast cumin seeds in a small skillet for 4 minutes or until they darken and pop.
3. Heat oven to 300 degrees.
4. Cook the bacon for 5 minutes in a large ovenproof pot or Dutch oven. Pour off all but 1 tablespoon fat (leave bacon pieces in pan), add olive oil, onion, carrot, and garlic and sauté for 5 minutes. Add remaining ingredients except the vinegar, salt, and pepper and stir gently to mix. Cover and bake for 3 hours. Add vinegar, salt, and pepper and stir gently to mix.
5. Replace cover and bake another 2 hours or until beans are very tender. If necessary, add additional chicken stock or water during cooking time to keep beans covered. When cooked, remove thyme sprigs and bay leaves, correct

seasonings (check salt level), and serve.

SERVES 8

VERMONT BAKED BEANS

Follow master recipe but substitute maple syrup for the molasses; add ¼ teaspoon ground cloves, ½ teaspoon ground cardamom, and ½ teaspoon ground allspice along with the salt and pepper.

BAKED BEANS WITH BOURBON AND BROWN SUGAR

Follow the master recipe but increase the bacon to 8 strips and cut them into ½-inch pieces. Use brown sugar instead of molasses and chicken stock instead of water. Add ½ cup bourbon along with the chicken stock.

Canned Bean Variation

These are a very far cry from the real thing and I do not suggest using this recipe except in a pinch. I also wouldn't call them baked beans since they don't take on the rich color and flavor of beans cooked for 5 hours. However, they are nicely flavored and this is a good, quick way to doctor up a couple of cans of beans.

1   tablespoon olive oil
½   onion, diced
½   carrot, diced
1   clove garlic, minced
2   (14-ounce) cans white beans, drained

⅓ cup chopped tomato
1 teaspoon prepared mustard
2 tablespoons molasses
1 bay leaf
2 sprigs thyme
2 tablespoons vinegar
Salt and freshly ground black pepper
to taste

Heat the oil in a large saucepan and sauté the onion, carrot, and garlic for 5 minutes over medium heat. Add the next 6 ingredients (beans through thyme). Bring to a boil, lower the heat, and simmer uncovered for 45 minutes. Add the vinegar, and salt and pepper to taste. (These beans will need little if any salt, since most canned beans are already salted.) Simmer another 15 minutes and serve.

Master Recipe for Bean Salad

Beans are much like rice in that they absorb flavors. Therefore, taste them just before serving. Additional vinegar, lemon, or lime juice along with a pinch of salt may be necessary to pick up the flavor. If you use raw corn kernels, make sure that they are tender and sweet. Tough winter corn won't do.

FOR THE SALAD
4 cups cooked beans (see master recipe page 91)
2 ribs celery, chopped
2 tablespoons finely chopped onion
⅓ cup finely chopped flat-leaf parsley or cilantro
3 scallions, finely chopped, or 2 tablespoons chopped fresh chives
1½ teaspoons salt
2 tablespoons lemon juice

OPTIONAL INGREDIENTS
1 cup peeled, seeded, and diced cucumber
1 cup cherry tomatoes, halved
½ cup fresh, sweet corn kernels, raw
1 cup green beans, boiled until just tender and cut into 1½-inch pieces
½ cup diced green, yellow, or red bell pepper

FOR THE DRESSING
¼ teaspoon salt
Freshly ground black pepper to taste
3 tablespoons high-quality white or red wine vinegar
2 cloves garlic, peeled and finely chopped with herbs below
1 teaspoon minced fresh tarragon, or ½ teaspoon dried
1 teaspoon minced fresh oregano, or ½ teaspoon dried
1 tablespoon Dijon mustard
¾ cup extra-virgin olive oil

Combine all ingredients for the salad including some or all of the optional ingredients. For the dressing, whisk the first 3 ingredients together in a small bowl. Add remaining ingredients and whisk until the mixture thickens, about 15 seconds. Toss with salad.

SERVES 8

Lentil Potato Salad

The idea of combining lentils and potatoes comes from Jacques Pépin, who also suggests serving this type of salad with sausage. Make sure that you thoroughly drain the lentils and potatoes. Otherwise, the salad will be watery.

1 cup dried lentils
1 pound waxy potatoes
½ cup finely chopped onion
2 tablespoons finely chopped fresh tarragon
¼ cup finely chopped fresh flat-leaf parsley
4 scallions, finely chopped
1½ teaspoons salt

FOR THE DRESSING
2 teaspoons finely minced garlic
2 teaspoons Dijon mustard
5 tablespoons extra-virgin olive oil
2 tablespoons good-quality red wine vinegar
½ teaspoon salt

1. Wash the lentils in a colander and then simmer in boiling salted water to cover for 15 to 20 minutes or until just tender. Drain thoroughly.
2. Wash potatoes, quarter them, and then either boil or steam them for about 15 minutes or until cooked but still firm. Drain thoroughly in a colander.
3. When the potatoes are cool enough to handle, cut them into thick slices and place them in a large serving bowl. Add the lentils, onion, tarragon, parsley, scallions, and salt. Whisk together the dressing ingredients and add to the bowl. Gently mix to combine. Serve while potatoes are still warm.

SERVES 6 TO 8

Marinated White Beans

Vinegar and cooked beans are a good combination, especially when left overnight to marinate. This dish can be served as a bean salad, as an accompaniment to meat, or even as a sauce over pasta.

½ master recipe for Cooking Dried Beans (use white beans, see page 91)
1 cup White Wine Vinaigrette (see below)
¼ cup chopped flat-leaf parsley
 Freshly ground black pepper to taste

Drain cooked beans, dress with vinaigrette and chopped parsley, and let marinate in refrigerator overnight. Taste and season with additional salt and freshly ground black pepper if necessary.

SERVES 4

WHITE WINE VINAIGRETTE

This is a simple vinaigrette. Note that the proportion of oil to vinegar is higher than for most recipes and therefore the oil can simply be whisked into the vinegar mixture without adding it drop by drop.

½ teaspoon salt
2 tablespoons white wine vinegar
½ cup plus 1 tablespoon olive oil
2 cloves garlic, peeled and lightly crushed (optional)
1 teaspoon Dijon mustard
1 teaspoon minced fresh tarragon, basil, marjoram, or parsley (optional)

Whisk together the salt and vinegar in a small bowl. Add remaining ingredients and whisk together for 15 seconds or until an emulsion forms. If using garlic, remove before serving.

Black Bean Soup with Sherry

This soup needs to be puréed; otherwise it is rather unattractive (although the flavor is quite good). Use a blender or food mill. Although modern cooks flinch at the notion of using salt pork, don't. It is crucial to building flavor.

1	pound (2 cups) dried black beans
¼	pound lean salt pork, coarsely chopped
1	quart chicken stock, preferably homemade or low sodium
2	large onions, peeled and diced, reserving 1 cup for garnish
2	garlic cloves, peeled and coarsely chopped
2	large carrots, peeled and coarsely chopped
1	medium potato, peeled and coarsely chopped
2	ribs celery, coarsely chopped
1	bay leaf
¼	teaspoon ground cloves
⅛	teaspoon grated nutmeg
½	teaspoon salt
¼	teaspoon Tabasco
¼	cup sherry
	Freshly ground black pepper to taste
2	tablespoons lemon juice
3	eggs, hard-boiled and chopped

1. Soak beans overnight in plenty of cold water. Drain. If you don't have time to soak them, simply increase the cooking time by 15 minutes.

2. In a large soup pot, combine the beans with 2 quarts of cold water. Bring to a simmer and cook uncovered for 45 minutes or until the beans are soft and edible. Add the salt pork and chicken stock, raise heat, and bring soup back to a simmer. Add the next 10 ingredients, reserving 1 cup of onion for garnish, and simmer for 1 hour or until beans and vegetables are very tender.

3. Remove bay leaf. Test soup for doneness by removing ½ cup and forcing it through a food mill; then return purée to the pot. If the mixture does not purée easily, continue simmering, checking every 10 minutes. When beans and vegetables are soft enough, purée the remainder in a food mill or blender. Return soup to the pot, add sherry, and simmer for 5 minutes.

4. Season to taste with additional salt if needed and freshly ground black pepper. Stir in the lemon juice and serve with a garnish of reserved diced onion and chopped hard-boiled egg.

SERVES 4 TO 6

Hash Brown Beans

This recipe was inspired by Stephen Schmidt, author of *Master Recipes*. He suggests making a skillet cake using beans, sausage, and onion and serving it in the morning along with eggs. It ain't diet food, but it's a good hearty breakfast when you plan on working outside all day. I prefer sweet Italian sausage meat for this recipe.

1	tablespoon vegetable oil
1½	cups sausage meat, removed from casing and crumbled
3	cups chopped onions
½	cup chopped red bell pepper (optional)
¼	teaspoon nutmeg
1	teaspoon sugar
½	teaspoon salt
3	cups thoroughly cooked dried beans, liquid reserved (see recipe page 91) Freshly ground black pepper to taste
¼	cup chopped flat-leaf parsley or chives

1. Place a large cast iron skillet over medium heat. When moderately hot, put in the oil, sausage, onions, and optional bell pepper and cook, stirring frequently, for 10 minutes or until sausage is no longer pink and onions are lightly browned. Add nutmeg, sugar, and salt and stir to combine.

2. Put beans on top of sausage mixture, mash with a potato masher, and cook without stirring for 6 minutes or until beans start to crust at the edges. Break up mixture with the edge of a spatula, then press into a new cake. Cook until edges start to crust up. Break up mixture and press into a new cake three more times, for a total cooking time of about 24 minutes. Cut and serve individual portions topped with a few grindings of pepper and sprinkled with either parsley or chives.

SERVES 6

Covered Dish Suppers

EVERY SUNDAY EVENING in the summers, I cook supper for a
variety of local Vermonters, who show up promptly at 5:30 (real
Vermonters are never late for dinner). Since I like to be outside all day,
either cutting hay or trying to repair a piece of equipment or just going for a
hike up our mountain, I have turned to simple casseroles as an expedient
solution. During the summer, I do most of the food preparation before church
when it's cool and then throw the covered dish into the oven about an hour
before serving.

When the food is set out, the farmers "get down to business," and there isn't
much conversation. Vermonters know that good food is to be eaten, not praised
and judged or regarded as a delicate art form. Compliments are few but country cooks know that requests for second helpings tell the real story. And it is the
essence of country life that nothing is singled out for praise, because the notion
of excellence is one that is foreign on a farm. It is dependability that is the
watchword, since there are no degrees of perfection. Hay is put in the barn or it
isn't, a tire is either flat or fixed, and either supper is on the table or farmhands
go hungry. This leads to both moderation and a quiet satisfaction with life,
since one truck is no better than another as long as it gets the job done, or one

house is not to be preferred over another with a better view. The view doesn't matter as long as the roof keeps the rain out and it is warm in January. (That's why real Vermonters don't have fireplaces — too much heat is lost up the flue.) Food, like everything else in life, is valued for its essence, for its basic purpose, which is to feed, to stoke the fires of those who labor. That it tastes or even looks particularly good is simply gravy for the meat, a pleasant surprise but not a fundamental characteristic to be judged, savored, or remarked on. But this does not mean that a hot dinner is to be taken for granted — quite the opposite. Since the essence of the thing is what matters, each meal is a blessing, like a tractor that starts on a cold day or a baler that doesn't break a shearing pin mid-afternoon. Perhaps that is why covered dish suppers are held in such high regard in the country. They are simple in design and purpose, practical, and by their very nature, modest, one well-worn casserole dish looking much like another from the outside. But when well-made, a covered dish supper conveys all the blessings of home cooking, the thrill of good food presented in a simple container. This marriage of modest expectations and excellence is at the heart of the matter, savoring simple pleasures when they are least expected.

COVERED DISH SUPPERS are still popular in Vermont. On Old Home Day or on Labor Day weekend when one of our neighbors has an all-afternoon open house, or even for a birthday celebration, neighbors bring over the sorts of dishes found in this chapter. In the old days,

however, these suppers were more common. Kitchen hops or dances were quite popular, especially in the summer, the parties held right in the kitchen with many folks sitting just outside the back door listening to the music. Another popular social event was the box social that was usually held at the town hall. Each of the young women in town made up a box lunch and the men had to bid on the right to dine with the young lady who made it. What made it interesting was that the men didn't know who made which box. I am sure that not all of the men were bidding blind, however, having been given hints by their sweethearts. In those days, it really paid to be a good cook.

In developing recipes for this chapter, I discovered that most covered dish recipes suffer from common difficulties, one of which is that a variety of ingredients all must be cooked for the same amount of time. This usually results in overcooked vegetables. To solve this problem, I have shortened the ingredient lists of many recipes and used frozen vegetables, such as peas and corn, without thawing. A second problem is that a deep casserole requires a good deal of baking to properly heat the ingredients. By using shallow pans and a hot oven, I find that cooking times can be dramatically shortened, which yields better texture. Finally, many old-fashioned casseroles call for a dense, floury sauce as a binder. I have lightened these considerably, which brightens both the texture and flavor of the dish.

Chicken Potpie

Say the words "chicken potpie" and most people run in the other direction, having tasted only store-bought, frozen pies with pasty fillings and overcooked chicken all stuffed under a tasteless, sodden crust. The truth of the matter is that a properly prepared pie is just short of heaven, a marriage of brightly flavored chicken and vegetable, bound in a thin well-seasoned sauce, hiding under a rich, luxurious crust.

I eliminated vegetables that can't stand prolonged cooking, hence no celery, which instantly turns to mush. I also found that frozen peas can be used without thawing or cooking, producing a fresher, more lively texture and flavor. I use a very thin sauce as a binder, foregoing the thick butter-flour–chicken stock combination used by most cooks. This brightens flavors considerably. Finally, I found that a high oven temperature combined with a shallow baking dish gets this recipe in and out of the oven in just 20 minutes, preserving much of the texture and flavor of the ingredients.

1	recipe American Pie Pastry (page 339), sugar reduced to 1 teaspoon
6	tablespoons butter
2	tablespoons olive oil
1	cup minced onion
2	cloves garlic, minced
1	cup sliced carrots (¼-inch rounds)
1¾–2	pounds skinless, boneless chicken breasts or thighs, trimmed of fat and gristle, cut into bite-size chunks
	Salt and freshly ground black pepper to taste
2	cups sliced white mushrooms
3	tablespoons flour
1¼	cups chicken stock, homemade preferred
¼	cup white wine
3	tablespoons dry sherry
1	tablespoon minced fresh thyme leaves or 1 teaspoon dried
2	cups (10-ounce package) frozen peas (not thawed)
1	egg yolk
1	tablespoon heavy cream

1. Make pie pastry, and refrigerate for at least 30 minutes before using. Heat oven to 425 degrees.

2. Heat 1 tablespoon each of butter and oil in a large skillet over medium heat, and when foam subsides, add onion. Sauté for 5 minutes. Add garlic and sauté for 1 minute. Add carrots and sauté for 4 minutes. Remove carrot/onion mixture to a large bowl. Add 1 more tablespoon of butter to the skillet and sauté chicken until browned, about 9 minutes. Season with salt and pepper and remove to bowl with a slotted spoon. Pour off pan juices and reserve. Put 1 tablespoon each of butter and oil into skillet and, when hot, add mushrooms and sauté until they release their juices and start to squeak when stirred. Season liberally with salt and pepper and remove to bowl.

3. Heat remaining 3 tablespoons of butter in the skillet; when foam subsides, add flour and stir with a wooden spoon, scraping up any bits from the bottom of the pan. Whisk for 1 minute. Add chicken stock and reserved pan juices, and whisk over medium heat until mixture thickens, about 3 to 4 minutes. Add white wine, sherry, and thyme and stir together. Pour over other ingredients in bowl and stir to mix. Taste for salt and pepper and adjust if necessary. Add frozen peas.

4. Pour mixture into a shallow casserole. Roll out pastry to the shape of the casserole and place over dish. Trim so that ½ inch of dough overlaps edges. Fold excess dough underneath the edges and crimp with your fingers or a fork. To glaze the pastry, beat together the egg yolk and cream with a fork and brush over top with a pastry brush. Cut 3 steam vents with a small knife. Place in oven and bake for 20 minutes or until crust is nicely browned. Serve immediately.

SERVES 6

Master Recipe for Shepherd's Pie

This recipe is quite similar to a potpie except that it uses ground meat and the casserole is topped with mashed potatoes instead of a pastry crust. I often make this dish first thing in the morning on blustery winter weekends, before we take the kids out to shovel off the pond for ice skating. About half an hour before dinner, I just pop the dish in the oven and that's it. Be sure to use a shallow baking dish or casserole so that the ingredients heat through quickly.

2	tablespoons olive oil
4	tablespoons butter
4	cups coarsely chopped onions
2	cups sliced carrots (¼-inch rounds)
2	pounds ground lamb, turkey, beef, or pork or a combination
1½	teaspoons salt
	Freshly ground black pepper to taste
1	tablespoon fresh thyme (for turkey or pork) or oregano (for beef or lamb) or 1½ teaspoons dried

1½	cups low-sodium chicken broth, homemade preferred
1	cup canned ground tomatoes or whole canned tomatoes, drained and chopped
4	teaspoons lemon juice
½	teaspoon Tabasco
2	teaspoons Worcestershire sauce
¼	cup brandy
2	cups (10-ounce package) frozen corn kernels
2	cups (10-ounce package) frozen peas
2	tablespoons minced fresh parsley
1½	recipes Mashed Potatoes (see page 70)

1. Heat olive oil and 1 tablespoon butter in a 12-inch skillet (a smaller pan will not be large enough) over medium heat. When foam subsides, add onions and cook for 5 minutes, stirring occasionally. Add the carrots and cook 5 minutes longer.

2. Add the meat, the salt, and a few grindings of black pepper. Cook and stir for 5 to 8 minutes, breaking up lumps of meat. If using beef, pork, or lamb, pour off most of the excess fat. Add the next 7 ingredients (herbs through brandy). Reduce heat to low and simmer for 20 minutes. Stir in still frozen corn and peas and the parsley.

3. Heat oven to 425 degrees. Pour mixture into a shallow baking dish or casserole, top with mashed potatoes. Melt remaining butter and brush it over potatoes. Bake for 20 minutes or until mixture is bubbling and potatoes are lightly browned.

SERVES 6 TO 8

New England Braised Dinner

At *Cook's Illustrated*, we researched how to make New England boiled dinner and found that commercially distributed corned beef was virtually inedible. Since corning is a method of preserving which was crucial for a farm but is no longer necessary, I prefer to simply cook a fresh piece of brisket, the same cut used for corned beef, in a small amount of liquid. (Corned beef can stand to be boiled, but brisket cannot. Brisket is a triangular piece of meat, a cut that comes from underneath the animal, just behind the front legs, and is usually cut in half, sold as a "point half" and a "flat half." Purchase the "point half" of the brisket, since it will be a bit more tender and flavorful.) If you cannot find brisket, use any good chuck roast such as a "top blade" roast. Be absolutely sure to bring all the ingredients to a simmer before placing the pot in the oven. Otherwise, it will take a very long time for the meat to cook. To crush juniper berries (they add a great deal of flavor to this dish and are worth including), place them in a small plastic storage bag on a cutting board and pound once or twice with the bottom of a heavy saucepan.

1   tablespoon vegetable oil
3   pounds beef brisket or chuck roast, preferably top blade
    Salt and freshly ground pepper to taste
½   cup dry white wine
1   medium onion, diced
4   cloves garlic, minced
2   medium tomatoes, coarsely chopped
½   cup chicken stock
¼   cup water
1   teaspoon dried thyme
1   teaspoon dried rosemary
1   bay leaf
12 juniper berries, crushed (optional)
4   carrots, peeled and cut into 3-inch pieces
4   medium parsnips, peeled, large diameter sections cut in half lengthwise, and cut into 3-inch pieces

1. Heat oven to 250 degrees. Put oil in a large Dutch oven over medium-high heat. Season brisket with salt and pepper and then brown well on each side.
2. Remove brisket, turn heat to high, and add white wine. With a wooden spoon, scrape bottom of pan and reduce wine for 1 minute. Add onion and cook over medium heat for 5 minutes. Add garlic and cook for 1 minute.
3. Return brisket to pan with all additional ingredients except carrots and parsnips. Bring to a simmer.
4. Cover, place in heated oven, and cook for about 2 hours, turning meat after 1 hour, or until the brisket is tender (about 200 to 210 degrees internal temperature). Add carrots and parsnips and cook an additional hour. (The vegetables can also be steamed or boiled separately and then served with broth along with the meat.) Discard bay leaf.
5. Remove brisket to a cutting board and slice against the grain into thin slices. Arrange on plates with carrots and parsnips, adding broth to each serving.

SERVES 4 TO 6

Master Recipe
for White Bean Casserole

Lamb and pork work best with this dish, since they have a good deal of flavor. I call for canned beans in this recipe as dried beans must be precooked, adding significantly to the preparation time. This is an excellent recipe for using up leftovers.

2	tablespoons high-quality olive oil
1	tablespoon unsalted butter
2	cups chopped onion
2	teaspoons minced anchovies (2 large fillets or 4 small fillets)
6	cloves garlic, minced
2	cups canned drained and chopped whole tomatoes
3	cups bite-size pieces of cooked chicken, lamb, pork, or beef
2	(15-ounce) cans white beans, drained and rinsed
1	cup low-sodium chicken stock
1	tablespoon lemon juice
1½	teaspoons salt
	Freshly ground black pepper to taste
⅓	cup minced fresh parsley

1. Heat oven to 400 degrees. Heat 1 tablespoon olive oil and the butter in a nonreactive Dutch oven. When foam subsides, sauté onion and anchovies for 5 minutes over medium heat. Add garlic and sauté for 1 minute.
2. Add all other ingredients except parsley and bring to a simmer. Taste for seasonings and adjust. Cover and bake for 25 minutes. Stir in parsley and serve.

SERVES 4

Skillet Frittata with
Potatoes, Bacon, and Leeks

This is very similar to the recipe for potato casserole on page 71. Just add eggs for the last half hour of cooking and you have an omelet or frittata. This makes a good supper with bread and a salad.

4	slices thick-cut bacon
2	tablespoons olive oil
¾	pound onions, thinly sliced
½	pound leeks, white part only, thinly sliced
2	pounds starchy potatoes, peeled and sliced ⅛ inch thick, placed in a bowl of water to cover
1½	teaspoons salt
	Freshly ground black pepper to taste
2	teaspoons minced fresh thyme, or 1 teaspoon dried
8	large eggs

1. Heat oven to 350 degrees. Cook bacon until browned in a well-seasoned 12-inch cast iron skillet or Dutch oven (a smaller skillet won't work). Drain on paper towels and reserve. Pour off all but 2 tablespoons fat.
2. Add olive oil to pan, heat, and add onions and leeks. Sauté over medium heat, stirring occasionally, for 8 minutes. Crumble bacon and add to onion mixture. Drain potatoes, reserving ¾ cup of water. Add 1 teaspoon salt to the water and stir to dissolve. Using a large rubber spatula, fold potatoes, salted potato water, pepper, and thyme into the onion mixture. Continue folding over medium heat until liquid starts to thicken.
3. Cover pan with aluminum foil and bake for 30 minutes.

4. Whisk eggs with the remaining ½ teaspoon salt and freshly ground black pepper to taste. Remove skillet from oven, uncover, and pour in eggs, lifting up the bottom layer of potatoes so that eggs flow to the bottom of the pan. Place back in oven and bake uncovered until eggs are set but not dry, about 20 minutes. Cut into wedges and serve.

SERVES 6 TO 8

Beef Stew with Beer and Parsnips

Making a beef stew with beer instead of wine is nothing new. In testing, I used a heavy, dark beer and found that the flavor was overpowering, so I recommend using a standard American beer such as Michelob. I also tested using homemade beef stock (see page 40) instead of chicken stock and the results were excellent. I have tested making stews at a variety of oven temperatures and find that low heat works best. I used to call for a 200 degree oven, but since most home ovens are not properly calibrated, many cooks would be using an oven cooler than 200 degrees. For this reason, I now suggest heating the oven to 250 degrees, which provides a good margin of safety in terms of getting the meat cooked in a reasonable amount of time. You do not have to purée the potato at the end of the recipe if you prefer a thinner sauce. I also found that it was best not to peel red potatoes, which have a very thin skin.

3	pounds stew beef (purchase chuck instead of round), cut into 1½-inch cubes
3	tablespoons olive oil
2	medium onions, cut into large dice
1	(12-ounce) bottle beer
2	large cloves garlic, minced
2½	cups chicken stock or homemade beef stock
2	canned tomatoes, seeded and chopped, or 1 tablespoon tomato paste
1	bay leaf
½	teaspoon salt
4	medium carrots, peeled and cut into 2-inch chunks
3	medium parsnips, peeled and cut into 2-inch chunks
4	waxy potatoes diced into 2-inch chunks (peeling optional)
1	teaspoon dried thyme or 1 tablespoon fresh
	Freshly ground black pepper to taste
2	tablespoons minced parsley

1. Heat oven to 250 degrees. Pat meat dry with paper towels. Heat 2 tablespoons of the olive oil in a large pot or Dutch oven set over high heat and brown meat in batches on top and bottom. Do not crowd. Remove meat to a bowl and pour off all fat from the pan.

2. Add the remaining tablespoon of olive oil to the pot over medium/high heat. When oil is hot add the onions along with ¼ cup of the beer. Sauté for 2 minutes, stirring constantly with a wooden spoon, scraping the bottom of the pan to remove the accumulated juices. Add the garlic and sauté for 1 minute, stirring constantly. Add the rest of the beer, the stock, the chopped tomato, the bay leaf, the browned meat, and the salt. Bring to a simmer. Cover and bake in preheated oven for an hour. Add the next three ingredients and cook another hour.

3. Add the dried thyme (if using fresh thyme, add it later) and continue cooking for another 30 minutes. Check meat. If tender, add the fresh thyme and cook another 15 minutes. If meat is still tough, continue cooking until tender, adding the fresh thyme for the last 15 minutes of cooking. Check seasonings and add freshly ground black pepper to taste. Remove the bay leaf.

4. Transfer ¼ of the potatoes and 2 cups of the liquid to a food processor or blender and purée. Return to the pot and stir to combine. Sprinkle each serving with parsley and serve with large hunks of country bread.

SERVES 6

Lamb or Irish Stew

According to James Beard, one of the first Irish stews to be published in an American cookbook was made with beef, not lamb, and served with a brown sauce! In a traditional Irish stew, however, a stock is made with lamb bones the day before the stew is prepared. Instead, I have opted to use chicken stock as a base — which is considerably simpler.

3	pounds boneless lamb, cut into 1-inch cubes from the shanks or shoulder
	Salt and freshly ground black pepper to taste
3	tablespoons olive oil
2	medium onions, cut into large dice
1	(12-ounce) bottle beer
2	large cloves garlic, minced
2½	cups chicken stock
4	medium carrots (about ½ pound), peeled and cut into 2-inch chunks
4 to 6	waxy potatoes (about 1 pound), quartered
2	teaspoons minced fresh thyme or 1 teaspoon dried
2	tablespoons parsley, minced

1. Heat oven to 250 degrees. Pat meat dry with paper towels and season liberally with salt and pepper. Heat the olive oil in a large pot or Dutch oven set over high heat and brown meat in batches. Do not crowd. Be sure that meat is browned on all sides. Remove meat to a bowl.

2. Put onions into the pot along with ¼ cup of the beer. Sauté for 2 minutes, stirring constantly with a wooden spoon, scraping the bottom of the pan to remove the accumulated juices. Add the garlic and sauté for 1 minute, stirring constantly. Add the rest of the beer, the stock, the browned meat, and ½ teaspoon of salt. Cover and bake in preheated oven for an hour. Add the carrots and potatoes and cook another 30 minutes.

3. Add the dried thyme (if using fresh thyme, add it later) and continue cooking for another 30 minutes. Check meat. If tender, add the fresh thyme and cook another 15 minutes. If the meat is still tough, continue cooking until tender, adding the fresh thyme for the last 15 minutes of cooking. Check seasonings and add pepper to taste and more salt if necessary.

4. Remove ¼ of the potatoes and 2 cups of the liquid to a food processor or blender and purée. Return to the pot and stir to combine. Sprinkle each serving with parsley and serve with large hunks of country bread.

SERVES 6

Noodles and Macaroni

I ONCE ATTENDED a cooking conference at which the speakers were describing the difference in tasting abilities from person to person. They explained that some of us have more taste buds than others and that different parts of the tongue, the front for example, perceive sweetness whereas other parts (the back portion) are sensitive to bitter flavors. As I was developing the recipe in this chapter for tomato sauce, I rediscovered the complexity of taste. I found that with just the right sort of canned tomatoes, prepared in just the right manner, a rich, sweet tomato flavor would burst on the tongue, followed by a kick of acidity, followed by a hint of garlic, an underlying layer of salt, a tongue-coating burst of olive oil, and the fresh scent of basil to finish. In cooking, we aspire to complexity, avoiding the consolidation of tastes and textures to achieve unexpected but rewarding marriages.

When she turned eight, I decided that my older daughter should learn a bit about hard work by helping out a local farmer. Her first job was to help us corral a few Belgians from the upper pasture above the old Lomberg farm so they would be ready for our Fourth of July parade. These were working animals, about sixteen hands high, the size of a good quarter horse, and they didn't much like the look of our rope halters. We funneled three of them into a small spot by the gate, large maples on one side and a steep bank on the other, but it was dangerous work, one of them spinning up on his hind legs, muscled forequarters up and over the back of a second horse, taking flight through the woods. It was no place for an eight-year-old, the men shouting, the horses with ears back, nostrils flared, grain spilled on the muddy road, jostling by chestnut animals weighing almost a ton each. Sent far up the bank, by an old sugar maple, my daughter waited until we were done, left out, not needed. I looked up, saw the tears just starting down her cheeks, and had a sharp memory of times on the farm when I was young, rebuked for running a tractor downhill out of gear, pulling a fully loaded hay wagon, or standing helplessly by while the old-timers hooked up the teams to the old-fashioned mechanical mowers, snapping the ancient wooden hames around the collars, sorting out the tugs and traces, pole straps and lazy straps, whipple trees and eveners, britchens and back pads. It was a lonely time in those moments, feeling unwanted and painfully aware that I was just a kid.

After the horses were safely in the barn, our family jumped into the pickup and went up to the swimming hole just past the Methodist church. It's not really a hole, but a series of pools and chutes, used by generations of town kids. It was late afternoon, the sun lighting up the crystal pools, turning the water a radiant green. I dove in, an icy baptism, came up to the surface and saw the dappled leaves, the rush of water, caught a hint of trout and moss-covered schist in the stream's moist, fresh scent, the sour taste of the heat of the day gone in an instant. And

then all three kids followed, my oldest daughter jumping into my arms, exhilarated, happy, immersed in the rush of the stream and the wildness of the moment, suspended in time by the swirl of water, the sparkle of sun through the waving birches.

It was a day of contradictions, of disappointment and joy, but, as it seemed later, the two events were intertwined, one needing the other. My daughter had tasted first of sour, then of sweet, the latter enhanced and made more joyous by the former. I remember that we all slept well that night, but I like to think that she slept best, on a day that ended with a full moon rising over the hollow, the sweet smell of fern in her hair, and a father who lay awake for just a moment, thinking of other summer days long ago.

AS FAR AS I can remember, nobody on the farm ever used the term "pasta." We might have a spaghetti dinner down at the local church or be served macaroni salad or macaroni and cheese. These were noodle dishes, not pasta, and were usually served in heavy crockery casseroles not on fancy dinner plates. For the most part, I have limited the recipes in this chapter to the sort of noodle dishes that might be found in a country kitchen.

I did, however, make tomato sauces, most often using canned tomatoes, since good local tomatoes can only be had for about six weeks if you have a good hot summer. I started my investigations trying to determine which brand and which type (crushed, diced, whole, etc.) was best. Having done a fair amount of testing in the kitchens of *Cook's Illustrated,* I knew that in terms of canned crushed tomatoes, I preferred Progresso, Muir Glen, and Redpack, in that order. But I soon discovered that in a quick-cooking tomato sauce, crushed tomatoes were disappointing; their lackluster flavor did not have sufficient complexity. Looking for a style of tomatoes that would work in any recipe, I next tested whole tomatoes, with mixed results. I then stumbled onto what was to be my clear favorite, Muir Glen Diced Tomatoes. To begin with, they are convenient because the entire contents of the can is used; with whole tomatoes, using all of the packing liquid resulted in substantially thinner sauce. Even better, the flavor is fresh and bright with a good balance of sweet and acid. (Incidentally, Muir Glen also sells ground tomatoes, which I did not like as much given that they had a flatter, duller flavor. This supported my finding that overly processed sauces tend to have less flavor.)

However, because Muir Glen Diced Tomatoes may not be available in your supermarket, I retested crushed versus whole tomatoes and decided that the latter were the clear winner. My favorite brands were Muir Glen once again, followed closely by Progresso. The thick purée used in the Redpack brand I found unappealing for the master recipe that follows, although the tomatoes themselves are high quality. While I was at it, I tested the claim of many cooks that seeding the tomatoes is important to remove bitterness, and found that seedless sauce tasted no different than the version with seeds. I also decided that, when using whole tomatoes, it is important to drain the tomatoes first, reserving the liquid, in order to prevent the finished tomato sauce from being too thin.

I then decided to create a good basic recipe for quick canned tomato sauce, since so many noodle recipes require this as a building block. At first, it seemed that trying to define the "best" quick tomato sauce is almost as silly as trying to settle on the best type of corn. (I am still partial to the old standbys, Silver Queen or Butter and Sugar, but others swear by the new supersweets: Kandy Korn, Kiss and Tell, or Peaches and Cream.) After some thought, however, I managed to define a style of sauce that would be particularly useful to an American home cook: a quick year-round sauce that would be best served over fresh-boiled pasta. I wanted to use the fewest number of ingredients possible, so I selected the key players — tomatoes, oil, garlic, and salt — and eliminated nonessentials such as carrots, meat, wine, and so forth. I wanted a tomato sauce, not tomato soup. This immediately eliminated a whole category of longer-cooked, full-bodied Italian sauces. The sauce had to be quick to make, twenty minutes or less from pantry to table. Finally, it had to taste first and foremost of tomatoes, with a nice hint of acidity and a light, fresh flavor.

With this fairly limited mission statement, a number of fundamental issues came to mind. How do you get a nice hint of garlic without overpowering the sauce? How does cooking time affect flavor? Do you need sugar to boost tomato flavor? And what about tomato paste?

After some initial testing I determined that butter tends to dull the bright, slightly acidic flavor of the tomatoes, tomato paste has a rather one-dimensional flavor, and more than two cloves of garlic and three tablespoons of olive oil for one twenty-eight-ounce can of tomatoes was too much. In general, shorter cooking times of ten to fifteen minutes produced a fresher, brighter tomato flavor. A large sauté pan was preferred to a saucepan because it hurried up the cooking.

I also came to some conclusions about overall flavor. The sauces I preferred tasted predominantly like tomatoes, not garlic, basil, or any other ingredient. The better recipes also had a nice balance between sweet and sour to give the sauce some depth. This layering of flavors in fact became the holy grail of this investigation. The proper balance between sweet and sour, smoothness and bite, tomato and garlic, basil and olive oil, were crucial to an exciting, multidimensional sauce.

With these decisions made, I then compiled a master recipe using one teaspoon of minced garlic, three tablespoons of olive oil, one can of diced tomatoes, eight chopped basil leaves, one-quarter teaspoon of sugar, and salt to taste. This made enough to sauce one pound of pasta.

The first test was aimed at finding the best method of preparing the garlic. Using a garlic purée that was diluted with water and sautéed briefly in olive oil provided a mild, even garlic flavor while greatly reducing the possibility of overcooking the garlic as compared to using minced garlic, simply crushing the cloves, using slices, or adding minced garlic just before serving without cooking it, or cooking minced garlic along with the tomatoes without sautéing it. Next I tried making sauces with no sweetener, with one-quarter teaspoon of sugar, and with

carrots instead of sugar. The no-sugar sauce had a reduced tomato flavor, the quarter teaspoon was judged to be just right, and the carrot method added too much cooking time.

The quantity of olive oil was also evaluated and judged to be ideal at three tablespoons. I also tested whether all of the olive oil should be added at the beginning of cooking or some withheld and added at the end to provide a nice burst of fresh flavor. As I suspected, it was best to use two tablespoons of olive oil for cooking and a third tablespoon at the end to finish the sauce. Not surprisingly, I preferred a high-quality, extra-virgin oil because it delivered a pleasant hint of fresh olives.

Now I was ready to taste the sauce on pasta. Much to my surprise, I found that it did not properly cling to the pasta, and the flavor was unexpectedly bland. My complex, well-balanced sauce, it turned out, was too delicate for the texture and flavor of the pasta. My first fix was to add back a quarter cup of pasta cooking water to the drained pasta once it had been returned to its original pot. This dramatically improved the consistency of the sauce and, to my great surprise, also improved the flavor.

I started off using two cups of sauce for one pound of pasta but this seemed insufficient for a quick, fresh-tasting sauce. By reducing the amount of pasta to three-quarters of a pound, the balance between sauce and pasta was clearly improved. As a final note, I found that adding the sauce, stirring to coat the pasta, and then heating everything for one minute was the most effective saucing method, giving the sauce better distribution and overall consistency.

Master Recipe for Quick Tomato Sauce

If you use whole canned tomatoes, avoid those packed in sauce or purée, which results in a dull, relatively flavorless sauce without the interplay of sweetness and acidity. If you choose Muir Glen Diced Tomatoes instead, use the can's entire contents, without discarding any liquid. The pasta and sauce quantities can be doubled, but you'll have to simmer the sauce for an extra five or six minutes to thicken it. Note that this recipe uses a great deal of salt because it is served over pasta, which needs it. If you intend to use this sauce for another purpose, just add salt to taste. Although three-quarters of a pound of pasta may seem an odd quantity, a full pound of pasta will dilute the sauce, resulting in a lack of flavor. You can, however, stretch the sauce to cover one pound of pasta if you make one of the more flavorful variations.

1	(28-ounce) can diced or whole tomatoes (*not* packed in purée or sauce) or 2 pounds fresh tomatoes, chopped
2	medium cloves garlic, peeled
3	tablespoons extra-virgin olive oil
2	tablespoons coarsely chopped fresh basil leaves (about 8 leaves)
¼	teaspoon sugar
1½	teaspoons salt
¾	pound pasta
1	tablespoon coarsely chopped flat-leaf parsley

1. If using diced or fresh tomatoes, go to step 2. If using whole canned tomatoes, drain and reserve liquid. Dice tomatoes either by hand or in workbowl of a food processor fitted with metal blade (three or four ½-second pulses). Tomatoes should be coarse, with ¼-inch pieces visible. If necessary, add enough reserved liquid to tomatoes to total 2 cups.

2. Process garlic through a garlic press into a small bowl. Add 1 teaspoon of water and stir to mix. Heat 2 tablespoons of the oil and the garlic mixture in a 6-quart Dutch oven, large skillet, or sauté pan. Cook over medium heat until fragrant but not brown, about 1 to 2 minutes. Stir in tomatoes; simmer until thickened slightly, about 10 minutes. Stir in basil, sugar, and ½ teaspoon of the salt.

3. Meanwhile, cook pasta until *al dente* in large pot of boiling salted water. Reserve one-quarter cup cooking water; drain pasta and transfer it back to cooking pot. Mix in reserved cooking water, sauce, remaining oil, and ½ teaspoon of salt; cook together over medium heat for 1 minute, stirring constantly. Taste and add up to ½ teaspoon additional salt if needed. Sprinkle with parsley and serve immediately.

DRESSES ¾ POUND OF PASTA: SERVES 3

TOMATO SAUCE WITH BACON AND PARSLEY

In a 10-inch skillet, fry 3 ounces of thick-cut bacon, cut into ½-inch pieces, over medium-high heat until crisp and brown, about 5 minutes. Transfer with a slotted spoon to a paper towel–lined plate; pour off all but 2 tablespoons of fat from pan. Follow master recipe above, omitting olive oil and heating garlic and ½ teaspoon crushed red pepper flakes in bacon fat until fragrant but not brown, about 2 minutes. Continue with master recipe, substituting 2 tablespoons chopped fresh parsley leaves for basil and adding reserved bacon along with parsley.

TOMATO SAUCE
WITH SPICY CANNED TOMATOES

Follow master recipe above for Quick Tomato Sauce, increasing garlic to 3 cloves and adding ¼ teaspoon red pepper flakes and 3 minced anchovy fillets along with garlic and oil. Substitute ¼ cup minced fresh parsley leaves for basil. Add ¼ cup pitted, sliced kalamata olives and 2 tablespoons drained capers to the sauce after the initial 10-minute cooking time. Simmer for 3 minutes.

QUICK TOMATO SAUCE
WITH AROMATIC VEGETABLES

Add the olive oil to the pan but do not add the garlic. Also add 1 each finely chopped onion, carrot, and rib of celery. Cook over medium heat for 8 minutes or until the onion is very soft but not browned. Add the garlic and cook for 1 minute. Stir in the tomatoes and proceed with the recipe. Serve with freshly grated Parmesan cheese and freshly ground black pepper to taste.

Spaghetti Sauce Cooked with a Steak or Chop

This sauce tastes just like the sauce all moms used to make if you lived in an Italian neighborhood. I find that the taste of pork is best, but beef also works well. The recipe can be completed in about an hour but has a deep, long-cooked flavor. Some chopped fresh herbs are a good addition before serving.

2	(28-ounce) cans diced or ground tomatoes or whole tomatoes *not* packed in purée or sauce (Muir Glen Diced Tomatoes preferred)
3	tablespoons high-quality olive oil
1	large, thick pork chop or 1½ pounds boneless beef chuck, steak preferred
1½	teaspoons salt
	Freshly ground black pepper to taste
1	medium onion, peeled and finely chopped
1	medium carrot, peeled and finely chopped
4	cloves garlic, peeled and crushed
½	cup red wine
3	tablespoons chopped fresh basil or parsley, or a combination

1. If using whole tomatoes, drain them, reserving the liquid, and chop. Reserve tomatoes and juice in a bowl.
2. In a nonreactive Dutch oven, heat the olive oil. Season the chop with salt and pepper and brown on both sides over medium-high heat, about 8 minutes total. Remove meat and set aside. Reduce heat to medium-low, add the onion and carrot, and sauté until softened, 6 to 8 minutes. Add the garlic and sauté for 1 minute. Return the meat and any accumulated juices to the pot and add the wine. Bring to a simmer and cook uncovered for 3 minutes.
3. Add the reserved tomatoes and their juice (if using crushed or minced tomatoes, just add them directly from the can) and salt and bring back to a simmer. Reduce heat to low to maintain a slow

simmer, partially cover, and cook until meat is tender, about 45 to 55 minutes, depending on the thickness of the meat. Remove meat and keep warm. Raise heat to medium and continue cooking sauce for about 5 minutes, or until thickened.

4. Stir in the basil and/or parsley and add freshly ground black pepper to taste (the sauce will be salty at this point; it will taste fine once added to pasta). Slice the meat and serve with the pasta and sauce.

DRESSES 1½ TO 2 POUNDS OF PASTA: SERVES 6 TO 8

Slow-Cooked Spaghetti Sauce with Ground Meat

Tomatoes are acidic, and that is why they have such an affinity for cream. I also tried this recipe with milk and half-and-half; I found that cream is considerably better. I also found that milk tends to separate and curdle after simmering.

1	(28-ounce) can diced or ground tomatoes or whole tomatoes *not* packed in purée or sauce (Muir Glen Diced Tomatoes preferred)
1	tablespoon butter
2	tablespoons olive oil
1	medium onion, finely chopped
1	carrot, finely chopped
1	stalk celery, finely chopped
1	clove garlic, minced
½	pound ground beef
¼	pound ground pork
½	cup white wine
1	teaspoon salt
1	teaspoon sugar

	Dash nutmeg
	Dash allspice
	Freshly ground black pepper to taste
¼	cup heavy cream (optional but recommended)
3	tablespoons chopped fresh parsley (do not substitute dried) (optional)

1. If using whole tomatoes, drain, reserving the juice, and chop them. Place tomatoes and juice in a bowl and reserve.

2. Heat the butter and oil in a large Dutch oven or sauce pot. When foam subsides, add the onion, carrot, and celery and cook over medium heat for 8 minutes or until onion is very soft but not browned. Add the garlic and cook 1 minute. Reduce heat to low and add the beef and pork, breaking it up with a wooden spoon. After 3 to 4 minutes add the wine and salt — the meat should still be pink inside. Simmer for 5 minutes and then add the sugar, nutmeg, allspice, and tomatoes with their juice. Simmer for 1 hour. Add pepper to taste.

3. Add the heavy cream and bring the sauce back to a simmer. Simmer for 3 minutes, add the parsley, and serve.

DRESSES 1 POUND OF PASTA: SERVES 4

Master Recipe for Raw Tomato Sauce

This sauce can be used not just on pasta but also with grilled fish or perhaps grilled boneless chicken breast. The sauce should taste a bit salty before serving with pasta. If using with meat or fish, reduce salt to ½ teaspoon.

2 pounds high-quality ripe tomatoes, seeded and chopped into medium dice
⅓ cup high-quality olive oil
2 cloves garlic, peeled and minced
¼ cup flat-leaf parsley, mint, or basil, or a combination, finely chopped
1 teaspoon salt
¼ teaspoon sugar
Freshly ground black pepper to taste

Combine all ingredients and let marinate for 1 hour.

DRESSES 1 POUND OF PASTA: SERVES 4

Macaroni and Cheese

Some pasta and cheese recipes are nothing more than eggs, butter, and cheese. Others call for mustard, dried bread crumbs, and, in one peculiar recipe, peanut butter. I prefer, however, to make a béchamel, the classic French white sauce, and then add cheese. It provides a creamier, more satisfying consistency. I also tried adding an egg, which makes the sauce unappealing if it sits for any amount of time. The trick is to have just the right amount of cheese; otherwise the sauce becomes gooey and stretchy.

4 tablespoons butter
2 tablespoons flour
1 cup milk
¼ teaspoon freshly grated nutmeg
½ teaspoon salt
1 teaspoon dry mustard, dissolved in 1 teaspoon water
5 ounces grated American cheese
5 ounces grated Monterey Jack, fontina, or Cheddar cheese
12 ounces elbow macaroni or bow tie pasta
¼ cup grated high-quality Parmesan cheese
Freshly ground black pepper to taste

1. Bring a large pot of salted water to a simmer.

2. Meanwhile, in a medium saucepan, heat 2 tablespoons butter. When foam subsides, add flour and whisk mixture for 1 minute over medium heat. Gradually add milk and continue whisking over medium-high heat until mixture thickens, 2 to 3 minutes. Remove from heat and add next 3 ingredients (nutmeg through mustard). Over low heat, add the American and Monterey Jack cheeses and stir with a wooden spoon until cheese is melted and mixture is smooth. Keep warm.

3. Cook pasta and drain. Add back to pot, add remaining butter, and stir to coat evenly. Add the cheese sauce and the Parmesan to the macaroni and stir to mix. Heat for 3 to 4 minutes or until mixture is hot and creamy. Serve with a sprinkling of freshly ground pepper and additional grated nutmeg if you like.

SERVES 4

Baked Macaroni and Cheese

I prefer this recipe to the basic recipe above, since the buttered breadcrumbs add a nice bit of texture to the macaroni. Be sure to omit the Parmesan cheese when making the basic recipe.

1   recipe Macaroni and Cheese (above) made without the Parmesan cheese
2   tablespoons butter
½   cup packed soft bread crumbs
¼   cup grated high-quality Parmesan cheese

Heat 2 tablespoons of butter in a large skillet over medium heat until foam subsides. Add the bread crumbs and cook, tossing to coat with butter, until bread crumbs just begin to brown. Let cool and stir in Parmesan. Adjust oven rack so it is 6 inches from the heating element and heat broiler. Pour cooked macaroni and cheese into a 2-quart ovenproof baking dish. Sprinkle crumbs evenly on top. Broil until crumbs turn deep brown, 2 to 3 minutes. Let stand 5 minutes and serve.

SERVES 4

Master Recipe for Noodle Casserole

This recipe works best with chicken or turkey and spaghetti, which is then a recipe for tetrazzini. According to James Beard, the name comes from a famous turn-of-the-century opera singer who was partial to both pasta and large quantities. Note that this dish is not covered or baked for a long time. For a fresher, less sodden texture and flavor, it is best to use a shallow baking dish, no cover, and a very hot oven. The ingredients warm quickly and the bread crumbs brown nicely. If done properly, this is quite a good dish, not just a way to make do with leftovers. Don't be stingy with the salt and pepper. This dish needs aggressive seasoning.

8   tablespoons (1 stick) butter plus extra for greasing baking dish
¾   cup fresh bread crumbs
2   cups sliced white button mushrooms
1   cup diced onion
     Salt and freshly ground black pepper to taste
¾   pound spaghetti, macaroni, or any similar pasta
¼   cup flour
2   cups low-sodium chicken stock, homemade preferred
3   tablespoons dry sherry
½   cup grated Parmesan cheese
¼   teaspoon freshly grated nutmeg
½   teaspoon salt
2   teaspoons lemon juice
4   cups boned cooked meat (chicken or turkey preferred) cut into bite-size chunks

1. Heat oven to 450 degrees. Heat a large pot of salted water. Butter a shallow casserole or baking dish and set aside. Melt 2 tablespoons of the butter and toss with fresh bread crumbs; set aside.
2. Melt 2 more tablespoons of the butter in a skillet and, when hot, add mushrooms and onion. Sauté over medium heat, stirring frequently, until the mushrooms release their juices and start to squeak when stirred. Season with plenty of salt and freshly ground black pepper to taste. Remove to a large bowl.
3. Snap strands of spaghetti in half and add to the boiling water. Cook until *al dente*, about 7 minutes. Reserve ¼ cup of cooking liquid, drain spaghetti, and return to the pot with the reserved liquid.
4. While spaghetti is cooking, heat remaining 4 tablespoons of butter in a medium saucepan. When foam subsides, whisk in

the flour over medium heat for 1 minute or until mixture loses the scent of raw flour. Gradually whisk in the chicken stock and cook over medium-high heat, whisking constantly, until mixture thickens, about 3 to 4 minutes. Remove from heat and whisk in the next 5 ingredients (sherry through lemon juice). Add sauce to bowl along with chicken. Mix.

5. Add spaghetti to the bowl and mix well. Taste and adjust seasonings, if necessary; be generous with the salt. Pour mixture into baking dish and sprinkle buttered bread crumbs on top. Place in oven for 8 minutes or until bread crumbs brown and mixture is bubbly. Serve at once.

SERVES 6 TO 8

TUNA NOODLE CASSEROLE VARIATION

Substitute two 6½-ounce cans of water-packed chunk light tuna, drained and flaked, for the meat.

Parsley Pesto

Parsley is available year-round at a reasonable price, whereas basil is expensive and extraordinarily sensitive to frosts. In New England, for example, it makes more sense to make pesto out of flat-leaf parsley (don't use curly parsley; it has less flavor) than basil. Freeze pesto in ice cube trays, pop out the frozen cubes, and then store them in a double thickness of heavy-duty freezer bags. They can be quickly thawed in a microwave (use 50 percent power and microwave for about 2 minutes).

¼	cup pine nuts (or walnuts in a pinch)
3	cloves garlic, crushed
2	cups chopped flat-leaf parsley (include stems that are not woody and tough)
1	teaspoon salt
	Freshly ground black pepper to taste
½	cup high-quality olive oil
½	cup grated Parmesan cheese

1. Toast nuts 3 to 4 minutes in a 400 degree oven until lightly browned. Check constantly to prevent burning. Walnuts will take a little more time than pine nuts.

2. Combine all ingredients except cheese in a blender. Process until combined but not puréed. Remove pesto to a bowl and stir in cheese. Serve over hot pasta with freshly ground black pepper and freshly grated Parmesan cheese.

DRESSES 1½ POUNDS OF PASTA;
SERVES 4 TO 6

Lasagne

No-boil noodles were brought to my attention by Jack Bishop, a *Cook's Illustrated* editor, when he was researching a piece on lasagne for the magazine. I was suspicious at first — they sounded gimmicky to me — but they really work and save a tremendous amount of time and effort, since they do not have to be precooked. They do absorb a bit more sauce than traditional lasagne noodles, but this was easily compensated for in the recipe. By making a full two recipes of the meat sauce, you will have enough left over to serve with the finished lasagne.

FOR THE MEAT SAUCE

2	recipes Slow-Cooked Spaghetti Sauce with Ground Meat (page 117)

FOR THE LASAGNE

1½	pounds ricotta cheese
3	eggs
2	cups grated mozzarella cheese
1½	cups grated high-quality Parmesan cheese
	Pinch of nutmeg
3	tablespoons chopped fresh flat-leaf parsley
½	teaspoon salt
	Freshly ground black pepper to taste
¾	pound no-boil lasagne noodles

1. Heat oven to 350 degrees. Mix together in a bowl the ricotta, eggs, mozzarella, 1 cup of the Parmesan, nutmeg, parsley, salt, and a few grindings of black pepper.

2. Spoon a thin layer (about ⅔ cup) of meat sauce over the bottom of a roasting pan and place a single layer of no-boil noodles over it, overlapping slightly. Spread with a second layer of meat sauce, then ⅓ of the ricotta mixture. Repeat twice, using noodles, sauce, and ricotta mixture. Finally add one last layer of pasta and then meat sauce on top. Sprinkle with remaining ½ cup Parmesan.

3. Cover tightly with aluminum foil and bake for 40 minutes. Remove foil and bake another 15 to 20 minutes until bubbly and browned. Remove from oven and allow to cool for 20 minutes before serving.

SERVES 6 TO 8

The Chicken Coop

MY MATERNAL GRANDFATHER, Dr. White, had a farm just west of Leesburg, Virginia, that was populated with at least two of most every farm animal, including pigs, cows, horses, burros, ducks, turkeys, and, of course, chickens. A full-time farmhand, Manuel, took care of the place, and his daughter, Mary Elizabeth, became good friends with my mother, Mary Alice. They exchanged presents every Christmas. One year Mary Elizabeth gave my mother a dried, blown-up pig's bladder to use as a toy, which horrified my grandmother, who was more comfortable at a dinner party back in Washington, D.C., than out on the farm. This was especially true when strong thunderstorms moved through the Blue Hills, and it took three people to close the front door because of the high winds. My grandmother was usually found hiding in a closet, waiting for the thunder and lightning to pass.

But it was the chickens that seem to have left their mark on our family. My mother owns a farm in northwest Connecticut and tends to over a hundred and fifty chickens in her spare time, including Silkies, who are good mothers; Polish with their distinctive topknots; Austerlorps, who are big, glossy black birds, good for laying and meat; and guinea hens, who are good watchdogs but bullies, hooting and hollering if they see a hawk or stranger coming. Guinea fowl are also known to chase other chickens, pecking out their tail feathers, hence the origin of the term "pecking order." As with all groups of animals, there is a clear hierarchy, one that is part of the daily ritual. At nighttime, when the chickens go back into the henhouse, they scramble to see who will get the top roost. It is always the birds at the top of the pecking order, the "kings of the roost," who prevail.

Over time, chickens and humans can develop quite a close relationship. My mother talks to them, calling them "girls," and if she sneezes in their presence, they take this as a sign of communication, immediately responding with a cacophony of clucking. But they also need a good deal of protection, since they are easy prey for hawks, red fox, coyotes, and raccoons. She once put a plastic owl on top of the henhouse in an effort to frighten off hawks and the next day she came out to find a hawk perched right next to it, unfazed by the store-bought threat. But she does lose birds occasionally and takes it personally, as if a member of her extended family had been taken away. After all, as she says, "I give them garbage and they give me eggs. Even humans can't do that."

In our Vermont town, chickens have always been raised for eggs and meat. The Woodcocks used to keep a few birds, and it was said that, just before suppertime, Eleanor Woodcock often stuck her .22 rifle out the kitchen window and popped one for dinner. Just across the street, our neighbor Jean still keeps a few hens and, in the summer, a small band of coyotes comes down off the mountains after midnight, screeching and yapping, trying to get at the birds. They have yet to be successful, but a few years ago a chicken thief stole two birds in the middle of the night, quietly stopping his car by the roadside henhouse and making a quick getaway. Other hens have been killed by neighbors' dogs or the red-tailed hawks that constantly circle our small valley.

But it is the relationship between farmer and animal that is curious. The gap between human and animal narrows over time, the two engaged in a mutually satisfactory two-way conversation. Back in the 1950s, our neighbor Floyd Bentley still mowed hay with a team of horses, making them turn on a dime with an offhand flick of the reins and a word or two uttered in the very back of the throat, almost below the range of human hearing. Floyd and his team, Duke and Dan, were like an old couple, able to finish each other's sentences before they even got started. After a lifetime of driving horses, he took to treating humans in much the same manner, quietly hunched over in the shadows of the kitchen of the yellow farmhouse, elbows on his knees, a lit cigarette in his hand. He'd look up at you with rheumy eyes and never utter the first word. When he did get around to saying something it took time; it was like watching him take a slow backswing with a bale of hay, just to start some momentum before hefting it up onto the wagon.

THE FIRST AND MOST important rule about cooking chicken is to purchase a good one. That doesn't sound too difficult, but most people grab whatever is on the supermarket shelf, usually a Purdue chicken, thinking that a chicken is just a chicken. Well, they are radically different. Some commercial brands have a slightly bitter, sour flavor and the texture is compressed, like wet sawdust. Others are bright with clear juices and a fresh, sweet taste. The one brand that I can strongly recommend which is generally available throughout most of the country is Bell & Evans.

It is also important to know how to cut a whole chicken into parts efficiently. To remove the thigh, grab it with your hand, pull it down and away from the body of the bird, cut through the skin between the thigh and carcass, and then keep bending down the thigh until the joint is visible and starts to separate. At this point, you can either cut through the joint, separating the thigh from the carcass, or you can make an additional cut to preserve the "oyster," a small, quarter-size piece of meat which connects the thigh to the backbone. To do this, cut along the middle of the backbone with a sharp boning knife, at the point where the skin from the thigh attaches to the body. The oyster is nestled in a small depression, on a small piece of curved bone. Follow the contour of this bone and then continue cutting the thigh from the body. The wings are easy to remove if you use a boning knife in one hand and pull the wing backward with the other. Working from underneath the bird, slowly cut away the skin, exposing the joint between the wing and the body. Cut through this joint. The leg may be removed from the thigh by turning the piece over, skin side down. Look for the line of yellow fat that separates the leg from the thigh. Using a chef's knife, cut the leg from the thigh at this point. Next, remove the backbone with either poultry shears or a large, sharp chef's knife. If you use the latter, be careful that the knife does not slip. The knife handle is likely to become slippery with chicken fat. Simply cut along either side of the backbone and remove. Now flatten the rest of the carcass with your hand. For the breast meat, you can simply cut between the two breast halves with a sharp knife or, for a cleaner job, remove the breastbone first. (This is dangerous since the breastbone is hard and your knife is usually slippery. Be sure to use a large, sharp knife and wash it thoroughly, especially the handle, to ensure a firm grip.) To do this, use a sharp paring knife to cut away the skin around the bone. Next, use your hands to crack either side of the top of the bone. Finally, pull at the round top end of the breastbone and pull it out. Now the breast halves can be separated.

A few notes about roasting chicken. It is best to roast a chicken unstuffed and untrussed. This allows the hot oven air to get inside the cavity, thus speeding up the time it takes for the inside of the thigh to cook. Basting should only be done before roasting, never during. Otherwise, the skin will end up rubbery. Use butter instead of oil for flavor and color. One last trick. You can make any chicken casserole in this chapter without the chicken skin, which will dramatically reduce the fat in the recipe. The meat will be less moist, but you may wish to consider the trade-off.

Sautéed Chicken Cutlets

The most important aspect of sautéing perfect chicken cutlets is the pan temperature. Too high and the butter will burn; too low and the meat will stew or poach. When the cutlets are first added, the pan will cool off quickly — this is a good time to keep the heat high. As the pan temperature recovers, reduce the heat until the cutlets are still sizzling but the pan is not smoking. Keep an eye on the heat throughout the cooking process and adjust accordingly. If you do not have a 12-inch sauté pan, you may have to prepare these cutlets in two batches, which will require additional olive oil and butter.

MARINADE

½	cup olive oil
1	clove garlic, peeled and minced
¼	cup lemon juice
1	tablespoon minced fresh rosemary or thyme or a mixture
	Freshly ground black pepper to taste

CUTLETS

4	boneless chicken breast cutlets (2 whole breasts split in half; boned and skinned, rinsed and dried, and pounded to an even thickness)
¼	teaspoon salt
½	teaspoon freshly ground black pepper
⅓	cup all-purpose flour
½	cup fine cornmeal
⅓	cup buttermilk
2	tablespoons unsalted butter
1	tablespoon olive oil

1. *For the marinade*, combine all ingredients in a large plastic zipper-lock storage bag.
2. Place prepared cutlets in plastic bag with the marinade, seal, and shake to cover. Let marinate in refrigerator for at least 1 hour and up to 3 hours.
3. *For cutlets*, place salt, pepper, flour, and cornmeal in a plastic bag and shake. Pat cutlets dry with a paper towel and then

dip in buttermilk. Add to the plastic bag and shake to cover.
4. Heat butter and oil in a heavy 12-inch skillet over medium-high heat. (If you use a smaller pan, cook cutlets in two batches, adding more oil and butter for the second batch.) As soon as butter stops foaming and turns a light brown, add cutlets one at a time, tenderloin side down. (The tenderloins are the small oblong pieces of flesh attached to the underside of the breasts.) Cover. After about 1 minute, reduce heat slightly to prevent the oil from smoking, while maintaining a sizzling-hot cooking environment. Turn over cutlets after 4 minutes of total cooking time. Cook covered another 3 to 4 minutes. Chicken is done when it is firm when pressed and, when cut, the juices run clear.

SERVES 4

Simple Roast Chicken

For *The Cook's Bible*, I roasted 14 different chickens to determine the best method. Although I slightly preferred a slow-roasted bird, it was time consuming and also required three different oven temperatures. As a result, I use this simpler method, which is also quite good. The trick is to preheat the roasting pan and to turn the bird twice after it goes into the oven. An instant-read thermometer is important since one has to check the inside part of the thigh after 50 minutes. The bird is cooked to 165 to 170 degrees.

1	(3- to 3½-pound) roasting chicken, giblets removed from cavity, rinsed and patted dry with paper towels

2   tablespoons butter, melted
     Salt and freshly ground black pepper

1. Place a shallow roasting pan in oven and heat oven to 375 degrees. Make sure that chicken is perfectly dry and then brush with butter. Sprinkle liberally with salt and pepper.

2. Remove heated pan from oven and place a roasting rack in it. Put chicken on its side on rack and place in oven. After 20 minutes, turn on its other side. After 20 additional minutes, turn breast side up. Roast another 10 minutes, then check breast meat with an instant-read thermometer. Once the breast reaches 155 degrees, measure the thigh temperature. When it registers between 165 to 170 degrees (I prefer the latter), remove from the oven. Let sit for 20 minutes on a cutting board before carving. Total cooking time will be about 1 hour depending upon the size of the bird.

SERVES 4

To check whether a roast chicken is properly cooked, insert an instant-read thermometer into the thickest part of the thigh. The gauge should read 165 to 170 degrees.

Crisp, Crunchy Fried Chicken

The objective with this recipe was to maximize the crunch of the outer coating. There are all sorts of tricks to this, including using ingredients such as corn flakes, but I find that eggs help thicken up the coating, and I let the coated chicken sit in the refrigerator for 2 hours (a tip that I picked up from *The Farmhouse Cookbook* by Susan Herrmann Loomis), which helps the mixture adhere to the chicken while frying. I also find that buttermilk makes the chicken slightly crustier, and a bit of cornmeal mixed with flour adds a bit of crunch. In order to improve the juiciness and flavor, I soak the chicken in salted water for 2 hours before coating it. This also guards against overcooking, since the meat is extra juicy even when cooked a bit too much. I prefer peanut oil for frying, although Crisco also works quite well. I also find that lard adds flavor and improves the texture of the chicken, but use it in combination with oil or Crisco since it has a very strong taste. A large cast iron Dutch oven is ideal for this recipe, since it will maintain the temperature of the oil. Don't use a thin, lightweight pan. I also find that an instant-read thermometer is helpful to determine when the chicken is cooked: about 165 degrees internal temperature.

½   cup coarse or kosher salt (or 6 table-
     spoons table salt)
3   quarts water
1   whole chicken cut into serving pieces
1½   cups all-purpose flour
¼   cup cornmeal
2   teaspoons dried thyme or oregano or
     pinch cayenne

1   teaspoon table salt
½   teaspoon freshly ground black pepper
2   eggs
½   cup buttermilk
     Peanut oil or solid vegetable
     shortening for deep-frying
     Lard (optional) (see Note)

1. In a large bowl or pot, dissolve ½ cup kosher salt in 3 quarts water. Rinse chicken pieces and add to bowl. Cover and refrigerate for 2 hours. Remove chicken pieces and rinse under cool water. Clear space in the refrigerator to accommodate a wire cooling rack.

2. Mix together the next five ingredients (flour through pepper) and place in a large zipper-lock plastic storage bag. Shake. In a medium bowl, whisk the eggs and then whisk in the buttermilk. Dip half the chicken pieces in the buttermilk, then place in the plastic bag. Shake, and place on a wire rack. Repeat for remaining pieces. Put the rack on a jelly roll pan or cookie sheet and place in the refrigerator for at least 1 hour but preferably 2 hours.

3. Put peanut oil or Crisco (and optional lard) in a large iron Dutch oven to a depth of ¾ inch. Place over medium-high heat.

4. When oil reaches 365 degrees (if you don't have a thermometer, simply wait until the oil just starts to smoke — I find that very hot oil is fine for this recipe), arrange chicken pieces in the pan, skin side down, and cover pan. After 5 minutes remove the cover. Adjust heat level if necessary so that oil bubbles at a moderate pace; not too rapidly and not too slowly. (Medium to medium-high is best depending on the heat conductivity of your pan.) Rearrange pieces if some are browning

more quickly than others. After 5 more minutes, turn the pieces over. Cook uncovered for 8 to 10 more minutes or until done. Meanwhile, thoroughly wash and dry the wire rack while chicken is cooking.

5. Remove fried chicken to the cleaned wire rack set over a cookie sheet or jelly roll pan. Let drain for 5 minutes and serve.

Note: For 4 cups of vegetable shortening, use no more than 1 cup of lard.

SERVES 4

Master Recipe for Milk or Cream Gravy

This is the classic recipe used by almost all country cooks for a quick pan sauce made with flour and milk. You can use this recipe any time you have 2 tablespoons of pan drippings or juices, whether it is from lamb shanks, fried chicken, or even fried green tomatoes. This recipe is easily doubled.

2   tablespoons fat or pan drippings
¼   cup diced onion
1   tablespoon flour
1   cup milk
     Salt and freshly ground black pepper
     to taste

Remove all but 2 tablespoons of fat from a pan that was used to sauté or fry any flavorful food such as meat or chicken. Over medium heat, sauté the onion for 3 minutes, stirring frequently. Sprinkle 1 tablespoon of flour over the onion and whisk constantly over medium heat for 1 minute or until you can no longer smell the flour.

Slowly stir 1 cup milk into the mixture, whisking constantly over medium high heat, until it thickens, about 4 or 5 minutes. Season to taste with salt and freshly ground black pepper.

MAKES ABOUT 1 CUP OF GRAVY

CHICKEN STOCK VARIATION

The recipe above is more or less a béchamel, a mixture of flour and butter cooked with milk until thickened. This is a velouté, which is a béchamel made with chicken stock instead of milk. Follow the directions in the master recipe above but simply substitute chicken stock for the milk.

Braised Chicken, or Chicken in a Pot

Chicken skin is very fatty and therefore the braising liquid in this dish is rather rich. I prefer not to make a sauce with it, serving the chicken and vegetables with just a bit of liquid. For a leaner dish, remove skin before cooking, although the chicken pieces will turn out drier.

3½	pounds chicken parts (skinning is optional)
	Salt and freshly ground black pepper
3	tablespoons olive oil
1	tablespoon butter
1	slice thick-cut smoked bacon, cut into matchsticks
1	cup chopped onion
2	cups coarsely chopped vegetables (a leek/carrot combination works well)
¼	cup white wine
1	cup chicken broth
½	teaspoon dried thyme or 1½ teaspoons fresh
1	teaspoon minced garlic
2	tablespoons minced parsley

1. Heat oven to 250 degrees. Rinse chicken parts and pat dry with paper towels. Season with salt and freshly ground black pepper. Heat 2 tablespoons olive oil and the butter in a large Dutch oven or skillet and brown chicken on both sides over medium-high heat in two separate batches. (Each batch will take about 10 minutes.) Do not overcrowd pan. Reserve browned chicken in a bowl and pour off all but 1 tablespoon fat.

2. Heat 1 tablespoon olive oil in pan, add bacon, and sauté 1 minute. Add onion; sauté over medium heat for 3 minutes, stirring occasionally. Add chopped vegetables, turn heat to medium high, and sauté for 3 additional minutes, stirring occasionally. Add white wine to pan with heat still on medium high; scrape up browned bits from bottom of pan and cook about 1 minute.

3. Add chicken back to the pan along with the chicken broth, ¼ teaspoon salt, and thyme (if using dried). Bring broth to a simmer, place a large sheet of aluminum foil over the top of the pan, cover, and place in heated oven. After 30 minutes, add thyme (if using fresh), garlic, and parsley. Cook another 15 minutes or until internal temperature of breast meat is 165 to 170 degrees. Serve with a small amount of liquid.

SERVES 4

Chicken Stew

This is a very flavorful stew, because it uses the chicken liver for flavoring. Be sure to sauté the chicken pieces over high heat. This will render as much fat as possible from the skin, which is then discarded. This will make for a lighter, less fatty sauce. If you like, you can remove the sauce after the chicken is cooked, strain it, and then let it sit for a few minutes. The fat will rise to the top. It can be spooned off or you can use a fat separator to pour off the defatted sauce.

2	slices thick-cut bacon, minced
1	(3- to 4-pound) chicken, cut into 10 pieces (reserve liver)
	Salt and freshly ground black pepper
4	tablespoons high-quality olive oil
1	large onion, peeled and sliced
1	raw chicken liver, minced
2	bay leaves
1	teaspoon minced fresh rosemary
4	whole cloves
1	tablespoon tomato paste
⅔	cup white wine
1¾	cups chicken broth, homemade preferred

1. Place a large skillet over medium-high heat. When hot, add the bacon and cook until brown and crisp, stirring frequently. Drain on paper towels and reserve.
2. Wash chicken pieces, pat dry with paper towels, and season with salt and pepper. Pour off all but 1 tablespoon fat from skillet and add 2 tablespoons olive oil. When hot, add the chicken pieces and brown, in batches if necessary, until nicely colored on all sides. (Use lots of heat and render as much of the fat from the skin as possible.) Remove and reserve.
3. Pour off fat and add 2 tablespoons olive oil to the pan. When hot, add the onion, chicken liver, bay leaves, rosemary, and cloves and cook, stirring, about 7 to 8 minutes or until the onion is soft and translucent. Return the chicken and bacon pieces to the skillet. Add the tomato paste and half the wine and stir to coat the chicken. Add the rest of the wine and the broth and scrape the bottom of the pan with a wooden spoon. Simmer for about 20 minutes, stirring occasionally.
4. Check the chicken for doneness. If not cooked through, simmer another 5 minutes or so. Add salt and pepper to taste. Remove chicken to a bowl and cover to keep warm. (At this point, you can degrease the sauce if you like by straining it into a fat separator or by letting it sit for a few minutes and spooning off the fat that rises to the top.) Simmer sauce another 8 to 10 minutes or until thickened. Add back the chicken pieces, heat through, and serve at once.

SERVES 4 TO 6

Master Recipe for Broiled Butterflied Chicken

Butterflying a chicken (removing the backbone and flattening it) accomplishes two tasks. It speeds up cooking time to 30 minutes (instead of an hour) and it also cooks the white and dark meat fairly evenly. However, all broilers are not created equal and therefore the cooking times will vary greatly. (This is one recipe for which an instant-read thermometer is crucial. The inside of the thigh should register 165 to 170 degrees when the chicken is done.) If you wish to butterfly a chicken yourself, use either poultry shears or a large sharp knife to cut out the backbone. (Be very careful if using a knife; the handle will quickly become slippery.) Then place the chicken, breast side up, on a flat surface. Press down hard with one hand on top of the other to flatten. By the way, this recipe does make a mess of your oven and produces a fair amount of smoke, although it is an easy and delicious way to cook a whole chicken.

1	(3- to 4-pound) chicken, backbone removed, and flattened
½	cup olive oil
4	cloves garlic, crushed
¼	cup lemon juice
1	tablespoon minced fresh rosemary or thyme
	Salt and freshly ground black pepper

1. Rinse the chicken and pat dry with paper towels. Combine oil, garlic, lemon juice, and rosemary in a large plastic zipper-lock bag. Add the chicken, press out as much air as possible, seal the bag, and turn to coat with oil. Marinate in the refrigerator for 12 hours.

2. Heat the broiler. Remove chicken and pat dry with paper towels. Season with salt and pepper. Broil about 15 minutes per side, starting skin side down, 4 to 6 inches from the heat. An instant-read thermometer inserted into the inside of the thigh should read 165 to 170 degrees.

LEMON PEPPERCORN VARIATION

Follow the recipe above but increase lemon juice to ⅓ cup, reduce olive oil to ¼ cup, omit garlic, and add 2 tablespoons crushed black peppercorns (place them in a plastic storage bag, put the bag on a cutting board, and crush with the bottom of a heavy saucepan or with a meat pounder).

STOVETOP VARIATION

Use either of the two marinades listed above, but instead of broiling the chicken, heat a large (12-inch) iron skillet until very hot, put 1 tablespoon of olive oil in the pan, and immediately add the butterflied chicken, skin side down. Put a pie plate on top and weight with heavy saucepans (cast iron pans are very good for this) or bricks. This will flatten the chicken so that it presses hard against the hot skillet. Cook over medium heat until done, about 15 minutes per side. Be sure to use an iron skillet for this recipe, as it heats evenly. Note that this recipe makes a royal mess of your stovetop — the chicken will splatter and sputter — but it's worth it. Also be sure to frequently check the internal temperature of the inner thighs. They should register 165 to 170 degrees when the chicken is done.

Chicken Fricassee

I don't much care for old-fashioned dishes that bathe chicken in cream sauces. They take too much time and I usually prefer the leaner, purer flavor of a simple roast chicken. So I was surprised by the intense, high-octane taste of this dish: a jolt of concentrated chicken stock married to a velvety but not overpowering sauce. The question was, how to streamline this dish for a simple mid-week dinner while modernizing the sauce for leaner palates.

First of all, fricassee simply means to stew gently in an aromatic liquid. A chicken fricassee is a cut-up bird essentially poached in water or stock, after which the liquid is reduced and a simple white sauce is made from it. The first problem was cooking time. Older cookbooks suggest poaching chicken for up to 1½ hours, whereas in my testing, I found that 40 minutes was just about right. In addition, I found that a brown fricassee, that is, browning the chicken pieces first, not only added tremendous flavor but also cut the poaching time to about 25 minutes, a small savings in time but key to intense flavor. As the chicken is cooked over high heat, the meat and skin release juices that help flavor the final sauce.

Many recipes suggest adding celery, carrots, and other vegetables to the poaching liquid. I found these additions unnecessary but I did find that using chicken stock instead of water was a tremendous improvement. This method makes a "double" stock, which is highly flavored, and also removes the need to boil down the poaching liquid to concentrate flavors, a time-consuming step. I also tested heavy cream, light cream, and half-and-half in the sauce and found that the latter was best. Since I did not have to reduce the cooking liquid, I also found that the sauce was considerably thinner but also lighter and more intensely flavored, with a higher ratio of chicken stock to dairy.

This recipe makes about 3½ cups of sauce, and I recommend that you serve the dish with either rice or mashed potatoes, providing a convenient excuse to soak up as much as possible. Be liberal with the parsley and be sure to use the more flavorful flat-leaf variety instead of curly parsley.

1	(3- to 4-pound) chicken cut into pieces (see recipe instructions)
	Salt and freshly ground black pepper to taste
2	tablespoons olive oil
3	tablespoons butter
3	cups chicken stock
2	cups chopped mushrooms (about 6 ounces)
½	cup finely chopped onion
3	tablespoons flour
1	cup half-and-half
	Freshly grated nutmeg to taste
¼	cup minced flat-leaf parsley

1. Cut chicken into 10 pieces (cut each breast half in half again), rinse, and pat dry with paper towels. Season with salt and pepper. Heat olive oil and 1 tablespoon butter in a very large, deep skillet. When foam subsides, add chicken pieces in two batches, starting skin side down, and brown on both sides over medium-high heat, a total of 10 to 12 minutes for each batch. Pour off fat. Return all chicken to the skillet, add stock, bring to a simmer, and cook gently, uncovered, for 25 to 30 minutes or until chicken is cooked through. Be sure that the thigh meat is thoroughly cooked. Remove chicken to a bowl and place in a 200 degree oven to keep warm. Strain cooking liquid through 4 layers of cheesecloth.

(You can skip straining the sauce for a less "refined" dish.) Return liquid to skillet.

2. While the chicken is cooking, melt 2 tablespoons butter in a separate skillet. When hot, add the mushrooms and onion and sauté and cook over medium-high heat, stirring frequently, until mushrooms release their liquid, 4 to 5 minutes. Add the flour and cook for 1 minute, stirring constantly. Stir in the half-and-half and season liberally with salt, pepper, and nutmeg. Whisk this mixture into the broth in the skillet over medium heat. Bring to a boil and cook for 5 to 6 minutes or until sauce thickens slightly (it will be the consistency of half-and-half). Arrange chicken on serving plates and cover with sauce. (This recipe makes 3½ cups of sauce. You will have leftovers.) Garnish with an abundance of parsley.

SERVES 4 TO 6

Chicken and Dumplings

I have tried many recipes for dumplings, some made with cottage cheese, others with potatoes. I find the cheese-based dumplings to be too wet and heavy, while the potato dumplings are good but take too much extra work for a simple supper. You can use the dumpling recipe below with any dish that has a fair amount of liquid, such as a stew.

1   (3- to 4-pound) chicken cut into pieces (see recipe instructions)
    Salt and freshly ground black pepper to taste
2   tablespoons olive oil
3   tablespoons butter

3   cups chicken stock
1   cup water
2   cups coarsely chopped mushrooms (about 6 ounces)
½   cup finely chopped onion
1   tablespoon flour
1   cup half-and-half
    Freshly grated nutmeg to taste
¼   cup minced flat-leaf parsley

FOR THE DUMPLINGS
2   cups flour
¾   teaspoon salt
½   teaspoon baking soda
1   egg
4   tablespoons butter, melted
¾   cup buttermilk, or more as needed

1. Heat oven to the lowest possible setting. Cut chicken into 10 pieces (cut each breast half in half again), rinse, and pat dry with paper towels. Season with salt and pepper. Heat olive oil and 1 tablespoon of the butter in a very large Dutch oven with a cover. When foam subsides, add chicken pieces in two batches, starting with the skin side down, and brown both sides over medium-high heat, a total of 10 to 12 minutes for each batch. Pour off fat. Return all chicken to the Dutch oven, add stock and water, bring to a simmer, and cook gently, uncovered, for 20 to 25 minutes or until chicken is cooked through. Be sure that the thigh meat is thoroughly cooked. Remove chicken to a bowl, cover with aluminum foil, and place in 200 degree oven to keep warm. Strain cooking liquid through 4 layers of cheesecloth. (You can skip straining the sauce for a less "refined" dish.) Return the liquid to the Dutch oven.

2. While the chicken is cooking, melt 2 tablespoons of butter in a skillet. When hot, add the mushrooms and onion and cook over medium-high heat, stirring frequently, until mushrooms release their liquid, 4 to 5 minutes. Add the flour and cook for 1 minute, stirring constantly. Stir in the half-and-half and season liberally with salt, pepper, and nutmeg.

3. For the dumplings, whisk together the first three ingredients. Whisk together the egg, melted butter, and buttermilk. Pour the buttermilk mixture into the flour mixture and stir with a rubber spatula to form a dough, much like a biscuit dough. If it needs a bit more buttermilk to moisten (it probably will), add it 1 tablespoon at a time until the dough comes together. Roll out the dough to ½-inch thickness and cut with a biscuit cutter. Bring the chicken broth to a simmer in the Dutch oven, add the dumplings, and cook covered for 15 minutes. Remove with a slotted spoon to a bowl and place in preheated oven.

4. Whisk the onion-mushroom mixture into the broth in the Dutch oven over medium heat. Bring to a boil and cook for 3 or 4 minutes or until sauce thickens slightly (it will be the consistency of half-and-half). Arrange chicken and dumplings on serving plates and cover with sauce. Garnish with an abundance of parsley.

SERVES 4 TO 6

CHICKEN AND RICE

Although there is no specific American tradition for a dish called "chicken and rice," the combination is neither surprising nor innovative. Perhaps closest to a jambalaya or paella, this dish is nothing more than chicken pieces sautéed until well browned and then cooked on top of the stove casserole fashion with sautéed onions and garlic, a liquid (chicken stock, water, or wine), and rice. Its appeal is obvious. It's a one-dish supper, it's easy, and it's eminently variable. Yet, after having made a dozen attempts at perfecting this recipe, I found two major problems. The white meat tends to dry out before the dark meat is cooked, and the rice is often heavy and greasy. I also wanted to devise a master recipe that lent itself to variations, perhaps a blend of Indian spices or a version with Latin overtones.

First, I tackled the problem of the overcooked breast meat. It turned out that the solution was rather simple. When the breast meat was added to the casserole 15 minutes after the thighs and legs, both cooked perfectly. Of course, one could make this dish with just dark or light meat but, like most cooks, I am most likely to have a whole chicken on hand rather than just thighs or breasts. In addition, our family of five has distinct and different taste preferences encompassing both kinds of meat.

The texture of the rice, however, was a more vexing issue. My first thought was to reduce the amount of olive oil used to sauté the chicken and onion from 2 tablespoons to 1. This simply was not enough fat to get the job done, and the resulting rice was only fractionally less greasy. I thought that perhaps the chicken skin was the culprit, but after making this dish with skinless chicken pieces, I was surprised to find that the rice was still heavy and the chicken, as I suspected, was tough and chewy. The skin is effective at maintaining succulent meat, especially during heavy sautéing.

I then thought that reducing the amount of liquid in the recipe would produce less sodden rice. I was using 1½ cups of long-grain white rice to 1½ cups of chicken stock plus 2 cups of water. By reducing the stock to a mere ½ cup, I had better results. The rice was indeed lighter, but the layer of rice on top was undercooked and dried out. This was solved by stirring the dish once when adding the breast meat so that the rice on top was stirred into the bottom, producing more even cooking. I then made four different batches using four different liquids: chicken stock (heavy, greasy rice), water (bland, flat tasting), a combination of wine and water (the acidity of the wine cuts through the fat, producing clean, clear flavors), and a combination of water, chopped canned tomatoes, and tomato liquid (the acid in the tomatoes punches up and enriches flavor). I then used a combination of white wine, water, chopped tomatoes, and tomato liquid with excellent results. By the way, as I discovered in prior taste tests of canned tomatoes, you should use only chopped or diced tomatoes, *not* ones packed in a purée or sauce. This will result in a cleaner, brighter flavor.

Finally, I tested different varieties of rice to see which held up best to this sort of cooking. A basic long-grain white rice was fine, with good flavor and decent texture; a medium-grain rice was creamy, with a risotto-like texture and excellent flavor (I found this version too heavy for my taste, but others on my tasting panel overlooked the dense texture for the improved flavor); basmati rice was nutty, with separate, light grains (this was by far the lightest version, but the basmati rice seemed somewhat out of place in such a pedestrian dish); and converted rice, which was absolutely tasteless, although virtually indestructible (the tasting panel agreed that since converted rice is tasteless it is also worthless). So basic long-grain white rice is a fine all-purpose solution, although both medium-grain and basmati rice can also be used with different but good results.

Master Recipe for Chicken and Rice

This is a basic chicken and rice dish with variations. Although I rarely suggest stirring rice during cooking, it is necessary in this dish so that the top layer of rice does not undercook and dry out. If you prefer, you can make this dish with either all breast meat or with just boneless chicken thighs. Be sure to use canned tomatoes that are packed in their own juices rather than in a purée or sauce.

2	pounds chicken pieces
	Salt and freshly ground black pepper
2	tablespoons olive oil
1	medium onion, chopped
3	cloves garlic, peeled and puréed or minced
1½	cups long-grain white rice or basmati rice

1   cup chopped canned tomatoes plus
        ½ cup tomato liquid
½   cup white wine
2   cups water

1. Rinse the chicken parts and pat dry with paper towels. Season chicken liberally with salt and pepper.

2. Heat the oil over high heat in a heavy, nonreactive casserole or Dutch oven. When hot, brown chicken parts (skin side down first; if making a double recipe, brown chicken in batches) on both sides, about 12 minutes total. Do not fuss with the chicken for the first 5 minutes of browning, but turn pieces 3 times during cooking. Chicken should be very dark. Remove chicken to a bowl. Pour off all but 2 tablespoons of fat.

3. Lower heat to medium, add the onion, and cook for 3 to 4 minutes to soften, stirring frequently. Add the garlic and continue to cook for 1 minute. Stir in the rice and cook, stirring, for an additional minute. Add tomatoes, wine, water, and 1 teaspoon salt. Scrape the bottom of the pot with a wooden spoon, add back the chicken thighs and legs (the breasts will be added later), and bring to a boil. Cover with a lid or aluminum foil and simmer gently for 15 minutes. Add the breast pieces, stir the ingredients gently so that the rice is thoroughly mixed, cover, and continue to cook for 10 to 15 minutes or until rice is done. Try to keep skillet covered as much as possible. Serve.

SERVES 4

CHICKEN AND RICE WITH INDIAN SPICES

This variation has many spices traditionally used in Indian cooking, including turmeric, cumin, and coriander. Follow master recipe above through step 2. At the beginning of step 3, add a 3-inch piece of cinnamon stick and stir with a wooden spoon over medium-high heat until it unfurls (about 10 seconds). Add the onion and garlic along with 1 teaspoon ground turmeric, 1 teaspoon ground coriander, 1 teaspoon ground cumin, and 2 green bell peppers, cored and chopped. Sauté until onion and peppers are just soft, 5 to 6 minutes. Add rice, stirring for 1 minute, then add remaining ingredients. Follow master recipe instructions.

CHICKEN AND RICE WITH SAFFRON, PEAS, AND PAPRIKA

Cook 1 diced green pepper along with the onions according to the master recipe. Add 4 teaspoons paprika and ¼ teaspoon saffron to the sautéed onion and garlic and cook for 1 minute. After the chicken and rice has completed cooking, stir in 1 cup frozen peas and ¼ cup chopped flat-leaf parsley. Cover the pot and let sit for 5 minutes.

CHICKEN AND RICE WITH JALAPEÑO, CILANTRO, AND LIME JUICE

Cook 2 seeded, stemmed, diced jalapeño peppers with the onions according to the master recipe. Add 2 teaspoons ground cumin, 2 teaspoons ground coriander, and 1 teaspoon chili powder to the sautéed onion and garlic and cook for 1 minute. (For more flavor, toast 2 teaspoons of cumin seeds in a nonstick skillet over medium heat for 3 to 4 minutes and then process in an electric grinder.) After the chicken and rice has completed cooking, stir in ¼ cup chopped cilantro and 3 tablespoons lime juice. Cover pot and let sit for 5 minutes.

CHICKEN AND RICE WITH ANCHOVIES, OLIVES, AND LEMON JUICE

Cook 5 anchovy fillets with the onions according to the master recipe. After the chicken and rice has completed cooking, stir in 1 teaspoon of minced lemon rind, 1 tablespoon lemon juice, ½ cup pitted imported black olives, and ¼ cup chopped flat-leaf parsley. Cover pot and let sit for 5 minutes.

The Meat Locker

A FEW YEARS AGO, I received a call from a Vermont neighbor, Jean, who said, "The fourth squirrel is in the freezer. See you Saturday night." For months, I had seen her hunkered down by the chicken coop at the side of the road with a .22 rifle loosely held across her lap. When queried about her objective, she admitted to a keen interest in squirrel hunting but after she'd bagged three fat specimens (gray squirrels, not the smaller, gamier red squirrels), the local population had been sufficiently decimated so that it took three months to bag the fourth and final quarry. As I soon found out, all of this small game hunting was in preparation for dinner: the classic American dish Brunswick stew, which is made from fresh lima beans, corn, tomatoes, onions, toasted bread crumbs, and, of course, squirrel.

Besides bagging the required number of squirrels (one per person), Jean had to skin them, and found instructions in the old *Joy of Cooking*. (Cut through the tailbone, make cuts in the back, turn the squirrel over, and stepping on the base of the tail, pull on the hind legs until the skin comes free.) All of this took some time; the hunting, the skinning, the boning, and the actual cooking. Being thrifty, and keenly devoted to living off the land, however, Jean found this perfectly natural — as normal as grilling a couple of T-bones on the backyard grill.

When that Saturday night arrived, my wife, Adrienne, and I walked down our driveway, past our lower field where we often pick wildflowers, including three of our favorites — joe-pye weed, butter-and-eggs, and queen of the meadow. We headed across the dirt road past a few grazing sheep, and then up the hilly path to Jean's house, a white clapboard farmhouse perched on top of a steep embankment which leads down to a small barn and chicken coop. Inside, the house displayed the simplicity of a true Vermont home. The dining room has a wide-plank wooden floor painted gray and is partially covered with a braided rug made by her mother, Dorothy. There are no curtains — the windows open onto a vast field of alfalfa framed by mountains — and the table was simply set with ironstone china, a small glass dish of homemade bread-and-butter pickles, an antique castor, and two beeswax candles.

The stew was excellent (squirrel is not oily like woodchuck or gamy like wild partridge, but mild and lean, reminiscent of dark turkey meat). After a second helping, a simple salad of spinach and wild leek, and a thick slice of coconut cake, it occurred to me that Vermonters, perhaps more so than most folks these days, have a clear sense of their place in the world, free from the turmoil that defines modern times. This sense of simplicity is seen most clearly in the clean, unadorned lines of an old clapboard farmhouse sitting honestly on the edge of a field, the grass running right up to the foundation, unrestricted by the suburban penchant for foundation plantings. It's a frugal life, but parsimony has its advantages, reducing clutter so that the substructure of daily life is clearer. We walked home that

evening past the horse barn, skipping over Baldwin Brook, and then past the beehives and through the lower hay field. The moon was almost full and the lines of our small farmhouse were clean and bright, a graceful beacon calling us toward a simpler time.

IN A WORD, the problem with most meat cookery these days is fat. There isn't enough of it. You can have your 90 percent lean ground beef (except for skillet hamburgers), your dry, tasteless pork, and your tough, chewy bottom-round roasts. Whether this is to be blamed on the self-proclaimed health experts or on ourselves for lacking the backbone and spirit to purchase and cook meat with sufficient fat to make it edible is for others to decide. For my part, I ain't buying. Although I am not partial to a heavy, fat-laden diet, most lean meat is hardly worth eating.

The other problem is the current fashion of cooking all meats either rare or medium-rare. (Contrary to what I had presumed, serving roast beef rare was all the fashion in the late eighteenth century in America.) I agree with this sentiment for most cuts, but I like an overcooked stringy pot roast, not a pink-in-the-center roast cooked in a pot. It is true that as meat is cooked past 140 degrees internal temperature it will lose moisture and weight and, in many cases, become tougher. But, as a friend of mine points out, what's the point of gravy if the meat is moist and tender? (At first I thought he was joking but I have to agree that there is some truth in this statement.) So for cheaper cuts (a pot roast or short ribs), I don't mind cooking meat to higher temperatures, especially if it is to be served with a simple pan sauce or gravy. More expensive cuts, however, should definitely be cooked rare or medium rare.

Understanding Cuts of Meat

Regardless of your preferences, there are some helpful things to know about purchasing and buying meat. The first step is to understand the cuts of meat. A butcher starts by splitting the animal, whether it's beef, lamb, pork, or veal, in half from neck to rump. Looking at each half, all animals have three major parts: the shoulder, the rib section, and the rump. In a small animal such as a pig, these three areas roughly correspond with the major cuts. The shoulder of a pig is referred to as the shoulder butt, the ribs are referred to as the loin, which contains all of the ribs, and the rump of the animal, really the upper portion of the leg, is called the ham. The spareribs and bacon are cut from the section directly beneath the loin (the belly). A larger animal, however, is divided into more sections because of its size. In a side of beef, the shoulder area is referred to as the chuck, the area from the shoulder to the pelvic joint is divided into two parts (the front portion is the rib and the rear portion, containing only one rib, is the loin), and the leg from the knee to the socket of the hip bone is referred to as the round. Underneath the chuck, the rib, and the loin are less expensive cuts including the brisket, the plate, and the flank.

TIPS ON MEAT COOKERY

Here are a few tips on meat cookery that are the result of much testing over the years:

- Most roasts should be cooked at low temperatures after an initial browning.

Higher oven temperatures will overcook the outer layers of meat before the inside is done. I recommend 250 degrees as the best temperature for roasting any thick cut of meat except for lamb, which requires higher temperatures. (When cooked at low oven temperatures, lamb becomes soft and cottony.) It is important, however, to brown the roast well on all sides first. As well as adding flavor, this will kill off any bacteria, most of which are likely to exist on the outside of the meat. Thinner, more expensive cuts, such as the tenderloin, can be successfully cooked at higher roasting temperatures.

- Generally speaking, the front portion of an animal, which is referred to as the chuck, has more fat and is more flavorful. Use a beef chuck roast instead of a round roast (the round is the knee up to the hip), as the round is lacking in fat and will be tough. When making meat loaf, or hamburgers that are to be grilled, never use ground round; always use ground chuck.

- An instant-read thermometer is a great help when roasting meat. It is difficult to tell what is going on inside a roast from looking at the outside. I even use an instant thermometer when cooking a steak.

- The choice of cut and the quality of the meat are more important than the recipe. (These are two different things. A particular animal might have high- or low-quality meat, and therefore the same cut from two different animals might be quite different.) Stew meat cut from the round will be tough whereas the same stew recipe made with cubes cut from the chuck will be a whole lot better. For more information on cuts, see my first book, *The Cook's Bible*.

- Letting a roast rest for 15 to 20 minutes after coming from the oven does allow the juices to flow back into the center of the meat. I have tested this and found it to be worth doing.

- Aging roasts, especially inexpensive cuts, in the refrigerator for 4 days on a rack uncovered does add tremendous flavor. You may have to trim off a bit of the outside before cooking (it will turn a darker color and dry out) but this is the easiest and best way to improve a roast. Be sure to age the meat totally exposed to the air without any sort of wrapping or covering.

- Defatting pan sauces is crucial to meat cookery. If possible, prepare the meat the day before (this works well with ribs and shanks), refrigerate the juices separately from the meat and vegetables, and then remove the solid white layer of fat on the surface the next day. When this is not practical, when making a pot roast for example, either use a defatting pitcher (it has a spout connected near the bottom of the container, which allows one to pour off the leaner juices beneath the floating layer of fat) or simply let the juices settle in a Pyrex measuring cup and then spoon off the fat which will rise to the top. If the juices are still rich and indigestible, I dilute them with chicken stock, using from a quarter to a half cup of juices per two cups of stock.

- Everything depends on the quality of the meat. I have made the short ribs recipe in this chapter and have had thick, rich pieces of tender meat falling off the bone. A few weeks later, I made it again with inferior ribs and the meat was tough, with lots of connective tissue and gristle. The most important step in meat cookery is the first one, buying the meat. The most reliable source of high-quality meat is a butcher, not a supermarket, especially one who supplies meat to the best restaurants in town. To find the best food suppliers, including butchers, ask local chefs where they do their shopping.

BEEF

Here is a list of cuts of beef and how to purchase them.

Ground Beef

This is usually leftovers — ground-up meat from any primal cut. The key is fat content, which is measured in percentage of lean, from about 72 percent to 90 percent (the latter often referred to as "diet lean"). You want a middle ground here — 80 percent is about right, if the burgers are to be cooked on an outdoor grill. I prefer using a less fatty, 90 percent lean ground meat if the hamburgers are to be cooked in a skillet rather than on a grill. On a grill, the excess fat simply drips onto the coals. In a skillet, the rendered fat pools up in the pan, making the resulting burgers quite greasy. The best cuts for ground beef come from the chuck, and I recommend the top blade cut, which either your butcher can grind for you or you can grind at home in a food processor.

Steaks

This designation really means nothing. Steak can come from the chuck, plate, flank, rib, loin, sirloin (a part of the loin), and the round. The most popular steaks, including sirloin and porterhouse, are cut from the hindquarter, although you can also purchase rib steaks, which are cut from the seventh to the fifth rib, and steaks from the chuck such as boneless top blade steak (from the chuck) and those from the round including top round steak, eye round steak, and cube steak. Later in this chapter (see page 150), I compare different inexpensive steak cuts for flavor and texture.

Roasts and Pot Roasts

The best cut and the most expensive is the rib roast, which is cut from the loin, from the tenth through the twelfth ribs. A two-rib roast will serve 4; a three-rib roast will serve 6. Rib roasts can be cut from any of the other ribs, however, such as from the chuck or rib section. You can also purchase less expensive cuts for roasting. Although the top round, a rump roast, an eye round roast, or a bottom round roast are cut from the round, avoid these cuts. Even when cooked at low temperatures, they will be tough. Always buy a roast from the chuck, such as a top blade roast or a chuck eye roast, instead of from the round. (A supermarket may refer to these roasts as "beef chuck top blade roast boneless" or "top chuck roast.") Don't be confused by "pot roasts." These are simply inexpensive boneless roasts that are cooked in a pot on top of the stove over low heat. Any boneless roast can be "pot roasted."

Ribs

Ribs cut from the chuck are the best, as they have lots of meat, whereas the ribs toward the rear of the animal have less meat and more fat. Short ribs are nothing more than short sections of any rib. Flanken ribs are those cut from the front of the animal, and they are known for having a thick layer of meat on them.

Stew Beef

You want as much fat as possible in stew meat; otherwise the finished product will be dry. I prefer stew meat cut from the shoulder, although it also comes from just about every other part of the animal, including the shank and the plate.

Master Recipe for Meat Loaf

On our farm back in the 1960s, we used to make hamburgers with a combination of beef and sausage, since we raised Black Angus cattle as well as pigs. The sausage added not only flavor but also juiciness. Today, however, I find most sausage to be too strongly flavored, with an overpowering taste of fennel. As a result, I simply use a combination of beef and pork. I also like the addition of veal, which diminishes the meaty, hamburger taste of most meat loaf. Make sure that the beef is 80 percent lean, which indicates that there is enough fat in the meat to be tasty and juicy. (Don't use ground beef that is 85 percent or 90 percent lean; it will be too dry and lacking in flavor.)

You will find that there is a good half-inch of fat collected on the bottom of the pan after cooking. Therefore, bake the meat loaf either on a perforated broiler

To prepare a meat loaf, wrap it with bacon slices, tucking them underneath the meat, and place on a rack in a roasting pan. The rack allows the fat to drain off during baking.

1	teaspoon fresh thyme or ½ teaspoon dried
1/4	teaspoon ground nutmeg
2	pounds ground beef (80 percent lean)
1	pound ground pork
1	pound ground veal
1	cup fresh bread crumbs
1	cup finely chopped onion
1	cup finely chopped celery
3	cloves garlic, minced
½	cup minced fresh flat-leaf parsley
1	cup grated Parmesan cheese
12	slices thin-cut bacon

tray or on a rack set in a roasting pan. This recipe uses 4 pounds of meat, double the standard meat loaf recipe. It is no more work and then you have plenty of leftovers for sandwiches the next day.

In testing meat loaves, I tried using oatmeal instead of bread crumbs; a big mistake, since the meat loaf tasted like oatmeal. I also started out soaking the bread crumbs in cream and found that they turned into a clump that was hard to break apart. By increasing the eggs from 3 to 4, I was able to eliminate the soaking of crumbs altogether, with the same taste and texture.

4	large eggs
2	teaspoons salt
	Freshly ground black pepper to taste
½	teaspoon Tabasco
1	teaspoon fresh rosemary or ½ teaspoon dried

1. Heat oven to 350 degrees. Whisk eggs with the next 6 ingredients (salt through nutmeg) in a large bowl. Add remaining ingredients (except bacon) and mix well. Form into a large loaf, 12 inches long and 7 inches wide, and place on the top portion of a broiler pan or onto a flat rack positioned in a roasting pan. (If the meat loaf is to be cooked on a rack, form the loaf first on a cutting board using wet hands. Place a large plate or platter on top, flip the loaf over, and then flip it back onto the rack.)

2. Cover the loaf with bacon strips, tucking one end of each strip under the loaf, draping it up and over the meat, and tucking the other end under the other side. (You may need to trim the bacon a bit if it is too long. You will want only a half inch or so tucked under each side. The portion of the bacon underneath the loaf will not brown.)

3. Bake for about 1 hour 20 minutes or until the internal temperature reads 150 to 155 degrees. (The USDA recommends 160 degrees.) Cool for 20 minutes and serve.

SERVES 8 TO 10

Master Recipe for Hamburgers

The first question one must ask about burgers is what is the ideal size? I find that truly gargantuan patties are unwieldy. Therefore, I prefer a hamburger that is 4 inches in diameter and ¾ of an inch thick, about 8 ounces. In terms of ingredients, many additions I found unnecessary or unwelcome, including cream (the burger tasted too creamy), raw onions or celery (the vegetables don't properly cook by the time the meat is done), cooked bacon pieces (better to simply place a piece or two on top of the burger when serving), grated cheese (the burger was a leaky, oozing mess), a thin slice of tomato and onion (these were sandwiched in the middle of the burger and, since they don't cook properly, are best simply added as garnishes after cooking), a parsley, onion, and egg combination (tasted like meat loaf, not a hamburger), and a whole lot of ground black pepper (this worked okay but masked the flavor of the meat). I also tried braising the burger in red wine, which prevented the outside of the burger from developing flavor during cooking; also, the red wine turned sour in the cast iron pan, my cooking implement of choice. I even tried putting large pieces of ice in the middle of the burger, a technique offered in more than one cookbook, which simply produced a burger with a cold, wet center. The selection of the beef was crucial. I usually prefer an 80 percent lean ground beef, but when preparing hamburgers in a skillet, the large amount of rendered fat made them greasy and unappealing. Therefore, I suggest using 90 percent lean beef. (However, the 80 percent lean variety is recommended if the burgers are to be grilled, since the fat will simply drip onto the hot coals.) For safety reasons, the USDA suggests cooking hamburger until it is well-done, or 160 degrees internally. The choice is yours.

2	pounds ground 90 percent lean beef (use 80 percent lean if grilling hamburgers)
1	teaspoon Worcestershire sauce
¼	teaspoon Tabasco
2	teaspoons Dijon mustard
1	clove garlic, minced
1	teaspoon salt
½	teaspoon freshly ground black pepper
1	tablespoon butter
2	tablespoons olive oil

Mix all ingredients except the butter and oil. Lightly form four 8-ounce patties, about ¾ inch thick and 4 inches in diameter. Place a large cast iron skillet over medium-high heat. When hot, add the butter and oil, and when the foam subsides, sauté patties for 3 minutes. Turn patties and sauté for an additional 3 minutes. Lower heat, turn patties, and cook for 2 minutes. Turn once more and cook for a final 2 minutes. For pink, juicy burgers, the total cooking time cannot be longer than 10 minutes.

SERVES 4

HAMBURGERS WITH BACON

Heat a cast iron skillet and cook 4 slices of thick-cut bacon until brown and crisp. Remove to paper towels to drain. Pour off all but 1 tablespoon of fat. Add the olive oil and eliminate the butter and proceed with the master recipe above. When burgers are cooked, serve with 1 slice of bacon topping each burger.

Slow-Cooked Roast of Beef

As Susie de Peyster, our unofficial town mayor, often points out, "People do dumb things for good reasons." That holds true for cooking a roast of beef, since most folks assume that moderate or high heat is the proper method. In fact, low-heat roasting makes more sense for this sort of cut. At higher temperature, the outside becomes overcooked before the inside is done. The choice of cut is also important. This recipe is best made with a boneless chuck roast, which has plenty of fat to produce a flavorful, juicy roast. There are five basic chuck roasts: the blade roast, the chuck eye roast, the underblade roast, the chuck fillet or chuck tender roast, and the shoulder roast. Choose the blade or chuck eye roast, since they are both full of juice and flavor. The former has a fair amount of connective tissue but it is not tough or stringy when cooked; the latter is a bit fatty although with tremendous flavor. The term "blade" refers to the shoulder blade, and the chuck "eye" roast is simply a boneless rib roast cut from the center of the first five ribs. If you have a roast from the round, I suggest that you follow the pressure cooker variation that follows, since the meat will turn out moister and more tender.

Although roasting meat is quite a simple task these days, since the invention of gas and electric ovens, in the old days meat had to be roasted in a fireplace. The most basic method was to hang the roast from a twisted piece of string which turned the meat as it unwound. But my favorite method was the spit-connected treadmill powered by the family dog. No matter how it was done, it was unpleasant work since the fire was often smoky, adjusting the heat was no easy matter, and the large fireplace meant that the house was drafty, since much of the heat escaped up the flue.

1   (3- to 4-pound) chuck roast, boned and tied
      Salt and freshly ground black pepper to taste
2   tablespoons olive oil

Heat oven to 250 degrees. Rinse exterior of meat and pat dry. Sprinkle with salt and pepper. Heat olive oil in a Dutch oven on top of the stove. Add roast and brown thoroughly on all sides. Place in oven and cook uncovered until internal temperature reaches 110 degrees, about 40 to 50 minutes. Increase oven temperature to 500 degrees and cook until internal temperature reaches 130 degrees, about 15 to 20 more minutes. Total cooking time will vary depending on the size of the roast. Remove from oven and let sit for 20 minutes before carving. This produces a perfect, medium-rare roast. If you prefer roasts more well done (although the more you cook it, the drier and tougher the meat), cook to 140 degrees internal temperature but no higher. After 140 degrees, the meat fibers lose a great deal of their juices and shrink, becoming tough and unpalatable.

SERVES 6 TO 8

This method is excellent for those who really like their roasts well done and is also the preferred method for less tender roasts such as those from the round. Be sure to start with a chuck roast as recommended in the master recipe, and pressure cook the roast a full hour instead of just 40 minutes. The meat will shrink considerably and turn gray and ropy but it will still be tender. Of course, you can also cook the roast to medium-rare by following the directions below.

Heat a 5- to 6-quart pressure cooker, uncovered, over medium-high heat. Add olive oil. Season the roast with salt and pepper and brown on all sides in cooker. Remove roast and place a rack in pressure cooker. Add 1 cup of water and place roast on rack. (Some cookers may require 2 cups of water for safe use. Check your instruction booklet.) Cover and lock. Let pressure cooker come up to high, then lower heat to maintain pressure. Cook for 35 to 40 minutes for a medium-rare roast. (The internal temperature should be 130 degrees. If you prefer your meat really well done, you can cook the roast for a full hour, as long as it is a good chuck roast with plenty of fat. The meat will be ropy and tender.) Quickly release pressure according to manufacturer's instructions. Remove meat from cooker and let sit 20 minutes before carving.

Braised Short Ribs

Braising is simply a method of roasting in a covered pot with a small amount of liquid. Although most cookbooks will tell you that braising produces moister meat or fish, I have tested this and found it not to be true. The inside of a piece of meat is not at all affected by the moistness of the cooking environment. (The origins of braising probably have more to do with preventing food from scorching when cooked in pans over a hot fire.) However, braising does produce a wonderful sauce. The problem is that this sauce is intensely rich and must be properly defatted.

But first, here is what you need to know about short ribs. These days, they are simply any piece of rib that is fairly short in length, no more than six or seven inches. Some short ribs are full of meat and others are mostly bone. (Ribs near the front of the animal, from the chuck or forequarter area, tend to have more meat and will be more tender. Short ribs should be cut from the chuck.) You will also find that they will vary tremendously in length. It is best, I find, to serve shorter pieces; otherwise they appear unappetizing on the plate. If necessary, ask your butcher to cut them into smaller pieces.

In terms of cooking method, James Beard liked to broil his short ribs, instead of browning them in the pan, before braising them. I tried this and found that it makes the recipe a bit more complicated than necessary since you need two pans and the oven has to be cooled off a bit after broiling and before roasting. Instead, I prefer simply to brown the ribs in a large cast iron skillet, cover the pan with a lid or aluminum foil, and then roast them in a

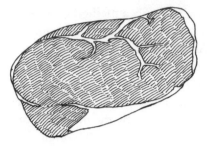

Top sirloin is the best cut from the rump or round for flavor and tenderness.

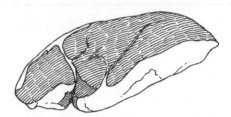

London broil is not a cut of meat, but is instead a method of cooking and carving meat. Although flank steak used to be the cut of choice for London broil, this cut is expensive and therefore butchers currently use most any inexpensive cut and label it "London Broil." This cut is from the chuck.

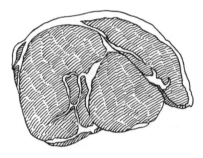

Shell steaks are cut from the sirloin and tend to be meaty tasting and dry when cooked as a steak.

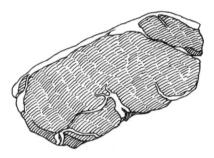

Short cut rump is cut from the loin, and although it was fairly juicy and tender, it had a very meaty, flat taste when cooked.

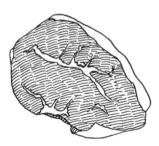

Top blade steaks are taken from the front of the animal, above the shoulder blade. They had very good flavor in our taste tests but were a bit dry.

Top round is a cut from the round, the area between the knee and thigh. It is tough, a bit dry, and has a very "livery" flavor. In general, cuts from the round tend to be tough and dry, and have a strong, somewhat unpleasant flavor. Cuts from the chuck are preferable.

Sirloin tip steaks were highly rated in our tasting with a moist, tender texture and good flavor.

Short ribs is a general term referring to any short piece of rib. Ribs cut from the chuck (front) end of the animal tend to have more meat than those cut from ribs farther back.

slow oven. I also tested using coffee as an ingredient, which was not judged to be a winner, and substituted chopped tomatoes instead, which I liked. Although ribs often come in a wide variety of sizes within each package, they all seemed moist and fork tender after 2 hours of cooking. You can also make this recipe with pork ribs, although I suggest you check them after 1½ hours since they are smaller and will cook faster. This is a good example of beef that should be well done rather than served medium rare, so that it becomes melt-in-your-mouth tender.

Defatting the sauce is the crucial step. The easiest method is to make this dish the day before, allowing the liquid to chill (separately from the ribs) in the refrigerator. A deep layer of fat will solidify on top of the natural juices. It can easily be removed and discarded. I also tested using a fat separator — a clear plastic or glass pitcher with a spout near the bottom of the device, which allows one to pour off the juices underneath the fat which naturally floats to the top. This works but is

less satisfactory since some of the fat is left behind, mixed with the sauce. However, I find that with either method it is best to mix the juices (you should have about 1 cup after defatting) with 2 cups of chicken stock. Without dilution, the juices will be too rich. This method yields a bright, relatively light sauce, a perfect accompaniment to the substantial ribs.

1	teaspoon dried thyme
1	teaspoon freshly ground black pepper
1	teaspoon table salt
5	pounds beef short ribs
1	slice bacon
2	tablespoons olive oil
2	large onions, coarsely chopped
3	large cloves garlic, minced
2	carrots, diced
½	cup canned or homemade beef stock
½	cup canned whole tomatoes, chopped
¾	cup dark beer
1	tablespoon brandy
3	bay leaves
2	cups chicken stock

¼ cup minced fresh flat-leaf parsley
(optional)
Coarse or kosher salt

1. Heat oven to 250 degrees. Mix together the first 3 ingredients and rub over meat.

2. Cook bacon in a large (cast iron is best) Dutch oven or skillet, at least 12 inches in diameter, that has a lid. Remove bacon. Add olive oil (if you are using a well-seasoned cast iron pan, you will not need to add the oil) and brown ribs in batches on both sides over medium-high heat. Remove meat and pour off all but 1 tablespoon of fat. Add onions, garlic, and carrots and sauté for 6 minutes.

3. Add the beef stock, tomatoes, beer, brandy, and bay leaves and scrape bottom of pot with a wooden spoon. Boil rapidly for 3 minutes, stirring occasionally. Return ribs to the pot, bring liquid back up to a simmer if necessary, cover top of pot or skillet with aluminum foil, and then cover with a lid if available (to prevent the liquid from evaporating). Immediately place in the 250 degree oven.

4. Cook for 2 hours or until ribs are fork tender. (Check after 1½ hours.) Remove meat and bay leaves, covering meat with foil, and then pour remaining liquid into a fat separator or a one-quart Pyrex measuring cup. If you wish to serve this dish immediately, allow the fat to rise to the top, about 10 minutes, and then either use the fat separator to pour off the non-fat juices or spoon off the top layer of fat. You should have about 1 cup of defatted juices which should then be combined in a small saucepan with the chicken stock and heated until simmering. Serve the ribs with the chopped parsley, some of the hot juices, and a sprinkling of coarse salt.
SERVES 6

Short Ribs with White Beans and Rosemary

Soak 2 cups of white beans overnight in plenty of water to cover. (If you forget to do this, simply proceed with the next step.) Drain the beans and cook them in 6 cups of water until tender. Add 1 teaspoon salt and simmer 3 minutes. Mince 1 tablespoon of fresh rosemary. For each person, place a serving of beans in a warmed shallow bowl and then add ½ cup of the defatted juices simmered with the chicken stock, sprinkle with a bit of coarse salt and minced rosemary, and top with a serving of short ribs. Sprinkle with parsley and serve.

WHAT ABOUT INEXPENSIVE STEAKS?

For most Americans, the best, most expensive cuts of steak come from the loin of the animal, the section between the ribs and the round. If one were to look at a side view of a beef carcass, the front section of the animal containing the first 5 ribs is the chuck, the next (moving toward the rear of the animal) is the rib section containing 7 ribs in all, next is the loin and sirloin (in human terms, this is the small of the back down to the pelvis), and finally the round, which is the leg from the hip socket down to the knee. Delmonico, T-bone, and porterhouse steaks all come from the loin section; the sirloin steaks come, of course, from the sirloin, which is slightly farther to the rear. There are many cuts of sirloin steak, including the pinbone, the flat-bone, the full-cut, the wedgebone, and the short sirloin.

On a farm, however, one is not likely to purchase and cook expensive meat. So I set out to determine if other, less expensive cuts are worth purchasing as steaks and cooking in an iron skillet.

(Any section of meat can be cut into a "steak," which is simply a cross-section containing bone and meat. If the meat is removed, leaving the bones, this is called "seaming out" the cut, and is how a boneless roast is prepared.) I chose cuts from the chuck, the loin, and the round and prepared them in a preheated iron skillet. Here are the results:

KITCHEN TEST: COOKING INEXPENSIVE STEAKS

Seven different cuts of steak were seasoned with salt and pepper and placed in a preheated iron skillet for 1 minute, turned, and cooked 1 minute on the other side. The heat was then lowered and the steaks were cooked on each side for an additional 3 minutes. All of the steaks were 1 inch thick.

STEAK TYPE	PRIMAL CUT	PRICE/LB.	TEXTURE	TASTE
London broil	Chuck	$2.49	chewy, dry	too "meaty"; flat taste
Top blade	Chuck	$2.39	tough, dry	good flavor
Shell steak	Loin	4.79	chewy, dry	too "meaty"; flat taste
Short cut rump	Loin	4.99	fairly tender; juicy	"meaty"; flat taste
Sirloin tip	Loin	4.69	fairly tender; juicy	nice steak flavor
Top round	Round	4.99	tough, a bit dry	very "meaty"
Round tip steak	Round	2.69	tough, dry	"meaty" flavor

WHAT TO BUY: Inexpensive steaks, with the exception of the sirloin tip steak, are not worth buying if you intend to cook them on top of the stove. Many of these cuts are fine if slow-roasted or braised, but quick, high-heat cooking tends to dry them out. They also have a very "meaty" flavor which, from an American perspective, is not what we are looking for in a steak. The expensive cuts from the loin, which contain a large section of the tenderloin muscle (this is what tournedos and chateaubriand are made from), contain meat that is soft and also light in the flavor department. Many cultures, the French and Italians for example, prefer stronger-tasting steaks and therefore tend to take cuts from the rib section. If you want a juicy but flavorful steak, order rib-eye steaks, although they will be more expensive (between $8 and $10 per pound) than the cuts in the chart above.

Skillet Steak

This is a common method of cooking a steak in Vermont. You do need a cast iron skillet for this method, since it retains heat much better than other pans. If the temperature of the pan drops too much once the steak is added, you will stew the meat rather than sear it.

4   1-inch-thick steaks, rinsed, dried with paper towels, and seasoned liberally with salt

Heat a well-seasoned 12-inch iron skillet over high heat until very hot, about 4 minutes. Place two steaks at a time in the pan (the pan should not be crowded) and sear for 1 minute per side. Reduce the heat to medium and cook for 3 minutes or so per side. Steaks are done when an instant-read thermometer registers 130 degrees when inserted into the middle. Or make a small cut into the meat with a small paring knife to check doneness.

SERVES 4

Master Recipe for Country Pot Roast

A pot roast is any cut of beef cooked over low temperature in a covered pot. This method is usually reserved for tough, inexpensive cuts, since it produces moister, more tender meat. Buy the top blade roast (the top blade is one of four muscles in the chuck), which is often labeled "beef chuck top blade roast boneless" or "top chuck roast." Do not purchase cuts from the round, because these cuts are low in fat and the pot roast will be dry unless you use a pressure cooker. (Older recipes for pot roast almost always called for a roast cut from the forequarter.) The chuck is the front of the animal and the round is the back leg up to the hip.

I have gone back and forth about how much to cook a pot roast and am now convinced that a "medium-rare" pot roast is an unholy marriage of modern *"al dente"* sensibilities and the soul of country cooking. I have also found that a pot roast that is still slightly pink in the center can be tough, although this varies with the cut. Therefore, I now suggest that you cook a pot roast longer, to an internal temperature of 200 to 210 degrees. It will be a bit drier but it will also taste like a real pot roast.

I have also gone back and forth about cooking potatoes or carrots along with the meat. I now prefer to simply steam or boil them just before serving instead of placing them in the pot along with the roast, since the latter method often overcooks them. I also like the contrast between the fresh, earthy taste of boiled new potatoes and the rich flavor of the meat and sauce. When cooked together, that contrast is lost.

As for the gravy, I sometimes serve the pot roast with the unthickened pan gravy, which is full of flavor. If you like a thinner sauce as I sometimes do, don't bother thickening it with the cornstarch.

½   teaspoon dried thyme
¼   teaspoon cloves
¼   teaspoon allspice
¼   teaspoon cardamom
1   teaspoon black pepper
½   teaspoon salt

1	pot roast (top blade roast or top chuck roast), 3 to 4 pounds
2	slices bacon
2	tablespoons olive oil
1	medium onion, diced
2	carrots, diced
¼	cup white wine
1	cup canned or homemade beef or chicken broth
1	tablespoon sherry
3	tablespoons tomato paste
1	bay leaf
2	teaspoons cornstarch mixed with 1 tablespoon water
	Steamed or boiled potatoes or carrots as an accompaniment (optional)
¼	cup chopped flat-leaf parsley

1. Heat oven to 250 degrees. Mix together the first 6 ingredients (thyme through salt) and rub over meat.

2. Cook bacon in a well-seasoned cast iron Dutch oven (preferably just large enough to hold the pot roast). Remove bacon (reserve for another recipe) and all but 1 tablespoon of fat. Add olive oil and brown pot roast on all sides over medium-high heat. Remove meat; add onion and carrots and sauté for 8 minutes.

3. Add the next 5 ingredients (white wine through bay leaf) and scrape bottom of pot with a wooden spoon. Boil rapidly for 2 minutes, stirring constantly. Return meat to the pot and cook over medium heat until liquid starts to simmer. (At this point, the liquid will look like a thick tomato sauce. During cooking, the meat will exude plenty of juice, thinning the gravy.) Ladle some of the liquid over roast, cover top of pot with foil (use 2 pieces if necessary), and then cover with lid. Immediately place in the preheated oven.

4. Cook until interior temperature of the meat reaches 200 to 210 degrees on an instant-read thermometer; this will take about 2 hours. Remove meat and cover with foil to keep it warm. Remove bay leaf. Pour remaining contents of the pot into a blender and purée until smooth. Return liquid to the pot, place over medium heat, and bring to a simmer. If a thickened gravy is desired, add the cornstarch mixture and whisk until thickened. For a thinner gravy, simply serve as is. Adjust seasonings. Serve sliced pot roast with gravy and optional boiled or steamed root vegetables. Garnish with chopped parsley.

SERVES 6 TO 8

Pressure-Cooked Variation

Using a 5- or 6-quart pressure cooker, follow the directions above. When the pot roast is returned to the pot after browning (step 3), place the roast on top of the trivet (most models have round metal trays that allow the roast to sit above the liquid — if you do not have one, simply place the roast on the bottom of the cooker), secure the top of the pressure cooker, and bring up to high pressure. Cook under high pressure, according to manufacturer's instructions, for 60 minutes. Remove from heat, allow pot to cool on stovetop, and when pressure subsides, remove cover and proceed with step 4.

Country Hash

The most important ingredient in hash is the right skillet. A well-seasoned 12-inch cast iron skillet is best, although a non-stick skillet also works. It is important to develop a nice crust on the bottom of the hash; the hash is then broken up, and the bottom is browned again. This is repeated twice. Precooking the potatoes and then chilling them yields the best texture and prevents the potatoes from breaking up during cooking.

1	tablespoon olive oil
1	tablespoon butter
1	medium onion, diced
½	cup diced red bell pepper
1	pound potatoes , boiled until just tender, chilled, peeled, and diced
2	cups diced cooked roast beef, corned beef, turkey, ham, or lamb
1	cup canned chicken stock
½	teaspoon salt
	Freshly ground black pepper to taste
2	teaspoons minced fresh thyme or 1 teaspoon dried
¼	cup minced fresh parsley

1. Heat a 12-inch nonstick or well-seasoned cast iron pan over medium heat. (A cast iron skillet of this size will take a few minutes to heat up.) Add oil and butter and, when the foam subsides, add the onion and diced pepper. Toss to coat with the oil/butter mixture and cook for about 5 minutes, stirring frequently, until the onions are translucent and just starting to brown. Add the potatoes and cook for an additional 5 to 7 minutes, stirring frequently, until the potatoes are lightly browned.

2. Add the meat, ½ cup of the chicken stock, salt, pepper to taste, thyme, and 2 tablespoons of the parsley. Stir to combine. Cook without stirring for about 7 minutes or until the bottom is browned and has a crust. Break up the hash, mixing the crust into the mixture, and repeat twice. Add additional stock ¼ cup at a time as the mixture starts to dry. After the last crust is formed, taste for seasoning and add more salt if necessary. Allow a final crust to form on the bottom, sprinkle with the remaining parsley, and serve in wedges with poached eggs.

SERVES 6

PORK

When I was a kid, we raised both Angus beef and pigs, the latter having been installed in a series of pens located on the backside of our old red barn out by the small creosoted silo. Most city people don't know that pigs are smart, real smart, and are also clean animals when not stuck in a mud wallow by a farmer who doesn't know any better. The challenge in pig farming is keeping them fenced in, since their noses are good for digging holes under a fence big enough to squeeze their coarse, pink bodies through. To avoid this problem, many farmers will have a ring put through their nose, making rooting painful.

I can remember many summer evenings sitting down to dinner, the plate of fresh-picked corn on the blue-checkered tablecloth covering the picnic table that we used for year-round dining, and we'd hear a car pull up. It would be a neighbor telling us that they just saw our pigs running down the road, their short legs scrabbling, making good speed for such poorly designed creatures. It would take at least an hour and more than one bucket of grain to get them back up the road and into the barn. But it was fun since this was one job that was well suited to kids, full of energy and pretty good at running around ourselves. We'd get back home as the sun was setting, the food cold, but it was an adventure that I still remember fondly.

We didn't live in the small white farmhouse next to the barn; our place was up in a field behind the Woodcocks'. My mother let the farmhouse out to the Squires, Bernie and Lucy, who looked after the place when we weren't around, fed the pigs and the cattle, helped check the fencing, and, on one occasion, got to a dead Angus quickly enough to bleed it so the meat wouldn't go bad. Bernie was one of the last old-time Vermonters. He wasn't a farmer; he was a logger with a pickle-barrel chest and massive hands permanently stained with chain oil and axle grease from his huge old Ford dump truck. His chain saw was the size and weight of a good-size jackhammer, with huge handles and a bar that was no dainty 16-incher like those we use today. To my young eyes, it had to stick out a good three feet, large enough to cut down an ancient oak that had been growing on a fence line since before Lincoln's time. But what I remember most about Bernie, besides his gentle soul and sense of humor, was his breathing. A heavy smoker, Bernie wheezed between words, struggling to suck in a breath of air, enough to keep him going to the end of the sentence. I can't say whether the wheezing slowed down his conversation or he just didn't have much

to say, but he was man of few words, which made him hard to figure. You couldn't read his broad, thick face too well, since he'd break out in a semitoothless grin when you least expected it, as if you weren't party to some secret inner conversation. But he knew how to look at a kid. He could look right through you, patient, not afraid of staring. He'd make flatlanders so nervous they would starting talking about most anything, making fools of themselves in the process.

One of my favorite Bernie stories is about the man from the Vermont Department of Wildlife who came down to see my mother, to consult on crops to grow to attract grouse and wild turkey. He got to the bottom of our road, where Bernie lived in the "corner house" before he moved up to our farm. Bernie was working on his truck, legs sticking out onto the dusty front yard, and the stranger asked if he knew where Mrs. Kimball lived. A good bit of time went by, Bernie rolled out from underneath to get a good look at this hapless out-of-towner, fixed him with one of his piercing stares, decided he wasn't good for much, and simply said, "Ay-uh," and then went back to work. The stranger finally made it to our place, but not with Bernie's help.

As we were growing up, our farm produced plenty of pork, covered with fat, juicy and tender. The roasts were truly grand, worthy of company, and my mother would also have the meat locker mix up a batch of hamburger meat, half Angus and half pork, wrapped in light green butcher paper and slapped with a label indicating weight. One day a week, we'd fill up two or three coolers with dry ice and our meat and make the rounds of local restaurants. Our pork sausage was sold under the label "The Whole Hog" to indicate that we didn't just use scraps. Each link was stuffed with the best parts, from the picnic ham to the Boston butt. This was high-class sausage. After the farm was sold and we went out of the pork business, I realized just how bad commercial pork had become. Since the early 1970s, pork producers have been struggling with the consumer's demand for lean meat, which has led to selective breeding intended to produce the leanest possible cut of pork. In my opinion, this has destroyed the industry and the meat. It isn't easy to find a pork roast worth eating these days. They are tough, dry, and without much flavor. I suppose that we have ourselves to blame. It's about time that we stood up and started asking producers to put the fat back in meat. Otherwise, we might as well cook tofu stir-fries and be done with it.

To overcome this problem, there are three possible solutions besides finding a small producer with a good product. The first is to brine a pork roast before cooking. This is a technique that many of us at *Cook's Illustrated* use for a variety of meats, including turkey. This simply means setting the roast in heavily salted water in the refrigerator for a few days. It requires advance planning, but is worth the trouble. One can also inject a flavored saline solution into the roast — this is what many pork producers do to make their meat more palatable — but when tested at *Cook's*, I found the meat to be wet and spongy. The final solution is to roast at low temperature, which helps prevent the meat from drying out. If you have the time, brining is well worth it,

and under all conditions, I suggest slow roasting (I use a 250 degree oven until the meat gets up to 110 degrees and then crank the oven to 500 degrees. This keeps the roast moist but also induces plenty of browning and flavor enhancement as a result of the high heat to finish).

BUYING AND COOKING PORK CHOPS
There are 4 distinct types of pork chops, each of which has its own flavor and texture characteristics. They are:

Blade Chops
These have 2 bones and a fair amount of connective tissue; they are a bit tough but flavorful. This cut comes from the front end of the animal, around the shoulder blade. Hence the term "blade" chop.

Center-Cut Loin Chop
This is a T-shaped bone with little connective tissue and a strip of fat running along one side. This is the premium cut: tender and flavorful.

Boneless Center-Cut Long Chop
Same as the above except without the bone. Doesn't have quite as much flavor without the bone.

Rib Chop
This cut has a curved bone along one side and a fair amount of connective tissue, and it can be a bit tough. However, it has good flavor and is relatively moist. In terms of cooking pork chops, I tested three distinct methods. I used a 1-inch-thick center-cut bone-in loin chop for each test. (Thinner cuts are tricky to cook, since they tend to dry out quickly.) First, I sautéed the chop 1 minute per

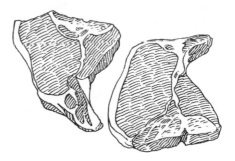

Ham hocks are usually found in the freezer section of the meat department and are most often smoked. They are excellent for flavoring soups, such as split pea, or beans, the cooked meat shredded and added back to the soup. Keep a few hocks in your freezer at all times.

Pork loin chops are the premium cut but are expensive.

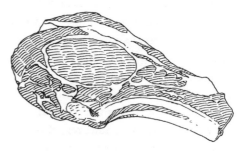

Pork boneless loin chops are the same as loin chops except without the bone.

Pork rib chops are also an excellent choice. They are usually less expensive than loin chops, and have more flavor but are a bit tougher.

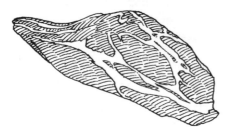

Pork boneless rib chops are the same as rib chops except without the bone.

Pork blade chops are cut from the forequarter of the animal from the shoulder blade area. These chops tend to be moist and flavorful but with a large amount of connective tissue. They are similar to a shoulder chop.

side, covered the skillet, reduced the heat to medium, and cooked 4 minutes per side longer. This produced a chop with nice caramelized flavors, but the texture was dry and stringy, even though the pork was still pink in the center. Next, I sautéed each side and then put the chop into a 250 degree oven for 10 minutes, covered. This was an excellent method since the browning added color and flavor and the low oven heat did not dry it out. Finally, I sautéed each side, added a small amount of chicken stock, brought the liquid to a simmer, covered the pan, and then simmered gently for 6 minutes. Although the meat was a bit juicier than the first method, it lacked flavor, tasting as if it had been steamed (which it had). I also noted that much of the browning from the sautéing had washed off during cooking. So the skillet sauté followed by a 250 degree oven was the winner.

I was still curious, however, about exactly how long to sauté the chops before placing them in the oven. I tested 2 minutes per side, 1½ minutes per side, and then 1 minute per side. The 2-minute version produced overcooked pork with an internal temperature of 178 degrees. The 1½-minute chops also turned out overcooked at 172 degrees internal. The 1-minute chops turned out nicely, the meat tender and juicy. I did test this recipe with both a cast iron skillet and an aluminum skillet and both worked equally well. The skillet must be very hot, otherwise the chops will not cook properly during the short sauté time.

Master Recipe for Pork Chops

Try to avoid thin pork chops. They dry out quickly. I prefer the center-cut loin chops, although thick rib chops are also good. If your pan cannot hold all of the chops at once (a 12-inch skillet will easily hold 4 chops), see the variation below. I prefer using a cast iron pan, since it retains heat well, but any heavy-duty ovenproof skillet will work.

4   (1-inch-thick) center-cut loin pork chops
    Salt and freshly ground black pepper to taste
1   tablespoon olive oil

1. Heat oven to 250 degrees. Heat a large cast iron skillet over high heat. Season the chops liberally with salt and pepper.
2. When the skillet is hot (it is crucial that the pan be *very* hot), add the olive oil, wait 30 seconds, and add the chops. Cook for 1 minute. Turn and cook for an additional minute. Cover the skillet (use aluminum foil if you do not have a regular cover) and place the skillet in the heated oven for 10 minutes. Remove skillet from oven, remove chops, and cover them. Let them rest for 5 minutes before serving.
SERVES 4

SMALL SKILLET VARIATION

If your skillet is not large enough to hold all 4 chops at once, place a roasting pan in the preheating 250 degree oven. Sauté 2 chops, then remove them to the pan (remove pan from oven) and cover them. Sauté the other 2 chops and then place all

4 chops into the preheated pan. Cover the pan, place it back into the oven, and cook chops for 14 minutes.

Pork Chops with a Simple Herb Sauce

Even though this recipe contains white wine, you can make the sauce in a cast iron skillet with no adverse effect on flavors (as long as the pan is well seasoned). This is a light sauce flavored with fresh herbs.

4	pork chops, about 1 inch thick
	Salt and freshly ground black pepper
1	tablespoon olive oil
½	cup white wine or ⅓ cup dry vermouth
1¼	cups chicken stock
2	teaspoons mixed herbs, chopped (rosemary, sage, thyme, oregano, or parsley or a combination)
1	tablespoon cold butter cut into 4 pieces

1. Place an ovenproof pan or dish in oven and heat oven to 250 degrees. Heat a large cast iron skillet over medium high heat until hot. Season chops with salt and pepper. Put olive oil in pan and, when hot, add the chops and brown well on both sides. The chops should be nicely browned. Arrange chops in the preheated ovenproof dish, cover tightly, and place in the heated oven for 14 minutes.
2. Meanwhile, add the wine to the skillet and, with a wooden spoon, scrape up any bits stuck to the bottom of the pan. Cook, reducing the wine by two thirds. Add the chicken stock and simmer for 5 to 6 minutes. Add the herbs and simmer for 3 to 4

minutes more or until the sauce has begun to thicken. Add ⅛ teaspoon of salt, and pepper to taste. When the liquid has thickened (a spoon should leave a clear trail on the bottom of the skillet), remove from the heat and stir in the cold butter. Serve immediately over the chops.
SERVES 4

Pork Chops with a Hearty Brown Sauce

This is a more full-bodied sauce than the recipe above, well suited to drizzling over mashed potatoes.

4	pork chops, 1 inch thick
	Salt and freshly ground black pepper
1	tablespoon olive oil
⅔	onion, diced
¾	cup red wine
1¼	cups chicken stock
1	tablespoon tomato paste
½	teaspoon sugar
2	teaspoons Dijon-style mustard
1	tablespoon cold butter cut into 4 pieces

1. Place an ovenproof pan or dish in oven and heat oven to 250 degrees. Heat a large cast iron skillet over medium-high heat until very hot. Season chops with salt and pepper. Put olive oil in pan and, when hot, add the chops and brown well, 1 minute per side. The chops should be nicely browned. Place chops in the preheated ovenproof dish, cover tightly, and place in the heated oven for 14 minutes.
2. Meanwhile, lower heat under skillet to medium. Add the diced onion and cook, stirring occasionally, for 5 to 7 minutes or

until it is translucent and soft but not browned. Add the red wine, and with a wooden spoon scrape up any bits stuck to the bottom of the pan. Reduce the wine by two thirds. Add the chicken stock and simmer for 5 to 6 minutes. Add the tomato paste, sugar, ¼ teaspoon salt, pepper to taste, and mustard and simmer for 1 to 2 minutes more or until the liquid has thickened (a spoon should leave a clear trail on the bottom of the skillet). Remove from the heat and stir in the cold butter. Serve immediately over the chops.

SERVES 4

ONION VARIATION

Increase the onions to 2 cups and cook them for 10 to 12 minutes instead of the 5 to 7 minutes called for in the recipe above. Simmer the sauce, after the tomato paste and other remaining ingredients are added, for 3 to 4 minutes instead of the 1 to 2 minutes called for.

Pork Chops with Cabbage and Apples

This recipe is best made with red cabbage and red onion. I tested it with green cabbage and yellow onion and the results were not as good.

4	pork chops, about 1 inch thick
	Salt and freshly ground black pepper
1	tablespoon olive oil
1	medium red onion, sliced (about 2 cups)
¼	head red cabbage, sliced (about 5 cups)
1	firm apple such as Granny Smith, peeled and cut into ½-inch slices
¼	cup cider vinegar
1	cup chicken broth, homemade preferred
1	teaspoon caraway
1	tablespoon sugar

1. Place an ovenproof pan or dish in oven and heat oven to 250 degrees. Heat a large cast iron skillet over medium-high heat until very hot. Season chops with salt and pepper. Add the olive oil to pan and when hot, add the chops and brown well, 1 minute per side. The chops should be nicely browned. Place chops in the preheated ovenproof dish, cover tightly, and place in the heated oven for 14 minutes.

2. Meanwhile, lower heat under the skillet to medium. Add the chopped onion and cook, stirring occasionally for 5 to 7 minutes or until translucent and soft. Add the cabbage and apple and stir to combine with the onion. Add the vinegar, and using a wooden spoon, scrape up any brown bits from the bottom of the skillet. Add the chicken broth and cook until the cabbage is soft, about 6 minutes. Add ½ teaspoon of salt, pepper, caraway, and sugar. Stir to combine and cook another minute or two. Serve at once with the chops.

SERVES 4

Master Recipe for Boneless Pork Roast

Pork tenderloin is too expensive for a country cook; most folks would use a simple loin roast, which is still not cheap. A center-cut roast is best (one end is the rib end and the other is the loin end) since the center has less muscle and is less chewy. Note that the USDA suggests that pork be cooked to 160 degrees for safety, although some experts claim that trichinosis is killed at 137 degrees. I am willing to take the risk and eat pork that is cooked to lower temperatures and I find that 150 is about right. These days, pork tends to be lean, and cooking to higher temperatures dries out the meat.

1	boneless center pork loin roast, 3 to 4 pounds
3	cloves garlic, peeled and cut into slivers
2	teaspoons dried thyme
	Salt and freshly ground black pepper to taste
2	tablespoons olive oil

1. Heat oven to 250 degrees. Rinse exterior of meat and pat dry. Cut small slits into the meat with a paring knife and insert garlic slivers. Coat roast with thyme and sprinkle with salt and pepper. Heat olive oil in a Dutch oven on top of the stove. Add roast and brown thoroughly on all sides, about 10 minutes.
2. Place roast in oven and cook uncovered until internal temperature reaches 110 degrees, approximately 20 minutes depending on the size of the roast. Increase oven temperature to 500 degrees and cook until internal temperature reaches 145 to 150 degrees, from 20 to 25 minutes longer. Total cooking time will be 35 to 40 minutes after browning depending on the size of the roast. Remove from oven and let sit for 20 minutes before carving.

SERVES 6 TO 8

SPICE RUB VARIATION

Follow the master recipe above but substitute the spice rub below for the salt, pepper, and thyme. Simply combine the spices below in a small bowl to make the rub.

2	teaspoons cumin
1	tablespoon chili powder
1	teaspoon cinnamon
½	teaspoon ground cardamom
1½	teaspoons brown sugar
2	teaspoons salt
¼	teaspoon crushed red pepper flakes
2	teaspoons freshly ground black peppercorns

PORK TENDERLOIN VARIATION

Follow the master recipe above using a boneless piece of tenderloin instead of the loin. Since they are approximately ¼ pound each, you may wish to cook 2 or even 3 to feed the same number of people. The cooking time will be about 7 minutes to 110 degrees and then 12 minutes to 145 degrees or 15 minutes to 150 degrees.

LAMB

There is an old gray-weathered barn about a half-mile from us, on the edge of a field, a good stone's throw from the road. It is owned by a friend of ours who is a weekend farmer. He keeps a young quarterhorse up in one of Junior Bentley's old barns so it can be tended to when he is not around. Once in a while I'll see Junior and our friend out in the field, sowing timothy or rye with an 1896 wooden seeder, drawn by a team scrabbled together from the herd that runs pretty much wild up above Marie's old place.

Our friend's brother lives full time in town and keeps a wide assortment of animals, although his sheep outnumber all the rest, including the cows, the llama, the rabbits, and the chickens. This ramshackle barn is used to house the sheep during the winter and, since I often go by the barn on my way to New York State to eat breakfast at Linda's on Saturday morning with the boys or to go over to Salem Farm Supply to get tractor parts, I began to notice a rather strange sight. Through the side windows of the barn, I could see the faces of sheep, staring across the open field toward the road. They were standing on a good three feet of dried hay and muck, the barn never having been cleaned out.

Lamb can be quite gamy, especially if the animals are fed a poor diet. Younger animals always taste milder than older specimens; that's why, when I want a leg of lamb, I try to purchase the smallest one available. I've also found when roasting lamb that low-roasting, my favored method for most meats, doesn't work well. The meat tends to get cottony, almost mushy.

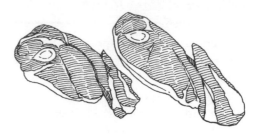

Lamb arm chops are inexpensive and cut from the upper foreleg of the animal. They are fairly tender, juicy, and flavorful when cooked although not as good as the more expensive loin or rib chop.

Lamb shoulder chops are another good choice for an inexpensive chop, being equal to arm chops in terms of tenderness and flavor.

When purchasing lamb chops, one has plenty of choices. Of course, the loin chop is the best: the meat is tender and the least gamy of all the cuts. The rib chops are also good, slightly tougher but with slightly more flavor. However, I wanted to test much less expensive cuts and tried the following:

Shoulder Chop
Consists of 2 bones with a fair amount of connective tissue. It is fairly tender, juicy, and flavorful.

Arm Chop
Same as above but with one small round bone.

Shank Chop
This consists of a large medallion-shaped chop with one small round bone. It has some connective tissue, is a bit tough, and is quite flavorful. Best braised as one might prepare osso buco (braised veal shanks).

In terms of cooking lamb chops, I tested three methods, identical to the methods for cooking pork chops. First, I sautéed them 1 minute per side in a cast iron skillet, then covered the pan, reduced the heat to medium, and cooked about 4 minutes per side longer. This produced great flavor from the sautéing, and the meat was juicy and pink inside. The second method, searing on both sides and then finishing in a 250 degree oven, was my first choice for pork, but lamb does not fare well at low oven temperatures. The higher-heat method, best when roasting a leg of lamb as well, won out for both flavor and texture. Finally, I tried sautéing the chop and then braising it. It tasted like a steamed or boiled lamb chop. This is definitely not recommended.

Skillet-Cooked Lamb Chops

Although finishing pork chops in a 250 degree oven works well, lamb suffers at lower oven temperatures. As a result, I cook lamb chops entirely in the skillet, starting with a quick sauté and then covering the pan and finishing over medium heat.

4   loin, rib, or shoulder lamb chops
     Salt and freshly ground black pepper
1   tablespoon olive oil

Rinse off chops, pat dry with a paper towel, and season liberally with salt and pepper. Place a large cast iron skillet over high heat. When hot, put in the olive oil and then the chops. Sauté for 1 minute per side. Cover (with aluminum foil if you do not have a lid), reduce heat to medium, and cook for about 4 minutes per side longer.

SERVES 4

THE SECRETS OF "POT ROASTING"

Braising meat — cooking it with a small amount of liquid in a tightly covered pot — is an easy method of meat cookery and one that also produces a flavorful sauce for no extra work. This method can be used for shanks, as in the dish osso buco, for pot roast, short ribs, and even, in this case, a boneless leg of lamb. Although most home cooks opt to cook their meat medium-rare, braising is well suited to preparing meat that is fall-apart tender since it is served with the accompanying pan sauce. The problem is that even when the meat is fully cooked, I have found that it often never gets tender, it just gets drier and tougher. I set out to discover the secret of tender "pot roast" meat.

I started with a boneless leg of lamb with all fat, sinews, and silverskin removed. I asked my butcher to butterfly it so that it was even in thickness and flat. I covered the meat with a simple stuffing, rolled it up, tied it with string, and then browned it in a cast iron Dutch oven. When browned, water and a few vegetables were added to the pot. The heat was reduced to the lowest possible setting, the pot was covered, and then the experiment began. Starting at 140 degrees internal temperature, and for every 20 degrees thereafter, I removed the meat from the pot and checked its appearance and texture. I discovered that lamb, unlike beef, can have a very unpleasant texture when undercooked. This was true at 140 degrees. The meat was almost raw and not edible. At 160 degrees, however, the meat was rare and very flavorful but not at all tender. At 180 degrees, the meat was medium rare and slightly more tender but still chewy. At 200 degrees, the meat had very little pink left and was becoming tender but still not at the "pot roast" stage. The internal temperature had to rise to 210 degrees for the meat to become well done and absolutely tender. (The scientific reason for this high temperature is that collagen, which surrounds meat fibers, takes a lot of time and heat to become tender. For more information, see the July/August 1998 issue of *Cook's Illustrated*.) So after years of serving tough, well-done shanks and roasts, I now realized that I simply had not cooked the meat long enough. Extraordinarily high internal temperatures are required to get the "pot roast" effect. In the interests of science, I did continue cooking the lamb another 10 degrees with no additional benefits.

The other issue was cooking time. I find that this varies tremendously depending on the type of pan and the cooktop. For this recipe, I find that 1½ to 2 hours is about right (the longer time for a real pot roast effect) but that is using a heavy cast iron Dutch oven. With other pans that do not retain heat as well, the time could be longer. You may also, after browning the meat on top of the stove and bringing the added water to a boil, place the covered pot in a 250 degree oven rather than cooking the meat entirely on top of the stove.

Pot Roasted Leg of Lamb

For a rare, but very tough, piece of meat, cook it to 145 degrees internal temperature. However, I prefer to cook it to the "pot roast" stage, a full 210 degrees.

1	boneless leg of lamb, 3½ to 4 pounds
1	tablespoon minced garlic
6	anchovy fillets, chopped
2	teaspoons capers
1	tablespoon pitted and chopped imported black olives (optional)
2	teaspoon minced fresh herb such as rosemary or thyme
½	teaspoon salt
1	tablespoon olive or peanut oil
2	medium onions, peeled and coarsely chopped
1	carrot, peeled and coarsely chopped
½	cup water
2	tablespoons minced fresh parsley or chives for garnish

1. Ask your butcher to remove all fat, sinews, and silverskin from the meat, butterflying it so it lies flat. Mix together the next 6 ingredients (garlic through salt) in a small bowl. Spread this paste with your fingers over the top surface of the meat. Roll up the roast and tie with kitchen string, spacing each piece of string about an inch apart. Also run a longer piece of string around the ends of the roast, weaving the string in and out of the shorter pieces tied around the circumference. Sprinkle the exterior with salt.

2. Heat a large cast iron Dutch oven over high heat. When hot, put in the oil and then brown the roast on all sides, about 15 to 20 minutes. When well browned, add the onions, carrot, and water. Cover the pot and reduce heat to the lowest possible setting. Check after 10 minutes. The liquid should be at a low simmer, not boiling rapidly. Cook until done (the inside of the roast should measure 200 to 210 degrees, using an instant-read thermometer to measure the internal temperature. The timing is very difficult to predict accurately, as the amount of heat in the pan will vary tremendously from one stove to another. However, it should take about 1 to 1½ hours.

3. Turn off the heat, pour off the juices into a 2-cup Pyrex measure (the vegetables are not served), and let sit for 15 minutes. Spoon off the fat that accumulates on the top. Remove meat from the pot, slice (leave as much string as possible on the roast as you slice or it will fall apart easily), and serve with the defatted pan juices and a sprinkling of parsley or chives.

SERVES 8

Lamb Shanks with White Beans, Carrots, and Rosemary

Shanks are notorious for varying cooking times and therefore you have to keep cooking them until they are tender, regardless of the specific oven times suggested in the recipe. The major problem with lamb shanks, however, is that the resulting sauce tends to be very greasy. The best solution is to prepare this dish the day before, refrigerate the sauce separately from the shanks, and remove the congealed layer of fat. Combine the shanks with the defatted sauce and reheat gently. You will also find that some stores sell long pieces of shank rather than 2-inch cross sections. Each of these larger pieces weighs about 1 pound. Rather than serve 1 piece per person, I usually remove the meat from the bone after cooking and divide it among 4 to 6 plates, placing the meat on top of the beans.

4	tablespoons olive oil
4	pounds lamb shanks
	Salt and freshly ground black pepper to taste
¼	cup all-purpose flour
2	medium onions, diced
2	medium carrots, cut into bite-size pieces
5	garlic cloves, peeled
1	cup dry white wine
3	tablespoons tomato paste
2	cups chicken stock
2	tablespoons sherry
2	teaspoons fresh rosemary or 1 teaspoon dried
2	teaspoons fresh thyme or 1 teaspoon dried
¼	teaspoon ground cloves

1   bay leaf
1   cup dried navy beans, soaked
    overnight
    Coarse or kosher salt

1. Heat oven to 250 degrees.

2. Heat 2 tablespoons of the oil in a large casserole or Dutch oven over medium-high heat. Season shanks with salt and pepper and dust them with flour. Brown shanks on all sides in oil, in batches if necessary — do not overcrowd pan. Remove shanks. Pour off all the fat.

3. Put remaining 2 tablespoons of oil in pan. Reduce heat to medium. Add onions and carrots and cook for 5 minutes. Add garlic and cook 1 minute more. Turn heat to high, add white wine, and cook for 1 minute, scraping bottom of pan.

4. Stir in all remaining ingredients except beans. Bring to a simmer, cover, and bake for 2 to 2½ hours.

5. Meanwhile, drain the beans and cook in 3½ cups of salted water for about 40 minutes or until tender but still firm. Drain. When the lamb is very tender, season with salt and pepper to taste, then add the beans and bake for 15 minutes.

6. Remove the shanks to a large bowl and cover to keep warm. Pour sauce through a strainer into a defatting pitcher (this is a container with a spout located near the bottom; the sauce can be poured off while leaving the fat behind) or any narrow container. Spoon off the fat on top of the sauce if using the latter. Discard bay leaf. Return the defatted sauce and the contents of the strainer back into the pan. Reheat until simmering. Check and adjust seasonings. With a large spoon, put a serving of sauce and beans on each plate. Add either a whole shank or a portion of the boneless meat. Top with a light sprinkling of coarse salt and a grinding of black pepper. Serve.

SERVES 4 TO 6

Braised Lamb Shoulder

The shoulder is actually quite similar to the shank, the latter being the foreleg of the animal. Both are fatty but exceedingly tender and delicious when cooked at low heat in a bit of liquid. The only problem with these cuts is that the resulting sauce is exceedingly rich and fatty. It is therefore best to make this recipe the day before, strain out the sauce, and refrigerate it overnight. The fat will congeal and can be easily removed. You can also try defatting the sauce using other methods (see the recipe for instructions), but the liquid will still be on the heavy side. It is best to have the shoulder boned and tied by your butcher. Forget about doing this at home. I have had this demonstrated to me by a variety of professional butchers and it is beyond the skill level of most home cooks, myself included. One could braise the shoulder with the bone, but carving is tricky and the resulting slices of meat will be a bit of a hodgepodge. I suggest serving the shoulder with plain boiled new potatoes or mashed potatoes. You need something simple and lean to balance the rich flavors of this dish.

1   (3½- to 4-pound) lamb shoulder,
    boned and tied, or 4 lamb shanks,
    ¾ to 1 pound each
    Salt and freshly ground black pepper
    Flour for coating meat
3   tablespoons olive oil

1   cup diced carrot
1   cup diced onion
½   cup diced celery
3   cloves garlic, minced
2   bay leaves
1   cup white wine or ⅔ cup dry vermouth
2   cups low-sodium chicken stock, canned
    or homemade
1   cup diced tomato, fresh or canned
1   teaspoon salt
1   teaspoon chopped fresh rosemary or
    ½ teaspoon dried
1   teaspoon chopped fresh thyme or
    ½ teaspoon dried
1   teaspoon chopped fresh sage or
    ½ teaspoon dried
2   tablespoons chopped fresh flat-leaf
    parsley for garnish

1. Heat oven to 300 degrees. Place a large Dutch oven over medium-high heat until very hot. Season the lamb with salt and pepper and lightly coat with flour. Put 1 tablespoon of olive oil into the hot pan and brown the meat well on all sides. Remove the meat and reserve.

2. Lower the heat to medium and add the remaining 2 tablespoons of olive oil. When the oil is hot but not smoking, add the carrot, onion, and celery. Cook, stirring occasionally, for 6 to 7 minutes. The vegetables should be soft but not brown. Add the garlic and cook for an additional 2 minutes. Add the bay leaves and the wine. Using a wooden spoon, scrape up any pieces stuck to the bottom of the pan. Return the reserved meat to the pan and add the chicken stock and the tomato. Let the mixture come to a simmer.

3. Cover the Dutch oven and place in the heated oven for 1 hour. Turn the meat, season with salt and a few grindings of black pepper, and cook covered for an additional 30 minutes. Add the rosemary, thyme, and sage and cook covered for an additional 30 minutes.

4. Remove the pan from the oven and check the meat. It should be tender and moist and the liquid should be aromatic. If not, return to the oven and check every 15 minutes. When ready, remove meat to a platter and let it rest for 15 minutes, covered loosely with aluminum foil. Strain the liquid from the pot into a tall, narrow container or a defatting pitcher. Remove as much of the fat as possible (it will float to the top) with a large spoon or small measuring cup. It can also be soaked off with paper towels. Discard the bay leaves. Return the defatted liquid and the vegetables to the pot and boil for 3 to 4 minutes or until thickened slightly. Carve the shoulder and serve with a small amount of the gravy. Sprinkle with fresh parsley.

SERVES 4 TO 6

VEAL

Veal is a by-product of dairy farming. When bull calves are born, most of them are not needed by a dairy farmer. In the old days, many of these calves were simply slaughtered or given away. The story is told in our town about a farmer, during the Depression, who left two bull calves by the side of the road with a FREE sign next to them. He came back later to find three. However, after a while, a dairy-based formula was invented, the calves were fed for 6 weeks, and then they were brought to market.

Traditional veal has little flavor but a wonderful, soft texture. It is a flavor carrier much like the tenderloin muscle in beef. The sauce or seasoning is what gives it interest. Today, some veal is "naturally" raised, which means that it is not penned and is fed a more varied diet. This veal is darker and tastes much like mild beef. Putting aside the moral issues for the moment, the home cook needs to recognize these two varieties when shopping. I prefer the more traditional veal for its mild character and texture.

In our town in Vermont, we don't eat veal, although every August we do have an "ox roast" for which we prepare a young heifer (about 6 months old) that weighs about 180 pounds. This is no calf, and the meat tends to be tough, dark-colored, and fairly beefy. Each steamship round (the leg from knee to hip) is quite heavy, weighing in at about 25 pounds. This sort of meat bears no resemblance whatsoever to the light-colored, tender veal that is only 6 weeks old.

If purchasing chops, one can choose them from the loin, which are inordinately expensive ($10 to $12 per pound). A thick loin chop is what is most likely to be served in an expensive Italian restaurant. However, there is another common cut one might try: the shoulder blade chop, with two bones and a fair amount of connective tissue. It can be quite large and is fairly tender and flavorful. This cut comes from the chuck, the forequarter of the animal. In terms of cooking chops, I tried all three methods tested on lamb and pork chops and found that sautéing the chops for 1 minute per side, covering, and then putting them into a 250 degree oven worked best. They were tender and juicy, and also had plenty of flavor from the stovetop searing.

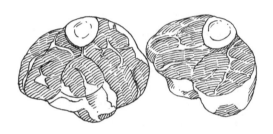

Veal round arm chops are a good alternative to the more expensive center-cut loin chops. A shoulder chop is roughly comparable in flavor and texture.

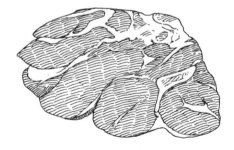

Veal shanks are the basis of the dish osso buco. The shank is the lower foreleg of the animal. Shanks should be cooked slowly at low oven temperatures, about 250 degrees.

Veal shoulder chops are similar in taste, price, and texture to arm chops.

Veal Chops

The oven time will vary depending on the thickness of the chops. Check them with an instant-read thermometer. It should register 145 degrees.

4 1-inch-thick shoulder blade chops or loin veal chops
   Salt and freshly ground black pepper to taste
1 tablespoon olive oil

Heat oven to 250 degrees. Rinse off chops, pat dry with paper towels, and season liberally with salt and pepper. Heat a large cast iron skillet and then put in the olive oil. Add all 4 chops and brown well on both sides. Cover pan (use aluminum foil if there is no lid) and place in heated oven. Cook for 10 minutes.

SERVES 4

Veal Shanks with Capers, Anchovies, and Sage

The perfume of fresh sage works well with this dish, along with the traditional lemon zest, which adds some zip. Be sure to cook the shanks long enough (up to 4 hours for very thick, large shanks). This dish can be made earlier in the day and then reheated on top of the stove over low heat (about 15 minutes). Be sure that none of the bitter pith — the white skin between the peel and the flesh — is attached to any of the lemon peel. I use a vegetable peeler instead of a knife, because it is easier to avoid taking any of the pith.

2½–3 pounds veal shank cut into pieces 1½ inches thick
       Salt and freshly ground black pepper
2   tablespoons unsalted butter
2   tablespoons olive oil
¼   cup all-purpose flour
1   medium onion, chopped
4   anchovy fillets, chopped
2   carrots, finely chopped
4   cloves garlic, finely chopped
½   teaspoon dried thyme or 1 teaspoon fresh
½   teaspoon dried marjoram or 1 teaspoon fresh
½   cup dry white wine
⅔   cup chicken stock
1   cup chopped canned whole tomatoes (optional)
1   tablespoon grated lemon rind
2   tablespoons capers
2   teaspoons minced fresh sage or 1 teaspoon dried
¼   cup minced parsley

1. Heat oven to 250 degrees. Tie a string around the circumference of each piece of veal (or have the butcher do it for you) to keep meat from separating from bone. Season shanks with salt and pepper.
2. In a 12-inch-wide Dutch oven or sauté pan with a lid, melt the butter with olive oil over medium-high heat. When the foam subsides and the fat is very hot but not smoking, lightly flour the seasoned shanks and place them in the pot. Sauté for about 4 minutes per side, shaking pan occasionally to keep meat from sticking. The shanks should be golden brown on each side. Remove shanks and reserve. Put the onion, anchovies, and carrots in the pan, stir, and cook for 2 minutes. Add the next 6 ingredients (garlic through

tomatoes) along with the veal shanks and bring mixture to a boil. Cover pan and place in oven.

3. Cook for approximately 2 hours (very large shanks can take up to 4 hours) or until the meat is very tender. The size of the shanks and the type of pot dramatically affect the cooking time. The internal temperature of the meat should be approximately 200 degrees.

4. Stir in lemon rind, capers, and sage. Bring to a simmer and cook uncovered for 4 minutes. Sprinkle each serving with minced parsley.

SERVES 4

The Summer Garden

LATE EVERY AUGUST, our family drives over to the Washington County Fair, where the kids flock to the bumper cars, the flying school bus, the spinning teacups, and the haunted double-wide trailer. For my part, I look forward to a quiet stroll through the barns, admiring the Ayrshires, Jerseys, and Holsteins with names like Becca, Winnie, Orea, and Brittany. Teenage girls tend to them in the night, forking away the fresh manure and straw and using electric razors to trim unsightly whiskers that might lose them points during the judging. In the 4-H tent, there is an exhibit of garden produce that includes beets, onions, carrots, peppers, tomatoes, and sweet corn as well as vegetable art featuring cabbage faces and squash monsters. Local trees are also featured, with leaves from slippery elm, basswood, sassafras, white ash, shag-bark hickory, larch, and red oak. I stop by the chopped silage exhibit, where the product is displayed in one-gallon glass jars so it can be judged for quality.

As twilight seeps over the fairgrounds, the lights of the midway grow brighter, and the incessant repetition of the barkers takes over. Loud rock and roll blares from the speakers as the mechanical rides whip back and forth. My two-year-old boards a small green train and my older daughter begs to go one more time on the ride that snaps her thin body around, her face contorted with centrifugal force and breathless fright, transported to another world. Her dreams are of lights, and noise, and blinding speed, of exhilaration at the end of a painted metal arm that slings her back and forth, up and down. My dreams are quieter these days, of the clicking of a horse-drawn mower, the clacking back and forth of the scythe bar, the hollow echoes of a workhorse's huge shod feet on the thick wooden floorboards of the stable.

As the county fair changes every year, I wonder what will become of the silence, the stillness of country life. I will miss those gallon jars of silage, small exhibits of the farming life to be put on a shelf forever, perhaps in a farm museum with the rope stretchers and milk testers. But for our family in a small valley in the Green Mountains of Vermont, the past is still the present. I still walk the barns of my childhood with my kids, explore the old cave at the mouth of the river, listen to the piercing, thin wailing of the coyotes as they come down out of the hollow toward the chicken coop just across the road. It is a haunting cry, bearing as much resemblance to the bark of a dog as the real West does to the rodeo at the fair. For now, the wild things still come out in the dark of night, two bears hoot at each other across the ridges behind our house, the red-tailed hawks circle in the late August afternoon, their keening a constant companion and reminder that there are things we still do not understand. As I walk with my nine-year-old daughter toward home one evening, through a field littered with fallen birch and poplar, she looks up at the circling hawk and senses the connection, saying, "I wish it would drop us a feather." Although still a child, she wants to reach out and touch the wildness, to carry the feather with her through life, so when the hawk is gone, and the silage jars are on museum shelves, and the wilderness has retreated to just a memory, she can remember those days at the close of the twentieth century when she walked with her dad through the darkening hollow, when she looked up and saw a ghost in the sky and wanted to reach out and touch it. When my turn comes, and I too am a ghost in the twilight, I hope to leave her a feather, memories of sudden storms, and tall corn, and quiet moments walking hand in hand back home after a long summer day. It is our solemn responsibility to do this for our children, for those who will live in a world after the last old-time Vermont farmer is dead and gone, committed back to the soil that will no longer raise crops or graze cows. I think that it is the earth itself we will miss most, the gravelly scrabble or the rich loam of the river valleys. I often dream that those old farmers will lie there through the long winters and dry summers, whispering to us from their stony graves, their wordless song carried by the murmur of a brook or the rustle of leaves before a storm, calling us until we awake from our discontent, and the pastures once again feel the roots of young buckwheat, pushing down into the earth seeking moisture and inspiration.

ONE OF THE GREAT joys of gardening is the summer herb garden filled with the standard culinary herbs — rosemary, thyme, parsley, basil, sage, mint, dill, chives, oregano, and tarragon — as well as a few old-time plants that were once favored for their medicinal and other properties. There was *tansy*, used as a dye and a remedy, also thought of as a weed; *salad burnet*, a cure for melancholy and used in salads; *wormwood*, used to get rid of worms; *hyssop*, used to make Chartreuse and cure head lice, and very bitter; *yarrow*, also called *Achillea mille-folium* because legend has it that Achilles used it to stop bleeding; *calendula*, used to cure upset stomachs; *rue*, an herb of sorrow and repentance and also used as the inspiration for the design of the "club" suit on a pack of cards; *horehound*, whose name comes from its reputation for curing dog bites — it was also used extensively as a cough cure; and my favorite, *costmary*, used as book marks in Bibles because its fragrance reputedly kept churchgoers awake (it is also called alecost and was used to spice up beer). It seems that we have stripped away much of the charm and diversity of nature in our desire to simplify and popularize. But there are still residents in our small town who can walk the woods finding scores of edible plants, from emerging fiddlehead ferns to dandelion greens, sorrel, wild leeks, lamb's quarters, Jerusalem artichokes, rose hips, purslane, milkweed, and wild peppery watercress, the latter growing in a small stream across our dirt road by a large culvert. A keener eye will also find winter cress, which can be added to salads raw in late winter before the leaves become bitter; young stinging nettles, which lose their poison during cooking; spotted touch-me-not, which advertises with large orange blossoms; wild marjoram; and burdock, treasured for its roots.

Our town also has plenty of wild mushrooms, from the more common chanterelles, morels, giant puffballs, and oyster mushrooms to horse mushrooms, shaggy manes, black trumpets, bear's head tooth, goat's beard, chicken mushroom, Oryad's saddle, and hen-of-the-woods.

As for the recipes in this chapter, I have confined them to the usual suspects, given the fact that most folks don't live on a farm and can't spend an hour foraging before dinner. For those who are home gardeners, however, I would like to share a few suggestions. Turnip tops, when they are no more than three inches long, add a wonderful peppery flavor to salads. I grow at least two and sometimes three crops of them, allowing a few plants to mature. Beet tops should never be discarded but should be cooked as well and either served with the beets or served with white beans. They can also be sautéed in olive oil and garlic and served as a side dish. When planting lettuce, I no longer carefully plant rows. I simply scatter a variety of different seeds in a small area and rake them into the dirt. I repeat this every two weeks throughout the summer, except during very hot weather, and we always have a fresh crop. I sometimes combine lettuce seeds with radishes and carrots. They also grow very close together, which avoids the problem of weeding. Brussels sprouts are easy to grow, mature in September, and hold just fine well into the fall, even after a frost, when they are slightly sweeter. Although store-bought varieties are virtually inedible — tough and dull-flavored — home-grown sprouts are tender, with a light, fresh taste. These are now our favorite garden vegetable. For small bug and mite infestations use a spray of Safer soap, which is acidic and quickly removes the pests. It is also safe, organic, and nontoxic. For those with good-size gardens, I suggest using a roll of black weed matting for the larger plants. Metal stakes hold the plastic in place (purchase the heavier rolls, which have a feltlike covering on the side that faces the soil — it weathers better and can be used year after year) and then holes are cut out for planting. This avoids all weeding and keeps the soil moist. Finally, a simple drip irrigation system is easy to install and worth the investment. Half-inch-diameter plastic pipes are laid down between the rows and then very small drip lines are punched into the piping and run to the plants. At the end of the drip lines are metal shut-off valves. This is not only convenient but better for larger plants than watering from above.

In terms of cooking, I find that steamer baskets are really not necessary. I simply place a small amount of water, about ¼ inch, in the bottom of a large skillet, bring it to a simmer, add the vegetables, cover, and then steam. I have not found any difference between boiling and steaming in taste or texture but I usually steam, since it is faster — less water must be heated. Remember that vegetable peelers do get dull over time and have to be replaced. A good vegetable cleaning brush is useful, especially for potatoes. Finally, I believe that vegetables should be fully cooked, not warm crudités that crunch and crackle as they are eaten. Overcooking is also a crime, especially with broccoli, which loses color and takes on an unpleasant odor, but the tendency these days to eat nearly raw vegetables is unfortunate.

As far as salad recipes go, I have avoided the traditional composed salads which were the mainstay of salad chapters in older cookbooks. Some of these recipes were remarkable in their complexity and design. One of the most curious recipes I have come across is Indian Salad, which is made from a hollowed-out tomato into which are placed a half dozen short stalks of cooked asparagus followed by rings of beet, green pepper, and red pepper which are stacked on top of the tomato rim and then topped with Indian Dressing, which itself is made from thirteen different ingredients. Instead, I provide a simple make-in-the-bowl salad recipe, coleslaws, and a mustard vinaigrette, which I prefer for either more bitter, heartier greens or for vegetables.

Steamed Asparagus

Asparagus comes in different thicknesses. The thin "pencil" asparagus that arrives early in the season cooks in just two or three minutes. The thicker-stalked asparagus requires longer cooking — up to six minutes — and the ends of the stalks must be peeled as well. Asparagus should be neither crunchy nor soft.

1   pound asparagus, washed and ends snapped
    Salt and freshly ground black pepper to taste

If using a steaming basket, bring 1 inch of water to a boil in a large pot. If you do not have any steaming equipment, bring ⅛ inch of water to boil in the bottom of large pot. Add asparagus, cover, and steam over medium heat for 4 to 6 minutes depending on the size of the asparagus. To test, simply remove one spear, wait a few seconds until cooled, and then bite into the large, snapped end. It should be firm but not crisp. Sprinkle with salt and freshly ground black pepper to taste.

SERVES 4 AS A SIDE DISH

Roasted Asparagus

This is an unusual preparation method, but it is easy and heightens the vegetable's flavor. Roasted asparagus is best served immediately, as it tends to soften after cooking.

1   pound asparagus, washed and ends
    snapped
    Olive oil
    Salt and freshly ground pepper
    to taste

Heat the oven to 400 degrees. Arrange prepared asparagus in a single layer in a roasting pan and brush with olive oil. Sprinkle with salt to taste. Roast for 10 minutes. Add freshly ground pepper to taste and serve.

SERVES 4 AS A SIDE DISH

Asparagus Soup

Leeks and potatoes give this soup body and depth of flavor. The onions and leeks are sweated — cooked covered over low heat — rather than sautéed so as not to compete with the delicate flavor of the asparagus.

2   tablespoons butter
1   tablespoon olive oil

1   medium onion, chopped
1   cup chopped leeks (white part only)
      (about 2 medium leeks)
3   cups chicken stock
1   medium potato, diced
2   stalks celery including leaves, chopped
1½   pounds asparagus, washed, tough
      ends removed, cut into 1½-inch pieces
½   teaspoon sugar
1   tablespoon chopped fresh chervil,
      mint, or marjoram
½   cup heavy cream
1   tablespoon brandy
      Salt and freshly ground black pepper
      to taste
¼   cup minced parsley, for garnish

Heat the butter and olive oil in a large pot. Add the onion and leeks and cook covered over low heat for 15 minutes — do not let onion and leeks brown. Add the chicken stock and potato, bring to a simmer, and cook for 5 minutes. Add the celery, asparagus, and sugar and simmer until the asparagus is tender and completely cooked, 6 to 7 minutes. Add the fresh herb, cream, and brandy and cook for 5 minutes. Purée in batches in a food processor or blender. Add salt and pepper to taste. Garnish with parsley.

SERVES 4

Master Recipe
for Steamed or Boiled Broccoli

The trick in cooking broccoli is how to prepare it. First, let's get the terminology straight. There are florets, stalks, and the stem. The florets are tender, flowery bunches at the end of the stalks. The stalks connect the florets to the stem and are both thin and tough. The stem is the

The Summer Garden **177**

trunk, much like the trunk of a tree. The trick is to leave the stalks behind. They are inedible unless peeled, which takes a great deal of effort. The other important technique is to trim the sides of the thick, fibrous stem, leaving only the tender inner heart. Now the florets and the trimmed stem will cook at the same rate.

You can now either boil or steam the broccoli; I can't tell the difference when it is cooked. Be sure not to cook broccoli more than 7 minutes, the point at which it begins to break down, resulting in a brownish tinge to the florets and the telltale sour odor. If you intend to cook broccoli a second time, in a skillet perhaps, you should blanch it first. Simply drop it into plenty of boiling salted water for 4 minutes, drain, and rinse under cold water to stop the cooking.

2   pounds broccoli

1. Place broccoli head-side-down on the work surface. Use the end of a sharp chef's knife to trim off the florets, leaving the thin, tough stalks behind, still attached to the stem. Trim off the top and bottom of the stem and then stand it straight up. Trim away about ⅛ inch of the sides of the stem, cutting away the tough outer skin and all the stalks. (The amount that needs to be trimmed will vary depending on the size and condition of the stem.) The remaining flesh should be tender. Cut stem in half lengthwise and then into ½-inch pieces. Either steam the florets and prepared stem pieces or place in a pot of boiling salted water. Cook covered for about 6 minutes or until just tender. Drain and serve, usually with a simple salad dressing.

2. If you wish to blanch the broccoli, cook it for about 4 minutes. Refresh under cold running water to stop the cooking, and drain. Now the broccoli can be cooked a second time to finish, usually sautéed in a skillet.

SERVES 4

Olive Oil and Lemon Juice Variation

After steaming or boiling a head of broccoli according to the master recipe, place it in a large bowl and toss with ¼ cup high-quality extra-virgin olive oil, 1 tablespoon lemon juice, salt, and freshly ground black pepper to taste.

Broccoli with Brown Butter and Toasted Walnuts

The broccoli needs to be dressed right before serving as the lemon juice will cause discoloration if left sitting too long.

⅓   cup walnuts or pecans
4   tablespoons (½ stick) unsalted butter
1   tablespoon lemon juice
1   bunch broccoli, prepared according
      to master recipe above and either
      steamed or boiled
      Salt and freshly ground black pepper
      to taste

1. In a 400 degree oven, toast nuts for about 4 to 5 minutes or until nicely toasted but not burned. Check frequently. A toaster oven also works well.
2. Melt the butter in a small saucepan over medium heat. When it turns brown

(the butter should still be golden, not blackish-brown), immediately remove the pan from the heat. Add lemon juice carefully, as the butter can splatter.

3. In a large bowl, toss the cooked hot broccoli with nuts and brown butter, season to taste with salt and pepper, and serve.

SERVES 4

Gratin of Brussels Sprouts

There is no comparison between the tender, nutty sprouts grown at home and the tough, woody, slightly bitter sprouts sold in most supermarkets. The latter are often not worth eating and the former are divine. Home-grown brussels sprouts are so delicate in both taste and texture that they can simply be steamed and served with a bit of butter or olive oil, salt, and fresh herbs. This recipe, however, works with just about any quality sprout, since they are flavored with bacon, cream, and cheese.

6	cups brussels sprouts
2	slices thick-cut smoked bacon cut into matchsticks
1	cup heavy cream
⅛	teaspoon freshly grated nutmeg
½	teaspoon salt
	Freshly ground black pepper to taste
⅓	cup freshly grated Parmesan cheese

1. Heat the oven to 400 degrees and set a rack in the middle position. Butter a 2-quart baking dish.
2. Trim the stems of the sprouts, remove any tough outer leaves, and make a small X in the stem of each sprout with a paring knife. Fill a 4-quart saucepan halfway with water and bring to a boil. Add the sprouts and cook for 5 to 10 minutes or until just tender. (Cooking time will depend on the size of the sprouts.) Drain, rinse with cold water, and reserve.
3. Cook the bacon over medium heat in a cast iron skillet until crisp. Drain on paper towels.
4. Put the bacon and the sprouts into the baking dish. Pour cream into the dish and add the nutmeg, salt, and pepper; toss lightly to combine. Sprinkle the top with cheese and place in the heated oven. Bake uncovered for about 30 minutes or until golden brown and bubbling.

SERVES 6 TO 8 AS A SIDE DISH

Master Recipe for Steamed Cabbage

Older recipes for cabbage often called for very long, slow cooking in cream or in a béchamel sauce. This is a fresher, simpler preparation method. The cabbage is steamed and then tossed with a dressing. A simple vinaigrette works well and I find that a bit of diced or grated ginger makes a nice addition.

1	head green, red, or Savoy cabbage
1	recipe Mustard Vinaigrette (below)

Remove the core and tough outer leaves of the cabbage. Cut into wedges or strips. Place in a steamer or on a rack in a large pot. Steam for about 6 minutes. (Strips will take less time than wedges; red cabbage will take longer than green.) Serve with Mustard Vinaigrette.

SERVES 4 TO 6

Mustard Vinaigrette

I use two kinds of vinaigrette. One has a high proportion of olive oil to vinegar and is best for tender greens. The other recipe is much stronger, with proportionally more vinegar, and also includes a good dose of garlic and Dijon mustard. The latter is paired with stronger-flavored greens such as escarole or used over steamed vegetables. The mustard seems to make this vinaigrette less acidic, creating a creamy, softer emulsion. A little bit of this recipe goes a long way.

2	teaspoons finely minced garlic
2	teaspoons Dijon mustard
3	tablespoons extra-virgin olive oil
1½	tablespoons good-quality red wine vinegar
¼	teaspoon salt

Whisk all ingredients together lightly in a small bowl for just a few seconds.

DRESSES 8 CUPS OF GREENS OR
6 CUPS OF STEAMED VEGETABLES

Summer Garden Coleslaw

This slaw has a little of everything from our summer garden with a creamy buttermilk dressing. If you want to make this slaw ahead of time, add the parsley or basil at the last minute so they don't wilt.

1	tablespoon poppy, caraway, or mustard seeds
½	head green cabbage, cored and sliced thin
1	cup onion, ends trimmed, cut in half across the equator, peeled, and thinly sliced
½	cup chopped basil or parsley leaves
2	carrots, peeled and grated

DRESSING

½	cup buttermilk
2	tablespoons olive oil
1	tablespoon fresh lemon juice
1	tablespoon cider vinegar
¼	teaspoon dry mustard
½	teaspoon salt
2	teaspoons sugar

1. Place a cast-iron skillet over medium heat until hot. Add the seeds and toast for 2 to 3 minutes until they are fragrant and lightly toasted. Shake skillet occasionally.
2. Toss together salad ingredients with seeds. Whisk together the dressing ingredients, pour over vegetables, and toss.

SERVES 8 TO 10

Pepper Slaw

This recipe comes from James Beard's *American Cookery* and is my favorite coleslaw recipe. I have reprinted it exactly as it appears, since it needed no improvement.

1	medium head of cabbage, finely chopped
1	medium onion, finely chopped
3	ribs celery, finely chopped
2	green peppers, finely chopped
1	medium carrot, finely chopped

FOR THE DRESSING

½	cup extra-virgin olive oil
1½	teaspoons salt
1	teaspoon freshly ground black pepper

2	teaspoons celery seeds
2	tablespoons sugar
3	tablespoons good-quality white wine vinegar
1	tablespoon Dijon mustard

Combine all the vegetables. Whisk the dressing ingredients together and toss with the vegetables. Allow to sit for at least 2 hours and toss again before serving.

SERVES 8

CORN

I plant almost a full acre of sweet corn in a small field just off the dirt road that heads toward town. I use an old Ford red-and-white planter which I found over in New York State through the *Pennysaver*. It hooks up to the three-point hitch on my tractor and has two buckets for seed and one large container for fertilizer. It plows two small furrows, drops in a seed every few inches, and then sprinkles two rows of fertilizer near the seeds. It's best to finish the field by using a large roller, which presses down the soil, making it a bit more difficult for birds to get at the seeds.

Although the supersweet hybrids are all the rage, I find that they lack the depth of flavor that I associate with older varieties. Last summer I planted a hybrid called Bodacious and it was extraordinarily sweet and light, but it was a bit like cotton candy: it melted in the mouth leaving a sweet but slightly unpleasant aftertaste. By comparing sugar levels, I realized that the new hybrids really are much sweeter. Old-fashioned "sweet" corn has 5 to 10 percent sugar, "sugar-enhanced" corn is 15 to 18 percent, and "supersweet" is 25 to 30 percent. Next year I am going to plant "sugar-enhanced," abandoning the supersweets entirely.

Regardless of the variety, I will continue to plant my corn patch every May. Watching the young plants sprout, measuring their height on July 4 (despite the saying "knee-high by the Fourth of July," the corn should be at least a foot taller than that in a good growing season), eagerly anticipating the moment that the stalks tassel and the ears sprout silk, all connect the farmer to the land, to the weather, to the endless cycle of growing seasons. Much has been written about the cycles of life and nature, to the point that one would be hard-pressed to offer a fresh thought on the subject, but driving by the field in my old pickup every day, the progress of the plants binds me to some other clock in a manner that provides a great deal of comfort, like watching a small child slowly mature. This window into the world of rain and loam, wind and hot sun, pests and honeybees, of long droughts and wet, cool springs, of the moment that the corn is ready to be picked, walking between the rows with paper bags half full of huge, coarse ears twisted off their mother stalk, soon to be husked and thrown into boiling water and eaten straightaway without butter or salt, has no equal, in my experience. Farmers move the earth with large, expensive machines, trying to leave their mark, to alter the course of events. But of course we leave nothing. Even a cleared field is soon dense with poplar and birch if not mowed. I like to think, however, that my memories of the first sweet bite of corn in August, or the look of the stalks after a hailstorm in July, will forever float about our farm, perhaps remembered by our children or picked up by a stranger a hundred years from now as he stands in my old cornfield. As I walk a line of trees in our woods and come across an old piece of barbed wire growing out of a large maple where a fence once stood, I sometimes feel close to old Charlie Tikander, who used to run dairy cows on our property. It's no great trick to dig up the trash he left in an old cellarhole — bits of broken bottles, an old pair of workshoes, or a rusted milk pail — but when I catch one of his memories, as I stand to watch the sun coming over the Green Mountains or the moon scuttle out from behind a cloud, he and I are standing there side by side for just a moment, an old Finn who didn't speak much English next to a cook and weekend farmer who has so much to learn. Years from now, when my turn has come and gone, I hope to stand beside my son in that field, and whisper in his ear, a ghostly memory of how the corn stood tall on an August afternoon at the close of the twentieth century. It is a great comfort to think that he may hear my faint voice, just a flicker of memory in an old cornfield.

Simple Boiled Corn

Corn can be cooked anywhere from 2 to 8 minutes depending on the type of corn and how fresh it is. To determine the proper cooking time, I put seven ears of corn (since most folks don't have fresh-picked corn available I used store-bought supersweets out of season) in boiling water and took one ear out every minute. The 4- and 5-minute ears were best; the former had a slight edge, although it is

hard to be precise because the sweetness and freshness of the ears may vary. When I tested locally grown, fresh-picked corn, I found that 2 minutes was best. (Good locally grown corn, despite the new hybrids, is always better than supermarket corn.) Basic "sweet" corn, however, needs 6 to 8 minutes to soften the kernels. My advice is to boil fresh corn for 2 minutes and then taste-test it; boil supermarket corn for 4 minutes before tasting. Corn can also be steamed, although I cannot tell the difference. By the way, there is a saying in our town that the harder it is to husk the corn, the harder the upcoming winter. Last summer (1997), the husks were particularly tough (but the winter was mild!).

8   ears corn, husked and silked

Bring a large pot of water to a boil. Boil fresh-picked supersweet corn uncovered for 2 minutes and supermarket supersweets for 4 minutes. Regular supermarket "sweet" corn, unless it is grown locally, is not worth eating. Or place husked corn in a large pot of boiling water and then remove the pot immediately from the heat. Let sit for about 5 minutes.

Creamed Fresh Summer Corn

Forget everything you think you know about creamed corn. This is a delicate, died-and-went-to-heaven dish made from just-picked corn with a little butter, a dash of cream, salt, and a few grindings of black pepper. I like this dish so much that I planted a full acre of sweet corn this year so I would have enough corn to see me through the season. Of course, you need to plant a lot of extra corn in Vermont, since the raccoons will plunder the field, knocking down stalks and taking a bite or two from each ear the night before the corn is fully ripe.

The key to this recipe is milking the kernels. If you simply trim off the kernels whole, none of the corn milk (the liquid inside the kernels) will be liberated. The easiest method is to use a "corn stripper," which both removes kernels and milks them at the same time. If you don't have one, use a large bowl and a sharp knife. Slice off the tops of the kernels over the bowl, also catching the milk. Then scrape down the cob with either a large spoon or the back of a large chef's knife. This will get more of the milk and the kernels. Don't bother making this recipe with old, store-bought corn. It has to be fresh, juicy, and delicate.

12	ears fresh-picked corn, husked and silked
4	tablespoons (½ stick) unsalted butter
½	cup heavy cream
¾	teaspoon salt
	Large pinch cayenne pepper or freshly ground black pepper to taste

Milk the corn (see above) and cut off the kernels, capturing both in a large bowl. Melt the butter in a cast iron skillet. Add the corn, all of its liquid, and the cream. Cook over medium heat, stirring occasionally, until mixture thickens and bubbles and the corn no longer tastes raw,

about 8 minutes. Add salt and a pinch of cayenne or plenty of freshly ground black pepper to taste. Serve.

SERVES 6 TO 8 AS A SIDE DISH

Onion and Bacon Variation

If the corn is very fresh and very sweet, don't bother with this variation. If, however, the corn is store-bought and needs some help, this version adds flavor.

Cook 4 pieces of thick-cut smoked bacon in an iron skillet until crisp. Remove to paper towels and pour off all but 1 tablespoon of bacon grease. Add only 3 tablespoons of butter to pan plus ½ cup of chopped onion. Sauté for 5 minutes over medium-low heat. Add corn and cream and proceed with above recipe but crumble reserved bacon and stir it into corn mixture just before serving.

Summer Corn Chowder

This is one recipe where a homemade chicken stock will make all the difference. I find that half-and-half is slightly better than milk, since it makes a creamier chowder. To remove the kernels, cut the thick end of a husked ear in half crosswise (so that you have a flat surface for the half-ear to stand on as you work) and then cut down along the outside with a large, sharp chef's knife, or use the "Kernel Kutter," which is a toothed metal ring with handles which slides down the outside of an ear of corn, quickly stripping off the kernels.

2	slices bacon
2	onions, diced
2	teaspoons minced garlic
1	quart chicken stock, preferably homemade
2	cups corn kernels
2	cups diced potatoes
2	cups half-and-half
½	teaspoon minced fresh thyme
	Salt and freshly ground black pepper to taste
	Dash of hot pepper sauce or pinch of cayenne (optional)

Fry the bacon in a large pot until crisp. Remove bacon and drain off all but 1 tablespoon of bacon fat. Add the onions and sauté over medium heat for 4 minutes. Add the garlic and sauté for 2 minutes. Add the chicken stock, corn kernels, and potatoes, bring to a boil, and simmer for about 30 minutes or until potatoes are cooked. Add the half-and-half and the thyme, bring back to a boil, then lower heat to a simmer for 5 more minutes. Add salt, black pepper, and hot pepper to taste.

SERVES 4 AS A MAIN COURSE,
6 TO 8 AS A FIRST COURSE

Cucumber Salad with Onions and Balsamic Vinegar

This salad is also very good with sweet onions (Vidalias or Walla Wallas — double the quantity if using one of these varieties). If you don't have balsamic vinegar, use red wine vinegar.

4	medium cucumbers
½	medium red onion, thinly sliced
1	medium tomato, seeded and diced

½	cup olive oil
2	tablespoons red wine vinegar
1	tablespoon balsamic vinegar
½	teaspoon salt
	Freshly ground black pepper to taste
2	tablespoons chopped chives or dill for garnish

Peel the cucumbers and cut them in half lengthwise. Scoop out the seeds using a metal teaspoon. Cut the cucumbers into ¼-inch-thick slices. Combine with all the ingredients except chives or dill and refrigerate for 1 hour before serving. Check seasonings and garnish with chives or dill.

SERVES 6 TO 8

Green Bean and New Potato Salad

Green beans are often sold too large with overdeveloped seeds. The best beans are small without spots or withered ends. Before cooking, trim off the ends with a knife or snap them off. (I find that a large chef's knife speeds up this operation considerably — just line up the ends so that you cut a half a dozen beans at once.) Green beans are very good lightly steamed and then quickly sautéed with olive oil and garlic or other flavorings. I admit that I find undercooked green beans to be unpleasant, reminding me of a crudité tray rather than a cooked dish. I suggest steaming 8 to 10 minutes.

New potatoes and green beans are both available in midsummer from the garden and are a classic combination. Some cooks roast their potatoes, but I prefer to steam or boil them to preserve their delicate, just-dug flavor. If you don't grow your own potatoes, purchase small red potatoes with thin, delicate skins. They are best when not much bigger than a golf ball. Potatoes are easy to grow, deer and other garden varmints don't eat the tops, and they produce a big crop in not much space. Potato bugs are, of course, a common problem. Having tested just about everything, and being wary of any sort of chemical spray (the nontoxic ones don't work very well), I find that simply picking them off and dropping them into a coffee can of kerosene works well although, like real Vermonters, I now simply squish them between my fingers, leaving a bright orange stain. But even squishing bugs is worth the effort for a good crop of these heavenly, earth-scented spuds.

1½	pounds new potatoes, cut into quarters or about 1-inch cubes
1½	pounds green beans, trimmed and cut into bite-size pieces
¼	cup good-quality red or white wine vinegar
1	teaspoon Dijon mustard (optional)
6	tablespoons high-quality olive oil
½	red onion, thinly sliced
2	tablespoons minced chives
¼	cup chopped parsley
½	teaspoon salt
	Freshly ground black pepper to taste

1. Steam the potatoes until barely tender, about 7 minutes. Add the green beans and steam for an additional 7 minutes or until just tender. Remove to a bowl with a slotted spoon and let cool for 15 minutes.
2. Whisk together the vinegar, optional mustard, and olive oil. Pour over the potatoes and beans. Add the onion, chives, and parsley. Add salt and pepper to taste. Toss and serve.

SERVES 6 TO 8

Greens Sautéed with Garlic and Bacon

You may add 2 cups of cooked white beans to this dish along with the greens during the last phase of cooking. The beans are a nice counterpoint to the sharp flavor of the greens.

2	pounds greens (kale, mustard greens, collard greens), stems removed, coarsely chopped
2	slices thick-cut smoked bacon
3	tablespoons high-quality olive oil
2	teaspoons minced garlic
1–2	anchovies, minced
¼	cup chicken stock
1	teaspoon white wine vinegar (optional)
	Salt and freshly ground black pepper to taste

1. Cook greens in boiling salted water for 5 minutes. Rinse under cold water, and drain well in a colander, or place in a kitchen towel and squeeze dry.
2. Cook bacon in a large sauté pan until crisp. Remove bacon to paper towels and pour off all but 1 tablespoon of fat. Add olive oil, garlic, and anchovies and cook over medium heat for 1 minute. Add greens, turn up heat, and sauté for 2 minutes. Add chicken stock and bring to a simmer. Lower heat to maintain a simmer and cover. Cook for about 5 minutes or until greens are tender. Add optional vinegar and salt and freshly ground pepper to taste. Serve with crumbled bacon on top.

SERVES 4 TO 6

The Summer Garden **185**

Master Recipe for Tender Greens

Bitter greens require precooking but tender greens can simply be sautéed.

3 tablespoons olive oil
3 large cloves garlic, peeled and smashed
2 pounds fresh tender greens (spinach, escarole, or chard), trimmed and washed
   Salt and freshly ground black pepper to taste

1. Heat the oil in a large skillet over medium-high heat. When hot, add the garlic cloves and sauté for 1 minute. They should just start to color.

2. Add the greens, cover, and cook for 2 minutes, stirring occasionally (chard may take an extra minute or two). The greens should be wilted. Season with salt and pepper and serve.

SERVES 4 TO 6

Tender Spring Greens with Sesame Seeds

By the time spring turns up in Vermont, everyone is desperate for something fresh from the garden. The earliest greens are always best; tender, small, and above all, sharp on the tongue and intensely alive. I admit that old Vermont cooks probably didn't use many sesame seeds and they certainly did not have toasted sesame oil, but these days, they are available everywhere.

1 tablespoon sesame seeds
1 pound tender spring greens (turnip, beet, broccoli rabe)

1 teaspoon toasted sesame oil
2 teaspoons high-quality olive oil
1 tablespoon lemon juice
   Salt to taste

1. Heat a small skillet and add sesame seeds. Toast, shaking the pan occasionally, until fragrant and light golden, 3 to 4 minutes. Do not burn.

2. Clean greens, removing any tough stems. Steam or boil until tender, 1 to 5 minutes depending on the greens.

3. Remove greens to a large bowl and add remaining ingredients. Toss and sprinkle with the toasted sesame seeds.

SERVES 4 AS A SIDE DISH

GREENS WITH ROASTED BEETS

Of course, the frugal country cook would simply use beet greens instead of spinach.

4 beets roasted (see recipe page 55) and sliced
3 tablespoons olive oil
1 medium onion, chopped
1 pound spinach or beet greens, stemmed and washed
   Salt and freshly ground black pepper to taste

1. Prepare beets according to the recipe. Heat the olive oil in a large skillet. Add the onion and cook over medium heat for 3 minutes.

2. Add the beets and greens and cook for 2 minutes for spinach, 4 minutes for beet greens.

3. Season with salt and pepper and serve.

SERVES 4

Dressed-in-the-Bowl Green Salad

Sonny Skidmore, son of Jenny and Harry, is a great bear of a man, with hands as wide as a dinner plate, but he could handle a backhoe like a scalpel, cutting through the earth within inches of a foundation. This delicate touch came to light in other ways as well. After digging a small pond for my mother up at the old Bartlett lot, he delivered his invoice. It was written in a fine, precise hand with perfect, cursive lettering.

But I can honestly say that, as far as I know, Sonny never ate a salad in his life. His diet consisted mostly of Pepsi and sandwiches made from luncheon meats, store-bought white bread, and mayonnaise. (He claimed that the huge stack of Pepsi cases in his back room was all that kept the ceiling up.) I don't know whether his aversion to greens was because he didn't know how to cook or he just didn't like them, but this recipe would have solved the first problem, since the easiest way to dress a salad is not to make an emulsion at all. A small amount of oil is drizzled around the salad bowl, the greens are tossed, and then a bit of vinegar is added and the greens are tossed again. This recipe is best made with very good vinegar, not the harsh, acidic brands sold in supermarkets.

        Mixed salad greens for 4
2½   tablespoons olive oil
1   teaspoon fresh herbs or ¼ teaspoon dried
1   tablespoon high-quality white or red wine vinegar, unflavored
        Pinch salt

1. Tear greens into bite-size pieces, discarding tough or bruised pieces. Or use a chef's knife to rough-cut the greens (this works best with tougher greens such as romaine). Wash greens and dry in a salad spinner.
2. Pour olive oil around inside of a large salad bowl. Add greens and herbs. Toss with your hands or a wooden fork and spoon. Add vinegar and salt and toss again. Taste. Add additional oil, vinegar, herbs, or salt as needed.

SERVES 4

Green Salad Vinaigrette

This is a basic dressing for use with salad greens. Unlike the recipe above, the oil and vinegar are briefly whisked together to form an emulsion. This tempers the flavors, especially the harshness of the vinegar as it is suspended in the oil. Use any herbs you like, including tarragon, summer savory, oregano, marjoram, or basil. One teaspoon of lemon or lime juice may be substituted for 1 teaspoon of vinegar. For a balsamic vinaigrette, substitute 2 teaspoons of balsamic vinegar for 1 tablespoon of red wine vinegar. For a milder garlic flavor, simmer 3 crushed cloves of garlic in the olive oil over low heat for 5 minutes. Discard the garlic, allow oil to cool to room temperature, and proceed with recipe.

1   clove garlic
½   teaspoon fresh marjoram, tarragon, basil, parsley, or summer savory or pinch dried
2   tablespoons white or red wine vinegar or lemon juice

Freshly ground pepper

1 teaspoon Dijon mustard

5 tablespoons olive oil

Finely mince garlic and fresh herbs together. Combine with vinegar, pepper, and mustard in a small bowl. Whisk in oil, drop by drop, until an emulsion forms (the mixture starts to thicken). Now add the rest of the oil in a thin stream, whisking constantly for 2 minutes.

MAKES ENOUGH DRESSING TO DRESS A GREEN SALAD FOR 8

Fresh Peas Cooked in Chicken Stock

Peas should be firm and not wrinkled. Remove a pea from its pod before buying — it should be fresh, crisp, and moist. The best peas are the small ones, which are light and delicate. Beware of the large, mealy peas that often find their way into supermarkets. Purchase about ½ pound of unshelled peas per person. Given the fact that fresh peas are not available for most of the year, most of us resort to frozen peas for most of our cooking. This is one vegetable that is worth growing if you have a garden.

2 pounds peas, unshelled
   (approximately 3 cups shelled)

2 tablespoons unsalted butter

½ cup chicken stock or water
   Salt and freshly ground black pepper
   to taste

Shell peas. Put the butter and chicken stock in a saucepan and melt over medium heat. Add peas, reduce heat to low, and simmer until tender, about 8 to 10 minutes. Add salt and pepper to taste.

SERVES 4

MINT AND ONION VARIATION

Add ½ medium onion finely chopped when putting the chicken stock and butter in the saucepan. Proceed with recipe above and toss with 1 tablespoon of chopped fresh mint before serving.

Creamed Spinach with Nutmeg and Parmesan

The problem with some creamed spinach recipes is that they do not have enough fat! The spinach is somewhat acidic, which results in a very unpleasant mouth-feel. This recipe, however, has no such problem. If you are looking for a health recipe, simply steam the spinach and be done with it.

2 cups heavy cream

12 tablespoons (1½ sticks) unsalted butter

3 pounds fresh spinach, trimmed and
   washed

1 cup chopped onion

1 teaspoon salt
   Freshly ground black pepper to taste

⅔ cup grated Parmesan cheese

⅛ teaspoon freshly grated nutmeg

1. Heat the heavy cream in a large sauté pan and let it simmer for 5 minutes or until it has started to reduce and thicken. Add the butter and heat until it melts.

2. Add the spinach and cook, stirring, for 5 minutes or until it is wilted and the cream starts to thicken further. Add the onion, salt, pepper, Parmesan, and nutmeg and stir until the cheese has melted.

SERVES 4

Fried Green Tomatoes

Last year, it was a cool summer, and I had bushels of green tomatoes. I pickled them, I made pasta sauces with them, I used them in casseroles, I stuffed and baked them, and then determined that they really weren't worth eating. This is clearly a case of not letting food go to waste, and I am sure that many New Englanders, given the weather, had plenty of unripe tomatoes come September and the first fall frosts. You can try ripening them by wrapping each tomato in newspaper, placing them in large paper bags, and storing them in the basement. This does work up to a point, but the tomatoes are still lacking in flavor. (That's why I have converted over to yellow cherry tomatoes, which ripen quickly and have plenty of fragrant tomato flavor.) However, they are worth eating fried. Of course, just about anything is worth eating fried, especially the fried funnel cakes served at country fairs, moist and hot inside, slathered with melted butter and dusted with plenty of sugar and cinnamon.

4	green tomatoes
1	cup cornmeal
1	teaspoon salt
1	teaspoon sugar

1	teaspoon dried oregano or
	2 teaspoons fresh, chopped
	Freshly ground black pepper to taste
½	cup buttermilk or milk
½	cup canola or olive oil

1. Wash and dry tomatoes. Remove the stem area using a sharp paring knife. Cut into slices about ¼ inch thick.
2. Mix together cornmeal, salt, sugar, oregano, and a few turns of freshly ground black pepper in a large, heavy plastic bag. Pour buttermilk into a bowl. Heat a 10-inch cast iron skillet. When hot, put in the oil.
3. Dip tomato slices one at a time in the buttermilk, then toss with the cornmeal mixture in the bag. Prepare only as many slices as can be accommodated in the skillet at one time. Fry over medium heat, turning once when slices are golden. Drain on paper towels or paper bags and sprinkle with additional salt. Serve at once.

SERVES 4 TO 6

Stuffed Zucchini

Although this zucchini recipe takes a bit of work, it is one of the better ways of preparing this garden "weed." The stuffing has lots of flavor and the baked zucchini isn't watery or bland.

2	medium zucchini (1½ to 2 pounds)
3	tablespoons olive oil
1	tablespoon unsalted butter
1	cup chopped onion
½	cup chopped red bell pepper
1	tablespoon minced anchovies

2   cloves garlic, minced
2   cups country bread, finely chopped or
    ground into coarse crumbs
1   cup lightly packed basil, chopped
2   tablespoons capers
¼   cup imported olives, pitted and
    chopped
1   large egg
    Salt and freshly ground black pepper
    to taste

1. Heat oven to 450 degrees. Trim ends off zucchini and cut in half lengthwise. Using a 1-teaspoon measuring spoon, scoop out the center of each half, leaving about a ½-inch shell. Chop the scooped-out flesh and reserve. Arrange zucchini halves cut side down on a baking sheet and brush the skin sides with 1 tablespoon of the olive oil. Roast until barely tender, about 12 minutes. Remove zucchini from the oven and reduce temperature to 350 degrees.
2. Heat the remaining 2 tablespoons olive oil and the butter in a large iron skillet over medium-high heat. When the foam subsides, add the onion, bell pepper, and anchovies. Reduce heat to medium and cook for about 8 minutes or until very soft and lightly browned. Add the reserved chopped zucchini and sauté for 3 minutes. Add the garlic and cook 1 additional minute. Remove from heat and transfer contents of skillet to a large bowl.
3. Add remaining ingredients along with plenty of salt and pepper. Mix thoroughly (this is best done with your hands) to be sure that the egg is incorporated. Stuff the zucchini halves and bake in heated oven for 20 minutes or until the stuffing is golden brown and firm to the touch.

SERVES 4

Sauté of Zucchini or Summer Squash

This is a very simple recipe, but one that all cooks should have in their repertoire given the abundance of zucchini in the summer. By salting the zucchini and letting it drain in a colander, much of the excess water is removed, which dramatically improves this dish.

1   pound zucchini or summer squash
2   teaspoons salt
2   tablespoons high-quality olive oil
1   tablespoon butter
1   clove garlic, minced
¼   cup chopped fresh flat-leaf parsley or a
    combination of fresh herbs such as
    basil, tarragon, thyme, etc.
    Freshly ground black pepper to taste

1. Slice zucchini into half-inch-thick rounds and discard the ends. Place in a colander and sprinkle with the salt. Toss to coat evenly. Leave for 30 minutes and shake the colander occasionally.
2. Heat a heavy skillet on medium-high heat. Add the olive oil and butter. When the butter stops foaming, add the garlic and sauté for 1 minute. Add the zucchini. Cook, stirring frequently, for 5 to 7 minutes or until the zucchini is light brown; tender but not mushy. Remove from heat.
3. Add the parsley or other fresh herbs and the pepper. Stir to combine. Serve hot or at room temperature.

SERVES 6 AS A SIDE DISH

Master Recipe for Vegetable Marinade

This is a good way of dealing with surplus vegetable produce. You can marinate the vegetables the day before, refrigerate overnight, and then throw some of the marinated vegetables into a salad or use them as a side dish. The best vegetables for this marinade are green beans, cauliflower, mushrooms, and carrots. You can prepare them separately or use a combination. The cooking times below will produce very crisp vegetables rather than thoroughly cooked specimens.

2	cups water
½	cup white wine
⅓	cup white wine vinegar
½	cup olive oil
4	cloves garlic, minced
½	teaspoon whole black peppercorns
4	whole cloves
2	bay leaves
1	teaspoon whole fennel seed
½	teaspoon mustard seed
2	teaspoons fresh oregano or 1 teaspoon dried

Bring all ingredients to a simmer in a large nonreactive saucepan and cook for 10 minutes. Add prepared vegetables and cook covered as indicated below. Remove from the heat and transfer vegetables and marinade to a large bowl or glass container. Let cool to room temperature and refrigerate overnight or at least for several hours. Serve vegetables as a side course or as part of a salad. The marinade can also be reduced — boiled down until reduced by half in volume — and then poured over the vegetables as a sauce.

To Prepare Cauliflower

Use a 1- to 1½-pound head, the florets only. Trim off stems and stalk. Cook for about 6 minutes.

To Prepare Carrots

Use 1 pound of carrots. Cut off tops and end. If large, cut into quarters lengthwise. If medium or small, halve. Cut into 2-inch pieces. Cook for 7 to 8 minutes.

To Prepare Mushrooms

Use up to 2 pounds of mushrooms. Wash and trim off ends of stems. Cook for 4 to 5 minutes.

To Prepare Green Beans

Use up to 1½ pounds and trim off ends. Cook for 5 to 6 minutes.

Country Bakery

THERE IS A STORY in *Old Squire's Farm* in which C. A. Stephens tells of his grandmother's mug-bread, so named because it was started in a lavender-and-gold-banded white porcelain mug. (This bread is an old Yankee recipe and was also called milk-yeast bread, patent bread, milk-emptyings bread, and salt-rising bread. A recipe for the latter can be found in *Beard on Bread*.) In the evening, his grandmother would mix "two tablespoons of cornmeal, ten of boiled milk, and half a teaspoonful of salt in that mug, and set it on the low mantel shelf behind the kitchen stove funnel, where it would keep uniformly warm overnight." At breakfast time, his grandmother would peer into the mug to see if the little "eyes" had begun to open in the mixture. If everything worked out as planned, water and flour were stirred in and the mixture was put back on the shelf to rise until lunchtime. It was baked into "cartwheels" — foot-wide, yellow-brown loaves just an inch thick that were served with fresh Jersey butter and all the canned berries a boy could eat. But some mornings, the mug would disappear suddenly and a strong sulfurous smell would linger in the kitchen. In that case, the wrong microbe had "obtained possession of the mug." One never knew how it was going to turn out. It was this element of chance, the not-knowing, that made that mug-bread taste so fine.

Even today, with standardized yeasts and flour, some breads rise faster than others, some rise higher, and some bake up lighter. All of the loaves I baked for this chapter proves that, although one can develop a standardized recipe that works admirably, no two loaves are exactly the same. Somehow, cooking, like everything else in life, is not an exact science. It is a bit of adventure and should be approached with a big helping of wild enthusiasm and risk-taking. As Harriet Van Horne once said, "Cooking is like love. It should be entered into with abandon or not at all."

For those growing up on a Vermont farm, the unknown was a constant neighbor, sharpening one's appetite for a host of activities from hunting to fishing, from hitching up a new team to boiling off maple sap. The sap might run well or it might not, the fish might be biting or not, a six-point buck might walk right past your tree stand or not, and that new team might hitch up well together or not, turning your wagon over in a ditch or running your seeder into a pile of rocks. Like the New England weather, one just never did know what was in store. That little stream, no more than a trickle in August, might wash out your culvert when the snows melted in the January thaw, or your crop of buckwheat might come in poorly if it didn't rain soon after planting. Our family used to hike up to the top of our mountain near the small abandoned barn on the ridge to pick blackberries. Some years we would get a bucketful and other years, even when the weather was good, we'd get no more than a quart of hard, small berries. It was a chance we were used to taking. But when the berries were fat and plentiful the sky was bluer, the air scented more sweetly with fern and pine, as if all the good memories of the lean years were collapsed into one enchanted summer.

These days, our small Vermont town has a "coming of age" ritual, which also has unexpected outcomes. There is a cave at the mouth of the Green River up in Beartown and it's located in a bend, the entrance hidden by a patch of stinging nettles. Dads take their sons and daughters up through the cave when they think they're ready to negotiate the long, dark passage. A few summers ago, it was time for my daughter Whitney, then seven years old, to make her first visit. She is a bit shy and never the first to rush into the unknown. I was apprehensive about the trip.

With some friends, we packed a bunch of local kids into the flatbed of our old Ford pickup. The truck was left at the end of the road and we walked up through an abandoned camp, then to the mouth of the cave, where each child was given a candle. I went first, with five kids in line behind me, Whitney in the middle of the pack. The entrance is small and the cave starts out narrow — about five feet high — and the stream that runs through it is deep and searingly cold. In the weak half-light of the candles, we scrambled back to a large circular room where we climbed up a funnel to the next level. The cave narrowed considerably at this point, and I made my way to the end, a small opening where the water bubbled up from a deep spring. I looked back and saw my daughter's mud-streaked face in the flickering glow. She looked confident, and gave me a quick, intimate smile that said, "I did it." The other kids were far behind in the darkness, too scared to follow.

Whitney called out, "Come on, what are you guys afraid of?" I was proud, of course, but also filled with the joy of the unexpected. It was the journey together that provided the yeast that day, struggling through the dark cave, not knowing if she would make it all the way to the end. Next year it would be her younger sister's turn, but that could wait. On that hot August day, the mug-bread had turned out just fine.

I HAVE BEEN attending the same church in Vermont since 1955. Built in 1877, it stands on the edge of a cornfield by the Green River, and if I sit in the right pew, I can look out over the pasture where we still harvest corn with a team of mules hitched to a mechanical corn binder.

Inside the church, things haven't changed much either. Hymns are played on an Estey pump organ made in the 1880s, and the carpet covering the foot pedals is now threadbare. The chandelier is Victorian but simple — gray metal scrollwork capped by large tulip globes. The pews themselves are original, made of oak that has turned dark over the years. It's a modest church — practical and spare — but it serves its purpose in the Yankee tradition of economy and function.

Since our town is without a restaurant or store, one of the church's functions is to serve as a meeting place. After the service, the congregation heads for the back room for coffee and gossip. At one such coffee hour, I was working on my second biscuit when Junior Bentley came up and asked, "What do you hear about those electric bread machines?" (For my response, see page 189.)

Now that was quite a question coming from a man whose toolbox contains a hammer, a pair of pliers, a grease gun, and a few yards of baling twine. He owns three vintage Farmall tractors (one of which he bought new in 1949); he knows how to keep them running and uses each for a specific purpose. Like a good cook, he prefers his equipment simple and well made — he doesn't pay for extras. Yet here he was, asking about a $250 piece of kitchen gadgetry that is supposed to replace the best tools any farmer can have: his hands.

Now I have kneaded bread by hand, in a food processor, and in a standing mixer. I have used a microwave oven to quick-rise the dough. I have made dozens of loaves of bread in bread machines. I once spent six months of weekends figuring out how to make a rustic, chewy loaf at home. And I have found that the secret to bread is that it is easy to make and endlessly forgiving, and the process of bread making is full of conventional wisdom, much of which is dead wrong.

Do You Really Need
to Proof Yeast?
If you are like most home cooks, you still believe that it is necessary to let yeast and water react with each other for 10 minutes before mixing a dough. What if you just skip this step? Well, I stopped proofing yeast years ago with no ill effect. I simply dissolve the yeast in water and then mix it in with the flour. I then followed up with phone calls to the King Arthur Flour company and to Fleischmann's Yeast to find out why proofing is still recommended. They agreed that proofing yeast is no longer necessary. I suppose that

many years ago either the yeast was not a sure thing — you might end up with a bowlful of flour, water, and dead yeast — or that the yeast needed more time in contact with water in order to get it started. Modern yeasts, however, have no such problem, so don't bother proofing.

Which Yeast Should I Use?

In a kitchen test using seven different yeasts (Fleischmann's Rapid-Rise Yeast, Fleischmann's Active Dry Yeast, Fleischmann's Cake Yeast, Red Star Quick-Rise, King Arthur Regular Instant Yeast, King Arthur Special Instant Yeast, and Red Star Instant Yeast) tested with a basic American bread, the staff of *Cook's Illustrated* determined that three Fleischmann's products rated very highly — the instant yeast, the cake yeast, and the rapid rise yeast. Since the instant yeast (instant yeast and rapid-rise yeast are not the same) and cake yeasts are often hard to find, I recommend using a rapid-rise yeast for any bread that uses fats and/or sugars. (There are two reasons why rapid-rise yeast is in fact more rapid. First, the enzymes in the yeast are more active, and second, this form of yeast has an open, porous structure which allows it to absorb moisture instantly.) This is a surprising result since I, and many home cooks, have assumed that a "rapid-rise" product would deliver inferior bread. It doesn't. In fact, in addition to cutting rising time by at least 50 percent and sometimes by two-thirds, the tasters also were convinced that the bread had more flavor and was sweeter. One theory is that a rapid-rise yeast provides less time for the creation of the acidic by-products of fermentation, hence a sweeter loaf. It is also true that

rapid-rise yeast has a superior enzyme structure (to regular active yeast) which converts starches to sugar faster than the regular-rise varieties. Most people do not realize that yeast is a plant, not a bacteria, and different types of yeasts have different qualities, just as do different varieties of, say, roses. Rapid-rise yeast was genetically engineered to reproduce the best characteristics of yeasts from around the world. Although genetic engineering often results in loss of flavor, our blind taste tests confirmed that, in this case, it produced an excellent product.

With breads made from just flour, water, salt, and yeast, slower methods of rising the dough can assist flavor development (see below). However, for most of the breads in this chapter, with the exception of the rustic country bread, rapid-rise yeast is fine. You make the substitution, using the same quantity of rapid-rise as for regular active yeast, and simply expect rising times to be about half as long.

Do Rising Times Affect Flavor and Texture?

If you want to develop more flavor in a European-style bread recipe that uses no fat, make a sponge and let it sit overnight. A sponge is a mixture of flour, water, and just a small amount of yeast (usually ½ teaspoon) which is allowed to develop slowly. This is the easiest means of producing a loaf with some depth of flavor. (For a recipe that uses 6 cups of flour, mix together 1 cup of water, 2 cups of flour, and ½ teaspoon of yeast. Cover with plastic wrap and let sit at room temperature overnight. The next morning, mix the bubbly sponge into the remaining ingredients and proceed with the recipe.) However, using this sponge method with breads that have stronger flavor ingredients such as butter, milk, or a sweetener may not be worth the trouble. I tested this notion when making a basic whole wheat loaf (see recipe, page 208) and found that a one-hour sponge produced a light bread, with a soft, cottony texture and mild flavor. A four-hour sponge had a nice rise but was also on the bland side, thus contradicting the notion of flavor development. Finally, I tested a bread that rose three times (instead of the regulation two-rise system) and this loaf edged out a first place over the basic master recipe with only two rises. The difference was very subtle and deemed not to be worth the extra time. So I would skip the sponge method for American-style breads, reserving it for leaner, simpler recipes with no fat. By the way, I came across an interesting recipe called "peggy tub" bread (the dough is kneaded, wrapped in a kitchen towel, and then immersed in a tub of water to rise). The *Cook's Illustrated* test kitchen tried it and found that the resulting loaf had a tight crumb, sour finish, and a very light texture. So much for this method.

Is Kneading by Hand Essential?
No. Kneading by hand is pleasurable and many people like to do it. But you can knead a basic bread dough in a food processor (using the metal blade) in *only 40 seconds!* You can also throw it in the bowl of a standing mixer. You can under-knead and overknead and still get good bread. Using a KitchenAid standing mixer, I have kneaded a whole wheat bread dough for four, eight, twelve, and sixteen minutes, respectively, *with no dis-*

cernible difference in the finished loaves. This confirmed my suspicion, based on previous bread testing, that kneading is far from the exact science that some cookbooks would have you believe.

What's the Difference Between Bread Flour and All-Purpose?
The difference is the wheat that the flour is made from. A bread flour is made from a "harder" wheat, which simply means that the kernel of wheat is physically harder. It also means that the wheat has a higher percentage of protein. Bread flour usually contains 12 percent to 14 percent protein, all-purpose is in the 10 percent to 12 percent range, and pastry and cake flours run under 10 percent.

When making bread, the gluten (protein) is developed through kneading. This creates a structure that is adept at trapping the gases caused by the yeast. This in turn results in a light, fine-textured bread. With less protein or gluten, the structure does not develop as well, and you end up with a slightly denser, coarser loaf. But the difference is modest at best and you can substitute all-purpose for bread flour without major problems. In my testing, I did find, however, that bread flour will absorb more water than all-purpose (so will whole wheat and rye flours). I suggest that if you do substitute all-purpose for bread flour, you reduce the liquid by 15 percent.

What Is Whole Wheat Flour?
A wheat berry contains three elements: the outer bran layer, the germ, and then the heart of the berry, the endosperm. In traditional whole wheat flour the whole berry is ground whereas all-purpose white

flour uses just the endosperm with the bran and germ removed. Whole wheat graham flour is similar to regular whole wheat flour but it is more of a medium grind than finely ground whole wheat flour. (Graham flour is often called for in older cookbooks, and the most probable origin of the name is a Presbyterian minister, Sylvester Graham, who was a believer in whole grains, especially whole wheat flour. An educated guess is that "graham" flour was no more than whole wheat flour. In addition, breads made from whole grain flour were often referred to as Graham breads. Over time, he developed quite a following, which gave birth to Grahamite societies, *The Graham Journal of Health and Longevity,* and grocery stores that sold his "health food" products.) Whole wheat flakes are simply the entire wheat berry put through a series of rollers to make flakes, a similar process to the one used to make oats for oatmeal. Wheat germ is simply the germ of the wheat berry which is separated from the rest of the berry through sifting.

Should I Purchase a Bread Machine?

The short answer is that bread machines are lousy ovens. The crust is pitiful and the interior is mediocre at best. They are, however, great kneaders and, to a lesser extent, proofing boxes. Just don't bake bread in them. Most newer machines have dough rising settings that allow you to remove the dough after it has risen once. Then place it in a bread pan (or shape it and let it sit in a rising basket — often referred to by professional bakers as banettons — or on a counter) and let it rise a second time. Finally, bake it in a regular oven. The results will be vastly better than when baked in a bread machine. That being said, I think that bread machines are unnecessary, expensive gadgets.

Don't Forget the Salt

I once made a loaf of bread and forgot to add the salt. It was inedible. Tasteless, flat, empty — completely lacking in appeal. (It is true that there are traditional Italian breads that use no salt at all. I suppose that if served with very salty foods, they might be fine, but I do not care for them. Bread without salt is like pastry dough without butter. It ain't got much taste.) In bread baking, salt is king. I use 1 slightly heaping tablespoon of *kosher* salt per 6 cups of flour. If you use table salt, try 2 teaspoons per 3 cups of flour. Kosher salt is not as salty as table salt when measured by volume. Don't forget that a little sugar or honey is also helpful. It will brighten the flavor of the flour and also help to brown the crust. I usually use 1 tablespoon of honey per 3 cups of flour.

Milk Versus Water

Lots of bread recipes use milk, eggs, or melted butter. These ingredients add fat, which yields a softer, more cakelike texture. A Parker House roll, for example, is a simple bread recipe with fat in it. It is very soft and pliable, not dense and chewy. So if you like bread with some tooth in it, don't add fat. If you like a nice soft sandwich or tea loaf, go ahead and add dairy products.

The Truth about Sourdough Bread

Many bakers tell you to make a sourdough sponge (this is flour, salt, and water which is allowed to sit around and attract wild yeast spores — this process takes a few days) and then use a part of it as a starter for baking bread. (You can also purchase a sourdough starter or add a small smount of commercial yeast to the starter to help it along.) You keep it in a refrigerator and have to feed it every week. If you don't, the bacteria will run out of food and die. This is great for professionals who bake bread daily or at least once per week but it is nonsense for most home cooks. It's like having a pet. If you go away for two weeks, somebody has to come over and feed your starter! If you are like me, your pet starter will have died a slow death in the refrigerator from lack of attention within 3 months. Nancy Silverton, of the La Brea Bakery in Los Angeles, claims that she can resuscitate a starter after a few months' inattention in the refrigerator. This may be the case, but it takes a few days to bring it back to life, which is not very practical for the home cook.

Is It Possible to Overknead Bread Dough?

Well, yes and no. A harder, high-gluten flour such as bread flour will maintain its strength and elasticity longer than an all-purpose flour, which is weaker. That is one reason why commercial bakers use such hard flour — it stands up well to the action of commercial machines. However, at home it is almost impossible to overknead dough, especially when using bread flour. It is possible to overdo it in a food processor, but you should have no trouble with a dough hook in a standing mixer. (If you do not have a heavy-duty mixer, I suggest that you use the "low" setting rather than the medium speed often called for. The latter can cause damage to lower-horsepower mixers when used with wet, sticky doughs.) I have also found that bread can be kneaded for just 7 or 8 minutes in a standing mixer and the resulting bread was as good as a 15-minute knead. Kneading time is not crucial.

What About Oven Temperatures?

For American-style breads, a moderate oven is best (350 to 375 degrees). European-style breads, such as the rustic Country Bread on page 201, should be baked in a very hot oven (450 degrees), since they contain a higher percentage of water and a hotter oven is necessary to develop a good crust. Also, the fats and sweeteners in American breads will tend to burn the crust if baked in very hot ovens.

Bread Baking Equipment

There are wooden peels and metal peels (peels are the large long-handled spatulas used by bread and pizza bakers to get bread in and out of the oven). I have both and don't have a preference, although the metal peels are slightly thinner and easier to slide under the loaf. Do not flour the peel — use cornmeal. A sticky dough will not slide off a flour-dusted peel but will glide right off a peel sprinkled with lots of cornmeal.

An instant-read thermometer is essential. Stick it into the bottom of the loaf to tell when it is properly cooked. (For breads baked in bread pans, you can insert the thermometer into the end of the loaf down at an angle into the center of the bread. This avoids the problem of having to remove the loaf from the pan to measure the internal temperature.) A wet dough needs to be baked to 208 degrees, but regular loaves are done at around 190. (Most books tell you to thump the bottom of the loaf until it sounds hollow, which is akin to predicting winter weather based on the toughness of corn husks, a common theory in our Vermont town. Use the thermometer unless you are a pro. See illustration on page 211.

DOES STEAM MAKE A BETTER CRUST? The key to a great crust, when baking a crusty European-style loaf, is steam. (Most American breads use fat and the crust is not supposed to be thick and chewy.) Some bakers throw ice cubes on the floor of the oven. Others pour hot water into a pan at the beginning of baking. Some use a spritzer and mist the outside of the dough every few minutes. My tests have shown that hot water is the best option. I find it best to place my water for steaming in a small *preheated* pan placed on a separate rack in the oven. The theory among bread pros is that you want steam immediately, in the first few minutes of baking. A cold pan will not do the trick — the hot water will just sit there. By using 2 cups of boiling hot water, you get both instant steam and enough residual water to keep a nice steamy environment throughout the cooking process. A preheated pan, however, will vaporize some of the hot water the second it is poured in, which leads me to the issue of safety. Wear thick oven mitts and a long-sleeved shirt when pouring the hot water into the pan — a long-spouted watering can works well.

SHORTCUTS, TIPS, AND ADVICE
- A wetter dough always produces a better crust and more air holes. A drier dough is easier to handle, but also gives you a thinner crust and a more refined texture. Try adding or subtracting flour a quarter cup at a time from any bread recipe if you want to vary the texture of the loaf.
- Rising times vary a great deal depending on temperature and other factors, including the number of yeast spores in the air. Therefore, do not rely on times provided by cookbook authors. Every kitchen is different.
- For denser bread, let the dough rise only about 75 percent during the second rise (not double).
- A serrated knife works well for slashing the top of a large loaf of bread.
- Use a very quick backward jerk to slide a bread loaf off the peel.
- Inevitably, bread crust will start to lose its crunch, especially in humid weather. Just pop the loaf back into a 400 degree oven for up to 10 minutes to restore it.
- If the baked loaf is dry, too much flour may have been added to the dough. I find that one way to avoid this problem is to slightly moisten your hands instead of adding flour to avoid sticking. You will also produce a slightly drier loaf if you substitute regular sugar for honey in a bread recipe without increasing the water.
- There are three reasons why bread doesn't rise properly. The water can be too hot, killing the yeast (temperatures over 125 degrees will kill some yeasts); too much flour may have been added to the dough, which made a heavy, squat loaf; or the bread was placed in a cool, drafty spot to rise. To cure the latter, heat your oven for 10 minutes at 200 degrees and turn it off. Now the oven can be used as a proofing box. Thanks to one of the *Cook's Illustrated* readers, I discovered that a microwave

oven can also be used as a proofing box. Fill a 2-cup Pyrex measuring cup almost full with water, place it in the microwave, and bring to a boil. Now place the dough (which is in a bowl covered with plastic wrap) in the turned-off oven, and the preheated water will keep the oven at the proper temperature for proofing. Also check to make sure that the expiration date on your yeast has not passed. I have made bread with yeast that expired 6 months before and found a noticeable lack of yeast activity.

- If the bread appears rippled with air pockets underneath the crust, the dough over-proofed before baking. That is, the dough was allowed to rise too much after it was shaped. If you notice that your dough has more than doubled in volume after shaping, punch it down, shape it a second time, and let it rise properly.
- If the bread doesn't rise in the oven, the dough was either under- or over-proofed. If you find, during the first rise, that the dough has risen too much, simply punch it down and let it rise a second time.
- If, after shaping the dough, you are not pleased with your efforts, simply let the dough rest for a few minutes, covered with a damp cloth. Now the dough is sufficiently rested and can be shaped a second time. Otherwise, the dough can be elastic and difficult to manage.
- If the dough appears sticky and wet, try to resist the temptation to add more flour. Many of my recipes use wet doughs that are almost "pourable." As the dough rises, it hydrates — that is, the water becomes more evenly distrib-

uted — and the texture will become very soft and smooth. Do not add additional flour.
- It is sometimes difficult to tell if a shaped loaf has doubled in volume as called for in a recipe. I use a plastic tub purchased from the King Arthur Flour Baker's Catalogue which has clear markings along the side that allow the home baker to measure the growth of the dough.

Molasses Country Bread

The choice of flour for this bread is not crucial — bread flour is best — but you do have a few alternatives. Regular supermarket bread flour has a protein content of 12 percent to 13 percent, whereas the flour I prefer to use is closer to 14 percent. (This type of flour is available from the King Arthur Flour Company. Call them at 800-827-6836 or write to The Baker's Catalogue, Box 876, Norwich, VT 05055-0876). If you wish to use this high-protein flour, increase the water in the dough from 1⅓ cups to 1½ cups, and I recommend that you knead the dough by machine. Hand-kneading with such a hard flour is quite difficult. You might also try making this recipe with King Arthur all-purpose flour by decreasing the water from 1½ cups to 1¼ cups. The results are good, although I find the bread to be a bit tougher in texture than I like.

THE SPONGE

½ teaspoon active dry yeast (not rapid-rise)
1 cup cool water
1 cup bread flour
1 cup whole wheat flour

THE DOUGH

½ cup rye flour
1 cup whole wheat flour (whole wheat graham flour preferred)
¼ cup wheat germ
1⅓ cups warm water
2 tablespoons molasses
2 teaspoons table salt
2¼ cups bread flour, or as needed
Coarse cornmeal for sprinkling on peel (optional)

1. *For the sponge:* Dissolve yeast in water in a medium-sized bowl. With a rubber spatula, mix in flours to create a stiff, wet dough. Cover bowl with plastic wrap; let sit at room temperature for at least 5 hours, preferably overnight.

2. *For the dough:* If you are kneading by hand, place the sponge and all dough ingredients, except the bread flour and cornmeal, in a large bowl. Stir mixture with a wooden spoon, about 5 minutes. Using the spoon, work in reserved bread flour and turn dough out onto a floured surface. Knead for 10 minutes, adding flour in 1 tablespoon increments only when absolutely necessary, being careful not to incorporate more than ¼ cup of additional flour. The dough will remain sticky but become smooth. Transfer dough to a large, lightly oiled bowl. Cover with plastic wrap; let rise until tripled in size, at least 2 hours.

3. Turn dough out onto a lightly floured surface. Lightly dust hands and top of dough with flour. Lightly press dough into a disk. Fold all four sides toward the center, overlapping edges slightly. Transfer dough, smooth side down, to a colander or basket lined with heavily floured muslin or a tea towel. Tent loosely with a large sheet of aluminum foil; let rise until almost doubled in size, at least 45 minutes.

4. As soon as dough begins to rise, adjust oven rack to low-center position and arrange quarry tiles to form an 18 x 12-inch surface (or larger). (You can also use a pizza stone.) On lowest oven rack, place a small baking pan or cast-iron skillet to hold water. Heat oven to 450 degrees.

5. Liberally sprinkle cornmeal over entire surface of a baker's peel (or place a large sheet of heavy-duty parchment paper on the baker's peel). Invert risen dough onto peel and remove muslin or tea towel. Use scissors or a serrated knife to cut three slashes on top of dough.

6. Slide dough, with a quick jerk, from peel onto tiles. Carefully pour 2 cups hot water into heated pan or cast-iron skillet. Bake until an instant-read thermometer, when inserted in bottom of bread, registers 205 to 208 degrees and crust is very dark brown, 35 to 40 minutes, turning bread after 25 minutes if not browning evenly. Turn oven off, open door, and let bread remain in oven 10 minutes longer. Remove from oven and let cool on a cake rack to room temperature before slicing, about 2 hours. To crisp the crust, heat in a 450 degree oven for 10 minutes.

MAKES 1 LARGE LOAF

FOOD PROCESSOR VARIATION

Mix half of sponge, half of flours, and half of molasses in a food processor fitted with metal blade. Pulse until roughly blended, three or four 1-second pulses. With machine running, slowly add ⅔ cup water through the feed tube; process until dough forms a ball. Let sit for 3 minutes, then add half the salt and process to form smooth dough, about 30 seconds longer. Transfer dough to large lightly oiled bowl, leaving metal blade in processor (some dough will remain under blade). Repeat process with remaining half of ingredients. Proceed with recipe.

STANDING MIXER VARIATION

In step 2, mix flours, water, wheat germ, molasses, and sponge in bowl of an electric mixer with a rubber spatula. Knead, using dough hook attachment, on lowest speed until dough is smooth, about 12 minutes, adding salt during final 3 minutes. Transfer dough to large lightly oiled bowl. Cover with plastic wrap; let rise until tripled in size, at least 2 hours. Proceed with step 3.

Oatmeal Rasin Bread

I can hardly see a loaf of homemade bread without thinking of the tens of thousands of loaves kneaded, proofed, and baked by Marie Briggs in the yellow farmhouse. A canvas cover was put over the dining room table to serve as a surface for kneading. A wire brush dipped into lard was used for greasing the sometimes rusty bread pans, which were then set, full of dough, on the top shelf of the Kalamazoo stove for rising. Finally, the loaves were baked in the wood stove and also in the back room where she had a small propane gas oven as well. But work was always stopped exactly at 4 P.M., when tea was served with just-baked country bread, often oatmeal raisin, or molasses cookies, or perhaps simply baking powder biscuits slathered with apple butter. She was all business, without one wasted movement, but she knew how to pace herself, stopping for lunch and tea at exactly the same time every day.

The recipe below is similar to Marie's; it is virtually foolproof and, if one uses rapid-rise yeast, it is also quick. In general, American breads tend to have more fat in the form of butter and milk than do comparable European loaves. This makes a more tender loaf suitable for sandwiches. Beware if you knead this dough in a standing mixer. It does have a tendency to climb up the dough hook, so you will have to stop the mixer a few times to scrape the dough back down into the bowl.

For those of you who knead by hand, I have developed a mixing method that uses only part of the flour to start so that this very loose dough can be mixed with a wooden spoon. This develops the gluten in the flour while making the mixing process easier. In the second stage, more flour is added and then the dough is kneaded by hand.

I decided to eliminate the use of hot water in the oven for steaming, which I find very useful for developing a crust on a chewier, crustier loaf, but this fattier bread recipe is softer and more refined. The simple, relatively tender crust is just fine for this tender bread.

3	cups unbleached all-purpose flour, or as needed
1	heaping teaspoon salt
2	tablespoons honey
1	cup warm milk (125 degrees)
⅓	cup warm water (125 degrees)
1	package rapid-rise yeast
¾	cup quick-cooking oats
2	tablespoons melted butter
¾	cup raisins tossed with a pinch of flour

1. Heat oven to 200 degrees for 10 minutes and then turn it off. After the oven is turned off, mix 1½ cups flour and the salt in a large bowl. Combine the honey, milk, and water, add the yeast, stirring to dissolve, and then add to the flour mixture. Add the oats and melted butter and stir with a wooden spoon for 5 minutes. Work in the remaining 1½ cups of flour and turn dough onto a floured surface.
2. Knead for 7 minutes and then press dough into a rectangle. Sprinkle the raisins over the surface, then fold the corners into the center and continue kneading for another 3 minutes, incorporating flour in 1-tablespoon increments but only when absolutely necessary. Do *not* incorporate more than ¼ cup additional flour. The resulting dough will be satiny smooth. Form it into a round and place top-down in a very lightly oiled bowl. Rub the top of the dough around the bowl to very lightly coat with oil. Turn dough right side up. Cover with plastic wrap and place in the warmed oven until dough doubles in size, about 40 minutes. Remove from

oven and heat oven to 350 degrees. Grease a 9 x 5 x 3-inch loaf pan.
3. Turn dough onto a lightly floured surface and gently press into a rectangle 1 inch thick and no wider than the length of the loaf pan. Roll it firmly into a cylinder, pressing gently with your fingers with each turn to make sure that the dough sticks to itself. Turn seam side up and pinch seam closed. Place dough in pan seam side down and press gently so that the dough touches all four sides of pan. Cover with oiled plastic wrap and set aside in a warm spot for 20 minutes or until dough doubles in size.
4. Place the pan on a middle rack in the oven. Bake until an instant-read thermometer inserted in the middle of the loaf registers 195 degrees, about 40 minutes. Remove from oven and loaf pan and cool on a wire rack.

MAKES 1 LOAF

Anadama Bread

This is my favorite of Marie's breads, the one I remember eating when I first heard the story about Claude and Chester Hayes. It seems that many years ago, when people still used horse-drawn carts, the Hayes brothers had decided to take their cart out at night to jack a deer since they needed some venison. They got lucky and shot a large doe, and as they were coming back through town, they realized that they were about to go by the old Hughes place. At that time, it was owned by old Charlie Randall, who had thick, wire-frame glasses and couldn't see too well. But he was curious, and peeked out through the front window each time someone went by. Well, Chester decided they had to do something to avoid getting caught, so he said to Claude, "Let's prop that old doe up between us so Charlie thinks it's just another person." Well, that's what they did and, sure enough, as they went by they could see the curtain pulled back and there was old Charlie's head peeking through the window.

The next day they were down at the country store and they ran into Charlie, who came right up to them and asked, "So who was that coming down with you last night?" Chester was quick, so he shot back, "Just a local girl." Charlie kind of squinted with a twinkle in his eye and said, "Kinda ugly, ain't she?"

By the way, the name of this bread comes from an often repeated story about a husband who returned home to find his wife gone and no dinner on the table. He concocted this recipe and it was named "anadama" a shortening of the invective "Anna, damn her!"

½	cup water
¼	cup cornmeal
3½	cups unbleached all-purpose flour, or as needed
1	heaping teaspoon salt
¼	cup molasses
¾	cup warm milk (125 degrees)
⅓	cup warm water (125 degrees)
1	package rapid-rise yeast
2	tablespoons melted butter

1. Heat oven to 200 degrees for 10 minutes and then turn it off. After the oven is turned off, heat ½ cup water in a small saucepan until boiling. Over medium heat, add the cornmeal and stir constantly for 4 minutes. In a large bowl, mix 1½ cups flour and the salt, and then stir in the cornmeal mixture and the molasses. Combine the milk and water, add the yeast, stirring to dissolve, and then add to the flour mixture. Add the melted butter and stir with a wooden spoon for 5 minutes. Work in an additional 1½ cups of flour and turn dough out onto a floured surface.

2. Knead for 10 minutes, incorporating flour in 1 tablespoon increments but only when absolutely necessary. Do *not* incorporate more than ¼ cup additional flour. The resulting dough will be satiny smooth. Form dough into a round and place top down in very lightly oiled bowl. Rub the top of the dough around the bowl to coat lightly with oil. Turn dough right side up. Cover with plastic wrap and place in the warmed oven until dough doubles in size, about 40 minutes. Remove from oven and heat oven to 350 degrees. Grease a 9 x 5 x 3-inch loaf pan.

3. Turn dough onto a lightly floured surface and gently press into a rectangle 1 inch thick and no wider than the length of the loaf pan. Roll it firmly into a cylinder, pressing gently with your fingers with each turn to make sure that the dough sticks to itself. Turn seam side up and pinch seam closed. Place dough in pan seam side down and press gently so that the dough touches all four sides of pan. Cover with plastic wrap and set aside in a warm spot for 20 minutes or until dough has doubled in size.

4. Place loaf pan on a middle rack in the oven. Bake until an instant-read thermometer registers 195 degrees, about 30 to 40 minutes. Remove from oven and loaf pan and cool on a wire rack.

MAKES 1 LOAF

Pullman Loaf
(White Sandwich Bread)

This bread is referred to as a pullman loaf or in France as *pain de mie*. Traditionally, it is baked in a pan with a sliding top, which produces not the typical rounded loaf but a rectangular, flat-topped bread. Since these pans are hard to find and cost close to $40, you can cover the dough with buttered aluminum foil, place a cookie sheet on top of the baking pan, and cover that with an iron skillet or other weights. (Be careful if you try this with a traditional loaf pan that measures 9 x 5 x 3 inches. You may find that the cookie sheet and weights are unbalanced and fall off easily. Use a larger pan that measures 10 x 5½ x 3 inches if you want to approximate a real pullman loaf. This pan is more stable.) Of course, you can simply bake this bread in any old bread pan if you don't care much about the shape of the loaf, which is what I do. (This recipe differs from the American white bread recipe in this chapter in that it uses a great deal of butter and little milk. Most original recipes for a pullman loaf use all water and no milk — I prefer a bit of milk for softer texture.)

6½	cups all-purpose flour
1	tablespoon salt
8	tablespoons (1 stick) cold unsalted butter, cut into small pieces
1½	cups water
1	cup milk
2	packages rapid-rise yeast
1	tablespoon sugar

1. In a very large bowl (or in the bowl of a food processor), whisk together the flour and salt. Cut the butter into the flour with a pastry blender, 2 knives, or your fingers. (If you have a food processor, pulse 7 or 8 times until the flour turns mealy and there are no bits of butter unincorporated.)

2. Combine the water and milk in a saucepan and heat until the temperature reaches 115 to 120 degrees. (The milk will be warm, not hot.) Remove from heat, add yeast and sugar, and stir to dissolve. Add the yeast mixture to the flour and stir to combine with a large rubber spatula or wooden spoon. If dough is too dry, add a bit more water. If too wet, add a bit more flour.

3. Knead the dough for 10 minutes by hand. (This can also be done in the bowl of a heavy-duty standing mixer equipped with a dough hook.) Do not add much extra flour. The dough should be smooth and elastic when done. Place in a lightly oiled bowl and cover with plastic wrap. Let rise in a warm spot for 40 to 50 minutes or until dough doubles in volume.

4. Punch down gently, knead for 3 minutes, and shape back into a ball. Let it rise again, covered, for about 20 minutes or until doubled.

5. Heat oven to 375 degrees. Grease a 16 x 4 x 4-inch pullman loaf pan or two 10 x 5½ x 3-inch pans for a pullman-style loaf or two 9 x 5 x 3-inch pans for a traditional loaf. If using the larger pan, gently press the dough into a rectangle, about one inch thick and no wider than the length of the pan. Roll the dough firmly into a cylinder, pressing with your fingers to make sure that the dough sticks to itself. Turn the dough seam side up and pinch it closed. Place the cylinder of dough in the prepared pan and press it gently so it touches all four sides of the pan. Cover with plastic and let rise 20 minutes or doubled in volume. If using the smaller pans, divide dough in half and follow the instructions above.

6. If you do not have a pan with a sliding top but wish to produce a rectangular sandwich loaf, butter one side of a piece of aluminum foil and place it over the dough in the pan. Cover the top of the pan with a baking sheet or any other ovenproof, flat object and weight the top with a heavy ovenproof saucepan. For a rounded loaf, skip this step.

7. Bake for 30 minutes and then remove lid or weighted top if you are using one. Bake an additional 15 to 20 minutes if using the larger pan size; 10 to 15 minutes if baking smaller loaves. The internal temperature of the bread when measured with an instant-read thermometer should be 200 degrees. Remove bread from pan and let cool on a rack before slicing.

MAKES 1 LARGE LOAF OR
2 SMALL ONES

FRIED BREAD

Any bread dough can be fried instead of baked. After the first rise, roll out the dough on a floured surface to an ⅛ inch thickness. Cut into strips 2½ inches wide and then cut into squares. Fry in hot oil, drain on a cooling rack, and serve with maple syrup.

PERFECT WHOLE WHEAT BREAD

If asked to describe the perfect loaf of whole wheat bread, you might say that it should be wheaty, but not grainy; chewy, but not tough; dense, but not heavy; and full-flavored, but balanced and not overpowering. In fact, you might come to the conclusion, as I did, that the perfect loaf of whole wheat bread is rather hard to define. There are literally hundreds of different types of loaves that use at least some whole wheat flour, but to earn the distinction of being a pure, shining example of whole wheat bread is entirely another matter.

After much testing, I devised a master recipe that had the elements I liked from a variety of whole wheat bread recipes. It contained 1 tablespoon of yeast, 2⅓ cups warm water, 4 cups whole wheat flour, 1¼ cups all-purpose flour, ¼ cup rye flour (to add complexity of flavor), 2 teaspoons salt, and 2 tablespoons of honey.

The results were good but the bread was too dense and it needed a boost of both salt and honey for flavor. So I made a new loaf in which I doubled the amount of both yeast and honey and punched up the salt to 2 tablespoons. The taste test results were encouraging, and the loaf was even better when I made another version with ½ tablespoon less yeast and the addition of ¼ cup of melted butter for flavor. But there were still problems. The wheat flavor wasn't really coming through properly and the texture was a bit dense. In addition, the flavor was a bit generic, reminiscent of a slice of whole wheat bread one might find at a diner, served with two individually wrapped pats of butter.

I then increased the total amount of flour in the following proportions: 3 cups whole wheat, 2¾ cups white, and ¼ cup rye. The flavor was excellent but still lacked the proper texture and wheatiness that I expected from a whole wheat loaf. I then added ½ cup of wheat germ, which turned out to be the ideal amount.

In terms of the proper sweetener, it was relatively hard to differentiate among the different types (sugar, honey, molasses, and malt), although the honey version was slightly better. For fats, I sampled loaves made with vegetable oil (a noticeable lack of flavor with a slightly "off" taste); melted lard (a strong flavor but unwelcome in this recipe); the standard melted butter (by far the best — good texture, sweet flavor); cold butter kneaded into the dough (denser, not as moist); and the addition of a whole egg (grainy, gritty texture — almost cottony). Finally, I decided to make two loaves, one with tap water and one with bottled water. To my great surprise, the bottled-water loaf was easily identified in a blind taste test as having a sweeter, fuller flavor. Of course, since more than 2 cups of water is used in this recipe, it makes sense that the flavor and quality of water should matter. So, if someone tells you to use good bottled water for breadmaking (or tap water if the local supply is high quality), don't immediately assume he or she is a culinary snob.

It did occur to me that perhaps the brand of whole wheat flour might make a difference. I had performed all of the tests to this point with King Arthur flour, but I also tried Arrowhead Mills Stone Ground Whole Wheat. This flour produced a loaf with a nice wheat flavor, but it was lighter in both color and texture. Next I made a loaf using Hodgson Mill Whole Wheat Graham Flour, which produced a wonderful loaf with a terrific nutty flavor. Graham flour is a coarser grind of whole wheat flour and, as I noted in the test, provided a nuttier flavor. Although the King Arthur was also very good, I felt that the Hodgson flour was best suited for this recipe.

Basic Whole Wheat Bread

This recipe works well in two standard 9 x 5 x 3-inch loaf pans, which produce regulation-size sandwich loaves. You can also twist two separate lengths of dough and proof them in the loaf pan to produce a more interesting "twisted" loaf. I also experimented with free-form loaves including a simple round loaf, a football-shaped loaf, and simple whole wheat dinner rolls. (See illustrations page 210.)

2⅓	cups warm water (115 to 120 degrees)
1½	tablespoons yeast
¼	cup honey
4	tablespoons (¼ cup) butter, melted
1½	tablespoons salt
½	cup toasted wheat germ
¼	cup rye flour
2¾–3	cups whole wheat flour, Hodgson's Whole Wheat Graham Flour preferred
2¾	cups white all-purpose flour

1. In a large bowl, using a large rubber spatula or wooden spoon, combine the warm water, yeast, honey, butter, and salt and mix well. Add the wheat germ, rye flour, and 1 cup each of the whole wheat and white flours. Beat to combine.

2. Add an additional ¾ cup whole wheat and ¾ cup white flour to the mixture and stir with a wooden spoon for 5 minutes. Add an additional cup each of both flours, stir to combine, and turn out onto a floured surface. Knead by hand for 5 minutes, incorporating no more than ¼ cup additional whole wheat flour. Dough will be wet and sticky but manageable.

3. Place in a lightly oiled bowl and cover with plastic wrap or a damp kitchen towel. Let rise for 60 to 75 minutes or until the dough has doubled in volume.

4. Gently punch down the dough and cut into two pieces. Shape the dough according to the instructions below. Let dough rise an additional 30 to 40 minutes or until doubled in volume. Heat oven to 375 degrees.

5. Bake for 35 to 45 minutes or until an instant-read thermometer inserted into the middle of a loaf reads 205 degrees. Remove immediately from the baking pans and let cool on wire racks until completely cooled.

MAKES 2 STANDARD LOAVES OR 16 ROLLS

STANDING MIXER VARIATION

In the bowl of a standing mixer, using a rubber spatula, combine warm water, yeast, honey, butter, and salt and mix well. Add the wheat germ, rye flour, and 1 cup each of whole wheat and white flours. Beat to combine. Using the dough hook, turn the mixer to the low setting (2 on a KitchenAid) and add the remaining flours, ½ cup at a time. The dough should be moist and tacky but the sides of the bowl should be clean. Add just enough flour to achieve this consistency. Increase the speed to medium (setting 4 on the KitchenAid) and continue to knead for 8 minutes. Continue with step 3 of the master recipe.

RAPID-RISE VARIATION

Substitute rapid-rise yeast for regular active yeast. Heat oven to 200 degrees and then turn off. Place dough in warm oven for first proofing. (Let oven stand for at least 10 minutes after it is turned off before using.) Allow about 40 minutes for the first rise and 20 minutes for the second.

SHAPING INSTRUCTIONS

For a Basic Sandwich-Style Loaf
Grease two 9 x 5 x 3-inch loaf pans. Divide dough into 2 equal pieces. Gently press each piece into a rectangle, 1 inch thick and slightly narrower than the length of the pan. Roll the dough firmly into a cylinder, pressing with your fingers to make sure that the dough sticks to itself. Turn the dough seam side up and pinch it closed. Place each cylinder of dough into a prepared loaf pan and press it gently so it touches all four sides of the pan. Cover with plastic and let rise 30 to 45 minutes or until doubled in volume.

For a Braided Loaf Baked in a Loaf Pan
Grease two 9 x 5 x 3-inch loaf pans. Turn dough onto an unfloured work surface, gently deflate the dough, and divide into 4 pieces. With your palms, roll each piece into fat cylinders, about 9 or 10 inches long. Place 2 pieces side by side and pinch together the ends of the rolled dough at one end. Starting at the sealed end, wrap one around the other to make a braid. Now pinch the other end to seal. Place in loaf pan and gently press down so that the dough is evenly distributed in the pan and is touching all sides. Repeat with the second loaf. Cover with plastic and let rise 30 to 45 minutes.

1. *To shape a basic American bread dough* before placing it in a loaf pan, press the dough into a rectangle, slightly narrower than the width of the pan. Use the pan itself as a guide.

2. Roll up the dough into a cylinder.

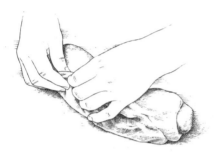

4. Now the dough is ready to be placed in the pan. Make sure than the seam is on the bottom of the loaf.

3. Pinch the seam shut, using your fingers.

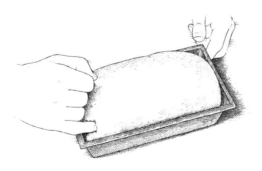

5. To check if the dough has risen enough, push your little finger into the dough.

6. If the hole remains when the finger is removed, the dough is ready for the oven.

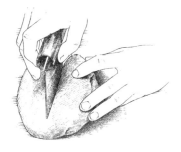

1. *For a braided loaf,* cut the dough in half using a dough knife, also referred to as a bench knife.

2. Roll each half into a cylinder using your fingers.

3. The dough should be longer than the pan.

4. Pinch the ends of the two cylinders together and braid them.

5. The braided loaf before rising and baking.

6. An easy way to check if bread is done is to insert an instant-read thermometer at an angle from the end of the loaf. (The tip of the thermometer should end up at the center of the loaf.) This will not disfigure the top of the loaf and makes it unnecessary to remove it from the pan.

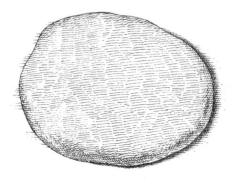

1. *For a football-shaped loaf* that is baked without a pan, pat the dough into a round.

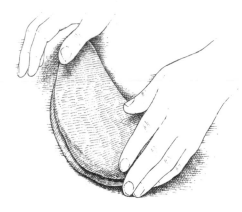

2. Fold the round in half.

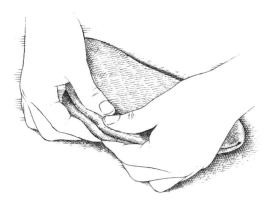

3. Now pinch the seam together with your fingers.

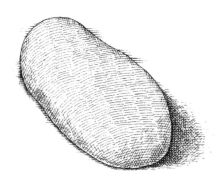

4. Turn seam side down and shape into a loaf. You may stop at this point to make a simple free-form loaf of bread.

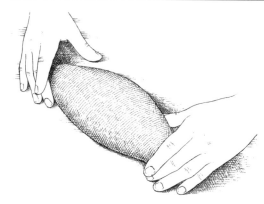

5. Now roll the ends of the loaf gently with your fingers to elongate them slighty.

For a Football-Shaped Loaf
Sprinkle fine cornmeal over a baking sheet or line with parchment paper. Deflate the dough gently and divide into 2 equal pieces. Press each piece into a round, then fold each piece in half and pinch together the sides. Now turn seam side down. Gently pull the ends so that they make a gentle point. Cover loosely with plastic wrap and let rise 30 to 45 minutes. Using a single-edge razor blade

or a serrated knife, make 2 slits length-wise, 1 inch on either side of the center. Liberally dust with white flour and bake for 30 to 40 minutes.

Basic Round Loaves

Sprinkle fine cornmeal over a baking sheet or line with parchment paper. Gently deflate dough and divide into 2 pieces. On an unfloured work surface, shape the dough into rounds, then tuck the sides of the dough underneath itself, rotating the ball of dough as you work. After a few tucks, the dough will form a tight ball. Turn the ball onto its side and pull together the bottom seams. Roll over these seams with the edge of your hand to create a taut seal. Place on prepared baking sheet. Cover loosely with plastic and let rise 30 to 45 minutes. Make three slashes with a razor blade or serrated knife.

Dinner Rolls

Sprinkle fine cornmeal over two baking sheets or line with parchment paper. Separate dough into 2 pieces, keeping one piece covered with a damp dishtowel while you work. On an unfloured work surface, flatten dough into a 10 x 6-inch rectangle. Using a knife, cut into 8 equal pieces. Roll one piece at a time into a ball between your outstretched palm and the work surface. Continue until the dough is shaped into a ball. Continue with remaining dough. Cover loosely with plastic wrap and let rise for 15 to 20 minutes. Using scissors, make 4 to 5 cuts in each roll like the spokes of a wheel. You should almost cut through to the center of the dough. Bake for 20 to 25 minutes.

QUICK BREADS

There are two types of breads: quick breads, which use baking powder or soda for leavening, and yeast breads. The great advantage of quick breads is that they are indeed quick; the batter can be thrown together in a just a few minutes and then popped into the oven. Older cookbooks are filled with a variety of these sorts of breads, including Kellogg's All Bran Brown Bread, Brown Bread, Orange Bread, Banana Bread, Date Bread, Nut Bread, Graham Bread, Grape-Nut Bread, Blueberry Bread, Prune Bread, Oatmeal Bread, Peanut Butter Bread. The chemical reaction caused by the leavener creates carbon dioxide gas, which causes the bread to rise. The disadvantage to these breads, however, is that one loses the depth of flavor that is the essence of the breadmaker's art. In the right hands, slow-rising yeast when paired even with the simplest of ingredients can produce a wonderfully complex loaf with superior texture and flavor, not unlike a fine wine.

The challenge with quick breads, therefore, is to find the right mix of ingredients to enhance both texture and flavor. Most recipes depend on baking powder and milk as building block ingredients. Through testing, I have found that baking soda and buttermilk make a better combination, providing both a more interesting flavor and also a lighter, less dense texture. (Buttermilk contains plenty of lactic acid, which reacts with baking soda to provide lift. Baking powder is nothing more than baking soda plus an acidic ingredient, which, in this case, is already provided by the buttermilk.) I also varied the amount of fat, using 1 egg instead of 2 and trying less butter. I concluded that the fat was indeed necessary for both flavor and texture.

Finally, to promote depth of flavor, I eliminate the buttermilk entirely when using bananas and zucchini for flavoring. They provide plenty of moisture and flavor without diluting them with more liquid. Lemon or orange zest is also helpful to boost flavor, and dried cranberries turned out sweeter and more flavorful than raw cranberries as suggested in some recipes.

Master Recipe for Quick Bread

This recipe should only be made with one of the variations below. It needs a strong ingredient such as cranberries or bananas to add flavor.

2	cups all-purpose flour
1½	teaspoons baking soda
½	teaspoon salt
8	tablespoons (1 stick) unsalted butter, melted
¾–1	cup sugar
2	eggs
1	cup buttermilk
1	teaspoon vanilla extract

1. Heat oven to 350 degrees. Grease a standard loaf pan with butter or spray with a vegetable oil spray. Whisk together the flour, baking soda, and salt. In a separate bowl, beat the butter, sugar, and eggs for 2 minutes either by hand with a whisk or at medium speed in an electric mixer. Stir in the buttermilk and vanilla.

2. Using a large rubber spatula, stir in the flour mixture. Mix until just combined. Do not overmix. Turn into prepared loaf pan and bake for 50 to 60 minutes or until top springs back when lightly pressed and a cake tester inserted in center comes out clean. Let cool in pan on a rack for 10 minutes before turning out onto rack to cool completely.

MAKES 1 LOAF

CRANBERRY NUT VARIATION

Use 1 cup sugar. Grate the rind of an orange and reserve. Juice the orange into a measuring cup and add buttermilk until you have 1 cup total; use this mixture instead of the buttermilk called for in the master recipe. Add the grated orange rind to the buttermilk and then stir into the egg mixture. In step 2, when the flour mixture is incorporated, also gently fold in 1 cup chopped dried cranberries and 1 cup chopped pecans or walnuts.

BLUEBERRY LEMON VARIATION

Use 1 cup of sugar. Grate the rind of 1 lemon. Add the lemon rind to the buttermilk. In step 2, when the flour is incorporated, fold in 1 cup of fresh blueberries. You may also add, if you like, ¾ cup chopped pecans along with the blueberries.

BANANA VARIATION

Use ¾ cup sugar. Add 1½ cups mashed ripe bananas. Omit buttermilk. After mixing the butter, sugar, and eggs for 2 minutes, add the mashed banana and mix for an additional 30 seconds. Proceed with step 2. For banana nut bread, gently stir ¾ cup chopped pecans or walnuts into the batter when the flour is incorporated. (One medium ripe banana yields about ½ cup mashed banana.)

ZUCCHINI VARIATION

Add ½ teaspoon cinnamon and ¼ teaspoon ground ginger to the dry ingredients. Omit the buttermilk. After beating the butter/sugar/egg mixture for 2 minutes, add 1½ cups packed grated zucchini (approximately 1 small zucchini) and mix for an additional 30 seconds. Proceed with step 2. You may also add ½ teaspoon finely chopped lemon rind if you like.

Johnnycake

Johnnycakes were originally called "journeycakes" since they kept well and were often served on long trips for breakfast or as a bread any time of day. Authentic johnnycakes were made from just cornmeal, water, and salt — no eggs, flour, baking powder, or sugar. They were cooked on a plank before the fireplace but, after the cookstove was introduced, they were cooked in a skillet like pancakes. This recipe is a modern hybrid, a far cry from the original but more suitable to modern palates. The batter is baked in an 8-inch square pan much like a cornbread. If you prefer to make pancakes out of them, see the variation below. If you do not have buttermilk on hand, substitute regular milk, eliminate baking soda, and

use 2 teaspoons baking powder instead. If you don't have molasses, simply increase sugar to ⅓ cup.

¾	cup cornmeal
1	cup flour
2	tablespoons sugar
¾	teaspoon baking soda
¾	teaspoon salt
1	tablespoon molasses
1	cup buttermilk
1	egg, beaten
4	tablespoons (½ stick) butter, melted

Heat oven to 425 degrees. Grease an 8-inch square baking pan with butter or a vegetable spray. Whisk together the first 5 ingredients (cornmeal through salt). Gently stir in the remaining ingredients until they are just mixed. Do not overmix. Bake for 20 minutes or until top springs back when lightly touched. Cool in pan.

MAKES 1 PAN

PANCAKE VARIATION

Johnnycakes were also cooked as pancakes. Simply prepare the batter in the recipe above, adding ¼ cup additional buttermilk, and cook ¼ to ⅓ cup of batter for each pancake on a greased electric skillet.

Spoonbread

Spoonbread is nothing more than a heavy soufflé made with cornmeal and served in a casserole or shallow baking pan. (It was also served as a simple quick bread, using baking powder for leavening. I find that version a bit too heavy for my taste.) I serve it as an accompaniment to a roast much as one would serve Yorkshire pudding. I have tried this recipe with buttermilk, but the slightly sour flavor is overpowering. However, you can substitute 1 cup of buttermilk for 1 cup of milk to add a bit of depth to the flavor. I tested this recipe with 3 eggs and found that there was insufficient structure and the taste was anemic. I also tried 4 whole eggs plus 1 additional white for lift, but I preferred the spoonbread with just 4 eggs. I find that a bit of sugar helps to build flavor and a few grindings of black pepper are also welcome.

2	cups milk
1	cup cream
¾	teaspoon salt
1	tablespoon sugar
2	tablespoons unsalted butter
1	cup cornmeal
4	eggs, separated
	Freshly ground black pepper

1. Grease a baking dish that is 9 inches square (and at least 3 inches high) or any similar size. Bring the milk, ½ cup of the cream, the salt, the sugar, and the butter to a simmer in a large saucepan. Sprinkle in the cornmeal and whisk over medium heat for 3 minutes, whisking constantly, or until the mixture thickens. Remove from heat and allow to cool for 10 minutes.
2. Whisk together the remaining ½ cup cream with the 4 egg yolks and a few grindings of black pepper. Stir into the cornmeal mixture. Whip the 4 egg whites until they hold a 2-inch peak and then stir, with a wooden spoon, about one quarter of the whites into the cornmeal mixture.

Now fold the remaining whites into the cornmeal using a large rubber spatula.
3. Using the spatula, move batter into the prepared dish and spread evenly. Bake for 25 to 30 minutes until the top has browned and the center is still a bit wet. It is better to undercook than overcook this dish. Serve immediately.

SERVES 6 AS A SIDE DISH

Sour Milk or Buttermilk Bread

Frugality made the notion of throwing out food anathema to any self-respecting farm family and therefore many old recipes included ingredients that would otherwise go to waste, such as sour milk, which was often used in breads, quick breads, doughnuts, and muffins. This recipe was inspired by a similar recipe from Jessie Batchelder, who is related to the family that founded the Batchelder Brothers Iron Works in Wallingford, Vermont. It has one interesting feature. Once the batter is mixed, it is allowed to sit for an hour before baking. I did, however, make a variety of changes in the recipe after the initial testing in order to produce a more savory all-purpose loaf. The original recipe (see below) called for ½ cup of sugar, which I cut back to only 3 tablespoons, and this recipe was made exclusively with whole wheat flour. I decided that a mix of white and whole wheat was preferable, with a bit of wheat germ thrown in for texture. However, the original recipe is also quite good and I have reproduced it below.

1½	cups all-purpose flour
1¾	cups whole wheat flour (whole wheat graham flour preferred)

½   cup raw wheat germ

1½   teaspoons salt

3   tablespoons sugar

1   heaping teaspoon baking soda

1¾   cups sour milk or buttermilk

1. Whisk together the first 6 ingredients (all-purpose flour through baking soda), then add the sour milk or buttermilk, stirring with a wooden spoon or spatula. Place dough in an ungreased loaf pan, wet the backside of a rubber spatula, and smooth the top. Let sit on the counter for 1 hour.

2. Heat oven to 375 degrees. Place pan in oven and bake about 1 hour or until the center of the loaf registers 190 to 195 degrees on an instant-read thermometer.

MAKES 1 LOAF

Jessie Batchelder's Sour Milk Quick Bread

This is the original recipe and is best eaten with perhaps a bit of cream cheese or simply on its own, much as one might eat a banana or date nut bread.

3¼   cups whole wheat flour (whole wheat graham flour preferred)

1½   teaspoons salt

½   cup sugar

1   heaping teaspoon baking soda

1¾   cups sour milk or buttermilk

1. Whisk together the first 4 ingredients (all-purpose flour through baking soda), and then add the sour milk or buttermilk, stirring with a wooden spoon or spatula. Place dough in an ungreased loaf pan, wet the backside of a rubber spatula, and

smooth the top. Let sit on the counter for 1 hour.

2. Heat oven to 375 degrees. Bake about an hour or until the center of the loaf registers 190 to 195 degrees on an instant-read thermometer.

MAKES 1 LOAF

Skillet Soda Bread

This is another quick bread, since it depends on baking soda, not yeast, for leavening. Many soda bread recipes use no butter and sugar and too little salt, which yields a dull loaf of bread indeed. The interesting aspect to this recipe is the use of a cast iron skillet for baking. Cast iron is a wonderful heat conductor and also serves to shape the dough as it bakes.

4   cups unbleached all-purpose flour

2   tablespoons sugar

1   teaspoon cream of tartar

1   teaspoon baking soda

2   teaspoons salt

4   tablespoons (½ stick) unsalted butter, softened

1¾–2 cups buttermilk

1   tablespoon butter, melted

1. Heat oven to 400 degrees. Whisk dry ingredients (flour through salt) together in a large bowl. With a fork or your fingers, stir softened butter into flour mixture until fully incorporated. Add 1¾ cups buttermilk and stir mixture with a large rubber spatula or your fingers until dough starts to come together. Add more buttermilk if necessary to produce a cohesive dough. Turn onto a lightly floured work surface and knead for 30 seconds, or until dough comes together. It should still be rough-textured and lumpy.

2. Shape dough into a round and place in a 9- or 10-inch cast iron skillet. Score top of dough with a knife or razor blade, making 2 or 3 slashes. Bake about 40 minutes or until an instant-read thermometer indicates an internal temperature of 180 degrees.

3. Remove from oven, brush with melted butter, and let cool for 30 minutes before serving.

MAKES 1 ROUND LOAF

Whole Wheat Soda Bread

This recipe is adapted from the Ballymaloe Cookery School in County Cork, Ireland. The test kitchen director at *Cook's Illustrated* spent a week there and suggested this recipe for the book. The dough can be made in less than 5 minutes with no kneading and then it goes right into the oven. It makes a soft, wheaty bread with a wonderful, mealy texture, totally unlike any quick bread I have had before. I also make this bread for breakfast since it goes so well with fresh sweet butter and homemade jam.

1½	cups all-purpose flour
1¾	cups whole wheat flour
⅓	cup wheat germ
1½	teaspoons salt
1	teaspoon baking soda
2	tablespoons butter, softened
1	egg
1½	cups buttermilk

1. Heat oven to 450 degrees. Whisk together the dry ingredients in a large bowl.

Using your fingertips, work the softened butter into the flour mixture. In a separate small bowl, whisk the egg and then whisk in the buttermilk. Make a well in the flour and add most of the buttermilk mixture (reserve ¼ cup), and mix together with your hands to form a loose dough. If dough will not come together, add some or all of the remaining buttermilk/egg mixture.

2. On a well-floured work surface, turn out the dough. Sprinkle with flour and shape into a 7- to 8-inch circle. Flatten slightly with the tips of your fingers. Score the top of the loaf, transfer to a baking sheet, and bake for 15 minutes. Reduce heat to 400 degrees for another 20 minutes. Check bread with an instant-read thermometer inserted halfway into the bottom. It should read 190 to 195 degrees. Let cool for 15 minutes and then serve.

MAKES 1 ROUND LOAF

IN SEARCH OF EASY, FULL-FLAVORED SKILLET CORNBREAD

A recent meal at a famous Boston restaurant brought me face to face with the reality of modern cornbread. It was cakelike; sweet, light, the sort of bread one might easily serve with whipped cream and sliced strawberries. Real cornbread, by contrast, is substantial, not too sweet, and can stand up to a thick soup or, if you are Southern, be crumbled into a bowl of potlikker and greens.

The first issue was the proportion of cornmeal to flour. Southern cooks use little if any flour, which produces a very heavy bread indeed. I prefer a lighter product, and when testing, I started with 3 parts cornmeal (1½ cups) to 1 part

1. *To make a loaf of Whole Wheat Soda Bread,* mix the ingredients together with your fingers or a large rubber spatula.

2. On a floured work surface, shape the dough into a round seven to eight inches in diameter.

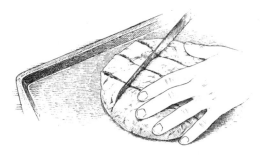

3. Score the top of the loaf with a bread knife, cutting about one-quarter inch into the loaf. Make three cuts in one direction and then make three cuts perpendicular to the first set.

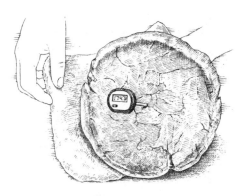

4. To check if the bread is done, insert an instant-read thermometer into the bottom of the loaf. It should read 190 to 195 degrees.

flour (½ cup), which was good but still a bit too dense for my Northern palate. I increased the flour to ¾ cup and produced a lighter but still substantial bread. Although Southern cooks also turn down their noses at sugar in cornbread, I find that a touch of sweetness is crucial to developing the flavor of the cornmeal. However, I use a mere 2 tablespoons, just enough to enhance flavor. To develop a moist, authentic texture, some older recipes suggest making a mush out of

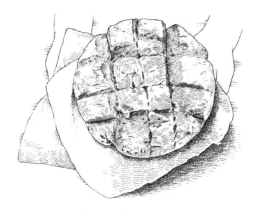

5. The finished loaf

boiling water and cornmeal and then whisking in the buttermilk and eggs. This is the method used by Pam Anderson in a recent article in *Cook's Illustrated* and I found that, indeed, it was successful. I also found that a bit of melted butter improved the flavor.

Some cornbread recipes add pork fat cracklings for flavor. Many food writers believe that cracklings are the skin or rind of the pig, cooked down during rendering of the lard. Although there may be some skin attached, real cracklings are the cubes of fat which rise to the surface during rendering. They are then skimmed off and set out on a table to drain. As one author noted, they should be the size of #1 buckshot and crispy without being tough or leathery. For this recipe I have adopted a more refined approach, simply using 1 teaspoon of bacon drippings to grease the pan. You can, however, also add cooked, crumbled bacon to the batter.

One final note. This cornbread is cooked in a preheated iron skillet, which produces a nicely browned bottom crust. It is very important to use a 9-inch skillet to produce the proper thickness and texture.

Skillet Cornbread

1	teaspoon bacon drippings or vegetable oil
1½	cups coarse cornmeal
¾	cup all-purpose flour
2	tablespoons sugar
1	teaspoon salt
2	teaspoons baking powder
½	teaspoon baking soda
½	cup boiling water
1½	cups buttermilk
1	large egg, lightly beaten
3	tablespoons melted butter or bacon drippings

1. Adjust oven rack to the middle position and heat oven to 425 degrees. Oil a *well-seasoned* 9-inch cast iron skillet (don't use a smaller or larger size; if you don't have one, use a greased 9-inch pie plate, not preheated, and bake for 30 to 35 minutes) with the bacon drippings or vegetable oil, using a paper towel and rubbing the entire interior surface of the pan. Set the skillet in the oven.

2. Place ½ cup of the cornmeal in a medium bowl. Sift the remaining 1 cup cornmeal with the flour, sugar, salt, baking powder, and baking soda in a small bowl or onto a piece of waxed paper.

3. Pour boiling water all at once into the half cup cornmeal and stir to make a stiff mush. Whisk in the buttermilk and egg. When the oven and skillet are hot, gently stir the dry ingredients into the batter. Do not overmix. Add the melted butter and stir to combine. Remove skillet from the oven, add the batter, and place back in the oven. Bake until golden brown and firm to the touch, about 25 minutes. Remove skillet and immediately turn cornbread onto a wire rack. (Cornbread can also be served directly from the skillet.) Cool for 5 minutes, cut into wedges, and serve at once.

MAKES ONE 9-INCH ROUND
AND SERVES 6

Steamed Brown Bread

If you have ever tasted good homemade brown bread, you have found that it is nothing like what can be purchased in a supermarket or offered in Americana-style restaurants. The combination of buttermilk, cornmeal, molasses, and whole wheat flour is unusual but delightful. When mixed together, the ingredients are steamed in a 1-pound coffee can for about 2 hours. Traditionally, brown bread was eaten with baked beans for a Saturday-night supper or with fish cakes for breakfast. The bread is sweetened with molasses and therefore pairs nicely with a savory dish, although I enjoy simply eating it alone with a smear of butter. I have found that it is becoming more difficult to find a 1-pound can of coffee. Many brands these days come in 12-ounce cans, although you can find the full 16-ounce variety if you look for it. I have also found that it is best to let this bread cool thoroughly before slicing; otherwise it has a tendency to fall apart.

½   cup rye flour
½   cup whole wheat flour
½   cup cornmeal
1   teaspoon baking soda
½   teaspoon salt
½   cup molasses
1   cup buttermilk
2   tablespoons unsalted butter, melted
½   cup raisins

1. Grease (with butter) a thoroughly clean 1-pound coffee can. Place a steamer rack inside a large pot (a stockpot works well) that is tall enough so that the coffee can sit on the rack and the pot still be covered. (If you do not have a rack, the coffee can may be placed directly on the bottom of the pot.) In a large saucepan, boil enough water so that it will fill the pot about halfway.

2. In a medium bowl, whisk together the first five ingredients (rye through salt). Stir in the molasses, buttermilk, and butter. When almost mixed, stir in the raisins and mix until combined. Pour batter into the prepared coffee can. Cover tightly with aluminum foil. Place can on rack (or on bottom of pot) and pour boiling water to come about halfway up the coffee can. Return water to a boil and lower to a simmer. Cover the pot. Steam for about 2 hours, adding more boiling water if necessary, until the bread is firm and a cake tester inserted in the center comes out clean.

3. Cool for 10 minutes and unmold. Let cool for 1 hour before slicing.

SERVES 6 TO 8

Farm Breakfasts

WEEKENDS ON THE FARM, the day starts early. On Saturdays, we are out of bed by 6 A.M., throwing on a few clothes to weed the garden or water the fruit trees or perhaps run the rototiller between the long rows of sweet corn. In the winter, the dark early-morning hours are used to do writing or paperwork, with a mug of coffee or tea, waiting for the sun to peek over the mountains to the east where the old town road used to run up the hollow, over a pass between two ridges, and then down to the road to New York State. But at 7:30, it is time to make a serious breakfast: buttermilk biscuits and scrambled eggs, or buckwheat pancakes with homemade peach butter or maple syrup, or corn muffins with a cheese omelet. The table is set with our own honey, our two hives providing at least 50 pounds, enough to last throughout the year, plus wild blueberry jam, blackberry jam, not-too-sweet strawberry jam, and our house favorite, a peach and brown sugar jam made from syrupy, heavenly Pennsylvania peaches trucked north in August.

But many of the old farmers, since the farmhouse cooks are long gone, make the trip down to the State Line Diner. It's not much of an establishment; just a double-wide trailer set near the town line with a large Pepsi sign out front and old-fashioned sleigh bells on the front door. The plastic-sheathed menu is peppered with ads for Day's Small Engine Repair, Downey's Rubbish Removal, Ushak's Supermarket, and Peabody & Bates Inc., the last offering screened and bankrun gravel. The waitress, in her best Vermont deadpan, offers each diner "two minutes to decide what to order and one minute to eat it." The food is no more than one might expect, but the company is good, from the farmers at the counter to the teenagers ordering up a mess of breakfast past noon.

One Sunday, I took my older daughter there for breakfast. After eggs sunny side up, a few breakfast links, and a heap of toast, we hopped in our old orange Ford pickup and drove home by the back road. As we climbed slowly through the small mountain valley, I had a vision of Whitney in the booth a few minutes before: quiet, beautiful, eyes wide open and self-assured. Little kids live in the moment, but as they mature they start living in the future, no longer content to sit at a Formica tabletop, consumed by food and the attention of a parent. That day, my daughter was watching the great flow of people, aware of the possibilities, eager, I think, to take a few first steps on her own, away from the watchful eye of her father.

As the truck came to a stop by the woodpile, I glanced across at her, noticing for the first time small changes in her face; a firmer chin, inquiring eyes, a hint of self-reliance and independence. These are the signs one looks for as a father, signals that a son or daughter has been raised well, trained to take his or her place in the world. We send them forth to do battle, hoping they will come back some-day to show us their trophies and scars,

having struck, I hope, a few shrewd blows for civilization. On that day, I will welcome her back, arms outstretched, a proud parent holding both her and a bit-tersweet memory of the first time she set out on her own one Sunday, jumping down from the cab, walking slowly away, her back turned to the yellow farmhouse.

TOWN MEETING is held across Vermont on the first Tuesday of March and it has become a symbol of the grassroots politics that still dominates the state. In fact, one of our neighbors from the 1950s, Norman Rockwell, painted Carl Hess, our local gas station owner, in *Town Meeting,* one of his better-known works. He also painted Floyd Bentley, one of the farmers I helped out occasionally, as he posed as the father of a boy going off to school in *Breaking Home Ties,* Floyd sitting hun-kered over on the sideboard of an old pickup, forearms on his thighs, cowboy hat in hand, a cigarette barely hanging to his lower lip, with a doe-eyed collie, mournful that the young man, Floyd's son in this picture, was going off to college. (The collie, Dixie, still lived at the yellow farmhouse when I was growing up.)

But real town meetings are anything but quaint. They are a rough-and-tumble exercise in local politics, the rules arcane and designed to favor locals. Weekenders, for example, cannot address the assem-bled residents without receiving express permission from the chairman. I've also noted that the really big votes, whether to build a town garage, for example, are saved for the end of the meeting so that only the diehard supporters are left. And being a selectman, of course, is not a popular position. Sonny Skidmore once asked Mark Christiansen, who was complaining about town politics, why he didn't jump into the selectman's race. Mark answered angrily, "Why do I need two holes in my head?" Sonny didn't miss a beat and shot back, "I guess one big one is okay!"

The best thing about town meeting, however, is that many of the locals bring homemade biscuits, muffins, and even doughnuts on occasion. Over the years I have found that these sorts of baked goods benefit from a light hand. Muffin and pancake batters should be barely stirred to the point that small streaks of unincorporated flour are still evident. Biscuit dough should also be treated gingerly, not pressed and kneaded like a loaf of bread. Otherwise, the baked biscuits will be short and tough. I have also found that buttermilk is a crucial ingredient for most breakfast baking, since its high percentage of lactic acid reacts violently with baking soda, producing plenty of carbon dioxide bubbles, which in turn promote lighter baked goods.

Since maple syrup is often served with breakfast, you should be aware that the lower, and cheaper, grades are best. I have always preferred the "dark amber" Grade B syrups since they have a fuller, smokier flavor. They are also cheaper than the "fancy" Grade A varieties favored by most producers. And a recent taste test in the kitchens of *Cook's Illustrated* found that the majority of tasters agree that the darker syrups are better. Of course in Vermont, almost everyone makes their own syrup, even the Carthusian monks who live in complete silence on top of a mountain in our town.

Cornmeal is a common ingredient in many breakfast recipes, including cornmeal mush, a basic farmhouse porridge, spoonbread, cornmeal muffins, and cornbread. However, it is available in different grinds and the terminology is not always consistent. First of all, there are many products made from corn, including cornstarch, hominy, cornmeal, and corn flour. Cornstarch is simply the starch that is extracted from corn using an industrial process. It is used as a thickener much the way flour, arrowroot, or tapioca is used, usually in very small quantities, most often to thicken milk-based recipes such as pastry cream or puddings. Hominy is dried kernels of corn which are cooked in water with an alkali to remove the skins. It is usually sold in cans packed in lightly salted water. Cornmeal is ground kernels of corn, and corn flour is finely ground cornmeal. Grits is simply a mush made from ground cornmeal, using either white or yellow corn. Of course cornmeal can be ground to varying degrees of fineness. Polenta, although nothing more than the Italian term for cornmeal, usually means a very coarse grind of cornmeal. Next, in terms of fineness of grind, are whole-grain cornmeals which include the germ. Other commercial brands, such as Quaker, are degermed and tend to be finer.

In order to assess the relative merits of different commercial varieties of cornmeal, I conducted a taste test using five different brands in a simple recipe for corn muffins. The chart on the next page summarizes the results.

MUFFINS

There are three basic techniques for preparing muffins. The dry and liquid ingredients can be mixed together quickly, the butter and sugar can be "creamed" (beaten with an electric mixer until light and fluffy) and then the dry and liquid ingredients mixed in; or the cold butter can be cut into the flour and then the other ingredients added. The first method is most common among country cooks; it's easy and produces an honest, toothy muffin. In the January/February 1997 issue of *Cook's Illustrated*, however, Pam Anderson, our executive editor, tested these three methods and decided on the second, preferring a lighter, more delicate muffin. Having tested all three methods, I am still a fan of the easier, throw-it-all-together school of muffin making. I don't like cupcakes for breakfast and I find that light, airy muffins, which are often too sweet for

KITCHEN TEST: USING DIFFERENT GRINDS OF CORNMEAL IN BAKING

Five different grinds of cornmeal were used in baking the cornmeal muffin recipe which appears on page 227.

NAME OF CORNMEAL	DESCRIPTION AND BAKING RESULTS
Corn flour	This is a very finely ground cornmeal. The muffins were much too cakelike and refined.
Quaker Cornmeal	This is a medium-grind cornmeal which has been degermed and has additives. It is slightly brighter in color than a whole-grain cornmeal. The muffins were okay, with a rather bland flavor, but with good texture, grainy and slightly crunchy.
Hodgson Mill Whole-Grain Stone-Ground Cornmeal	Hodgson Mill has both a lighter color and texture than the Quaker cornmeal. Whole grain means that the germ has been left in and therefore it is preferred for flavor and health reasons. The muffins had a nice corn flavor and the texture was coarse with a mild crunch.
Arrowhead Mills Hi-Lysine Cornmeal	This cornmeal has a nuttier and more savory flavor than the Hodgson Mill brand. In the muffin, the nuttiness masked the flavor of the corn.
Polenta	This is nothing more than the Italian term for cornmeal, yet I find that it is usually sold in a very coarse grind with actual bits of ground-up corn visible rather than being a powdery flour. This was the clear winner in the tests, since the corn flavor was most pronounced and the muffins had the crunchiest texture.

WHAT TO BUY: Purchase polenta whenever possible, since the coarse grind makes for excellent corn flavor and good crunchy texture.

my taste, are best served with chocolate icing, not alongside a plate of bacon and eggs. I like just a hint of sweetness and a bit of bite to the muffin, so that it calls out for a rich smear of yellow butter and some of our honey or peach jam.

But Pam did make an interesting discovery. When the dry ingredients are added to the melted butter and eggs, the flour is coated with fat, which delivers a more tender muffin. The development of gluten, which is promoted by the presence of liquid, is inhibited. Gluten is the protein found in flour. So I have adjusted my basic recipe, taking Pam's advice and rearranging the order in which the ingredients are mixed. Note that I use about half as much sugar as most muffin recipes call for. These muffins need jam or honey, which is the best reason to make them in the first place.

Master Recipe for Muffins

These are not sweet confections, but sturdier farmhouse muffins that need a thick spread of honey or homemade jam and plenty of soft, sweet butter. Many cooks confuse cupcakes with muffins, and these are definitely the latter. Remember that muffin batter needs a light hand to turn out light, not tough muffins; overmix this dough at your own risk.

8	tablespoons (1 stick) butter, melted
2	large eggs
½	teaspoon vanilla extract
3	cups all-purpose flour
¼	teaspoon ground nutmeg
2	teaspoons baking powder
½	teaspoon baking soda
½	teaspoon salt
1¼	cups buttermilk
½	cup plus 1 tablespoon sugar

1. Heat oven to 375 degrees. Grease a 12-cup muffin tin with butter or coat with vegetable oil cooking spray.
2. Whisk together the melted butter, the eggs, and the vanilla in a large bowl. In a smaller, separate bowl, whisk together the next 5 ingredients (flour through salt). Gently stir the flour mixture into the egg mixture until the batter looks about half-mixed. Add the buttermilk and sugar and mix gently with a large rubber spatula. Do not overmix. The batter should still have small streaks of flour in it and be lumpy.
3. Using a medium ice cream scoop or a ⅓ cup measure, divide batter evenly among the muffin cups. Bake about 25 minutes or until tops are golden brown. Remove pan from oven and set on a wire rack to cool for 5 minutes. Remove muffins from tin and serve.

MAKES 12 MUFFINS

CORNMEAL MUFFINS

Substitute 1 cup cornmeal for 1 cup flour and eliminate the nutmeg.

LEMON CORNMEAL MUFFINS

Substitute 1 cup cornmeal for 1 cup flour and add 1 tablespoon grated lemon zest and 2 tablespoons lemon juice along with the eggs. Eliminate nutmeg.

BLUEBERRY MUFFINS

Toss 1½ cups blueberries with 1 table-spoon flour and gently fold into the batter along with the buttermilk and sugar.

FRESH PEACH MUFFINS

Substitute brown sugar for white, add ¼ teaspoon ground allspice along with the flour, and add 1½ cups finely chopped fresh ripe peaches along with the butter-milk and sugar.

PECAN NUTMEG MUFFINS

Substitute 1 cup whole wheat flour for 1 cup flour, use brown sugar instead of white, increase nutmeg to ½ teaspoon, and add 1 cup chopped pecans to the batter along with the buttermilk and sugar.

Master Recipe for Skillet Potatoes

Recipes for potatoes cooked in a cast iron skillet on top of the stove are as common as recipes for baking powder biscuits. Even the Italians make potatoes this way. I did find, however, that it is best to precook the potatoes in boiling water and then chill them. This gives them a creamier texture and also cuts down cooking time in the pan. Some recipes call for cooking these potatoes in the oven, but I found that the stovetop is preferable, since the potatoes can be frequently turned, which improves the browning of the exterior.

1¼   pounds potatoes, washed and cut into
      1-inch cubes

1   tablespoon olive oil
2   tablespoons butter
1   medium onion, cut into large dice
      Salt and freshly ground black pepper
      to taste
1   tablespoon chopped fresh chives, tar-
      ragon, thyme, or rosemary (optional)

1. Boil potatoes following master recipe on page 66 and drain. Reserve and chill for at least 1 hour in the refrigerator.
2. Heat a 10-inch iron skillet over medium heat. Add olive oil and butter and cook until foam subsides. Add onion and potatoes and toss to coat. Season liberally with salt and pepper. Cook over medium-high heat, stirring frequently, until exterior is crisp and well browned, about 15 to 20 minutes. Adjust seasonings, sprinkle on optional fresh herbs, and serve.
SERVES 4

ONE-STEP SKILLET POTATOES

Do not precook potatoes but increase cooking time in the skillet to 25 minutes.

PEANUT OIL SKILLET POTATOES

Substitute 2 tablespoons peanut oil and 1 tablespoon bacon fat for the olive oil and butter in the master recipe.

SKILLET POTATO FRITTATA

Once the potatoes are cooked according to the master recipe, they can be folded together with eggs and cheese and then returned to the skillet to make a quick and easy frittata.

1   master recipe for Skillet Potatoes
    (page 228)
2   large eggs, beaten
2   tablespoons grated cheese, Parmesan
    preferred
½   teaspoon salt
    Freshly ground black pepper to taste
1   tablespoon olive oil or butter

Follow master recipe but when potatoes are cooked, place them in a large mixing bowl with eggs, cheese, salt, and pepper. Fold mixture together. Add the olive oil or butter to the same skillet used to cook the potatoes and place over medium heat. When hot, add the potato mixture to the skillet and cook over medium-low heat. Using a large pancake turner, flip when the bottom is lightly browned. Repeat flipping until both sides are nicely browned and the eggs are puffy and cooked through.

SERVES 4

BUTTERMILK PANCAKES

It doesn't need to be said that pancakes and waffles are dependent on using the best maple syrup. And there is nothing like maple syrup, drawn into a small cup from a spigot, warm and sweet. When I was a kid, we used to fire up the evaporator in the sap house by old Charlie Bentley's farm and Herbie, a local farmhand, would come down in sugaring season to help out. Sugaring requires a fair amount of skill, since the wood fire has to be just right and if there isn't enough sap available, the evaporator, the metal contraption that holds the sap as it cooks down, will burn out. My sister and I would pour the half-full sap buckets into a huge round collection vat mounted on top of a flatbed

pulled by Duke and Dan, Floyd's favorite team. After two or three days of work, keeping the fires stoked, slowly moving the sap from one end of the evaporator to the other, judging the syrup as it dripped off the edge of the scoop to see if it was thick enough to be considered done, much of the syrup would be taken off by a local family, leaving Herbie with most of the work and not enough syrup even for breakfast. One year, he was seen walking down the road heavily loaded with a 7-gallon bucket of maple syrup. When questioned, he shot back with fire in his eyes, "Guess I'll have enough for my pancakes now."

The other secret of great waffles and pancakes is buttermilk. I use 1¾ cups of buttermilk plus ¼ cup of regular milk per 2 cups of flour. The buttermilk provides a thick, fluffy pancake and the small amount of milk helps to thin out the batter, although this recipe produces extraordinarily thick, fluffy cakes. Please note that the thickness of the buttermilk you use will affect the recipe. (On the farm, buttermilk was the milk that was left over after making butter. It is actually quite low in fat. Today, however, buttermilk is made from cultured milk, which is an entirely different product.) The batter should be thick but just pourable. If it is too thin, cut back on the amount of buttermilk by 2 tablespoons. If it is too thick, add 1 tablespoon of extra milk. Note that this recipe does not call for any melted butter or vegetable oil. I find that not only is this addition unnecessary, but that I prefer the texture and look of the pancakes without them. If you intend to serve your pancakes without butter and syrup, either plain or with just a bit of jam, go ahead and add 2 tablespoons of melted butter to the buttermilk mixture along with the egg yolks. It's best to use an electric griddle for pancakes — set it to 350 degrees, not 375 or 400 degrees as suggested by many manufacturers. (These are very thick pancakes and require a lower temperature for thorough cooking.) Finally, I have listed a variation that does not require separating the eggs and beating the whites but this version is definitely inferior to the master recipe. Use it only in an emergency!

Master Recipe for Buttermilk Pancakes

2	cups all-purpose flour
2	tablespoons cornmeal (optional)
½	teaspoon salt
¼	teaspoon baking soda
2	eggs, separated
1¾	cups buttermilk
¼	cup milk

1. Heat an electric griddle. Whisk dry ingredients together in a medium bowl. Whisk egg yolks with buttermilk and milk.
2. In a separate bowl, beat egg whites until they hold a 2-inch peak. Add liquid ingredients to dry ingredients in a thin, steady stream while gently mixing with a rubber spatula; be careful not to add liquid faster than you can incorporate it. (This is best done in a narrow bowl.) The batter should be very rough at this point, really half-mixed, with large streaks of flour and puddles of buttermilk. Now gently fold in the whites to complete the mixing process. The batter will be very thick and lumpy. Do not overmix.

3. Pour ⅓ cup of batter on the heated griddle for each pancake, spacing the cakes well apart. Bake until the top of each pancake has many bubbles; turn and cook until the underside is light brown. Serve immediately.
SERVES 4

SHORT-CUT VARIATION

This version saves one step but is not nearly as good as the master recipe, although it still makes a very good pancake. Follow master recipe but do not separate the eggs, whisking them into the buttermilk and milk. Increase baking soda to ½ teaspoon.

WHOLE MILK VARIATION

If you are out of buttermilk, try this regular whole milk variation. Add 4 teaspoons of cream of tartar to the dry ingredients and substitute a scant 1½ cups milk for the buttermilk for pancakes and 1⅝ cups for waffles.

BUCKWHEAT CAKES

Buckwheat flour has a wild nutty flavor which I find overpowering if used in a ratio higher than 1 part buckwheat to 2 parts all-purpose flour. However, these are light, fluffy pancakes and I like to serve them spread with a homemade jam or preserve instead of maple syrup.

Follow the master recipe but substitute ⅔ cup buckwheat flour for ⅔ cup all-purpose flour and add 3 tablespoons vegetable oil along with the buttermilk. Whisk the egg yolks together with 1 tablespoon molasses and then add to the buttermilk.

BUTTERMILK WAFFLES

Follow the directions for the pancakes but eliminate the milk and use 1⅞ cups of buttermilk. Bake the waffles in a waffle iron, following the manufacturer's recommendation. You can make toaster waffles out of leftover batter — undercook the waffles a bit, cool them on a wire rack, wrap them in plastic wrap, and freeze. Pop them in the toaster for a quick breakfast.

Buttermilk Baking Powder Biscuits

This was Marie Briggs's signature recipe, the high-rise, fluffy biscuits often tucked into a round red tin for storage, layers separated by wax paper. The recipe below is my take on her recipe, which produces light, fluffy rounds of baked dough. If you do not have buttermilk, you can substitute regular sweet milk as indicated below. I have not included a recipe for beaten biscuits, which are thin, relatively hard biscuits, made without leavening, usually served in the mid-Atlantic states. Many years ago, at a wake, I was served beaten biscuits by a good Maryland cook and found them to be more of a cross between a cracker and a biscuit. The dough is actually beaten, quite vigorously, hence the name, and they are usually pricked on top with the tines of a fork. They keep better than the lighter, leavened biscuits, but this is insufficient reason, to my mind, for

Baking powder biscuit dough should be rolled out as lightly as possible to produce a light, airy biscuit. Use a biscuit cutter or the mouth of a drinking glass or jar to cut out biscuits.

Place cut biscuits on a baking sheet and bake in a hot, 425 degree, oven for ten to twelve minutes. Do not overbake.

The baked biscuits should be high, light, and fluffy.

giving up the pillowy texture of a good buttermilk biscuit.

> 2 cups flour
> ½ teaspoon salt
> 2 teaspoons baking powder
> ½ teaspoon baking soda
> 4 tablespoons (½ stick) chilled butter
> 3 tablespoons chilled vegetable shortening
> ⅔–¾ cup buttermilk

1. Heat oven to 425 degrees. Combine the flour, salt, baking powder, and baking soda in the bowl of a food processor. Process for 2 seconds to mix.

2. Add the butter, cut into 1 tablespoon bits, to the flour and pulse 7 times for 1 second each. Add shortening and pulse another 6 times or until mixture looks like coarse meal (the flour should take on a slightly yellowish hue from the butter).

3. Place mixture in a large bowl. Using a rubber spatula, fold mixture together while adding buttermilk in a very thin stream. When mixture starts to hold together, press the dough with the side of the spatula. Note that you may use a little more or less than the ⅔ cup buttermilk called for in this recipe.

4. Turn onto a floured surface and use a rolling pin to roll out dough very gently to a thickness of ½ inch. (You can also simply flatten the dough with your outstretched hands instead of using a pin.) Use a biscuit cutter to cut out rounds, pushing the cutter straight down without twisting. Arrange biscuits at least 1 inch apart on a cookie sheet and bake in the preheated oven for about 10 minutes,

turning sheet front to back after 5 minutes in oven. Serve hot.

MAKES TEN THICK 2¾-INCH BISCUITS
OR SIXTEEN 2-INCH BISCUITS

SWEET-MILK VARIATION

Substitute milk for buttermilk, add 3 teaspoons cream of tartar, and reduce baking powder to 1 teaspoon.

Cheap Biscuits

The only place I have ever seen a recipe for these biscuits is in *American Cookery* by James Beard, who claimed that this was one of his mother's specialties. (He referred to them as cream biscuits.) When no shortening was used in recipes for biscuits, doughnuts, and other quick breads, they were often referred to as "cheap," since they did not use butter or lard, which was often hard to come by. This recipe must have been derived from chuck wagon biscuits, which also used nothing more than flour, baking powder, and salt combined with heavy cream, buttermilk, or sour milk to make a dough. They can be dipped in melted butter as Jim suggests or simply baked as is. They have more tooth than a shortening biscuit and are easier to make. The only change I have made to the recipe is to reduce the amount of baking powder.

> 4 tablespoons (½ stick) unsalted butter (optional)
> 2 cups all-purpose flour
> 2 teaspoons baking powder
> ½ teaspoon salt
> ¾–1 cup heavy cream

1. Heat oven to 450 degrees. Melt butter (if using) in a small saucepan. Place next 3 ingredients (flour through salt) in a large bowl and whisk together. Gradually add ¾ cup cream, stirring with a large fork or rubber spatula until dough holds together. If necessary, add more cream in 1-tablespoon increments. Press gently into a large ball and then coat lightly with flour. **2.** On a floured surface, roll dough until it is ⅜ inch thick. Use a biscuit cutter or other tool (mouth of a small jar, metal lid, etc.) to cut out individual biscuits. Dip each biscuit into optional melted butter if desired and place on a baking sheet. Bake about 12 minutes or until bottoms and tops are lightly browned. Remove immediately from baking sheet and serve hot.

MAKES 10 TO 15 BISCUITS,
DEPENDING UPON SIZE

Dewey Buns

This recipe is taken from Marion Cunningham's *The Breakfast Book* and is truly spectacular. These are light, puffy rectangles of fried dough filled with thick vanilla cream. The dough can be made the night before; the next morning, it is rolled out, cut, fried, and then filled. This recipe takes some time but is worth every minute of it. I do not bother to sift confectioner's sugar over the buns as suggested in the original recipe since the filling is already quite sweet (although you may wish to do so). Marion tasted Dewey buns many years ago in a food market in Lancaster, Pennsylvania, and liked them so much that she set to work to create her own recipe. Neither of us knows the origin of the name.

FOR THE BUNS
1   cup milk, warmed
⅓   cup sugar
1   teaspoon salt
¼   cup vegetable oil
3   cups all-purpose flour
1   package regular active yeast
¾   teaspoon nutmeg
1   egg
       Oil for frying

FOR THE DEWEY CREAM
1   egg white
2½   cups confectioners' sugar
4   tablespoons (½ stick) butter,
       room temperature
1   tablespoon nonfat dry milk
1   tablespoon vanilla extract
¼   teaspoon salt
½   cup heavy cream

1. Mix the warm milk with the sugar, salt, and oil and stir to blend.
2. Stir together 2 cups of the flour, the yeast, and the nutmeg in a mixing bowl. Add the milk mixture and beat with an electric mixer for about 3 minutes. Add the egg and remaining 1 cup flour and beat for 2 minutes. Cover and refrigerate for 4 to 8 hours or overnight.
3. Lightly dust a board with flour and turn dough onto it. Roll the dough into a rectangle about ¼ inch thick. Cut it into squares that are 2½ by 3 inches. Heat oil to 365 degrees. Fry the squares, a few at a time, until golden on both sides. Put the buns on paper towels and pat free of excess oil.
4. *For the Dewey cream:* Beat the egg white, confectioner's sugar, and butter in a mixing bowl with a hand-held electric

mixer for 3 minutes on high speed. The mixture should be very smooth. Stir the nonfat dry milk, vanilla, and salt into the cream and add to the sugar mixture. Beat until smooth and creamy.

5. Cut the fried buns in half lengthwise and, using a spoon, scoop out a shallow pocket from the inside of one of the halves. The pocket should be large enough to hold 1½ tablespoons of filling. Fill with the Dewey cream and thinly spread the cream out to the edges. Put the two halves together and gently press the bun edges so that the halves will bind.

MAKES ABOUT 18 BUNS

Rapid-Rise Variation

Using rapid-rise yeast, the recipe can be made from scratch before breakfast. Substitute rapid-rise yeast for regular active yeast. Allow dough to rise at room temperature until doubled in size, no more than an hour. Punch down and then continue with the recipe, starting with step 3.

Skillet Scrambled Eggs

An article by Elaine Corn in *Cook's Illustrated* in which she suggested cooking scrambled eggs quickly over medium-high heat was intriguing and the results were different from the low-heat method, but excellent. After about 10 seconds in the hot skillet, the eggs are pushed along with a wide wooden spoon or spatula. This constant movement keeps the eggs moist, produces wonderful rolling custardy curds, and also takes less than a minute.

3	tablespoons cream or buttermilk
2	eggs
	Salt and freshly ground pepper to taste
¼	teaspoon dried tarragon or
	½ teaspoon fresh, minced
1	tablespoon butter

1. Whisk together the cream and eggs with a fork. Add salt and pepper to taste. Add the tarragon and whisk to incorporate.

2. Heat a well-seasoned cast iron or non-stick skillet. Add the butter and swirl to coat the bottom and sides. Add the egg mixture and, over medium-high heat, push the eggs in swaths from one side of the pan to the other using a wooden spoon or no-melt plastic spatula. The eggs should roll up into large curds. Serve as soon as eggs are cooked but still moist.

MAKES 1 SERVING

Puffy Omelet

As with any omelet, you have to use a good nonstick pan or well-seasoned cast iron skillet. This is a quick and easy recipe (I think of it as a country quiche), and since it can be stuffed with almost anything, it's good for a substantial breakfast. Some might suggest that this would make a good brunch dish, but I've yet to meet a Vermonter who eats breakfast much later than 7 A.M.

6	eggs, separated
1	teaspoon salt
½	teaspoon freshly ground pepper
½	cup cream
1	teaspoon minced chives (optional)
4	tablespoons (½ stick) butter

ADDITIONAL INGREDIENTS
(CHOOSE ONE OR A
COMBINATION)

- ½ cup diced ham
- ½ cup diced cooked bacon or crumbled and browned sausage
- ½ cup diced onion or sliced scallions, sautéed in 2 teaspoons butter for 5 minutes
- ½ cup diced Swiss, Gruyère, or mozzarella cheese
- ⅓ cup grated Parmesan cheese

1. Place a well-seasoned cast iron or non-stick skillet over medium heat. Heat oven to 350 degrees.
2. In a medium bowl, beat yolks for about 4 minutes or until light-colored and thick. Add the salt, pepper, and cream and beat to combine. In a large bowl, beat the whites until they hold a 2-inch peak (they should still be soft and glossy looking). Fold the yolks along with the optional chives and any of the additions into the whites.
3. Add the butter to the skillet and, when foam subsides, add the egg mixture. When the mixture is just set, in about 3 minutes (if using a nonstick pan, the omelet will move around in one piece when the pan is lightly shaken), place the pan in the pre-heated oven. Bake for about 10 minutes or until the top is puffy and set and light brown.

SERVES 4 TO 6

Cornmeal Mush

This recipe is great for breakfast with a bit of maple syrup and some milk or cream. It should be made in the microwave since it is fast, about 8 minutes, and also fool-proof. Note that this recipe does not work well with a fine-grind cornmeal such as Quaker, as it will clump and be uneven in texture. I find that the best type to use is a polenta-style cornmeal, which is very coarse, almost like small pellets.

- 1 cup medium- or coarse-grind cornmeal (do not use fine cornmeal)
- 3½ cups water
- 1 tablespoon vegetable oil or melted butter
- ½ teaspoon salt
  Maple syrup and milk or cream for serving

Place first 4 ingredients in an 8-cup glass measuring cup and stir lightly. Cover tightly with microwave-proof plastic wrap and microwave on high for 5 minutes. Uncover, stir with a wooden spoon (be sure to get at the more cooked layer on the bottom of the measuring cup), and then whisk to blend. Cover and cook an additional 3 minutes on high. Uncover, whisk again, and serve with maple syrup and milk or cream.

SERVES 3 TO 4
AS A HOT BREAKFAST CEREAL

HALF RECIPE

Reduce all ingredients by 50 percent but cook at 60 percent power for 4 minutes, whisk, and then cook another 4 minutes at the same power setting. Stir and serve with maple syrup and milk or cream.

Buttermilk Doughnuts

On rainy days, when we weren't mowing, tedding, raking, or baling hay, I would spend a few hours at the small yellow farmhouse that served as Marie Briggs's bakery. Of all the items that she baked and bagged for sale at the local country store, the farmhands were keenest on her doughnuts, substantial rounds of nutmeg-spiced dough, fried in lard so the outside was crisp and rich in flavor. Years later, those of us who spent time in that tiny farmhouse remember the doughnuts best, for their toothsome chew, their hint of crunch on the first bite, and their long-lasting sturdiness. I wanted to re-create the recipe, finding the best method for making a substantial country doughnut, not some airy Dunkin Donuts confection, with a good crunch on the outside and a moist, nutmeg-spiced interior.

Testing Ingredients

I started by cobbling together a master recipe that offered the best of both worlds using buttermilk, eggs, flour, sugar, baking powder, baking soda, melted butter, salt, and ground nutmeg. I then set out to test each ingredient, starting with the buttermilk. As is often the case, buttermilk provided a superior doughnut to those made with regular milk; the latter were denser, firmer, and less crisp. I also tried skim buttermilk and there was no noticeable difference, so you can use either. My master recipe used both baking powder and baking soda, so I tested leaving out the baking powder altogether (increasing the baking soda to a full teaspoon) and I also tried decreasing the amounts of both leaveners; neither test was satisfactory.

The master recipe had a slightly better chew than either test.

I had some luck with adding one extra egg yolk. This made a moister dough, and the extra fat also created a more tender doughnut. Increasing the butter, however, did improve the flavor, but bumping the sugar to 1¼ cups from 1 cup simply made the doughnuts brown up more readily, which was not necessarily an improvement. Besides, they were sweet enough as is, although not nearly as sweet as most commercial doughnuts. At first I liked the addition of vanilla, but after a few tastings it became clear that this extra flavor overpowered the delicate taste of nutmeg, the spice of choice. When bread flour was substituted for all-purpose, the dough was firmer and drier, which resulted in a doughnut that was less crisp on the outside. Bleached flour made no noticeable difference. I also tried adding an additional ¼ cup of flour to the recipe and determined that this drier dough does make a less crispy but also less greasy product. It is also a bit firmer and more chewy inside, but the lack of crackle on the outside placed this variation in second place.

Frying Methods

Next, I had to settle on the proper pot for frying. The best implement by far is a cast iron kettle, and I found that the 12-inch-diameter model was superior to the 10-inch because it maintains a nice steady heat, keeping the oil at the proper temperature without having to adjust the burner. The first fats I tried were soybean oil, corn oil, and canola oil (the latter coming in dead last), all of which were given mediocre ratings by my tasters. However,

I went on to test peanut oil and safflower oil, both of which were well liked. I then did a head-to-head taste-off between these two oils and peanut oil came in first, with rich flavor and good texture as well. The doughnuts were on the greasy side, though, so I called an old friend of mine, Drew, who runs Mrs. Murphy's Doughnuts, a store located in the next town. He suggested that I try a commercial shortening used by doughnut makers called Super Fry. I ordered the minimum quantity (a whopping 50 pounds!) and in a blind taste test, it won hands down. The doughnut fried in peanut oil was greasy in comparison. I then tested Crisco, a hydrogenated vegetable oil, and, to my surprise, this was a close second to the Super Fry because it absorbed much less oil than the peanut oil, my reigning favorite. I also found that doughnuts fried in the vegetable shortenings (Super Fry or Crisco) held up better than those fried in oil. I did note, however, that Crisco has a slightly off flavor; one taster noted that the doughnuts tasted a bit like circus food. But the lack of greasiness more than made up for the slight imperfections in flavor.

I also thought that I would test lard, since Marie Briggs swore by lard for her doughnuts. I had found that a combination of lard and oil works very well for most fried foods. But I also knew that lard has changed over the years. In the old days, lard used in cooking was "leaf" lard, the fat around the kidneys. This is a superior lard, one without a strong flavor. Today, lard is the fat from any portion of a pig and, generally speaking, it is much stronger and of lower quality than the lard Marie was probably using on the farm.

However, I pressed on with the tests and started off by using all lard, which was much too meaty tasting. I then cut back and used 5 ounces of lard to 5 cups of Crisco. This was good, very similar to the Vermont country doughnuts I grew up with, but compared to the doughnuts fried just in Crisco, the differences were slight. I then increased the lard to 2 ounces per cup of shortening, and this resulted in a nice boost of flavor. Lard is purely an optional ingredient.

In terms of cooking temperature, it is best to start out with the oil at 375 degrees, since the temperature will fall back to 360 or 365 as soon as the dough is added. At 350 degrees the dough absorbs too much oil; at 385 degrees the outside starts to burn before the inside cooks through. Also be sure to bring the shortening back up to temperature between batches. Finally, I wanted to find out if the shortening was reusable. Although I had been successful when reusing peanut oil, Crisco just didn't hold well; the second batch of doughnuts, made the next day, suffered a good deal in terms of flavor.

COOKING TIMES
Many recipes call for cooking doughnuts for 1½ minutes per side, a time that I found to be much too long. Once the doughnuts had been placed in the hot shortening and flipped, I tested 40 seconds, 50 seconds, 60 seconds, and 70 seconds and found that 50 seconds was ideal. The center was just cooked and the doughnut did not take on that dry, catch-in-your-throat texture. As a general rule, fry doughnuts until they are light brown unless they are particularly thick, in which

case they will have to be cooked a bit longer. The big surprise, however, was that doughnuts cooked longer were also greasier. The shorter the frying time, the less chance the shortening had to penetrate the dough.

FINAL THOUGHTS

If you prefer more of a country doughnut — firmer, chewier, less greasy, and crispy on the outside — add ¼ cup of flour to the recipe. As I discovered, drier doughs make firmer doughnuts. One last word of advice. When rolling out the dough, make sure that it is no more or less than ½ inch thick, about the width of the last joint of your little finger. Thinner doughs make doughnuts that are squat, with insufficient height to provide contrast between the exterior and interior. Dough that is rolled out to ⅝ inch or more will produce a bloated orb that is undercooked on the inside.

Buttermilk Doughnuts

3½	cups all-purpose flour, plus additional for dusting
1	cup sugar
½	teaspoon baking soda
2	teaspoons baking powder
1	teaspoon salt
1½	teaspoons ground nutmeg
¾	cup buttermilk
4	tablespoons (½ stick) unsalted butter, melted
2	eggs
1	egg yolk
6	cups vegetable shortening (Crisco) for frying
6	ounces lard for frying (optional)

1. In the bowl of a standing mixer, combine 1 cup of the flour, the sugar, baking soda, baking powder, salt, and nutmeg. (The first two steps of this recipe can also be completed by hand using a large bowl and a wooden spoon.)

2. In another bowl, whisk together the buttermilk, melted butter, whole eggs, and yolk. On medium speed (the number 4 setting on a KitchenAid), pour the liquid into the dry ingredients and beat for 10 seconds to make a homogenous batter (if you have a paddle attachment, use it). Lower speed and add the remaining 2½ cups of flour; mix until just combined, about 30 seconds. Using a wooden spoon or rubber spatula, give the dough a thorough mix in case liquid on the bottom of the mixing bowl has not been thoroughly combined. The dough will be quite moist and tacky, somewhere between a thick cake batter and a cookie dough.

3. In a large cast iron Dutch oven, heat vegetable shortening and optional lard to 375 degrees. Use a candy thermometer fitted to the kettle to keep track of the oil temperature as you work.

4. While the oil is heating, dust the work surface and a rolling pin *liberally* with flour. Roll out the dough to just ½ inch thick, about the width of the last joint of your little finger. Cut out doughnuts using a well-floured doughnut cutter and be sure to flour between cuts. (To flour a doughnut cutter, dip it into a container of flour.) You can gather the scraps and roll them out again to make more doughnuts. (We found that subsequent doughnuts were slightly drier and less crisp than the first batch.) Let the cut doughnuts sit for 5 minutes before frying as they will begin to rise. Cut doughnuts can sit for up to 2 hours.

5. When the oil reaches 375 degrees, fry doughnuts 4 or 5 at a time, depending on the size of your pot. As the doughnuts rise to the top (about 10 seconds), flip them using a slotted spoon. Let the doughnuts cook for 50 seconds (or until well browned) and flip again. Fry for the same amount of time on the other side. Remove and place on absorbent paper towels. Let the oil return to 375 degrees before frying subsequent batches. Doughnuts are best eaten warm. They cannot be successfully reheated.

MAKES 12 TO 14 DOUGHNUTS

Sour Cream Coffee Cake

This recipe is adapted from *Beard on Bread* by James Beard. I reduced the yeast by half and also increased the amount of filling, but otherwise his is an excellent recipe. Most coffee cakes are too sweet for me, but this one is more breadlike, contrasting nicely with the sweeter filling. The dough can be made in the evening and stored in the refrigerator overnight if you substitute regular active yeast for the rapid-rise. Since this makes a double recipe, you can make one cake right away and leave the other half of the dough in the refrigerator as long as it is punched down twice a day and the dough is made with regular yeast. You can also make half a recipe for just one cake, halving all ingredients and using 2 egg yolks instead

of 3. Although buttermilk doughnuts are very popular with the coffee-hour crowd at our Methodist church in Vermont, this coffee cake comes in a close second.

FOR THE DOUGH

2	packages rapid-rise yeast (or regular active dried yeast if you wish to make the dough the night before baking)
½	cup sugar
½	cup warm water (115 to 120 degrees)
1	teaspoon salt
½	cup milk
3	egg yolks
1	cup sour cream
2	teaspoons lemon juice
1	teaspoon vanilla extract
5–6	cups all-purpose flour
3	sticks (¾ pound) unsalted butter, softened

FOR THE FILLING

1½	cups currants or raisins
½	cup bourbon, rum, or brandy
3	tablespoons unsalted butter, melted
⅓	cup sugar
1½	teaspoons ground cinnamon
¼	teaspoon ground nutmeg
½	teaspoon ground allspice
1½	cups walnuts or pecans, chopped

FOR THE GLAZE

1	cup apricot jam or preserves
1	tablespoon brandy or bourbon

FOR OPTIONAL ICING

1	cup sifted confectioners' sugar
2	tablespoons milk

1. In a medium bowl, mix together the first 9 ingredients (yeast through vanilla

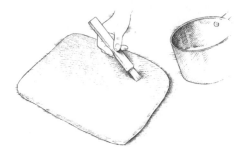

1. *To make Sour Cream Coffee Cake,* shape the dough into a rectangle, 10 by 14 inches. Brush with melted butter, leaving a one-inch border along one of the 14-inch sides unbrushed.

2. Place the filling on the dough, leaving the same one-inch border uncovered. Lightly press filling into the dough with a rolling pin. Roll up dough from the nearest 14-inch side.

3. Continue rolling dough into a cylinder.

4. Pinch seam to seal.

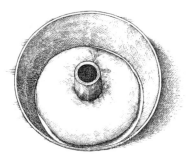

5. Lay the dough into a well-buttered tube pan like a coil of rope.

6. Make sure the the ends touch so that, when baked, the coffee cake is even and well proportioned. Cover with a damp towel and let rise for twenty minutes before baking.

extract). In a very large bowl, add 5 cups of the flour and then work in the softened butter with your fingertips (you can also pulse the flour and butter together in a food processor with a large workbowl) until the flour takes on the texture of a coarse meal. Add the yeast mixture and stir to combine with a large rubber spatula, wooden spoon, or your hands. Knead the dough in the bowl, adding more flour if necessary to produce a relatively smooth dough that holds together but is not overly sticky. Remove to a lightly floured board and knead for 6 or 7 minutes. (The dough can also be kneaded in the bowl of a large standing mixer using a dough hook.) Shape into a ball, place in a very lightly oiled bowl, and cover with plastic wrap. Let rise in a warm place until doubled in volume, about 45 minutes. (You may want to make this dough using regular active yeast and, at this point, let it sit in the refrigerator overnight. Using this method, the dough is easier to work with in the next step.)

2. About 1 hour before continuing with the recipe, soak the currants or raisins (for the filling) in the liquor.

3. Divide dough in half and roll out each piece into a rectangle, about 10 by 14 inches. Brush both pieces with the melted butter, leaving a 1-inch border along one of the 14-inch sides. Stir together the sugar and the 3 spices and then sprinkle over the dough except on the 1-inch border. Drain the currants or raisins and sprinkle over dough along with the nuts, once again leaving the border uncovered. Use a rolling pin to press filling into dough. Roll up the rectangles of dough from the wide end without the border. Pinch the dough along the seam to seal.

4. Heavily butter two 9-inch tube pans. Lay each roll in a pan like a coil of rope, fitting the ends together so they join closely. Pinch the ends of the coil together to join. The cylinders will coil around the center tube. Cover with a damp kitchen towel and let rise until doubled in bulk, about 20 minutes. Meanwhile, heat oven to 375 degrees. Bake for 45 to 55 minutes until golden brown and the internal temperature registers 205 degrees when measured with an instant-read thermometer. Cool for 15 minutes in the pans and then invert onto a rack. (This coffee cake can also be baked on a parchment-lined jelly roll pan and formed into a ring. Pinch the ends to seal. Using scissors, cut about ¾ of the way through the ring, dividing the coil into 8 to 12 evenly spaced segments. Twist each segment with your fingers about a quarter turn to expose the rings of filling. Let double in volume and bake about 30 minutes following the instructions above.)

5. Melt the apricot jam over low heat. Add the liquor and stir to blend. Let simmer for 2 minutes. Strain. Brush on glaze while cakes are still warm. If using the confectioners' sugar icing, place 1 cup sifted confectioner's sugar and 2 tablespoons milk in a small saucepan. Stir to combine. Bring mixture to a boil, reduce heat, and simmer for 3 minutes. Drizzle on coffee cake after it is glazed.

MAKES 2 LARGE CAKES

CINNAMON ROLL VARIATION

Use a half recipe. After the dough has been filled and rolled (it should be about 14 inches long), trim away ½ inch on either end and then cut it into 1½-inch-wide slices. Generously butter a 10-inch pie plate or a 10-inch round or 9-inch square cake pan. Place rolls cut side up in the prepared pan and cover with a kitchen towel until doubled in size, about 25 minutes. (This will take a bit longer if using regular, not rapid-rise, yeast.) Bake in a 350 degree oven for 20 to 25 minutes or until the tops are golden brown and are firm to the touch. Let cool for 10 minutes. Make a glaze with 1 tablespoon milk whisked into ⅔ cups confectioners' sugar and drizzle over the tops. Serve immediately.

MAKES 9 ROLLS

Quick and Crumbly Coffee Cake

Unlike the recipe above, this coffee cake uses baking powder and soda rather than yeast and can therefore be made at the last minute. This is a rich, moist coffee cake and is very good when made with ripe peaches.

STREUSEL TOPPING

½	cup flour
½	cup packed brown sugar
1	tablespoon granulated sugar
¾	cup toasted and chopped pecans or walnuts
½	teaspoon cinnamon
½	teaspoon nutmeg
4	tablespoons (½ stick) softened, but firm, unsalted butter

FOR THE CAKE

2	cups flour
½	teaspoon baking powder
½	teaspoon baking soda
½	teaspoon salt
12	tablespoons (1½ sticks) unsalted butter at room temperature
1	cup granulated sugar
1	egg plus 2 yolks
1½	teaspoons vanilla extract
¾	cup sour cream
1	apple or 2 peaches, peeled, cored or pitted, and cut into ¼-inch slices (optional)

1. Heat oven to 350 degrees. Grease and flour a 9-inch springform pan. Adjust oven rack to the middle position. Combine all ingredients for the streusel topping in a medium bowl and mix with an electric mixer until the mixture is crumbly and the butter is thoroughly combined, 3 to 4 minutes.

2. For the cake, sift the first 4 ingredients (flour through salt) onto a piece of wax paper. Put the butter in a large bowl and beat for 1 minute with an electric mixer. Add the sugar gradually and beat on high speed for 3 minutes or until the mixture is light-colored and fluffy. Add the egg and yolks one at a time and beat for 20 seconds after each addition. Add the vanilla and beat for 10 seconds.

3. Add ⅓ of the flour mixture and ⅓ of the sour cream and stir with a large rubber spatula or mix on low speed until combined. Repeat twice, scraping down the sides of the bowl as necessary. Be careful not to overbeat.

4. Add ⅔ of the batter to the prepared pan. Smooth the top with a rubber spatula. Add ½ of the streusel topping and all of the optional fruit. Add the remaining batter in globs on the top and, starting in the center, spread the batter gently to cover the surface. Sprinkle with the remaining streusel topping.

5. Bake for 50 to 60 minutes, checking after 40 minutes. If the top is becoming too browned, cover the cake with a sheet of aluminum foil for remainder of the baking time. The cake is done when the top is rounded and firm to the touch and a cake tester inserted in the center comes out clean.

SERVES 8 TO 10

The Cookie Jar

OUR COUNTRY STORE is a real workingman's hangout, not some tourist destination. Like a charmed and bottomless wine jug out of Greek myth, this store has everything from sulfite-free white wine to 15-amp fuses. If you are in need of tools for painting, car repair, or rough carpentry, they have them. You can also find stacks of duct and masking tape, road flares, Tung-Sol auto lamps, and Goof Off paint remover. If you are sick they have shelves packed with all the usual pharmaceuticals plus Dr. Seltzer's Hangover Helper and a box of ginseng tablets for energy. Hunters purchase their licenses here by the day, week, or year. If you need ammunition, that's no problem either, from .22 shorts to 12-gauge shotgun shells for dove and quail (number 8 shot), rabbit and squirrel (number 6), and pheasant (number 4). You can also buy plenty of supplies for black powder rifles, including Pyrodex powder, .50-caliber lead saboted boat tail bullets, ramrods, nipple wrenches, cleaners, and patches, as well as standard rifle cleaning equipment such as bore butter. Fishermen can find a broad assortment of Umpqua flies, including a Gray Yellow Hackle, an Elk Caddis, and a Trico Spinner. There is plenty to chew on, from Skoal Long Cut to Red Man Tobacco, or you can roll your own with Zig-Zag papers.

The proprietors, Doug and Nancy Tschorn, have lots of merchandise to attract the kids as well. You can find Yardstick Bubble Gum, Hacky Sack Footbags, Wolf Pack Bang Snaps, Assorted Color Smoke Bombs, Tippy Toes Finger Puppets, Jetfire Gliders, a jumbo bag of My Farm animals with sixteen pieces, an Explorer H20 Rocket, a Woody Woodpecker Magic Draw, removable tattoos, Giant Outdoor Chalk, and a Bible Song Sing Along. For candy, there are bags of jelly beans, gumdrops, candy watches, and the original hard-chew Bazooka Joe bubble gum.

The real attraction, however, is the round table in the back right next to the coffee shelf, which also offers prepackaged boxes of Gramps Restaurant Style Nachos with a white plastic dispenser for Gehl's Cheese Sauce. Here is the heart and soul of the town, especially early in the morning, as the carpenters, electricians, and plumbers stop by for a cup of coffee and the opportunity to complain about the town selectmen or the new town garage or the secession of our sovereign rights to the United Nations. (In fact, there is an informal "round table club," which is made up of early morning regulars.) A book entitled *Redneck Classics* lies open on the table and it offers plenty of good advice. I read that you are a redneck if "your bra size is larger than your IQ" or if "you have lots of hubcaps on your house but none on your car." You can always read a paperback if you are alone at the table, including *Campfire Thrillers, The Invisible Man,* and *The Official Italian/Polish Joke Book.* Former patrons have left a wall of hats behind, advertising everything from the Mall of America, Daytona Bike Week, Wilcox Lumber, Tri State Mega Bucks, UPS, and Salem cigarettes. Although out of place, "Cat in the Hat"–style headgear abounds as well, stuffed onto the head of a mannequin sporting hunting gear and propped onto the head of a buck, towering over its branched eight-point antlers. A postcard of the board of directors is posted right above the table: four donkeys staring out of a desert scene.

The back table also has plenty of magazines, including *Easyrider,* the magazine for motorcycle enthusiasts or anyone who enjoys seeing naked women on hot bikes, and *Women's Physical World,* which features G-string–clad bodybuilders with overdeveloped muscles that appear to need corrective surgery. You can also purchase copies of *Bass & Walleye Boats, 4 X 4 Power, Vermont Deer Camp Recipes,* and *American Astrology.*

For food, the selection is mostly dry goods, although the freezer section does offer Wolfgang Puck's 4-Cheese Pizza as well as the more popular Celeste Large Size Pepperoni Pizza. Great glass cookie jars stand on the counter next to the register or you can purchase Nilla Wafers from the back shelves. For pasta, you can stick with Chef Boyardee canned ravioli or ante up for the pricy Spring Hill Vermont Pasta that comes in egg, spinach, and tomato flavors. Real woodsmen might purchase a can of Armour Sliced and Dried Beef or B&M Brown Bread. No real country store is much without a broad selection of beer, from the budget-minded Genesee to a 25-ounce can of Fosters to Long Trail Blackberry Wheat to Heck's Cider.

But what really makes a Vermont country store is the unexpected. You can still buy a small green can of Antiseptic Bag Balm for your cow, a one-dollar postcard grab bag, Larvex Cedarized Moth Balls, a candy apple kit, or a bumper sticker that reads "My Kid Beat Up Your Honor Student" or "Just When You Think Life's a Bitch It Has Puppies." When the door opens, the old cowbell still rings with its deep, low clang. And as you walk in you can't help but see the sign that reads "If We Don't Have It, You Don't Want It."

When I was a kid, a trip to the store meant a handful of Mallo Cups, dark chocolate rounds spiked with crispy coconut and filled with gooey marshmallow, or a box of Black Snake fire tablets or a green plastic water pistol that would last about 24 hours, the trigger breaking after just a few fill-ups, hanging loose from the fingerguard. I usually stopped by after milking for an orange or grape soda, my T-shirt stuck with small spikes of hay. Although the Mallo Cups disappeared a few years back, the water pistols and snake tablets are still there, as are the balsa airplanes, smoke bombs, and cap pistols. I sit out on the porch with a can of soda and an oversized oatmeal cookie, watch the cheap American flag flutter occasionally in the hot breeze, listen to the clank of the cowbell, and wait for my children, excitedly flitting from one attraction to the next, trying to decide between candy lipstick and bubble gum tape or the small yellow plastic bank and the miniature finger puppets. I feel as if I have been sitting on that porch for forty years now, winters and summers having come and gone, my kids first as newborns, soon to be teenagers and then off on their own journey beginning on the road by this old country

store. They may go left or right, drive slow or push forward with great anticipation and speed, but somehow this old country road always comes back around and you find yourself, many years later, sitting on that narrow front porch, hefting a big-as-your-fist homemade cookie, knowing that your grandchildren will sit there someday listening to the dull clang of the same cowbell that greeted you so many years ago.

OLD-TIME country bakers, those who didn't use electric appliances, had massive biceps. I remember watching Marie Briggs mix up cookie dough by hand. Compared to today's standards of health and beauty, Marie wasn't much to look at, since she was quite pale, almost pasty, in complexion, spending most of her time indoors before the hot wood-fired stove. Like any real Vermonter, she never "exercised," since she burned plenty of calories in one long day, getting up before sunrise, making three meals for the farmhands, baking bread and cookies, and doing a score of odd jobs around the house. But Vermonters are deceiving, since they move slowly and their outward appearance is softened by a starchy diet unrelieved by many fresh fruits or vegetables. Under the loose folds of doughy draping lies cast iron, the kind of wiry strength that can free up a frozen lug nut, toss a large bale of hay high up onto a pickup, or move a 4 x 8-foot sheet of ⅝-inch Sheetrock without a grunt. City folks with their exercise machines, health clubs, and expensive running shoes have the appearance of strength, but deep down they just can't go the distance. I am particularly fond of inviting health-obsessed weekend guests to help out with a half-day of haying. After the fourth load, the local farmer has yet to break into a sweat while the high-fiber crowd has that vacant thousand-yard stare, having had to come face to face with a drastically revised self-image, one that has been sweated out of them in the hot sun. If we aren't haying, I invite guests on a short hike, which turns out to be a steep climb to 2,500 feet along an old logging road. It starts out with a gentle upward slope, the unsuspecting family dressed in well-pressed khaki shorts and carrying small backpacks filled with water, dried fruit, and nuts. About halfway up, where the incline starts to get serious, they start to ask how far we have to go or whether we shouldn't turn back in time for lunch. At this point, my wife (who is piggybacking our thirty-five-pound 2-year-old-son), our two daughters (who are running out ahead), and I (who am usually stuck with the Stihl chain saw to help clear the road) put our heads down, keep on marching, and tell them we will meet them at the top. This eliminates the possibility of negotiation and becomes a pure test of will. They all make it, eventually, although some guests don't ever invite themselves back. It's the sort of humor understood by Vermonters, who never tire of embarrassing flatlanders, especially when it comes to matters of endurance. One old bachelor, Owen Hayes, once told me that he had broken his leg and had a cast put on. He got such a bad case of cabin fever that he went out with a small crew one day and cut twenty-four cords of wood before nightfall. That's a Vermonter for you.

Over the years, I have had plenty of ex-perience with this sort of humor, having been put through a series of initiation rites. My first day on the job with the local dairy farmer, when I had just turned ten, started with an instruction to go out and bring in a cow with her newborn calf. The rest of the herd was already in the barn for the afternoon milking. I went out to the back pasture and soon found the wayward cow, horns long and untrimmed, standing protectively in front of her three-day-old. This wasn't the first time I had been around cows, but I was used to slow-moving docile beasts, the kind that might step on your foot if you weren't careful, but I had never witnessed aggressive behavior. Knowing that I was being watched from the barn, I hitched up my pants and went right after her, confident that a slap on the rump and a few throaty "git-along" sounds would soon get the job done. When I was about thirty feet away, she lowered her massive horns, actually pawed the ground like a dyspeptic Texas long-horn, and came right after me. I was lucky, since the barbed wire fence was nearby, and I scrambled under it, like a crab scuttling out of reach of the net, and found myself in a dense patch of milk-weed and thistle. I looked up and saw her huge head, red eyes bulging out of the massive bony sockets, a long ropy string of drool hanging from her lips. For the next twenty minutes, I scooted out from the safety of the fence, made a series of wild herding movements with my arms, and then ran like crazy for safety. We finally worked our way around the perimeter of the pasture, the cow chasing me back to the great red barn, when the farmer, wearing a faded green cap and just the hint of a grin, grabbed a thick leather milking strap, came to my aid, gave the cow a couple of good whacks, and she turned toward the barn, docile and defeated. I'll never forget that he managed to keep from laughing in the face of my utter humiliation, but that story is still told in our town, some thirty-five years later, since it so clearly defines what it means to be a Vermonter.

Although I was slow to pick up the finer details of farming, I did learn a thing or two about baking, since I spent many a rainy afternoon in the old yellow farmhouse, helping out Marie Briggs. I found that mixing cookie dough by hand is, for many recipes, actually preferable to using an electric mixer. A chocolate chip cookie dough, for example, can easily liquefy, producing flat, dull cookies. This is one category of recipe where a wooden spoon works just fine. In recent years, I have done a great deal of cookie testing and have found a few other interesting facts.

The most important of these is the difference between chemical leaveners. Baking powder is nothing more than baking soda (about one-quarter to one-third of the total makeup) mixed with an acid and double-dried cornstarch. The acid produces carbon dioxide when it comes into contact with the baking soda, and the cornstarch keeps the two elements apart during storage, preventing the premature production of the gas.

Many cooks believe that since only one-third of baking powder is baking soda — the actual leavening agent — then full-strength baking soda must be a more powerful leavening agent. Although it seems logical, this is incorrect. Baking soda is only fully effective if there is an acid component in the batter for it to react with and create carbon dioxide. In an alkaline (low-acid) batter, a teaspoon of baking powder will be a more effective leavener, since the baking soda in the powder combines with the leavening acid, also contained in the powder itself, to produce a more complete chemical reaction. This is the reason why recipes that contain acidic ingredients such as buttermilk usually call just for baking soda. That being said, even in the absence of an acid, baking soda will decompose during baking and throw off some carbon dioxide gas, but far less than baking powder. Generally the choice of whether to use baking soda or baking powder depends on the acidity of the batter rather than on the issue of leavening horsepower.

There is one other major difference between these two leaveners. Most baking powders are double acting, which means that two different chemical leavening acids are used in the mixture: one works at room temperature and the other works best at oven temperatures. In a cake, for example, it is important to have an early release of carbon dioxide during the batter preparation so that small bubbles are created to form the nuclei of the cell structure. These cells expand during baking because of additional carbon dioxide production caused by the action of the second leavening acid, and the dough firms up into the final cake structure. In a stiff cookie batter, however, especially one that has a good deal of structure from butter and eggs, the double-acting issue is less critical.

To test the relative merits of baking powder and baking soda, the test kitchen at *Cook's Illustrated* baked six batches of the oatmeal chocolate chip cookie recipe in this chapter, using one-quarter tea-spoon, one-half teaspoon, and one full teaspoon each of baking powder and then repeated the exercise with baking soda.

The cookies baked with one-quarter teaspoon of leavener were too flat, regardless of whether they used baking powder or baking soda. Curiously, the cookies made with a full teaspoon of baking soda were also flat, while those made with a full teaspoon of baking powder rose nicely. After some research, I discovered that this was because a full teaspoon of baking soda was *too much* leavener; the bubbles of carbon dioxide got too big, ran into each other, floated to the top of the mixture, and then popped, causing the cookie to deflate.

I also noticed that the baking soda cookies were all slightly darker and the outer crust crisper, particularly those baked with the larger amounts of the leavener. This, I discovered, is because baking soda increases the pH of dough more than baking powder, since after baking, some sodium bicarbonate is left over in the cookie. This kicks up the pH level of the cookie and leads to browning as well as a crispier exterior. This is why professional bakers add baking soda — about one-quarter teaspoon per cup of flour — to cookie dough: to encourage browning. However, in my tests, I found that the baking soda cookies had an unpleasant, quite bitter flavor as opposed to the clean, pure taste of the baking powder cookies. Finally, I found little difference in either lift or flavor between cookies made with a full teaspoon of baking powder versus a half teaspoon, so I voted for the lesser amount. In other tests, I found that if you

like a thick cookie, letting the dough sit in the refrigerator for a couple of hours helps. The dough will sit up on the baking sheet better, without quickly puddling into a large flat cookie. I use parchment paper on my cookie sheets simply because I can quickly slide off a baked batch and then slide on a new one. The bottoms also seem to be less prone to burning. You can purchase reusable baking sheet liners. Some look like metallic gold wax paper and others appear to be thin black mats. Contact The Baker's Catalogue at 800-827-6836 for more information. I also found in testing that parchment paper makes a better cookie, chewier and with more body. One last trick. Ice cream scoops (these come in many different sizes; use one that is about half as large as the common ice cream shop variety) are good for scooping dough and placing it on cookie sheets. These scoops are also good for muffin batter. Be sure to review the Country Kitchen chapter in this book (pages 3–33) before you purchase cookie sheets. I tested and rated eight different models and found two different brands for under $10 that worked fine.

Master Butter Cookie Recipe

Every time I think of cookies I remember this story about an extremely obese woman from our town who happened to be pregnant. She went in for an ultrasound and when the doctors unfolded a layer of fat to properly place the scope on her abdomen, they stopped in surprise. There, nestled in one of the folds, was a Twinkie. When she was asked about this strange phenomenon, she told them it was really quite simple. She and her husband liked to play "Hide the Twinkie"!

This recipe is a good all-purpose butter cookie, which is moist and cakey with a strong butter flavor. I found that the butter needs to be whipped for quite a long time, otherwise the batter becomes too stiff when chilled. I also found that a lower oven temperature was necessary to allow the cookies to bake through without becoming too dark on the bottom. This recipe can also be made with regular all-purpose flour, although cake flour is preferred.

2	cups plus 2 tablespoons cake flour (use all-purpose in a pinch)
½	teaspoon salt
2	sticks unsalted butter, softened
¾	cup sugar
2	egg yolks
1	teaspoon vanilla extract

1. Sift together the flour and salt onto a sheet of wax paper.
2. Place butter in a large bowl and beat with an electric mixer on high speed for about 5 minutes or until pale yellow and fluffy. (Be sure to beat butter for the full 5 minutes.) Add the sugar and beat on medium-high speed until mixture is very pale and very light, about another 2 to 3 minutes. Scrape down sides of bowl and add the yolks and vanilla. Beat for 30 seconds or until incorporated. Add the flour mixture and beat, slowly at first, for about 20 seconds, or until mixture forms a rough dough. Shape the dough into a round (if making refrigerator cookies, dough must be shaped into logs at this point), wrap in plastic, and refrigerate dough for at least 2 hours or up to 3 days.

3. Heat oven to 350 degrees. Line 1 or 2 cookie sheets with parchment paper.
4. Shape cookies (see below), arrange them ½ inch apart on the cookie sheet, and bake for 7 to 15 minutes depending on the shape of the cookie. If your oven is uneven, turn the cookie sheet halfway through baking. The bottom of the cookies should be lightly browned, while the tops should barely take on color. Let cookies sit on a cooling rack for 1 hour to set.

MAKES 40 DROP COOKIES OR
65 REFRIGERATOR COOKIES

DROP COOKIE VARIATION

Shape rounded teaspoons of dough into a ball using your palms and place onto baking sheet about 2 inches apart. Brush with egg white and sprinkle with sugar. Bake for 10 to 12 minutes or until lightly browned.

THUMBPRINT COOKIES

Shape rounded teaspoons of dough into a ball using your palms and place onto baking sheet about 2 inches apart. Make an indentation in the middle of the dough with your thumb and fill with ¼ teaspoon jam. Bake for 10 to 12 minutes or until lightly browned.

REFRIGERATOR COOKIE VARIATION

Divide the dough into 4 pieces. Take each piece and place it on a sheet of wax paper. Mold each piece of dough into a log shape and then wrap with the wax paper.

Twist the ends to seal. Chill for 2 hours or up to 3 days. To make cookies, unwrap and cut ¼-inch-thick cookies with a thin knife. Wet knife every few cookies to facilitate cutting. Arrange 1 inch apart on baking sheet. Bake about 14 minutes or until lightly browned.

ROLLED COOKIE VARIATION

Refrigerate dough for an extra half hour (for a total of 2½ hours). On a lightly floured surface, roll dough out until it is ⅛ to ¼ inch thick, depending on the thickness desired (⅛ inch is about as thick as a quarter). Cut into shapes with a cookie cutter. A ⅛-inch cookie will take 5 to 6 minutes to bake; thicker cookies take 8 to 9 minutes.

JAM SANDWICHES

Follow the directions for the rolled cookies, rolling out the dough to ⅛ inch thickness. Cut dough with a round cookie cutter and place half of the circles on cookie sheets. Spread a thin layer of jam (apricot and raspberry are good choices) over the circles. Using a smaller-diameter cookie cutter, cut a hole in the remaining rounds of dough and place on top of the cookies on the sheets. Bake 10 to 12 minutes or until lightly browned.

ALMOND VARIATION

Add ½ teaspoon almond extract along with the egg yolks. Add 1 cup toasted, slivered almonds to the dough mixture before the last 5 seconds of mixing.

ORANGE AND LEMON VARIATIONS

Add ½ teaspoon orange oil (available by mail order and at specialty stores) and 2 tablespoons grated orange zest with the liquid ingredients. For lemon cookies, use ½ teaspoon lemon oil and 2 tablespoons lemon zest.

Molasses Spice Cookies

At noon, the farmhands would meet at the old yellow house just by the town line and sit down to a classic New England meal of meat, potatoes, gravy, home-baked bread, fresh milk served in a white pitcher draped with a blue checkered napkin to keep out the flies, the occasional vegetable and, of course, big, large as a boy's fist, molasses cookies, with floured bottoms and a rich, chewy center a ten-year-old could get lost in. Although the local baker passed away a few years back, I was determined to find a method for preparing these rich, perfect rounds of baked dough at home for my kids.

I started with a recipe given to me by Rosemary Brophy, whose son makes her molasses cookies for a Boston restaurant. After one bite, I knew that they were much like the cookies I enjoyed in the old farmhouse. To get them just right, however, I performed a series of tests, beginning with how to deal with the butter and sugar. Creaming them (beating them together until they were light and fluffy) produced a lighter-textured cookie than using melted butter. Another trick I use for making thick chewy cookies, chilling the dough before baking, worked here as well. The cold dough doesn't spread out as readily, resulting in a thicker cookie. The proper amount of sugar was also crucial. Too little and the cookies tended to be hard and dry. I tried different quantities and settled on 1 cup of sugar to ¼ cup of molasses. I tested using baking soda and baking powder in different quantities. When I used a full 2 teaspoons of soda, the cookies browned too quickly and spread out flat on the baking sheet. I discovered that this excessive amount of baking soda caused too much of a chemical reaction (the soda reacted with the acid in the molasses, producing carbon dioxide bubbles which produced lift). This caused the delicate cookie structure to rupture, resulting in fallen cookies. I ended up using 1 teaspoon of baking powder, which produced just the right amount of lift and a nice thick cookie. The most important factor, however, was the size of the cookie. Roll the dough into large, 1¼-inch-diameter balls. This ensures that the inside of the cookies will remain moist when the outside becomes properly cooked. Smaller cookies will cook through, resulting in drier, tougher confections.

12	tablespoons (1½ sticks) unsalted butter, softened
1	cup sugar, plus extra for dipping
1	egg
¼	cup molasses
2¼	cups flour
1	teaspoon baking powder
¼	teaspoon salt
½	teaspoon cloves
1	teaspoon cinnamon
1	teaspoon ground ginger

1. Beat the butter and 1 cup sugar in the bowl of an electric mixer until creamy and smooth, about 3 minutes. Add the egg and molasses and beat until fully incorporated. In a separate bowl, whisk together the remaining ingredients and then stir into the butter-sugar mixture. Chill dough for 2 hours.

2. Heat oven to 350 degrees. Line 2 cookie sheets with parchment paper.

3. Shape dough into large, walnut-size balls. Dip tops in sugar. Place 3 inches apart on lined baking sheets. Bake for about 12 minutes. Cookies will appear undercooked when removed from the oven; the centers will still be very moist and light. As they cool, the cookies will harden.

MAKES 20 TO 24 COOKIES

Gingersnaps

I tested making gingersnaps with baking powder and also with baking soda. As my test cook, Jeanne Maguire, said, the ones made with the powder were "ginger-NO-snaps." The baking soda produces a crispier, snappier cookie.

12	tablespoons (1½ sticks) unsalted butter, softened
½	cup granulated sugar, plus extra for dipping
¾	cup packed dark brown sugar
1	large egg
¼	cup molasses
2½	cups flour
½	teaspoon baking soda
½	teaspoon salt
2	teaspoons ground ginger
½	teaspoon allspice
½	teaspoon cinnamon

1. Beat the butter and sugars in the bowl of an electric mixer until creamy and smooth, about 3 minutes. Add the egg and molasses and beat until fully incorporated. In a separate bowl, whisk together the remaining ingredients and stir into the butter-sugar mixture.

2. Chill dough for 2 hours. Heat oven to 350 degrees. Line 2 cookie sheets with parchment paper.

3. Shape dough into large, walnut-size balls and dip tops in granulated sugar. Place 3 inches apart on lined baking sheet. Bake for about 12 minutes. Cookies will appear undercooked when removed from the oven; the centers will still be very moist and light. As they cool, the cookies will harden. Store in an airtight container.

MAKES ABOUT 24 COOKIES

Oatmeal Chocolate Chip Cookies

The original version of this recipe was forwarded to me by my sister Kate, who found it on the Internet. It is the famous "Neiman Marcus" cookie recipe. A customer was charged $250 for it, not $2.50 as she had assumed when requesting it, and was so furious that she published it on the Internet as a form of revenge. I have made many revisions, including eliminating the baking soda entirely (using only baking powder), increasing the salt level, changing the oven temperature, decreasing the amount of both sugars as well as the oats, and rewriting the directions. The original was good but a bit dry and too sweet. Do not be put off by the use of oatmeal. This is an outstanding chocolate chip cookie — chewy, rich, and thick, since they do not spread much during baking.

1½	cups rolled oats
2	sticks (½ pound) butter, softened but still firm
¾	cup granulated sugar
¾	cup packed brown sugar
2	eggs, room temperature
1	teaspoon vanilla extract
2	cups flour
1	teaspoon baking powder
¾	teaspoon salt
12	ounces chocolate chips
4	ounces grated semisweet chocolate
1½	cups chopped pecans or walnuts

1. Heat oven to 350 degrees. Place oats in a blender or food processor and blend until very fine.

2. With an electric mixer, beat the butter and both sugars until light, about 3 minutes. Add the eggs one at a time and beat 20 seconds after each addition. Add the vanilla and beat for 15 seconds to blend.

3. Whisk together the flour, processed oats, baking powder, and salt. With a large rubber spatula or wooden spoon, blend the dry ingredients into the butter mixture. (This will be difficult since the batter is very stiff.) Add the chocolate chips, grated chocolate, and nuts. (The easiest method of grating chocolate is to use a heavy-duty food processor, such as the KitchenAid or Cuisinart models, fitted with the metal blade.)

4. Form dough into balls about 2 inches in diameter and place on a baking sheet covered with parchment paper. (The parchment paper is optional). Bake 14 to 15 minutes on the middle oven rack or until the bottoms are lightly browned. The cookies should still feel a bit soft at this point. (They will not spread very much and will look undercooked. *Do not over-cook or they will become hard and dry when they cool.*) They will harden as they cool. Remove from oven and let cookies cool for 2 minutes on the baking sheet before removing to cooling racks. Cool at least 30 minutes before serving.

MAKES 30 TO 36 LARGE COOKIES

Rich, Thick Chocolate Cookie

This is a thick, sturdy cookie that is moist and not overly sweet.

8	ounces semisweet chocolate, coarsely chopped
1	cup flour
½	cup unsweetened cocoa powder
1	teaspoon baking soda
½	teaspoon salt
12	tablespoons (1½ sticks) unsalted butter, softened but still firm
1	cup packed light brown sugar
¼	cup granulated sugar plus extra for sprinkling
3	eggs
1	teaspoon vanilla extract
12	ounces chocolate chips (optional)
12	ounces toasted chopped walnuts or pecans (optional)

1. Melt chocolate either in a saucepan in a 250 degree oven for 15 minutes or in a glass bowl in a microwave oven at 50 percent power for 3 minutes, stirring after 2 minutes. If you like, chocolate can also be melted in the top of a double boiler. Sift together the flour, cocoa, soda, and salt onto a piece of wax paper.
2. Heat oven to 350 degrees. In a large bowl, cream the butter with an electric

mixer on high speed for 4 to 5 minutes or until very pale and fluffy. Add the sugars and beat an additional 2 to 3 minutes or until light and fluffy. Scrape down the sides of the bowl. Add the eggs one at a time, beating 30 seconds after each addition or until each egg is just incorporated. Add vanilla and beat to incorporate for about 20 seconds. Add the melted chocolate and beat another 30 seconds. Scrape down the sides of the bowl. Add the dry ingredients and beat on the lowest speed until well mixed. With a wooden spoon, stir in optional chips and nuts.
3. Drop mounds of dough, about 2 tablespoons each, on a parchment-lined cookie sheet and sprinkle with granulated sugar. Bake for about 18 minutes, rotating the cookie sheet halfway through cooking. Do not let the cookies become too browned on the bottom. Remove to a cooling rack to set and cool.

MAKES 30 TO 36 COOKIES

Hermit Bars

These are the sort of cookies that might have been served at a dance hall in the old days, since they both keep and travel well. Our town had at least three dance halls that I know of, most of them built in the latter part of the last century when the town still had a sufficient number of residents looking for entertainment. But, according to the stories, they could be rough places. I once asked Cliff McKee, a well-known old-timer, about the first time he went to a dance. He said that he started climbing the stairs when a fellow came tumbling down backward, head over heels. When he started climbing again, a

Hermit bars are shaped into long loaves much like the Italian biscotti.

As they bake, they will spread on the baking sheet. When cool, they are easily sliced into individual bars.

second young man followed the first one. Cliff was so disgusted that he turned around and went home. He also remembers the time that the dancers were getting ahead of the calls, so the caller stood up and said, "Well, if you ain't gonna wait for me I'll just run along home." He was also there when a man called Moffitt got hit over the head at a dance, and when his wife showed up to say a few last words before he died, she told him, "You damned old fool, you got drunk and came here looking for a fight and you got it." So much for the good old days.

As for the recipe itself, I use a technique favored by biscotti bakers. I fashion the dough into logs, bake them up, and then slice them into individual cookies. These are good, solid cookies; they last well, and are a staple of any country baker's repertoire.

8	tablespoons (1 stick) unsalted butter, softened
½	cup sugar
2	eggs, room temperature
½	cup molasses
2	cups flour
½	teaspoon baking soda
½	teaspoon baking powder
½	teaspoon salt
¼	teaspoon allspice
½	teaspoon cinnamon
¼	teaspoon mace
½	teaspoon ground cloves
1	cup raisins
1	cup pecans or walnuts, coarsely chopped (optional)

1. Heat oven to 350 degrees. Line a cookie sheet or jelly roll pan with parchment paper.
2. Beat the butter and sugar in the bowl of an electric mixer until creamy and smooth, about 3 minutes. Add the eggs and molasses and beat until fully incorporated. (The mixture may appear grainy at first; keep beating until smooth and dull in appearance.) In a separate bowl, whisk together the remaining ingredients, except the raisins and nuts, and then gently stir into the butter-sugar mixture until just

incorporated. Stir in raisins and optional nuts.

3. Using a rubber spatula, form the dough into 2 logs on the prepared pan, about 2 inches wide by 14 inches long. (When baked, the logs will spread out to 5 inches in width so leave plenty of room between them.) Bake for 15 minutes or until the top of the log springs back and they are lightly browned. Let cool for 15 minutes. Cut at an angle into slices about 2 inches long. Hermits hold well in an airtight container and can also be successfully frozen.

MAKES ABOUT 16 BARS

Raspberry Rectangles

This recipe started out as date squares, but the flavor of the filling (dates are sweet and mellow) didn't contrast sufficiently with the crust. Raspberry preserves are a bit tarter and make for a brighter, livelier cookie. I also tested a variety of jams including apricot, strawberry, and blackberry, none of which had the bright strong flavor of raspberry, which stands up nicely to the oats and nuts. Make sure that these cookies cool completely before cutting.

1¼	cups quick-cooking oats
1½	cups flour
½	cup granulated sugar
½	cup packed brown sugar
¾	teaspoon baking soda
¼	teaspoon salt
½	cup chopped pecans or almonds or a mixture

12	tablespoons (1½ sticks) butter, softened
1	cup raspberry preserves

1. Heat oven to 350 degrees. Butter a 9 x 9-inch baking pan. Whisk together the first 7 ingredients (oats through nuts). Blend in the softened butter with a fork or with an electric mixer on slow speed for 3 to 4 minutes or until the mixture is blended well and looks like wet sand. Place two-thirds of the mixture in the prepared pan and press onto the bottom. Spread with the preserves, using a rubber spatula. Sprinkle the remaining crust mixture on top.

2. Bake for 30 minutes, turning pan once after 15 minutes. Cool in the pan completely before cutting.

MAKES 24 RECTANGLES

Snipdoodles

According to James Beard, snickerdoodles were called by many different names, depending on the region of the country the recipe was found. Along the Hudson River Valley they were called schnecken doodles, yet snipdoodles or snickerdoodles were also common names. I am partial to the name snipdoodles as well as to this recipe. I add a bit of nutmeg to the batter, which adds a gentle perfume to what is a very simple cookie. I tested them with Crisco instead of milk and the cookies were flatter, more spread out, and a bit crispier. I prefer a more delicate, softer snipdoodle and therefore used the milk. The texture of these cookies is heavenly:

light but with a nice chew. They bake up nice and thick, almost like a macaroon.

8	tablespoons (1 stick) unsalted butter, softened
1½	cups plus 3 tablespoons sugar
2	eggs
1	teaspoon vanilla extract
¼	cup milk
3	cups flour
¾	teaspoon baking soda
1	teaspoon cream of tartar
½	teaspoon salt
½	teaspoon ground nutmeg
1	tablespoon cinnamon

1. Beat the butter and 1½ cups of sugar in the bowl of an electric mixer or with a wooden spoon until creamy and smooth, about 3 minutes. Add the eggs and vanilla and beat until fully incorporated. Add the milk and stir to incorporate. In a separate bowl, whisk together the next 5 ingredients (flour through nutmeg) and then stir into the butter/sugar mixture. Chill dough for 2 hours.
2. Heat oven to 350 degrees. Line 2 cookie sheets with parchment paper.
3. Shape dough into large, walnut-size balls, about 1¼ inches in diameter. Mix together the remaining 3 tablespoons sugar and cinnamon in a small bowl. Dip tops in sugar/cinnamon mixture. Place balls 3 inches apart on lined baking sheet. Bake for about 12 minutes. Cookies will appear undercooked when removed from the oven; the centers will still be very moist and light. As they cool, the cookies will firm up.

MAKES 20 TO 24 COOKIES

Southern Pecan Bars

This recipe comes from Pillsbury's fifth $100,000 Bake-Off Contest, which was run in 1954. A Mrs. Pope from Aberdeen, South Dakota, won a $1,000 prize for her pecan bars, which are both light and chewy, a cross between a cookie and a candy. I have faithfully reproduced the recipe below without alteration since, when tested, they needed no improvement.

1	cup flour
¼	teaspoon baking powder
4	tablespoons (½ stick) butter, softened
⅓	cup firmly packed brown sugar
¼	cup pecans, finely chopped

FOR THE TOPPING

2	eggs
¾	cup dark corn syrup
¼	cup firmly packed brown sugar
2	tablespoons flour
½	teaspoon salt
1	teaspoon vanilla extract
¾	cup pecans, chopped

1. Heat oven to 350 degrees. Grease a 9 x 9-inch pan. Sift together the flour and baking powder onto a sheet of wax paper. Using an electric mixer, beat the butter and brown sugar together for 3 minutes. Add the flour mixture and continue beating until mixture resembles coarse meal. Stir in the pecans and mix with a wooden spoon. Pat firmly into prepared pan and bake for 10 minutes. Remove from oven.
2. For the topping, whisk eggs in a medium bowl until foamy. Add the next 5

ingredients (corn syrup through vanilla) and whisk until combined. Pour over baked crust. Sprinkle with chopped pecans. Bake at 350 degrees for 25 to 30 minutes. Let cool in pan, then cut into bars.

MAKES ABOUT 36 BARS,
EACH 1½ INCHES SQUARE

Farmer's Cookies

This recipe comes from Sweden and was given to me by Jeanne Maguire, my test cook. They are thin, crisp almond cookies and are wonderful with ice cream.

14	tablespoons (2 sticks less 2 tablespoons) butter, softened
¾	cup plus 1 tablespoon sugar
2	cups plus 2 tablespoons flour
1	teaspoon baking soda
¼	teaspoon salt
1	tablespoon water
1	tablespoon corn syrup
⅓	cup almonds, finely chopped

1. Beat butter and sugar in a medium bowl with an electric mixer or wooden spoon until light and fluffy. In a small bowl, whisk together the flour, baking soda, and salt. Add the water, corn syrup, flour mixture, and nuts to the butter/sugar mixture. Mix until thoroughly combined.
2. Divide dough in half and place each piece on a piece of parchment or waxed paper. Form dough into logs 1½ to 2 inches wide, and roll paper around logs, twisting the ends to seal. Refrigerate for at least 2 hours or up to 3 days.
3. Heat the oven to 400 degrees. Line 2 cookie sheets with parchment paper. Unwrap dough, slice into ¼-inch slices, and place on parchment-lined cookie sheets, 1½ inches apart. Bake 8 to 10 minutes or until very lightly browned, turning pans once after 4 minutes. Remove parchment paper with cookies and cool on a cake rack. Repeat until all cookies are baked.

MAKES ABOUT 60 COOKIES

Cakes

THE FIRST SUNDAY in August, our small Methodist church celebrates Old Home Day, a time for present and former members of the congregation to visit, to sing hymns, to read the list of those who have passed on, their seats now vacant or taken by a visitor or a weekender unaware of those who had filled the pews before. The minister starts the service by asking those present to call out favorite hymns by number and then we sing two verses; always the first and usually the last. Last summer, we began promptly at 1 P.M. with "Precious Lord, Take My Hand," Martin Luther King's favorite hymn and one well known by the congregation. The man just ahead of me in the next pew called out "My Faith Looks Up to Me," and then we sang "Because He Lives," followed by "What a Friend We Have in Jesus," "Be Thou My Vision," "Here Am I," and "For All the Saints." We sang well that day, voices given freely, the melody floating out across the field of alfalfa and down to the Green River to the old Baptist hole where I had gone swimming so many times as a kid.

The first Methodist church in our town stood across the street, moved from Ash Grove, New York, back in 1782. The current structure was raised in the 1870s, a modest church that holds no more than 150, although any sort of crowd is unusual these days. The congregation usually runs no more than 25 on a given Sunday, our family sometimes making up a good percentage of those present. The walls are pressed tin painted white, the windows are high and narrow with the original, imperfect lights, the Green Mountains filtered in small bubbles of distortion, a child's attention held by the play of light and wavy glass. The artwork, *Christ Blessing Little Children* and *Suffer Little Children to Come Unto Me,* is modest, inexpensive prints of the same biblical event. A few plaques also adorn the walls; the most practical reads "Oil Burner Installed in May of 1972, John W. Lunquist." Out in the small foyer, there is a smattering of mementos from the church's history: a Perkins Hollow Report Card from 1916 and photographs of Old Home Day, 1964, depicting hearty, broad-faced women with easy smiles and large flower-print dresses serving up dinner on long oilcloth-draped tables. I am drawn to those photos time after time, thirsty for the simplicity of those lives, faces open and expressive, sculpted over time by experience, like a large granite outcropping, weathered to a smooth, pleasing finish. My favorite photo is Eleanor Lomberg shown in early October in a bright red sweater and blue skirt, feeding a young doe by hand. (Her husband, Willy Lomberg, used to take in weak, malnourished deer in the springtime, keep them in his garage, and then let them go when they were fattened up.) At first, the skirt seemed out of place in the woods, but over the years I have come to realize that she was comfortable in it, her smile projecting an ease and energy that overcomes any sense of incongruity. Although she is

buried up the hill in the old cemetery, I expect her to come walking in the door one Sunday morning, picking up the order of service on the small table under the photograph, stepping to the right to take her place in the middle pew.

As I sit Sunday mornings with head bowed, I remember that our tiny church has lifted so many up to the clouds, taking with them bits of memory, small moments recalled over a lifetime. When I am lifted up, I like to think that there will be a seat reserved for me at the long table, the women serving up fresh corn and coleslaw and grilled chicken, a large glass of cold iced tea, and a sheet cake inscribed with my name and a large, hearty WELCOME! written in pale blue icing. I can hear the congregation singing in full voice to the tune of the old Estey organ, voices and hearts joined together, a cloud of witnesses for all time.

ANY SORT of baking can be difficult, since small changes in ingredients or pan sizes or even baking temperature can radically affect the outcome. This is particularly true of cakes, since they require just the right amount of lift during baking combined with the formation of sufficient structure to hold the height once the cake is done. This requires a balance between leavening agents, cell structure, fat, flour, eggs, and oven temperature.

Most cakes are quite similar. A basic yellow cake, the variety used as the building block for most recipes, is made with both egg whites and yolks. The lift is provided by baking powder and soda, and the structure is also enhanced by beating softened butter and sugar together in a process called "creaming." This is the same method used for the chocolate cake in this chapter. A white cake has no yolks but is otherwise similar in construct. This produces a finer, lighter cake akin to a Duncan Hines box cake.

Some cakes use whipped egg whites for lift. These include angel food cake, sponge cake, and chiffon cake. The three cakes are quite similar, the first using all egg whites, the second using a few yolks as well, and the third using yolks, vegetable oil or butter, and then some baking powder for lift, since the batter is heavier and fattier than either an angel food or sponge cake. I have reprinted a recipe for the latter from *The Cook's Bible*, since it is required to make the trifle recipe on page 371.

Here are a few tips that should help you avoid common cake-making mistakes:

- Be sure to use the correct pan size. An 8-inch round cake pan cannot always be substituted for a 9-inch pan. The relative volumes of the pans are quite different, requiring different baking times and sometimes different oven temperatures, and the resulting cake may end up sinking in the middle. As a general rule, if you use a smaller pan, lower the oven temperature by 25 degrees, and expect the baking time to increase.
- It is best to butter a cake pan and then insert a round of parchment or wax paper on the bottom. This will make it easier to remove the cake later. You can purchase precut rounds of parchment paper from cookware stores or cut them out yourself. For all baking, parchment paper is an essential item.

- A small flour sifter is helpful for flouring pans. It provides a fine, even coating.
- Butter must be at the proper temperature for creaming (beating with an electric mixer). If it is too cold, the batter will not come together properly and will separate. The butter should be soft and malleable, but *not* room temperature. You can use an instant-read thermometer to measure it — it should read 65 to 67 degrees. It should be the texture of a soft putty, but not as liquid as mayonnaise. Butter temperature is the most common cause of mistakes made by novice bakers.
- Eggs should also be warm. I take them from the refrigerator and place them in a bowl of warm water and let them sit until I need them. They can also be placed in a small bowl in a microwave oven and heated at 30 percent power for 10 seconds.
- If your butter and eggs were too cold, the batter may appear very shiny and look curdled. If this happens, warm up the bowl a bit by passing it briefly over a stovetop heating element or immersing the bottom in hot water. A properly made batter should look thick and dull and cohesive. If you are using a metal mixing bowl, you can check on the temperature of your batter by simply placing your hand along the outside bottom of the bowl. If it is chilly, you have a problem.
- A large rubber spatula is helpful in folding together batter ingredients. Smaller spatulas or wooden spoons require many more strokes, which are inefficient and can overwork a batter.

Whisking dry ingredients combines them thoroughly and quickly. Many bakers prefer to sift dry ingredients when using baking powder or baking soda to make sure that no small clumps of leavener are left undispersed in the flour. To avoid using extra bowls, simply sift ingredients onto wax paper.

If a recipe calls for sifting flour, you can use a fine sieve as well as a flour sifter.

To accurately measure flour, use the "dip and sweep" method. Dip a measuring cup into flour and then sweep off the top with a knife for a perfect measure.

A foolproof method for separating an egg is to crack it open in your outstretched palm, letting the white slip between your fingers into a bowl and leaving the yolk behind. It is best not to add eggs directly to other ingredients in the event that one has gone bad. Simply crack them into a small bowl first, then transfer.

Egg whites that are underbeaten.

Egg whites that are beaten to soft peaks. Although whites beaten to this stage are not at their full volume, tests with soufflés revealed that they will make up the difference during baking.

Egg whites that are beaten until stiff but still moist and glossy. For most recipes, this is the preferred method.

Egg whites that are overbeaten. Note that they appear clumpy and dry.

To measure the temperature of butter for creaming, simply use an instant-read thermometer. For perfect results when creaming (whipping butter, usually with sugar), the butter should read 67 degrees. Properly creamed butter should appear dull and smooth

- When working with batters, use the largest bowl possible. If is difficult to mix a batter in a bowl that barely contains it.

- Many cake recipes require that the flour and liquid be added to the batter in three parts, folding between additions. Sift the flour and other ingredients directly onto wax paper. The paper can then be picked up and one third of the flour can easily be poured into the mixing bowl.

- *Never trust baking times,* even those in my recipes. All ovens are different. Most ovens are not properly calibrated, which means that you may be cooking at 25 or even 50 degrees hotter or colder than you think, even if you have checked the oven with a thermometer. (Cheap oven thermometers are not reliable.) Always set the timer for two thirds of the baking time, check the cake, gently turn it around in the oven, and then start checking every five minutes or so thereafter. If the top of the cake is browning too rapidly, reduce the oven temperature by 25 degrees and place a baking sheet on a rack just above the cake.

- I find cake testers to be unreliable, and therefore I also press a fork flat against the top of the cake to see it if springs back when the fork is removed. If the depression remains, the cake is not done. In addition, not all cakes will start to shrink from the sides of the pan when they are done. Much of this shrinking can occur after the cake is removed from the oven.

- Don't panic if the tops of your baked cake layers are not even. It is not uncommon to find a layer that is slightly sunk in the middle. For a two-layer cake, use the best layer for the top. The imperfect bottom layer will never be seen. A bit of extra filling will disguise any depressions in the cake.

- When frosting a cake, first place four 2-inch wide strips of wax paper around the perimeter of the cake plate. Place the bottom cake layer on top of these strips so that about 1 inch of paper is sitting underneath the cake and the rest is sticking out. After frosting, simply pull out these strips and the plate will be perfectly clean.
- Cake flour and all-purpose flour are quite different products. The former has a relatively low gluten level, which simply means that it is made from a softer, lower-protein wheat, the actual kernels being less hard than those used for all-purpose or bread flours. This produces a finer, softer texture. If you want a bit more chew to a cake, for example, you can use all-purpose instead of cake flour. On the other hand, if you want a softer, finer product, use cake flour instead. Although different flours with different protein levels require slightly different ratios of liquid to flour, this is not a significant factor when making cakes.
- Self-rising flour already has a leavener included with the flour. Never use self-rising flour unless it is called for in a recipe, otherwise you will have too much leavener. This will cause overproduction of carbon dioxide gas, which may result in a cake rising too much and then deflating. The other problem with self-rising flour is that the amount and type of leavener (baking powder and/or baking soda) depends heavily on

what else is in a cake batter. For example, a batter that uses milk will probably require the use of baking powder, which also contains an acid, to help produce the chemical reaction that provides lift. (Milk has little acid in it.) One that is based on buttermilk, which contains a great deal of lactic acid, might not need the acidic ingredient found in baking powder and therefore use baking soda or a combination of powder and soda.

Buttermilk Chocolate Cake

This is similar to a recipe I developed for *The Cook's Bible* but I have done some additional work on it. I tried adding another egg and the cake was too loose and the texture was not as good. When I substituted oil for the butter, the cake was greasy and too moist. Sour cream, in place of the buttermilk, created a drier cake that was less chocolatey. It also did not rise quite as well. I then added a bit of oil to the sour cream, to solve the dry texture problem, and the resulting cake was moist, but the flavor was not as good as the buttermilk version. Finally, I tried sifting the cake flour and this created a wonderful cake, slightly moister than the master recipe from the *Bible*. You can bake this cake either in two 8-inch pans or one 9-inch pan. (Make sure that the 9-inch pan is at least 2 inches high.) By the way, if you frost a chocolate cake with orange icing it is called Black-Eyed Susan Cake.

1½	cups sifted cake flour
½	cup unsweetened Dutch-process cocoa
2	teaspoons instant espresso or instant coffee
¼	teaspoon baking powder
½	teaspoon baking soda
½	teaspoon salt
12	tablespoons (1½ sticks) unsalted butter, softened
1¼	cups sugar
2	eggs, room temperature
1	egg white, room temperature
1½	teaspoons vanilla extract
1	cup buttermilk

1. Grease the bottom of two 8-inch round baking pans or one deep (about 3 inches) 9-inch pan. Line the bottom with parchment or wax paper. Grease paper and lightly flour pans; turn pans upside down and lightly tap to remove excess flour. Preheat oven to 350 degrees. Adjust oven rack to middle position.

2. Sift the flour, cocoa, instant coffee, baking powder, baking soda, and salt together onto a sheet of wax paper. Put butter in the bowl of an electric mixer and beat for 1 minute or until light colored. Add sugar gradually and beat on medium-high speed for 3 minutes until mixture is very light-colored and fluffy (scrape down 2 or 3 times). Add whole eggs and egg white one at a time, beating for 20 seconds after each addition. Add the vanilla and beat for 10 seconds.

3. Add the flour mixture in three parts alternately with the buttermilk. Beat on low speed after each addition and scrape down the sides of the bowl with a rubber spatula. Stir by hand to finish. Do not overbeat.

4. Spread the batter into pan(s) and bake 25 to 30 minutes (about 10 minutes longer if using only one pan). Cool for 15 minutes, then remove cake from pans onto wire rack. Let cool fully before frosting.

Mocha Variation

Substitute ½ cup of strong brewed coffee for ½ cup of buttermilk.

Sponge Cake and Boston Cream Pie

The coming of springtime in Vermont has all the usual keynotes: the firming up of muddy roads, an ocean of red buds sprayed across the mountainsides, the roar of the brook through the culvert, the early white blossoms of the plum and pear trees, and, for our family, the making of a Boston Cream Pie. This occurs in late April when we have a small birthday party for a neighbor who is partial to this cake. Over the years, I have made it with a standard yellow cake, a chiffon cake, a sponge cake, and even a genoise. Never quite satisfied, I realized that I had been searching for a light cake, one with a springy but delicate texture that stands up nicely to a rich custard filling and a sweet chocolate glaze. It should not be dry or tough, the curse of many classic sponge cakes, nor should it be difficult to make. I was seeking a basic building-block cake recipe, one that offers an alternative to a classic American layer cake but which is just as dependable and useful, having a texture that lends itself to a variety of desserts, standing up to different fillings and toppings. In fact, it should be so tender and flavorful that it can simply be eaten on its own with perhaps a bit of whipped cream and fresh, sweetened fruit.

The first step was to understand the different types of cakes most likely to be used with Boston Cream Pie and how they are made. The first realization is that angel food, genoise, sponge, and chiffon cakes are all "foam" cakes. They depend on beaten eggs (whole or separated) to provide lift and structure. Although each of them uses an egg foam for structure, they differ in two ways: the addition of fat (butter, milk, or oil) and whether the foam is made from whole eggs, egg whites, or a combination.

The leanest of the foam cakes is the angel food cake, which is made only with egg whites, using no yolks or added fat. A genoise is made by whipping whole eggs, with the addition of melted butter. A sponge cake calls for beating whole eggs, and yolks and then folding in whipped egg whites. Traditionally, no other fat was added. A chiffon cake, the sturdiest of the lot, is a sponge cake with a good deal of added fat, usually a half cup or so of oil or butter.

The problem with these definitions is that cookbook authors ignore them, often using the terms foam and sponge interchangeably, referring to the whole category of foam cakes as "sponge-style" cakes. The recipe for sponge cake in the new *Joy of Cooking*, for example, is actually a genoise since it calls for beaten whole eggs and says nothing about beaten egg whites. I found the same problem in the sponge cake recipe that appears in *Classic American Desserts* by Richard Sax. Despite these inconsistencies, I concluded that a classic sponge cake must call for beating at least some of the whites sepa-rately and then folding them into the whole egg foam; otherwise it is nothing more than a classic genoise. (To make this category of cakes even more confusing, there are variations on classic sponge cakes that add fat in the form of milk and/or butter. One very common variation is the "hot-milk" sponge cake. Although, technically speaking, this qualifies it as a chiffon cake, it seems that the determining factor is the amount of fat. The addition of just a few tablespoons of milk or butter still qualifies it as a sponge cake; adding a half cup or so of fat transforms it into a chiffon cake.)

To get things started, I asked the *Cook's* test kitchen to try a variety of Boston Cream Pie recipes using different foam cakes and a traditional layer cake. The winner was a variation on a genoise. It was delicate but springy, light but firm. But, as I soon discovered, a genoise is anything but simple. This aerated mixture is dependent on the temperature of the ingredients, the ratio of eggs to flour, and even the speed with which the cake is whisked into the oven. During testing, I discovered that if the milk was added at room temperature, not hot as is suggested by most recipes, or if the eggs were a bit over- or underbeaten, the cake would not rise properly. It is a professional baker's cake, not the simple everyday cake recipe I was looking for.

My next thought was to turn to a sponge cake, which is similar to a genoise, but some or all of egg whites are beaten separately, which delivers a more stable batter and a more foolproof recipe. I started by making a classic American sponge cake, which adds no fat in the form of butter or milk. Using my own recipe that calls for 8 beaten egg whites folded into 4 beaten egg yolks, the cake certainly was light but lacking in flavor and the texture was dry and a bit chewy. Our test kitchen director, Susan Legozzo, suggested a recipe for a hot-milk sponge cake (a small amount of melted butter and hot milk are added to the whole egg foam) and this turned out much better on all counts. The added fat provided not only flavor but it tenderized the crumb. This particular recipe also used fewer eggs than my sponge cake recipe.

I was now working with a master recipe that used ¾ cup cake flour, 1 teaspoon baking powder, ¾ cup sugar, and 5 eggs. I started by separating out all five of the whites and found that the cake was too light and had insufficient structure, resulting in a slightly sunken center. I then beat just three of the whites and the resulting cake was excellent. When all-purpose flour was substituted for cake flour, the cake had more body and it was a bit tougher than the version with cake flour. I then tried different ratios of the two flours, finally settling on two-thirds cake flour to one-third all-purpose. I also tested the proper ratio of eggs to flour and found that 5 eggs to ¾ cup flour (we tested ½ cup and a full cup) was best. Six eggs produced an "eggy" cake; four eggs resulted in a lower rise and a cake with a bit less flavor.

I thought that the baking powder might be optional, but it turned out to be essential to a properly risen cake. Although angel food and classic sponge cakes, which use no added fat, do not require chemical leavening, the addition of milk and melted butter combined with the relatively small amount of beaten egg whites

in proportion to the flour make baking powder essential. Two tablespoons of melted butter was just the right amount; three tablespoons made the cake a bit oily and the butter flavor was too prominent. As for the milk, 3 tablespoons was best; larger quantities resulted in a wet, mushy texture.

A host of other tests were performed, including adding lemon juice, which is probably a holdover from angel food cakes, to whiten the color of the cake (I noticed no benefit in either color or texture), sifting the flour more than once (many professional bakers suggest this step; we found no improvement), and beating the whole eggs and sugar over warm water (this is a classic French technique that was both awkward and unnecessary; that being said, we found that the eggs must be room temperature to beat up into a thick foam).

I also played with the order of the steps. Beating the whole egg foam first, and then the whites, allowed the relatively fragile foam to deteriorate, producing less rise. I found that beating the whites first was vastly better. After much experimentation, I also found it best to fold together, all at the same time, the beaten whole eggs, the whites, and the flour, and then, once the mixture is about half mixed, add the warm butter and milk. This eliminated the possibility that the liquid would damage the egg foam and made the temperature of the butter/milk mixture less important than it was with a genoise.

To better understand egg foams, I called a variety of scientists and discovered that foam cakes, of which this recipe is a good example, depend on the proper aeration of both whole eggs and egg whites. When egg whites are beaten into a foam, their proteins partially unwind around air bubbles. (This unwinding also occurs during cooking.) These bubbles are lined with unwound protein strands which are loosely connected to one another. When the batter is heated, these bubbles increase in size and the loose, elastic strands allow this expansion without breaking their bonds. (If one over-beats egg whites, for example, the protein strands become inelastic and the mixture cannot expand.) This aeration is a good thing for leavening but it creates a less stable, more fragile structure, since the protein has been partially denatured through the beating process.

Any experienced baker will tell you that a whole egg foam is a great deal more sensitive and unstable than an egg white foam. This is because the two foams are actually quite different. A whole egg foam is based on the process of emulsification, not on a film of protein that traps air as in the case of egg whites. Through emulsification, water and air are held together by the phospholipids found in lecithin, an ingredient in egg yolks. This produces a more fragile and complex structure, since the continuous phase, the water, and the discontinuous phase, the air, are not naturally inclined to bond.

By folding in an egg white foam to a whole egg foam, I have increased the protein content of the batter, which makes it more stable. The beaten egg whites also set at a lower temperature than the whole egg foam, meaning that the cake structure firms up more quickly during baking. I also decided to add the flour, a stabilizing influence, to this mixture before adding the melted butter and milk (additional fats that often destabilize egg foams).

Three baking temperatures were tested: 325, 350, and 375 degrees. The middle temperature was best. I also discovered that this recipe can be made successfully in either an 8-inch or 9-inch pan, although making the entire recipe in one pan (one with high sides) is not recommended. The cake falls in the center. Determining when a sponge cake is properly cooked is a little more difficult than with a regular American layer cake. It should, however, provide some resistance and not feel as if one just touched the top of a soufflé. Another good test is color. The top of the cake should be a nice light brown, not a pale golden, nor should it be a dark, rich, brown.

How to handle the cakes once they are out of the oven was also tested. When left to cool in the baking pans, the cakes shrank away from the sides and the edges became uneven. It is best to quickly remove them onto a cooling rack. This is tricky, since the cake pans are very hot. I found that the best method was to place the hot cake pan on a towel, cover it with a plate, and then use the towel to invert the cake. Finally, slip the cake back onto a cooling rack.

Foolproof Sponge Cake

The egg whites should be beaten to soft, glossy, billowy peaks. If beaten too stiff, it will be very difficult to fold in the whole-egg mixture.

½   cup cake flour
¼   cup all-purpose flour

1	teaspoon baking powder
¼	teaspoon salt
3	tablespoons milk
2	tablespoons unsalted butter
½	teaspoon vanilla extract
5	eggs, room temperature
¾	cup sugar

1. Adjust oven rack to lower middle position and heat oven to 350 degrees. Grease two 8- or 9-inch cake pans and cover pan bottom with a round of parchment paper. Whisk flours, baking powder, and salt in a medium bowl (or sift onto waxed paper). Heat milk and butter in a small saucepan over low heat until butter melts. Off heat, add vanilla; cover and keep warm.

2. Separate three of the eggs, placing whites in bowl of standing mixer fitted with the whisk attachment (or large mixing bowl if using hand mixer or whisk) and reserving the 3 yolks plus remaining two whole eggs in another mixing bowl. Beat the three whites on high speed (or whisk) until whites are foamy. Gradually adding 6 tablespoons of the sugar, continue to beat whites to soft, moist peaks. (Do not overbeat, as stiff, dry egg whites will be difficult to incorporate into the batter.) If using a standing mixer, transfer egg whites to a large bowl and add yolk/whole egg mixture to mixing bowl.

3. Beat yolk/whole egg mixture with remaining 6 tablespoons sugar. Beat on medium-high speed (setting 8 on a KitchenAid) until eggs are very thick and a pale lemon color, about 5 minutes (or 12 minutes by hand). Add beaten eggs to whites.

4. Sprinkle flour mixture over beaten eggs and whites; fold very gently 12 times with a large rubber spatula. Make a well in one side of batter and pour melted butter mixture into bowl. Continue folding until batter shows no trace of flour and whites and whole eggs are evenly mixed, about 8 additional strokes.

5. Immediately pour batter into prepared baking pans; bake until cake tops are light brown and feel firm and spring back when touched, about 16 minutes for 9-inch cake pans and 20 minutes for 8-inch cake pans.

6. Place one cake pan on a kitchen towel; run a knife around pan perimeter to loosen cake; cover pan with a large plate. Invert pan and remove it. Then invert cake onto cooling rack. Repeat with remaining cake. Remove parchment and continue with one of the recipes that follow.

Sponge Cake with Blackberry Jam

A simple sponge cake filled with jam and dusted with confectioner's sugar used to be called a Washington Pie after Martha Washington. Seedless black raspberry jam is best.

1	recipe Foolproof Sponge Cake
1	jar (8 ounces) blackberry jam
	Confectioner's sugar for dusting

1. Make Foolproof Sponge Cake.
2. Place one cake layer on a cardboard round on a sheet of waxed paper. Evenly spread jam over cake. Place second layer over jam, making sure layers line up properly. Dust cake with confectioners' sugar and serve.

Sponge Cake with Rich Lemon Filling

This is another way to dress up a sponge cake for company. The cake is filled with the filling used for lemon meringue pie.

1   recipe Foolproof Sponge Cake

RICH LEMON FILLING
1   cup sugar
¼   cup cornstarch
⅛   teaspoon salt
1⅜   cups cold water
4   large egg yolks
2   teaspoons zest from 1 lemon
½   cup lemon juice from 2 lemons
2   tablespoons unsalted butter
     Confectioner's sugar for dusting

1. Make Foolproof Sponge Cake.
2. *For the filling:* meanwhile, bring sugar, cornstarch, salt, and water to simmer in a large nonreactive saucepan over medium heat, whisking occasionally at beginning of process and more frequently as mixture begins to thicken. When mixture starts to simmer and turn translucent, whisk in egg yolks, 2 at a time. Whisk in zest, then lemon juice, and finally butter. Bring mixture to a good simmer, whisking constantly. Remove from heat, and transfer to another container to cool to room temperature, placing a piece of plastic wrap directly on the surface of the filling to prevent a skin from forming. Let cool to room temperature. (Can be refrigerated overnight.) To ensure that lemon filling does not thin out, do not whisk or vigorously stir it once it has set.
3. Carefully spoon filling over bottom

layer and spread evenly up to cake edge. Place the second layer on top, making sure layers line up properly. Dust with confectioners' sugar and serve.

Boston Cream Pie

The foundation for Boston Cream Pie was a cake referred to by James Beard as the One-Egg Cake and by Marion Cunningham in *The Fannie Farmer Cookbook* as the Boston Favorite Cake. It is made with cake flour, sugar, butter, milk, one or two eggs, vanilla, baking powder, and salt. Using this simple building-block recipe, many different variations were created, including, according to James Beard, Washington Pie, filled with jam and topped with powdered sugar; Boston Cream Pie, filled with a pastry cream and topped with powdered sugar; Martha Washington Pie, which is either the same as Washington Pie or split into three layers, one filled with jam and the other with pastry cream; and Parker House Chocolate Cream Pie, which is Boston Cream Pie topped with a thin layer of chocolate butter icing. The latter was invented either by a French chef, Sanzian, who was hired by Harvey Parker at his hotel's opening in October 1855 at the extraordinary annual salary of $5,000 (a good chef in Boston could be hired at that time for eight dollars per week) or by a German baker named Ward, who, shortly after the hotel opened, was also credited with inventing Parker House rolls. However, it is not clear whether, as Beard suggests, the term Boston Cream Pie already existed before the Parker House version. My guess is that Beard is right since Fannie Farmer also lists a recipe for "Boston Favorite Cake," suggesting that Boston Cream Pie is merely a variation. As for why it is called a pie, Jim Dodge, author of *Baking with Jim Dodge*, suggests that the cake was originally baked by early New England cooks in a pie pan. (He offers such a recipe in his book.) Why were pie plates used? My best guess is that pie plates, which predated cakes in the American kitchen, were common kitchen equipment, cake pans being less widely available. No matter the origins, the editors of *Cook's* found, in a blind tasting of 5 different cakes, that the sponge cake recipe was ideal for Boston Cream Pie. I fill it with a thick pastry cream and then drizzle on a healthy layer of chocolate glaze. As with many more-modern Boston Cream Pie recipes, I allow the glaze to drip down over the sides of the cake.

| 1 | recipe Foolproof Sponge Cake (page 270) |

PASTRY CREAM

2	cups milk
6	egg yolks
½	cup sugar
¼	teaspoon salt
¼	cup cornstarch, sifted
1	teaspoon vanilla extract
1	tablespoon rum
2	tablespoons unsalted butter, optional

RICH CHOCOLATE GLAZE

1	cup heavy cream
¼	cup light corn syrup
8	ounces semisweet chocolate, chopped into small pieces
½	teaspoon vanilla

1. Make Foolproof Sponge Cake.

2. *For the pastry cream:* meanwhile, heat milk in a small saucepan until hot but not simmering. Whisk yolks, sugar, and salt in a large saucepan until mixture is thick and lemon-colored, 3 to 4 minutes. Add cornstarch; whisk to combine. Slowly whisk in hot milk. Cook milk mixture over medium-low heat, whisking constantly and scraping pan bottom and sides as you stir, until mixture thickens to a thick pudding consistency and has lost all traces of raw starch flavor, about 10 minutes. Remove from heat; stir in vanilla, rum, and optional butter. Remove from heat, and transfer to another container placing a piece of plastic wrap directly on the surface of the filling to prevent a skin from forming; let cool to room temperature. (Can be refrigerated overnight.) To ensure that pastry cream does not thin out, do not whisk or vigorously stir it once it has set.

3. *For the glaze:* bring cream and corn syrup to a full simmer in a medium saucepan. Remove from heat; add chocolate, cover, and let stand for 8 minutes. (If chocolate has not completely melted, return saucepan to low heat; stir constantly until melted.) Add vanilla; stir very gently until mixture is smooth. Cool until tepid, so that a spoonful drizzled back into pan mounds slightly. (Glaze can be refrigerated to speed up cooling process, stirring every few minutes to ensure even cooling.)

4. While glaze is cooling, place one cake layer on a cardboard round on cooling rack set over a jelly roll pan. Carefully spoon pastry cream over cake and spread evenly up to cake edge. Place the second layer on top, making sure layers line up properly.

5. Pour glaze over middle of top layer and let flow down cake sides. Use a metal spatula if necessary to completely coat cake. Use a small needle to puncture air bubbles. Let sit about 1 hour or until glaze fully sets. Serve.

Chiffon Cake

A chiffon cake is quite similar to an angel food or sponge cake with one major difference. Chiffon cakes use oil and therefore less sugar is called for (in proportion to the other ingredients), providing a tender but not overly sweet cake. (Both fat — in this case oil — and sugar tenderize proteins such as those found in eggs. Since an angel food cake has little fat, a large amount of sugar is called for to make a tender cake. In this type of recipe, less sugar is necessary, since the oil does much of the tenderizing.) Although an angel food cake relies exclusively on whipped egg whites for leavening, a chiffon cake contains both flour and fat, which need a chemical leavener (baking powder) to raise the structure.

My original recipe for chiffon cake called for inverting the pan after baking. On one occasion when I used vegetable oil instead of butter, I watched the cake simply slide right out of the pan! I suspect that butter may make the cake adhere better to the sides of the pan, since it causes the sides of the cake to brown better than when oil is used. Out of curiosity, I then made a chiffon cake and did not invert the pan after baking. It turned out fine, so I suggest that you do *not* invert the pan for this recipe. The amount of fat is relatively high compared to that in an angel food cake and you may have trouble.

2¼	cups cake flour
1½	cups sugar
2	teaspoons baking powder
½	teaspoon salt
8	tablespoons (1 stick) butter, melted, or ½ cup corn oil (butter is preferred)
6	egg yolks
½	cup water
2	teaspoons vanilla extract
9	egg whites
1	teaspoon cream of tartar

1. Heat oven to 375 degrees. Sift together the flour, 1 cup of the sugar (reserving ½ cup), the baking powder, and the salt into a large bowl. Whisk to blend.

2. In a separate bowl, whisk together the butter (or oil), egg yolks, water, and vanilla. Pour the liquid ingredients into the flour mixture and beat until smooth (this can be done by hand with a whisk or wooden spoon).

3. Using an electric mixer, in a clean bowl whip the egg whites until frothy, then add the cream of tartar. Beat until soft peaks just begin to form. Add the remaining ½ cup sugar and beat until whites hold a 2-inch peak. Do not overbeat; whites should be billowy and glossy.

4. Stir one quarter of the beaten whites into the batter to lighten. Then fold the remaining whites into the batter and pour into an ungreased 10-inch tube pan. Bake for 30 to 40 minutes. Press lightly with a fork. If the top of the cake does not spring back, bake for an additional 5 to 10 minutes (check every 5 minutes).

5. Remove pan from oven and let cool on

a rack for at least 1 hour. Run a thin knife around the outside of the cake before removing, since it is sticky and will adhere to the sides.

Citrus Variation

Replace ½ cup of water with ½ cup of orange juice. Add 1 tablespoon of grated lemon zest. Reduce vanilla extract to 1 teaspoon.

Master Recipe for White Cake

Homemade layer cakes are often heavy, lacking the pillowy, melt-in-your-mouth texture of a store-bought Duncan Hines box cake. I was looking for a recipe that combined the reliability and ease of a basic yellow cake with the ethereal texture of an angel food or sponge cake. It had to be sturdy, since I intended to fill and frost it, but also so delicate that it might just rise up off the plate.

A basic yellow cake is made with both egg whites and yolks. The lift is provided by baking powder (and sometimes baking soda), and the structure is also enhanced by beating softened butter and sugar together in a process called "creaming." A white cake, however, uses no yolks. The basic method is simple. Butter and sugar are creamed and then you fold in two separate mixtures: one of milk (or water), egg whites, and vanilla extract and the other of flour, baking powder, and salt. Some recipes opt for beating the egg whites and others, as noted above, use water instead of milk.

In my tests, I found that beating the egg whites produced a drier cake and also one not sturdy enough to use as an all-purpose layer cake. I also wanted an extremely tender crumb and therefore went with milk instead of water. I cut back on the sugar about 20 percent from more traditional recipes, slightly increased the amount of baking powder, and also reduced the ratio of butter to flour.

I suggest that you use the Meringue Frosting (page 277) or the Sour Cream Chocolate Frosting Whipped Variation (page 281) with either the basic recipe or one of the variations. If you want to make a Sunshine Cake, a classic American dessert, make a three-layer cake (two of yellow cake and one white cake layer) and frost it with a simple white icing such as Meringue Frosting.

	Butter and flour for preparing cake pans
1	cup milk
6	egg whites (use large eggs)
2½	teaspoons vanilla extract
3	cups cake flour
4	teaspoons baking powder
1	teaspoon salt
12	tablespoons (1½ sticks) unsalted butter, softened
1½	cups sugar

1. Heat oven to 350 degrees. Set rack in middle position. Coat two 9-inch cake pans with butter and sprinkle with flour. Roll pans in all directions to coat, shaking out excess.

2. Stir together the milk, egg whites, and vanilla with a fork. Sift together the next three ingredients (flour through salt) into a medium bowl.

3. Beat the butter in a large bowl with an electric mixer on medium speed for 30 seconds. Continue beating, gradually adding the sugar. Beat until light and fluffy, 2 to 3 minutes. Scrape down the sides of the bowl when necessary.

4. Add ⅓ of the flour mixture and ⅓ of the milk mixture and beat on low speed or by hand until just incorporated. Add the remaining flour and milk mixtures in 2 separate batches, beating between additions to fully incorporate. Scrape down the sides of the bowl and stir by hand to finish.

5. Divide batter between prepared pans. Smooth surface with a rubber spatula. Place pans in oven, a few inches apart, and bake 25 to 30 minutes (check cake after 22 minutes) or until top of cake springs back when lightly pressed in the center and a cake tester comes out clean.

6. Remove pans to a cooling rack. Let rest for 5 minutes. Run a small metal spatula around the sides of the pan and invert cakes onto greased racks. Reinvert cakes onto cooling rack. Let cool for at least 1½ hours.

ALMOND VARIATION

Reduce vanilla extract to 1 teaspoon and add 2 teaspoons almond extract.

CITRUS VARIATIONS

Reduce vanilla extract to 1 teaspoon and add 1 teaspoon orange or lemon extract plus 2 tablespoons freshly grated orange or lemon zest. Add zest along with extracts.

Old-Fashioned Coconut Layer Cake

I have made this cake with both sweetened supermarket coconut and unsweetened coconut, which may be found at a health food store. The latter is substantially better, with more coconut flavor and less sweetness. It is also best to toast the coconut first. When toasting, watch it closely, as it burns quickly and easily. This cake can also be filled with Rich Lemon Filling (page 272).

1	master recipe for White Cake (page 275)
1	recipe for Meringue Frosting (page 277)
2½	cups lightly packed unsweetened shredded coconut

1. Prepare cake according to instructions and let cool to room temperature on racks.

2. If you prefer to use toasted coconut (this step is optional), heat the oven to 350 degrees. Spread coconut on a cookie sheet and bake about 7 minutes. Watch the coconut closely, as it burns easily.

3. Prepare Meringue Frosting and fold in 2 cups of the coconut. Place one cake layer on a cake plate, frost the top, add the second layer, and frost the top and sides. Sprinkle ½ cup reserved coconut over frosted cake.

Meringue Frosting

This is a classic recipe for an Italian meringue. A hot sugar syrup is poured over beaten egg whites which are then whipped a bit longer to incorporate the syrup. This sets the whites, giving them lots of body. An instant-read thermometer is helpful in determining when the sugar syrup is properly cooked, although the traditional soft-ball test will do in a pinch. (A bit of the hot sugar syrup is dropped into a glass of cold water. If it sets up into a soft, gummy ball, it is done.)

3	large egg whites
1	teaspoon vanilla extract
¼	teaspoon cream of tartar
⅛	teaspoon salt
1¼	cups sugar
⅓	cup water

1. Beat egg whites in a medium bowl with an electric mixer or by hand with a large whisk for 45 seconds. Add the vanilla, cream of tartar, and salt. Increase speed to high and beat until stiff but still glossy. Whites should still be moist, not dry and cottony. (This can be done by hand, without an electric mixer, but will take a few minutes of intense beating with a large whisk.)
2. At the same time, combine sugar and water in a small saucepan. Bring to a boil, swirling pan occasionally to wash down sides of pan. Boil until sugar mixture reaches 238 degrees on a candy thermometer or until a drop of the syrup makes a soft, gummy ball when dropped into a small bowl of cold water. This will take about 7 minutes. Remove from heat and let cool for 5 minutes.

3. With the mixer on medium high, add the sugar syrup to the egg whites in a thin, steady stream. Continue beating until the frosting can hold a 2-inch peak and is very shiny. Cool to room temperature.

Maple Meringue Frosting

If you can't find maple sugar, substitute 1 cup granulated sugar and ¼ cup water. After beating the cooled syrup into the whites, add ¼ cup of dark maple syrup. In old cookbooks, this sort of frosting was often referred to as a "foam."

3	large egg whites
¼	teaspoon cream of tartar
⅛	teaspoon salt
1¼	cups maple sugar (not syrup)

1. Beat egg whites in a medium bowl with an electric mixer or by hand with a large whisk for 45 seconds. Add the cream of tartar and salt. Increase speed to high and beat until stiff but still glossy. Whites should still be moist, not dry and cottony. (This can be done by hand, without an electric mixer, but will take a few minutes of intense beating with a large whisk.)
2. At the same time, place maple sugar in a small saucepan. Bring to a boil, swirling pan occasionally to wash down sides of pan. Boil until sugar mixture reaches 238 degrees on a candy thermometer or until a drop of the syrup makes a soft, gummy ball when dropped into a small bowl of cold water. This will take about 7 minutes. Remove from heat and let cool for 5 minutes.
3. With the mixer on medium high, add the sugar syrup to the egg whites in a

thin, steady stream. Continue beating until the frosting is very stiff and shiny. Cool to room temperature.

Master Recipe for Yellow Cake

This is without doubt the most basic and most important cake recipe in any home cook's repertoire. Unlike the basic white cake, the yellow cake uses yolks and is therefore sturdier and works with a variety of different fillings and frostings. It also lends itself to a wide variety of flavorings, which might overwhelm a delicate white cake. I started with a master recipe that I had been using for years and then performed a series of tests to see if I could improve it.

First, I tried using cake flour in place of all-purpose. This did produce a finer-textured cake as expected but it was still a bit tough. I then reduced the flour to 2½ cups from 3 and found that the texture was significantly lighter. My master recipe used 5 large eggs and I found that different proportions of yolks to whites were not as good, being either too eggy or not rising properly. I was using only 1½ cups sugar; larger amounts produced a cake that was too sweet. Increasing the butter from 12 tablespoons to 16 made a very greasy and unpleasant cake. I also tried various combinations of ingredients, using higher amounts of both sugar and butter. The results were not as good as the master. So the only changes worth making were using cake flour instead of all-purpose and reducing the amount to 2½ cups.

Butter and flour for preparing cake pans
2½ cups cake flour
1 tablespoon baking powder
1 teaspoon salt
12 tablespoons (1½ sticks) unsalted butter, softened
1½ cups sugar
5 large eggs
1 cup milk
2 teaspoons vanilla extract

1. Heat oven to 350 degrees. Set oven rack in middle position. Coat two 9-inch cake pans with butter or vegetable shortening and sprinkle with flour. Roll pans in all directions to coat, shaking out excess flour.
2. Sift together flour, baking powder, and salt.
3. Beat butter in a large bowl with an electric mixer at medium speed for 30 seconds (or by hand). Continue beating and gradually add sugar. Beat until light and fluffy, 2 to 3 minutes. Add eggs, one at a time, beating after each addition. Scrape down sides of bowl when necessary.
4. Add about ⅓ of both the flour mixture and milk and beat on low speed or by hand until just incorporated. Add the vanilla and then the remaining flour and milk in 2 separate batches, beating between additions. Scrape down sides of bowl and stir by hand to finish.
5. Divide batter between prepared pans. Smooth surface with a rubber spatula. Place pans in oven, a few inches apart, and bake about 30 minutes (check cake after 22 minutes) or until top of cake springs back when lightly pressed in the center and a cake tester comes out clean.

6. Remove pans to a cooling rack. Let rest for 5 minutes. Run a small metal spatula around the sides of the pan and invert cakes onto greased racks. Reinvert cakes onto cooling rack. Let cool for at least 1½ hours.

Buttermilk Cake

This is almost identical to the recipe above but uses buttermilk instead of regular whole milk. The texture is slightly coarser but tender and the cake has a slightly tangy flavor from the buttermilk. If you try to bake this cake in an 8-inch pan, you may find that it will sink just a bit in the middle during baking. The 9-inch pans are best.

	Butter and flour for preparing cake pans
2½	cups cake flour
2	teaspoons baking powder
½	teaspoon baking soda
1	teaspoon salt
12	tablespoons (1½ sticks) unsalted butter, softened
1½	cups sugar
5	large eggs
1	cup buttermilk
2	teaspoons vanilla extract

1. Heat oven to 350 degrees. Set rack in middle position. Coat two 9-inch cake pans with butter or vegetable shortening and sprinkle with flour. Roll pans in all directions to coat, shaking out excess flour.
2. Sift together flour, baking powder, baking soda, and salt into a medium bowl.
3. Beat butter in a large bowl with an electric mixer at medium speed for 30 seconds

(or by hand). Continue beating, gradually adding sugar. Beat until light and fluffy, 2 to 3 minutes. Add eggs, one at a time, beating after each addition. Scrape down sides of bowl when necessary.
4. Add about ⅓ of the flour mixture and buttermilk and beat on low speed or by hand until just incorporated. Add the vanilla and then the remaining flour and buttermilk in 2 separate batches, beating between additions. Scrape down sides of bowl and stir by hand to finish.
5. Divide batter between prepared pans. Smooth surface with a rubber spatula. Place pans in oven, a few inches apart, and bake about 30 minutes or until top of cake springs back when lightly pressed in the center and a cake tester comes out clean. Check cake after 22 minutes.
6. Remove pans to a cooling rack. Let rest for 5 minutes. Run a small metal spatula around the sides of the pan and invert cakes onto greased racks. Reinvert cakes onto cooling rack. Let cool for at least 1½ hours.

Fresh Strawberry Cake

This cake requires very ripe berries for best results. Also, the cake is a bit messy since it tends to fall apart when sliced. However, it is a wonderful cake to serve during strawberry season.

1	recipe Yellow Cake or Buttermilk Cake (above)
1	recipe Magic Whipped Cream Frosting (page 281)
1	quart fresh strawberries, washed, dried, and hulled
1	teaspoon sugar

1. Prepare cake layers according to instructions and cool to room temperature on racks. Prepare frosting. Slice three-quarters of the strawberries in half lengthwise. Place in a medium bowl with sugar and toss gently to combine. Let sit for at least 20 minutes before using.

2. Place one cake layer on a cake plate. Top with a thin layer of whipped cream frosting. Top with halved strawberries (use all of them) and then add a second layer of frosting. Add second cake layer and frost top and sides. Decorate with remaining whole strawberries.

Creamy Chocolate Glaze

This is a simple glaze, which is poured over the cake when it has been placed on a wire rack. It's easier to use than a frosting and provides an elegant, glossy look. Determining when the glaze is ready to be poured over the cake is the only crucial step. To test this, drizzle a spoonful of the glaze back into the pan. When the glaze is ready, it should mound up a little as it touches the glaze in the pan. It's like drizzling honey into honey, although the glaze won't be quite that thick.

8	ounces semisweet chocolate
1	cup heavy cream
¼	cup light corn syrup
½	teaspoon vanilla extract

1. Chop the chocolate into small pieces, using a large knife. (You can also chop it in a heavy-duty food processor.)

2. Combine cream and corn syrup in a saucepan. Bring to a simmer. Remove from heat and add chocolate. Let stand for 8 minutes. (If chocolate is not completely melted, place mixture back over low heat and stir constantly until melted.)

3. Add vanilla and stir very gently until mixture is smooth.

4. Allow glaze to cool until tepid. Drizzle a spoonful of glaze back into the pan. When it mounds a little, the glaze is ready for pouring over the cake. (You can refrigerate the glaze to speed up this process but check every few minutes, stirring the mixture gently. Otherwise, it may set up too quickly.)

5. Place cake to be frosted on a wire rack set on a sheet of wax paper to catch the drippings. Pour contents of saucepan over middle of cake. Use a metal spatula if necessary to completely cover cake. Use a needle to puncture air bubbles. Let sit about 1 hour or until glaze fully sets.

Sour Cream Chocolate Frosting

You can make this recipe according to the basic directions below or whip it after it has firmed up a bit, which is how I prefer to serve it. (See variation below.) Whipping produces a lighter (both in color and texture) frosting, which is similar to the fluffy frosting one remembers from childhood. This is not a supersweet frosting, but is very tangy from the large amount of sour cream. It also sets up quickly given the large amount of chocolate.

12	ounces semisweet chocolate
1	teaspoon instant espresso or instant coffee (optional)
1⅔	cups sour cream

¼ cup light or dark corn syrup
¼ teaspoon vanilla extract

1. Chop the chocolate into small pieces with a large knife (or in the bowl of a food processor). Combine the chocolate and optional instant espresso in the top of a double boiler or in a heatproof bowl set over a saucepan of simmering water. Let sit for 5 minutes or until the chocolate has melted. Remove from heat and let cool until tepid.

2. Place sour cream, corn syrup, and vanilla in a medium bowl and stir to combine. Add the tepid chocolate and stir until the mixture is uniform. Let cool in the refrigerator (this should take no more than 30 minutes) until frosting is of spreadable consistency. If the frosting becomes too cold and stiff, simply leave it at room temperature until it is easy to spread.

WHIPPED FROSTING VARIATION

Once the mixture has cooled in the refrigerator and is ready to spread, beat with an electric mixer on high speed for 3 minutes or until the frosting is light in color and fluffy.

Magic Whipped Cream Frosting

Most whipped cream frostings don't hold up well, so I favor this version, which uses a bit of dissolved unflavored gelatin to give the whipped cream some stiffness and staying power. However, the frosted cake is still best kept in the refrigerator to preserve the texture and shape of the frosting.

1 teaspoon unflavored gelatin
2 cups heavy cream
½ cup confectioners' sugar
½ teaspoon vanilla extract

1. Chill bowl and beaters of an electric mixer in the freezer for at least 10 minutes.

2. Sprinkle gelatin over 2 tablespoons water in a small saucepan. Let dissolve for 4 minutes. Over very low heat, melt gelatin mixture, about 3 minutes.

3. Place heavy cream and melted gelatin in the chilled bowl. Beat on low speed for 30 seconds until gelatin is thoroughly mixed into cream. Increase speed to high and beat until cream just starts to take shape. Add sugar and vanilla and beat until stiff.

BOOZY VARIATIONS

Add 1 tablespoon of any liquor such as dark rum, bourbon, brandy, or Cointreau along with the heavy cream.

ALMOND, ORANGE, AND LEMON VARIATIONS

Use ½ teaspoon of almond extract, orange extract, or lemon extract in place of the vanilla.

Master Recipe for Upside-Down Cake

The trick with this recipe is having the proper size iron skillet. An 8-inch skillet is too small and a 12-inch skillet is too large. The ideal size is 9 to 10 inches. If you do not have an iron skillet of the proper size, simply heat the butter/sugar mixture in any saucepan for 4 minutes, add the fruit, stir until the sugar is completely dissolved, and then pour it into a 9 x 3-inch cake pan. Pour the batter on top. The cake pan method produces a straight-sided cake whereas the skillet will make a cake with sloping sides.

FOR THE FRUIT

2	cups fruit (peaches, plums, or pineapple) cut into ½-inch slices
1	tablespoon lemon juice
4	tablespoons (½ stick) unsalted butter
¾	cup packed dark brown sugar

FOR THE CAKE

⅔	cup buttermilk (see Note below)
3	whole eggs plus 1 egg white
1	teaspoon vanilla extract
½	teaspoon almond extract
1½	cups all-purpose flour
¾	cup sugar
1	teaspoon baking powder
¼	teaspoon baking soda
¼	cup cornmeal
½	teaspoon salt
6	tablespoons unsalted butter, room temperature

1. Heat oven to 350 degrees. Toss fruit with lemon juice and set aside. In a 9- or 10-inch iron skillet, melt the 4 tablespoons butter. Add the brown sugar and, stirring occasionally, heat for 4 minutes. Add the fruit and stir until the sugar is totally dissolved. Remove from heat.

2. Stir together ⅓ cup buttermilk, eggs and egg white, and extracts with a fork. In a large bowl mix the next 6 ingredients (flour through salt) until blended. Add butter and remaining ⅓ cup buttermilk and beat on low speed or by hand until moistened. Beat on medium for 1½ minutes. Scrape down sides of bowl and add half of buttermilk mixture. Mix for 30 seconds. Scrape down sides of bowl, add remaining buttermilk mixture, and beat for 30 seconds. Scrape down sides and beat 20 seconds more.

3. Pour batter over fruit in cast iron pan and smooth top. Bake about 30 minutes or until top of cake springs back when lightly pressed in the center. Check cake after 25 minutes.

4. Remove skillet to a cooling rack. Let rest for 3 minutes. Place a serving plate over top of skillet and invert. If any of the fruit sticks to the pan, remove and place on top of cake.

   Note: To make this cake with regular milk, not buttermilk, simply substitute one for the other, eliminate the baking soda, and increase the baking powder to 1½ teaspoons.

Pound Cake

Although it sounds simple, a good pound cake is in fact quite difficult to make perfectly if the ingredients are not at the proper temperature. The butter needs to be at just the right temperature (about 65 degrees) so that it is malleable but not quite room temperature, at which point it is too soft. The eggs must also be warmed. (The best way to warm up cold eggs is to place them in a bowl of very warm water.) If the ingredients are too cold, the batter will separate and the proper structure will not be formed. A perfect batter should be dull and thick without a grainy or shiny appearance.

1⅔	cups cake or all-purpose flour (cake preferred)
½	teaspoon salt
2	sticks unsalted butter, softened but still firm
1½	cups sugar
5	large eggs, room temperature
1½	teaspoons vanilla extract
1	teaspoon lemon zest

1. Heat oven to 325 degrees. Grease (with soft butter or vegetable oil spray) and flour a standard loaf pan, 9 x 5 x 3 inches. Sift together the flour and salt onto a large piece of wax paper.

2. Place the butter in a large mixing bowl and beat until smooth, light-colored, and creamy. This can be done by hand, about 1 minute, or in an electric mixer, about 30 seconds. Gradually add the sugar and beat until the butter turns almost white and is very fluffy, about 5 minutes by hand and 3 minutes with an electric mixer.

3. Add the eggs one at a time, beating for 20 seconds after each addition. The mixture should be dull and smooth. (If the batter appears grainy or separated, the butter or eggs were too cold. If this hap-

pens, simply let ingredients sit a few minutes until they warm up.) Add the vanilla and lemon zest and beat 10 seconds.

4. Add the flour in three equal parts, folding it into the mixture with a large rubber spatula until the batter is well mixed. Scrape up from the bottom of the bowl frequently.

5. Pour batter into prepared pan and bake for 1 hour and 10 minutes. The top should be split and nicely browned and a cake tester or straw inserted into the center should come out clean. If not, continue baking and check every 5 minutes. When done, empty cake upside down onto one covered hand (use two potholders) and then place the cake right side up onto the cooling rack. Cool at least 1 hour before slicing and serving.

Lemon Pudding Cake

This recipe is not likely to be served at a dinner party, but it is just fine for family fare, perhaps offered as a simple sweet for Sunday supper. During baking, this dessert separates into two layers, the bottom ending up a custard whereas the top becomes a cake. I tested many variations of this recipe and found that most published recipes are rather similar. They all use 3 eggs, which I found to be the right amount. I tried 3, 4, and then 5 tablespoons of flour and found that 4 tablespoons was best: less flour produced too much pudding and 5 tablespoons produced too much cake. I did add a bit of cream of tartar to this recipe, which lightened up the texture of the cake. A quarter of a cup of lemon juice was fine; larger quantities dramatically increased the pucker factor. Finally, a small bit of salt and vanilla, ingredients often not included in this recipe, helped to punch up flavors.

¾	cup plus 2 tablespoons sugar
¼	cup cake flour
¼	teaspoon salt
3	eggs, separated, at room temperature
1	cup milk
1	tablespoon lemon zest (about 1 lemon)
¼	cup lemon juice
½	teaspoon vanilla extract
½	teaspoon cream of tartar

1. Heat oven to 325 degrees. Adjust rack to center position. Butter and flour an 8-inch square baking pan.

2. In a medium bowl, combine ¾ cup sugar, flour, and salt. In a small bowl, beat the egg yolks, milk, lemon zest, lemon juice, and vanilla. Pour the egg mixture over the flour mixture and blend well with a rubber spatula.

3. In a clean bowl, beat the egg whites until they foam and bubble. Add the cream of tartar and beat until they hold soft peaks. Add the 2 tablespoons sugar and beat until they hold a 2-inch peak. Fold the egg whites into the yolk mixture with a rubber spatula.

4. Pour batter into baking dish. Bake 35 minutes or until the surface of the cake is lightly browned and springs back when lightly pressed. Serve immediately.

Blueberry Boy-Bait

This is my all-time favorite recipe name. It comes from Renny Powell, a teenager from Chicago, who submitted this recipe in 1954 to the Pillsbury $100,000 Recipe & Baking Contest (now known as the Pillsbury Bake-Off Contest) and won second prize in the junior division. This is a very light one-layer cake with blueberries and a simple crumble topping. Ms. Powell evidently found it useful in attracting members of the opposite sex and, based on my testing, I would have to agree that it's pretty good bait. I made a few changes from the original, including reducing the sugar level (recipes from the 1950s are usually too sweet), cutting back on the amount of topping, and increasing the volume of blueberries. We now use this recipe at the farmhouse, so that when neighbors stop by for a cup of coffee we have something to serve with it.

2	cups flour
1¼	cups sugar
10	tablespoons (1¼ sticks) cold butter
2	teaspoons baking powder
1	teaspoon salt
2	eggs, separated
1	cup milk
1½	cups fresh blueberries, washed, drained, and blotted with paper towels (or frozen blueberries that have been thoroughly thawed and drained)

1. Heat oven to 350 degrees. Grease a 13 x 9-inch pan with butter and then flour it lightly. Sift together the flour and sugar into a large mixing bowl. Cut the butter into pieces, then work into the flour mixture using your fingertips or a pastry blender. (If you have a food processor, place the flour and sugar in bowl and

pulse to mix. Add the butter, which should be cold and cut into pieces, and pulse 7 or 8 times until the flour takes on the texture of coarse meal.) The flour should take on the texture of coarse meal, with a few pea-size pieces of butter still visible, and turn slightly yellow. Reserve ½ cup of this mixture to use as a topping.
2. Add the baking powder, the salt, the egg yolks (reserve the whites), and the milk to the flour mixture still in the bowl. Beat with an electric mixer on low speed for about 3 minutes. (This can also be done by hand with a wooden spoon.)
3. In a separate bowl, whip the egg whites until they hold 2-inch peaks. Fold gently into the batter. Spread batter in the prepared pan. Sprinkle blueberries (make sure they are dry) on top, then sprinkle with the reserved ½ cup crumb mixture.
4. Bake for 40 to 50 minutes or until the center of the cake bounces back when pressed with the flat side of a fork. Let cool for 30 minutes before serving either as a coffee cake or a dessert, the latter with whipped cream.

Gingerbread

Most gingerbread recipes call for ground ginger, which makes for a very dull cake indeed, sweet, heavy, and flat-tasting. However, a few years ago I was lucky enough to order the gingerbread at the Ginger Island restaurant in Berkeley, California, which, I soon discovered, was made from fresh ginger. What a difference. It transformed this somewhat childish treat into an adult dessert, complex and with plenty of bite.

So I started my testing by eliminating the ground ginger and substituting a full quarter cup of fresh minced ginger. This was very good but too sharp and not complex enough in taste. I then cut back the fresh ginger to 3 tablespoons and added 2 tablespoons of chopped crystallized ginger, which added both depth and balance.

I also noticed that most old-fashioned gingerbread recipes call for the addition of ½ a cup or so of boiling water. This is a common feature of many simple one-layer cakes which depend on baking soda for lift. It is thought that the heat helps to activate the baking soda. (A similar recipe, applesauce cake, usually calls for hot applesauce and a small quantity of hot water in which the baking soda is dissolved.) After much testing, I found that the temperature of the milk or water made no difference. I also preferred milk (instead of water) to soften the crumb, making a more tender cake.

Pan size and cooking time are very important for this recipe. You can either use a 9 x 9-inch or an 11 x 7-inch pan, the latter being preferable but harder to find. Other sizes may cause the cake to fall a bit in the center after baking. After making this cake a dozen times, I have also found it extremely important to thoroughly cook the center of the cake; if it is even slightly undercooked it will have a tendency to sink as it cools. Do not trust cake testers — they are worthless. You need to press on the center of the cake with the flat side of a fork. It should spring back immediately.

I also tested using melted butter instead of creamed butter and found that the latter was preferable for a slightly lighter texture. It is very important that the butter be softened but still quite firm, about 67 degrees when measured with an instant-read thermometer. Also, the butter/sugar mixture should be light-colored and fluffy after beating. If it isn't, touch the side of the bowl. (It is best to use a metal bowl.) If it is very cold, then warm it for just a few seconds over a gas flame or run hot water over it to warm the contents. Be careful here. You don't want to actually melt the butter.

I also cut back on the amount of spices. Many old-fashioned recipes go overboard, using large quantities of cinnamon and the like. I use just ½ teaspoon each.

2½	cups flour
½	teaspoon cinnamon
½	teaspoon cloves
½	teaspoon nutmeg
½	teaspoon allspice
½	teaspoon baking soda
½	teaspoon salt
2	sticks (½ pound) butter, softened but still firm
½	cup packed dark brown sugar
½	cup granulated sugar
2	eggs, room temperature
1	cup molasses
3	tablespoons minced peeled fresh gingerroot
2	tablespoons minced crystallized ginger
½	cup hot milk

1. Heat oven to 325 degrees. Grease a 9-inch square baking pan. Line the bottom with parchment or wax paper, grease the paper, and flour the pan.
2. Sift the first 7 ingredients (flour through salt) onto a piece of wax paper.
3. Put the butter in a large bowl and beat with an electric mixer for 1 minute or until light-colored. Add the sugars gradu-

ally while beating. Beat for 3 minutes or until the mixture is light and fluffy, scraping down the sides of the bowl 2 or 3 times. Add the eggs one at a time, beating for 20 seconds after each addition or until smooth. Beat in the molasses. Add the dry ingredients, the fresh ginger, and the crystallized ginger. Beat on the lowest speed until combined. Add the hot milk and mix with a rubber spatula to combine.
4. Pour batter into the prepared pan and transfer it to the center of the hot oven. Bake for 55 to 60 minutes, until the top springs back when lightly touched or when a cake tester inserted in the center comes out clean. Cool on a rack for 20 minutes. Cut into squares and serve plain or with a dollop of sweetened whipped cream.

HONEY CAKE

Beekeeping is about more than just honey. It is an art and one that has to be learned slowly, since there are few books on the topic and most of the really useful tips have to be garnered firsthand. I remember taking a lesson from a young man who gave a good lecture and then led us out to the beehives for more practical training. He told us always to smoke a hive first, make sure that it is a sunny, warm day, and to be sure to fully cover any exposed skin. (A smoker is a small canister with attached bellows that produces a fair amount of smoke from grass clippings or wood chips. The hive cover is removed, smoke is blown across the top of the hive, and the bees retreat into the hive, becoming less aggressive.) On this particular day, it was cool and overcast, which makes bees ornery. The instructor did not bring his smoker, and he had a good part of his arms exposed, since he was wearing only a T-shirt and gloves. Well, as soon as he removed the hive cover, about 500 bees swarmed him, stinging him at least a dozen times. He maintained his composure, replaced the cover, and announced in a very faint but controlled voice that he would be back. He returned a few minutes later with a full set of overalls and a fired-up smoker. It is an unpredictable hobby. Of course there are beekeepers who seem to have a charmed relationship with bees. An old farmer friend told me that one day a bee inspector showed up at his house wearing nothing other than a pair of white painter's pants — no shirt, no shoes, no gloves, no headgear. (Inspectors come around every year or two to make sure that the hives are healthy.) They spent an hour or so checking out twenty hives and he didn't get stung once.

But the real joy of beekeeping is watching the bees work, whether building the comb or swooping into the hives in midsummer, heavily laden with pollen, sometimes crash-landing before the hive entrance. In winter, I reduce the size of the entrance to the hives and also wrap them with insulation. Bees beat their wings furiously all winter to stay warm and to expel excess moisture that builds up in the hive. Of course bees can be cruel by our standards. I have often watched a half dozen bees dragging an infirm but still alive worker out the front entrance, dumping her onto the snow to die.

And the honey itself is wonderful, and full of flavors not found in the store-bought variety. I am always looking for recipes that use lots of honey and so I researched honey cakes. Versions of this recipe are common in many cultures including Eastern Europe. Some recipes for honey cake use quite a lot of spices, which I felt competed unfavorably with the subtle flavor of the honey itself. However, I did like the addition of strong coffee as an ingredient, and a bit of Scotch didn't hurt either.

Honey Cake

This cake is designed to stand nicely on its own as a square to be served with coffee or tea as an afternoon snack. I have increased the amount of butter, eggs, and honey to make this a full-flavored, sturdy cake; lighter versions seemed a bit too delicate. By the way, if you don't particularly enjoy the flavor of honey, I do not recommend this cake.

¼ cup strong brewed coffee
2½ cups cake flour
½ teaspoon salt
1 teaspoon baking powder
½ teaspoon baking soda
2 sticks (½ pound) unsalted butter, softened but still firm
¼ cup packed brown sugar
¼ cup granulated sugar
3 eggs, room temperature
¾ cup honey
2 teaspoons finely chopped lemon zest
1 tablespoon Scotch or bourbon (optional)
⅔ cup raisins (optional)

1. Heat oven to 350 degrees and adjust oven rack to the middle position. Grease and flour a 9 x 9-inch baking pan or a deep 9-inch cake or springform pan. Brew a small amount of strong coffee or mix ¼ cup boiling water with 2 teaspoons instant coffee or espresso.

2. Sift the next 4 ingredients (flour through baking soda) onto a piece of wax paper.

3. Put the butter into a large mixing bowl and beat with an electric mixer for 1 minute or until very light colored. Add the sugars and beat for 3 minutes on high speed until the mixture is light and fluffy. Scrape down sides of bowl 2 or 3 times as you work. Add eggs one at a time, beating for 20 seconds after each addition. Continue beating until mixture is smooth. Add the next 3 ingredients (honey through Scotch) and beat to combine.

4. Add the flour mixture and beat on lowest speed to mix, or combine with a large rubber spatula. Do not overmix. Stir in the optional raisins.

5. Pour batter into the prepared pan and bake for about 30 minutes or until the center of the cake springs back and a cake tester or straw inserted into the center comes out clean. Cool on a rack for at least 30 minutes. Cut into squares and serve plain or with a dusting of confectioners' sugar.

Light Carrot Cake

A classic carrot cake has many problems, the greatest of them being the signature heavy, wet texture. This is caused primarily by the carrots themselves, which contain a great deal of water. An article in *Cook's Illustrated* by Marie Piraino and Jamie Morris solved a good deal of this problem by suggesting that grated carrots be tossed with sugar and then allowed to drain in a colander. The result was a much lighter cake, although I thought it was a bit too far removed from the original recipe. To find a happy middle ground, I tested a variety of ingredients, including apple sauce (the texture was very wet), honey (the honey flavor was too strong and unwelcome in this cake), whole wheat flour (the soft texture of the cake was lost and the flavor was too earthy), cooked carrots (the texture suffered and the carrot flavor was weaker), and coconut (dry, flaked, unsweetened coconut did add a bit of texture and improved the flavor; don't use the sweet supermarket variety). I also decided to use mostly dark brown sugar to produce a darker cake with a richer flavor. I also thought that the amount of grated carrots in the *Cook's* recipe was a bit excessive, so I reduced the quantity to 5 cups from 7. Most recipes use a combination of butter, cream cheese, confectioners' sugar, and sour cream for the frosting. I am not fond of buttercreams, I find them too rich, so I use only 4 tablespoons of softened butter (as opposed to a whole stick or more) to 16 ounces of cream cheese, 2 tablespoons of sour cream, and 2 cups of confectioners' sugar. The other interesting feature of this recipe, one suggested by Piraino and Morris, is that the butter for the cake be melted and browned. This does add a lot of extra flavor and therefore I use the same method below.

FOR THE CAKE

5 cups coarsely grated carrots, about 6 large

1 cup granulated sugar

1	8-ounce can crushed pineapple packed in its own juice, strained well (about ¾ cup)
2⅔	cups cake flour
4	teaspoons baking powder
½	teaspoon baking soda
2	teaspoons cinnamon
1	teaspoon salt
2	sticks butter
1½	cups dark brown sugar
5	eggs
1½	teaspoons vanilla extract
¾	cup toasted chopped pecans
⅔	cup unsweetened, dried, flaked coconut, optional (do not use the sweet supermarket variety)

FOR THE CREAM CHEESE FROSTING

16	ounces cream cheese, softened
3	tablespoons butter, softened
2	cups confectioners' sugar
3	tablespoons sour cream

1. Heat oven to 350 degrees and adjust rack to the center position. Grease two 9-by 2-inch cake pans. Line the bottom with parchment paper (this cake has a tendency to stick). Place the grated carrots in a large bowl and toss with the granulated sugar. Move carrots to a colander and place over the bowl to drain. Drain pineapple. Whisk together the next 5 ingredients (cake flour through salt) in a medium bowl.

2. Melt butter in a large saucepan or skillet over medium-low heat, stirring frequently. Cook until the butter turns golden brown, about 10 minutes, and has a nutty aroma. There should be small brown flecks on the bottom of the pan. Do not allow these flecks to turn very dark, otherwise the cake will have a burnt, bitter flavor. Pour melted butter into a large bowl and let cool for 2 minutes. Whisk in the brown sugar. Whisk in the eggs, one at a time. Add the vanilla and whisk for 10 seconds. Add the flour mixture and whisk until it is three-quarters incorporated. Using a large rubber spatula, gently fold in the carrots, pineapple, pecans, and optional coconut until the batter is well mixed.

3. Divide the batter evenly between the prepared pans. Smooth top surfaces with the rubber spatula. Bake until cake feels firm in the center when pressed lightly, about 40 to 50 minutes. Check cakes after 30 minutes. Remove from oven and run a knife around the perimeter of each pan. Invert cakes onto a large plate and then back onto a cooling rack. Allow to cool completely before frosting. Remove cream cheese and butter from refrigerator 1 hour before frosting.

4. To frost, beat the softened cream cheese and butter with an electric mixer on low speed until homogenous, about 3 to 4 minutes. Add the confectioners' sugar and sour cream and beat until well blended, up to 2 minutes longer. To frost the cake, place one layer on a cake plate, anchoring it with a small dab of frosting, and frost the top. Add the second layer, frost the top, then the sides, and then garnish with extra pecans or coconut if desired.

Butterscotch Brownies

When these brownies are done, the tops are cracked and lightly browned. The optional butterscotch chips may seem superfluous but add that extra touch that makes these brownies memorably decadent.

8	tablespoons (1 stick) unsalted butter, softened
1	cup packed dark brown sugar
¼	cup granulated sugar
1½	teaspoons vanilla extract
1	tablespoon molasses
2	large eggs
1	cup all-purpose flour
½	teaspoon salt
¾	cup pecans, broken or coarsely chopped
½	cup butterscotch chips (optional)

1. Heat oven to 350 degrees. Butter an 8-inch square baking pan. (This is one recipe for which the size of the baking pan is important. Do not use a larger or smaller pan.)

2. Beat the butter and sugars in the bowl of an electric mixer or with a wooden spoon until creamy and smooth, about 3 minutes. Beat in the vanilla and mo-lasses. Add the eggs one at a time, beating well after each addition. Beat mixture on high speed (or vigorously by hand) until it is very smooth.

3. In a small bowl, whisk together the flour and salt. Add the flour mixture to the butter/sugar mixture and stir on low speed or by hand until incorporated. Use a rubber spatula to scrape down sides of bowl and finish mixing batter. Stir in nuts and optional chips. Transfer batter to buttered pan. Spread top with a spatula to make it smooth and even.

4. Bake for 30 to 35 minutes, turning pan halfway through. Start checking after 23 minutes. When done, the center of the mixture should be firm but still moist, the top will be cracked, and the sides will start to pull away from the pan. Let cool in pan and then cut into squares.

MAKES 16 SQUARES

LIGHT, CAKELIKE VARIATION

This produces a much lighter brownie, a bit more cake-like in texture. It doesn't have much chew and is a bit more delicate all around. Simply add ¼ teaspoon of baking soda to the flour.

The Dairy

WHEN I TURNED ten years old, I started working summers for Junior Bentley, who at that time was renting a long red dairy barn down by the paved road that ran into New York State. The going rate was 75 cents per hour, and when we had finished up just before suppertime, I'd feel flush with my earnings but also a day's work done, the cows milked, the gutters cleaned, the pails of milk carried to the cooler, a small shack built onto one end of the long red barn. In those days, milk was stored in large cans, set into a thick metal cooler filled with cold water, waiting for the next pickup. Today, since the herds are larger, the milk is piped directly into large holding tanks. No more pouring of the warm, sweet milk from the milker to the pail, a whiff of something rich, almost intimate, just sucked out of a large, docile animal held in place by a rusted metal stanchion.

Those afternoons milking the small herd produced plenty of memories, from kicking open a few bales of hay once the cows were called into the barn, distributing it along the row, to the sound of water troughs filling, cows sucking down the cool water, the rhythmic beat of the compressor pumping in the corner, flies, thousands of them, buzzing around my head, the acrid, mind-filling stew of ripe hay and fresh urine and old manure, the clank of the metal stanchions, and the cows themselves: large, hot sacks of cud and gas and milk.

I would sit hunkered down by a large Holstein, my head up against her short white-and-black hide, the hairs smooth but not soft, one hand checking the teats and the other on the tail, holding it tight to the haunch, to avoid a quick, painful swat in the face that could quickly bring the sting of tears.

On rainy afternoons, I might grab my .22 rifle and head out to one of the many barns owned by the Bentleys in our town, barns used mostly for storing hay, but some still used for overwintering the horses or storing old carriages, sleighs, and haying equipment. They were faded gray structures, the paint long worn off by rain and wind and fierce winter storms. Much of the siding was loose, boards curled outward around the foundation, doors propped open with half-rotted boards, hanging on by only one set of hinges. My job was to decimate the rodent population, the rats tunneling into feed bags, making a mess. I'd sit as still as old Floyd on his mower, waiting for a flicker of movement, and then take careful aim, squeezing the trigger slowly until the gun seemed to go off by itself. Often, when I was hunting, a thunderstorm would come through, the artillery of thunder pounding through our valley, marching right up over Swearing Hill and down toward the small farm. At the height of the storm, the darkness would swallow the barn and the fields, a violent wall of rain would form a running curtain outside the drip line of the eaves, and undulating waves of mist and water would roll through the noise and the lightning, making their way like a Civil War regiment down the valley. As the

seconds between lightning and thunder grew shorter, the whole world became smaller, just the crashing, the intervals of silence and echoes, the violent hiss of the rain, the deep shadows of the barn, and the ripe, hot smells of fresh-baled hay and old leather and a whiff of dry manure.

Today, the old red barn is long gone, a victim of corporate farming, low prices, and competition. It was a hard life, rising at 4:30 A.M. to head down for the first milking or sitting atop the old red Farmall tractor on a bitter day in February, pulling the manure wagon with the wind whipping down out of the valley, the faded green farming cap not low enough to cover the ears. But to this day, that farmer still keeps horses and cattle, and gets up early to put out the hay, going about his business as if nothing has changed. I am not one to say that a hard life is always a good life. But hard physical labor doesn't leave much time for idleness, for hanging out at a mall, or thinking about what's coming next. It's repetitive, even boring work, but throwing hay up onto a pickup or crouching down by the side of a milker is a good time to let the mind wander a bit, thinking of a sudden storm blowing up across the valley or the sound of bees that fill a large, round apple tree in May, the humming drowning out idle thoughts. We become wedded to a place, to fields and small brooks, to the sunlight filtering in through slats in a barn, to the sound the house makes in the dead of winter, the stovepipe popping with exploding creosote. We take our place in the cycle of things, happy I expect, in the vista from the curved metal seat on top of the tractor. For some, it may not be much of a view, but for others, it happily encompasses all one needs to know or be.

COOKING WITH milk, cream, and eggs isn't easy, since a delicate balance must be struck between creating sufficient structure to hold the liquid in a custard, for example, without tightening that structure to the point that the liquid is released. In simplest terms, eggs are required because they contain protein, which forms itself into a mesh as it bakes. This honeycomb holds liquids somewhat as a sponge does. Too few eggs per cup of milk and the structure will not set up properly. Too many eggs and the mixture will taste too "eggy" and be less delicate. In my testing, I have found that 4 whole eggs per 3 cups of liquid, usually a combination of milk and heavy cream, is about right. But the biggest challenge faced by the home baker is to determine when a custard-based dessert is properly cooked. It must be taken from the oven before the center is fully cooked and is still a bit wobbly. Additional cooking will take place out of the oven. This is the secret to great custard desserts. Overbaking will result in disaster as the water will be squeezed out of the custard as the proteins start to tighten. This is what has happened when you cut into a baked custard and find that it is watery.

I also find that a mix of milk and heavy cream or the use of half-and-half is better than either all milk or all cream. All-milk custard desserts tend to be slippery, passing by the tongue without enough time to stop and say hello. All-cream variations are heavy, dulling the other flavors in the dessert. Finally, I have found that lower

oven temperatures are best, from 275 to 325 degrees. The egg proteins are less likely to toughen (a cheesecake, for example, is less likely to end up with a cracked top crust), and this provides the cook with a larger time window during which the dessert should be pulled from the oven.

It should also be noted that the milk, cream, and butter we enjoy today bear little resemblance to what was available on a working farm. In the summer, the cream and butter were richer, the latter a deep, natural yellow without the colorings added during winter months. (However, it should be noted that some small farmers were known for their frugality, even when it came to feeding their own milkers. The milk, especially in winter months, had a distinct bluish hue. It was so "nonfat" that one could not make yogurt or butter out of it. When our family needed milk with high butterfat content we would purchase milk from Jersey cows, which were well fed.) Of course real unpasteurized cream is altogether different from the tasteless, overprocessed product available today. A cream or custard pie made with the real thing is just short of divine.

American Baked Custard

No, this is no fancy flan, crème brûlée, or caramel custard. This is a simple, all-purpose baked custard that is tender and delicious, and makes a nice gift for a neighbor who is feeling poorly and needs a little nourishment. It is also my favorite recipe when I have to bring something along for a potluck supper. I tested it using half-and-half for the heavy cream and also tried an all-milk version. The heavy cream was clearly superior: silky, smooth, and tongue-coating. The all-milk version was thin, almost slippery in texture. Fewer yolks produced a custard that was not as smooth. Less sugar simply meant less flavor.

2	cups milk
1	cup heavy cream
2	egg yolks
3	whole eggs
½	cup sugar
⅛	teaspoon salt
1	teaspoon vanilla extract
	Nutmeg

1. Heat oven to 325 degrees. Butter a 1½- or 2-quart baking dish or 8 custard cups. Bring a kettle of water to a boil. Heat the milk and heavy cream until bubbly around the edges.

2. Whisk together the yolks and eggs. Stir in the sugar, salt, and vanilla, then whisk in the hot milk/cream mixture. Pour through a fine sieve into a large glass measuring cup or bowl with a pouring spout.

3. Place the prepared dish or cups in a roasting pan, pour in the custard mixture, top with a dusting of freshly grated nutmeg, and then place in the oven. Pour the hot water into the pan to a depth of 1 inch. Bake 15 to 20 minutes for cups and 40 to 50 minutes for the baking dish. The center should still be wobbly and barely set. Remove from oven and let stand until cooled. The custard may be served warm or refrigerated first.

SERVES 8

Master Recipe for Cheesecake

Over the last 15 years, I have been involved in two different in-depth cheesecake tests, both of which proved that a water bath is indeed necessary to produce a moist, tender cheesecake without cracks. Since a water bath is troublesome, you do need extra-wide aluminum foil for this process to prevent leaking. I have also found over the years that low oven temperatures are best to gently cook the egg protein. That is why the cake is left in the oven for 2 hours after the initial baking time; it finishes cooking at a very low temperature. This recipe is light — I don't like dense cheesecakes — but if you want a more substantial texture, simply don't separate the eggs. See the variation below. Flavor variations for cheesecake are difficult. A ginger cheesecake, for example, never had enough true ginger flavor, and the chocolate variation below is good but the overwhelming amount of dairy in the recipe diminished the chocolate to a mild flavoring, not a burst of intense chocolate flavor. The amount of chocolate was bumped to 12 ounces to help remedy this, but you will still find that this is not an intense chocolate experience. I am no fan of white chocolate — it always tastes artificial to me — yet I made a half dozen attempts to come up with a good white chocolate cheesecake recipe. I found that it took a very long time to set up, never really achieving the texture I was looking for, and have therefore not included it here. For maximum flavor, I suggest that you refrigerate the cheesecake for several hours before serving; the flavors seem to pick up. For half a recipe, you can cut all of the ingredients in half except the eggs (use 3) and reduce the baking time to 40 to 50 minutes. An easy technique for making graham cracker crumbs is to place a cracker in a zipper-lock bag and then crush it with a rolling pin.

1	tablespoon unsalted butter, melted
2	whole graham crackers, crushed into fine crumbs
2	pounds cream cheese, at room temperature
1¼	cups sugar
5	large eggs, separated
1	teaspoon minced lemon zest
1½	teaspoons vanilla extract
½	cup heavy cream
1	cup sour cream
½	teaspoon cream of tartar

1. Adjust oven rack to the middle position and heat oven to 275 degrees. Remove the bottom from a 10-inch springform pan. Cut a large piece of aluminum foil (it is best to use an extra-wide roll for this) and place the bottom of the pan on top of it. Fold the excess foil up around the edges. Reassemble the pan with the aluminum foil–coated side of the bottom facing upward. (The cheesecake will bake directly on the foil.) Now fold the excess foil up around the sides of the pan. (The foil should reach most of the way up the sides, since the pan will be sitting in a water bath during baking. The foil prevents leakage.) Brush bottom and sides of pan with melted butter and then sprinkle with graham cracker crumbs, tilting the pan to coat evenly. Set pan in a large roasting pan and bring a kettle or large saucepan of water to a boil.

2. Beat cream cheese with an electric mixer or by hand until smooth. Gradually

add sugar and continue beating, about 3 minutes if using an electric mixer, about 6 to 7 minutes by hand. Add yolks, one at a time, and beat until just incorporated, frequently scraping down the sides of the bowl. Stir in the next 4 ingredients (lemon zest through sour cream) with a wooden spoon or rubber spatula.

3. Beat the egg whites with the cream of tartar until they hold soft peaks. Fold whites into the batter with a large rubber spatula. Pour into prepared pan (the batter should not come up more than ¼ inch from the top of the pan) and then pour enough boiling water into roasting pan to come halfway up the pan. Bake for 1 hour to 1 hour and 10 minutes or until cheesecake is puffy, slightly browned, and the center is still a bit wobbly. Turn off oven and let cheesecake sit in oven, door closed, for another 2 hours.

4. Remove springform pan from the water bath and set on a wire rack to cool to room temperature. Cover and refrigerate for several hours (until completely chilled). To serve, run a thin knife around the inside of the pan and remove outer ring. To make slicing easier, run a sharp knife under hot water in between slices.

SERVES AT LEAST 12

THICK, RICH CHEESECAKE VARIATION

Don't separate the eggs. Beat in whole eggs, instead of egg yolks, as called for in the recipe above.

Chocolate Cheesecake Variation

Melt 12 ounces of semisweet baking chocolate. (This is best done in a glass measuring cup in a microwave oven: 50 percent power for 2 minutes, stir, and then an additional 1 to 2 minutes at the same power level; *or* place the chocolate in an ovenproof glass bowl and put it in the oven just as you turn it on for preheating — remove after 6 to 7 minutes.) Combine the melted chocolate with ⅓ cup of very strong hot coffee (or combine 1 tablespoon of instant coffee or espresso with ¼ cup hot water). Add this mixture along with the sour cream. Omit the lemon rind. Add 5 to 10 minutes to the initial baking time.

Master Recipe for Bread Pudding

This is a standard recipe from the American repertoire. There are different techniques for handling the bread. The Coach House in New York, for example, made this pudding with slices of French bread, which were coated with confectioners' sugar and then glazed under a broiler. However, I find that version too sweet. I have reduced the sugar a bit and bake this dish at a modest 325 degrees rather than at higher temperatures. This ensures a more tender custard. Many cooks prefer to use crustless bread; I prefer the look and taste of slices with the crusts left on. I also find that it is important to soak the bread in the custard mixture for 10 to 15 minutes before baking; otherwise the dish will consist of a thick layer of custard with bread floating on top. You will note that I call for a whopping 1 teaspoon of ground nutmeg. It's not a misprint.

I also tested how many eggs were necessary to set up the custard without making it too "eggy." With 3 eggs the texture was too loose; 4 eggs was excellent, with both good flavor and texture; and 5 eggs made the custard too rich. Using all milk, the custard was too thin, with a shiny, wobbly texture and appearance. An all-cream version was much too rich, even for me. Equal amounts of milk and cream (2 cups each) was very good. However, further testing showed that it was best to reduce the overall amount of custard and that 2 cups of milk to 1 of cream made an even better, livelier bread pudding. This also required a reduction in the amount of sugar.

4	large, ⅜-inch-thick slices country bread, about 4½ cups when cubed
3	tablespoons unsalted butter, room temperature
2	cups milk
1	cup heavy cream
4	large eggs
⅔	cup sugar
1	teaspoon vanilla extract
1	tablespoon brandy, rum, or bourbon
¼	teaspoon salt
1	teaspoon ground nutmeg

1. Heat oven to 325 degrees. Butter a 1½- to 2-quart baking dish. Coat bread slices with 2 tablespoons of butter. Remove the crusts if desired. Cut into ¾-inch cubes and reserve.
2. Whisk together the remaining ingredients and then add the bread cubes. Combine with a rubber spatula and let soak for 15 minutes.
3. Pour into the prepared baking dish and

bake for about 45 minutes or until the sides are firm and a knife inserted in the center comes out clean. Let stand for at least 20 minutes before serving.

SERVES 6 TO 8

RAISIN VARIATION

Some folks just can't stand raisins in puddings and therefore I offer this only as a variation. Soak ½ cup raisins in ¼ cup rum and let stand while the bread is soaking. (I prefer to use the Pavich Family Farms brand found in health food stores, or Dole; both are plumper and moister than Sunkist.) Add to the bread mixture just before pouring into the prepared dish and eliminate the liquor called for in the master recipe.

INDIAN PUDDING

When I was a kid, I used to accompany my mother when she made her rounds, delivering our homemade sausage to restaurants and stores around our part of Vermont. I always liked the trip to Weston, since I got to visit the Ortons' country store. I can still remember the hand-cranked peep show, which is there to this day. My mother would tell me when the clerk wasn't looking and I would jump up on a crate and peer in, cranking furiously. By today's standards, it is pretty tame stuff, but for a Vermont kid around 1960, it was pretty saucy. After stocking up on penny candy — watermelon slices, root beer barrels, and candy cigarettes, the kind that puff "smoke" (powdered sugar) when you blow through them — we had lunch at the restaurant next door. The prize dish on the menu was, and still

is, the Indian pudding. When properly made, it is rich and creamy, balanced by the slightly sour tang of molasses.

Indian pudding is nothing more than a version of hasty pudding, which was simply cornmeal mush either cooked as a porridge and served hot for breakfast or allowed to cool (like polenta) and then sautéed or fried. To make Indian pudding, molasses and spices were added and milk or cream was used instead of water. The term Indian, according to Richard Sax in *Classic Home Desserts*, simply referred to the use of cornmeal ("Indian meal"), not to a recipe patterned after a Native American tradition. The American settlers were less than interested in the local cooking.

The problem with this recipe — one that is unavoidable — is that it takes long, slow cooking. I did find recipes that called for a 350 degree oven and a baking time of only 1 hour, but other more traditional preparations suggested a 275 degree oven and 3 hours of baking. Testing proved that the latter was preferable. I also discovered that frequent stirring with a whisk was crucial to a creamy result. Simply letting the pudding bake unattended produces a tougher, less desirable texture. Almost all recipes call for eggs, but I found that omitting them yields a more delicate result. Instead of using all milk, I use a combination of milk and cream. The cornmeal does have to be whisked into the hot milk and then cooked and whisked into the pudding mixture until smooth. This is crucial to removing lumps. I also limited the spices to ginger and nutmeg; cinnamon only muddied the flavors.

Slow-Cooked Indian Pudding

1   quart milk
¼   cup granulated sugar
¼   cup lightly packed dark brown sugar
¼   cup molasses
1   teaspoon salt
3   tablespoons butter, room temperature
1   teaspoon ground ginger
½   teaspoon ground nutmeg
½   cup yellow cornmeal
1   cup heavy cream
     Vanilla ice cream or additional heavy
     cream for serving

1. Heat oven to 275 degrees. Whisk together 2 cups of the milk with the other ingredients, *except* the cornmeal and heavy cream and reserve. Butter a 2- to 3-quart casserole or soufflé dish.

2. Heat the remaining 2 cups milk in a medium saucepan over medium heat and slowly whisk in cornmeal. When mixture is smooth, whisk in the reserved pudding mixture and, whisking constantly, bring mixture to a boil over medium-high heat. Turn heat to low and simmer for 5 minutes, stirring frequently, until the mixture is quite thick (like a thick pea soup) and leaves a thick coating on the back of a spoon.

3. Pour into the prepared casserole, pour heavy cream over the mixture, and bake uncovered for 3 to 3½ hours, whisking or stirring every half hour for the first 2½ hours. The pudding is done when it is just set in the middle and still soft. Let cool for 20 to 30 minutes and serve with vanilla ice cream or additional cream.

SERVES 6 TO 8

Master Recipe for Tapioca Pudding

I started researching tapioca pudding by making it with the old-fashioned pearl tapioca. I discovered that this type of tapioca requires soaking for 1 hour and then needs about a half hour of cooking. (If you want to make a tapioca cream instead of simply a pudding, the mixture must be cooled and folded into beaten egg whites.) The whole process took over 2 hours and the result was marginal at best, given the large "fish-eye" pieces of tapioca floating in the mixture. With the invention of Minute tapioca, anyone, in my opinion, who uses the larger, pearl variety is simply out of his or her mind. The former is a vastly better product that works quickly and distributes itself more evenly throughout the pudding.

I then tried the recipe on the back of the Minute tapioca box and found that it wasn't half bad but the manufacturers called for too much of their own product, to stimulate consumption. As a result, the pudding was overly gelatinous. I reduced the tapioca from 3 tablespoons to 2 and the resulting pudding still set but was more tender. The basic recipe calls for milk only — no cream — and I thought it was a bit thin in both flavor and mouthfeel. Therefore, I substituted 1 cup of cream for 1 of milk. I also slightly upped the amount of sugar and worked up a few simple variations. If, however, you like a less creamy dessert, go ahead and use all milk.

1 egg
⅓ cup plus 1 tablespoon sugar
2 tablespoons Minute tapioca (do *not* use the pearl variety tapioca)
1¾ cups milk
1 cup heavy cream
1 teaspoon vanilla extract

Whisk the egg in a 2-quart saucepan until well beaten. Whisk in the remaining ingredients except the vanilla and let stand 5 minutes. Over medium heat and stirring constantly, cook the mixture until it reaches a full boil. The mixture will still be thin. Remove from heat and stir in vanilla. Cool 20 minutes, stir, and then spoon into individual serving dishes or glasses. Chill before serving.

SERVES 4 TO 6

TAPIOCA PUDDING WITH ORANGE PEEL AND ALMONDS

There is an established tradition of adding fruits or other flavorings to tapioca pudding, the most common ingredients being almonds, raisins, citron, currant jelly, and sherry. This is a simpler approach, pairing only orange and almond. To make it, simply add 1 teaspoon minced or grated orange peel and 2 tablespoons finely chopped almonds to the master recipe when adding the vanilla.

TAPIOCA PUDDING WITH ROSE WATER, PISTACHIOS, AND CARDAMOM

Add ½ teaspoon rose water, ¼ teaspoon ground cardamom, and 2 tablespoons finely chopped pistachios to the master recipe when adding the vanilla.

Chocolate Mousse

The essence of chocolate mousse consists of four elements: semisweet chocolate, egg yolks, whipped egg whites, and heavy cream. The chocolate is melted, the egg yolks are whisked in, and then both the whites and the heavy cream are whipped and folded in. Some recipes add butter, others a bit of strong coffee or liquor for flavoring, and some even use gelatin for setting the mousse. The trick is balance. Too much chocolate and the texture becomes dense and the flavor dull. Too little and the flavor fades quickly on the tongue.

Most recipes start with four eggs, which I borrowed as a reasonable starting point. After some experimentation, I decided on 8 ounces of semisweet chocolate. Some recipes use 4 and others 6; if I am going to make a chocolate mousse, I want the full chocolate experience. However, the texture suffered a bit (as the melted chocolate cools it hardens and this affects texture), so I had to also increase the amount of heavy cream from the standard ½ cup to ¾ cup. This maintained serious chocolate flavor but also perked up the texture.

I did find that a bit of butter added silkiness to the mousse and I settled on 4 tablespoons, which is melted along with the chocolate. I am not enthusiastic about overly sweet desserts and therefore added only 2 tablespoons of sugar, since I was using sweetened chocolate to begin with. In my opinion, more sugar flattens the taste profile of the chocolate; in this recipe one can taste deeper, earthier chocolate tones. Finally, I tested beating the egg yolks separately with some sugar rather than whisking them into the melted chocolate. This was time consuming and simply added more volume to the final mixture, which reduced the chocolate flavor. I also found that it was best to let the mousse sit a few hours in the refrigerator before serving, allowing time for the flavors to blend. Most chocolate mousse lovers serve it with additional whipped cream, which is a pleasant counterpoint to this rich chocolate experience. (Please note that this recipe uses raw egg whites, which the USDA claims presents a health risk. Although some cookbook authors suggest that you heat the whites to 160 degrees before using them — this is, in my opinion, one of the more absurd recipe directives in recent years — I just go ahead and use raw eggs for those recipes that need them. However, be aware that you are taking a small risk, although the USDA and other government agencies seem incapable of quantifying the magnitude of the problem.)

8	ounces semisweet chocolate
4	tablespoons (½ stick) unsalted butter
⅛	teaspoon salt
1	teaspoon vanilla extract
4	large eggs, separated
½	teaspoon cream of tartar
2	tablespoons sugar
¾	cup heavy cream
	Additional whipped cream for serving (optional)

1. Melt chocolate with the butter in a microwave oven. (Use 50 percent power for 2 minutes, stir, and then go another 1 to 2 minutes until done.) If you do not have a microwave, melt them in a glass bowl placed over a saucepan containing 1 inch of simmering water. Stir in salt and vanilla and then whisk in yolks, one at a time. Set

mixture aside. It must cool to room temperature before you fold in the egg whites.
2. Beat egg whites with cream of tartar until soft peaks just begin to form. Add sugar and beat until whites are firm but still glossy and smooth. Whisk one quarter of the beaten whites into the chocolate mixture. Fold in remaining whites with a large rubber spatula.
3. Whip the heavy cream until firm and fold into chocolate mixture. Spoon into individual serving dishes or glasses or into a large bowl. Cover and refrigerate for at least 2 hours. Serve with additional whipped cream.

SERVES 8

Mocha Variation

For a mocha flavor, add 1 tablespoon instant coffee mixed with 2 tablespoons hot water. Stir into the melted chocolate/butter mixture along with the salt and vanilla.

Rum or Bourbon Variation

Add 2 tablespoons of rum, bourbon, or other liquor to the melted chocolate along with the salt and vanilla.

Master Recipe for Prebaked Pie Shell

I provide two methods here. The first is done all by hand and the second, and by far the easiest and most reliable method, uses a food processor. If using the hand method, a simple box grater works well

1. *To make pie pastry without a food processor, grate frozen butter into the flour using a flat grater set over a bowl. It is vastly preferable, however, to use a food processor to achieve consistent, foolproof results.*

2. Use your hands to toss the butter (and Crisco) with the flour.

3. Gently and quickly work the shortening into the flour until the flour turns a light yellow and ressembles a coarse meal in texture. Do not overwork the butter or it will melt, ruining the pastry. You can also use a pastry blender.

4. Sprinkle the mixture with three tablespoons of ice water to start.

5. Use a rubber spatula to work in the water, pressing the dough together into a ball. Add up to one tablespoon additional water if needed. It is better to have a dough that is slightly too wet than too dry.

6. Lightly flour the ball of dough, flatten into a disk about four inches wide, and wrap with plastic wrap. Let rest in the refrigerator for at least thirty minutes. (An overnight rest is best, especially for beginners.)

7. Roll out dough using only light pressure. Turn the dough an eighth turn between each roll of the pin. Always roll away from you, beginning at the center of the dough, in order to avoid overworking the dough.

8. Every thirty seconds or so, lift the dough onto the pin using a dough scraper. Reflour the work surface and then flip the dough over, back onto the counter.

9. An easy way to measure whether the pie dough is of the correct diameter is to place the pie plate upside down on top of the dough. The dough should extend beyond the edge of the plate by two inches.

10. The easiest method of moving the dough into the pie plate is to drape it over the rolling pin.

12. For a single-crust pie, trim the dough to one-half inch from the rim of the pie plate. For a two-crust pie, trim the dough flush with the pie plate. The top crust is trimmed to a one-half inch overlap and then tucked under the bottom crust.

11. Lift up the outer edges of the dough and gently push it into the sides of the pie pan. This will reduce shrinkage during baking.

13. Fold the excess half inch of dough back under itself all around the pie plate.

14. To finish the edging, you can simply press gently with the tines of a fork.

15. You can also create a fluted edge by pressing the forefinger of one hand into the space created by the thumb and forefinger of the other hand.

16. Another simple method is to press the edge between your thumb and the side of your forefinger. This is called a "rope" edging.

for cutting up the butter and shortening. Since the butter and Crisco are grated, be careful not to work them too much into the flour mixture. They will quickly turn warm and soft and the dough will become soft, sticky, and impossible to work with. On the other hand, make sure that your dough is not too dry or it will be impossible to roll out. If you need to add a bit more water to form a cohesive ball of dough, don't be afraid to use it. This recipe is enough for one single-crust pie shell. Note that I use less butter and shortening for this recipe than I do with the apple pie on page 331. This is because a somewhat lower ratio of fat is preferable for a prebaked pie shell in order to maintain the distinct shape of the edging. (With higher ratios, the edging tends to "melt.") With a two-crust pie, however, this is less of an issue. In addition, you want the top crust to settle down onto the filling, leaving no air pockets, and this occurs with a higher-fat recipe. If you do not wish to wait 1 hour for the dough to rest before rolling it out, place it in the freezer for 20 minutes. (The refrigerator method is preferable.)

1¼	cups all-purpose flour
½	teaspoon salt
1	tablespoon sugar
5	tablespoons unsalted butter, put in freezer for 30 minutes
3	tablespoons vegetable shortening (Crisco), put in freezer for 30 minutes
3–4	tablespoons ice water

1. Mix flour, salt, and sugar in a large bowl with a whisk for 30 seconds. Grate the butter and shortening into the bowl containing the flour mixture. Gently toss the grated butter and shortening with your fingers to coat with the flour. Do not overmix at this point or the butter will melt and the dough will become sticky and hard to handle.

2. Sprinkle 1 tablespoon ice water onto the mixture and gently toss with your fingers to mix. Add an additional tablespoon and toss and then a third. Check the mixture by taking a handful and squeezing. If the dough holds together, it is done. If not, add the last tablespoon of water, toss, and squeeze a handful to check. Gather the dough into a ball and flatten into a 4-inch disk. Dust lightly with flour, wrap in plastic, and refrigerate for at least 30 minutes before rolling. (If you are not experienced with pie dough, I highly recommend that the dough be refrigerated overnight. This will allow time for the dough to properly hydrate, making it easier to roll out and prebake.)

3. If dough has spent more than 1 hour in the refrigerator, let it warm up a few minutes on the counter before proceeding. Roll out dough and place into an 8- or 9-inch pie pan (see steps page 304). Push dough gently down the sides of the pan. Trim dough around edge of pan leaving a ½-inch border. Fold excess dough underneath edge and shape edge using a fork or fingers (see steps page 305). Place in refrigerator for at least 40 minutes or in freezer for 20 minutes.

4. Heat oven to 375 degrees. Remove pie shell from freezer and fit a double thickness of heavy-duty aluminum foil (the extra-wide rolls are best; if the foil is too narrow, use two sheets) over shell, pressing foil carefully into bottom of pie shell and against the sides. Add pie weights or dried beans, enough to generously cover bottom of pie shell. Pile up the weights around the sides of the shell to help hold them in place.

5. Bake on lower rack for about 20 minutes or until sides of pie shell are set. (They should be firm and not moist.) Remove foil and bake another 6 to 8 minutes if shell is to be baked a second time with filling. The baked shell should have just the slightest amount of color. If not, bake until shell is a rich nut-brown, 35 to 40 minutes in total (another 15 to 20 minutes). Remove from oven and cool on a rack.

MAKES 1 PREBAKED SHELL

FOOD PROCESSOR VARIATION

Mix flour, salt, and sugar in a food processor fitted with the steel blade. Cut chilled but not frozen butter into ¼-inch pieces and scatter the pieces over the flour mixture, tossing to coat. Cut butter into flour with 5 one-second pulses.

Add shortening and continue cutting in until flour is pale yellow and resembles coarse cornmeal with butter bits no larger than small peas, about 4 more 1-second pulses. Turn mixture into a medium bowl. Sprinkle 3 tablespoons of water over the mixture. With blade of a rubber spatula, use a folding motion to mix, then press down on dough with the broad side of the spatula until dough sticks together, adding up to 1 tablespoon more water if dough will not come together. Shape dough into a ball with your hands, then flatten into a 4-inch wide disk. Dust lightly with flour, wrap in plastic, and refrigerate for 30 minutes before rolling.

New England Cream Pie

One of my neighbors, Jean, inherited a recipe from her mother, Dorothy, which in turn came from her aunt Nellie Newton. It is called Cream Pie and is made from fresh cream from a Jersey cow, sugar, nutmeg, and 1 egg. This is something quite apart from a custard pie, which usually has 1 egg per cup of milk or cream. The trick with this recipe is to use a very low oven and an extremely long baking time (7 hours), unlike a custard pie, which I bake at over 400 degrees for less than half an hour. This produces a delicate, light custard, rich from the intense flavor of the Jersey cream. Over the years, I tried as hard as I could to get the recipe but Dorothy would make me guess the ingredients, giggling like a ten-year-old every time I would try and, of course, I always got it wrong. She passed away a few years ago, and now her daughter Jean

has the recipe, which she recently shared with me.

The original recipe calls for using an unbaked crust and a cold filling, starting out at an oven temperature of 425 degrees and then lowering it after 10 minutes to about 250 degrees, which often produced a soggy crust. Instead, I use a hot pre-baked crust and also heat the cream in a saucepan on top of the stove. This yields a very good, crisp crust even during the extended baking time. I have tested starting the pie at higher oven temperatures, around 350 degrees, and found that it puffs up and starts to bubble, which produces a less delicate texture. I have also reduced the sugar from 1 cup to ¾ cup and have doubled the amount of eggs and flour in order to make sure that the pie sets properly.

You'll note that the recipe is rather simple with no vanilla or other flavoring ingredients other than cream, sugar, and nutmeg. This is a simple pie and, as Jean emphatically states, it should stay that way. Jean makes it with fresh Jersey cream which, of course, is heavenly and more flavorful than a pie made with ultra-pasteurized cream from a large dairy, although the supermarket product is less cloying and to most home cooks, probably preferable in terms of texture. If you can, try to find an organic brand of cream, which I find has the most flavor. Make sure that you use a very deep pie plate in order to accommodate the full quart of cream.

1   hot partially prebaked 9-inch deep-dish pie shell

FOR THE FILLING

2	tablespoons flour
¾	cup sugar
1	quart heavy cream, non-ultrapasteurized preferred
2	large eggs
½	teaspoon freshly grated nutmeg

1. Bake the pie shell according to the recipe on page 302. While it is baking, gently whisk together the first 3 filling ingredients in a heavy saucepan and heat, stirring frequently, until mixture begins to steam. Remove from heat. Whisk the eggs in an 8-cup Pyrex measuring cup or any other large heatproof pitcher.

2. When the pie shell is almost ready, whisk ½ cup of the heated cream mixture into the beaten eggs, then whisk in the remaining hot cream. Open the oven door and set a timer for 3 minutes. Reduce oven to 250 degrees. With the oven rack pulled a third of the way out, pour the cream mixture into the pie shell and very gently slide the rack back into place. Leave oven door open just a crack until the timer goes off. (The door will have been open for a total of 3 minutes.) Close oven door and bake for 5½ hours. (The top will be a caramel color and, when jiggled, the cream will still be wobbly.) Turn off oven and let pie bake an additional 1½ hours. Remove from oven, sprinkle top with freshly grated nutmeg, and cool on a wire rack for 2 hours. (The pie will still not be completely set at this point.) Chill in the refrigerator until set. This pie is best served either cold or cool in small slices. It goes well with strong coffee.

Butterscotch Pie

Most butterscotch pies simply substitute brown sugar for white. In Fannie Farmer's original cookbook, however, I found a recipe that called for using a caramel sugar syrup, which adds a great deal of extra flavor. Be warned that sugar syrups are tricky. They can turn from light brown to black and burnt rather quickly, so keep your eye on it. Also be very careful when pouring the syrup into the hot milk/cream mixture. Do so very slowly and carefully, as the mixture will violently bubble and froth.

1	hot partially prebaked 8- or 9-inch pie shell
4	large eggs
⅔	cup packed brown sugar
1½	teaspoons vanilla extract
⅛	teaspoon salt
2	cups milk
1	cup heavy cream
¼	cup granulated sugar
3	tablespoons water

1. Make the prebaked shell (see page 302) and place it in the oven. While it is baking, whisk together the eggs, brown sugar, vanilla, and salt in a large Pyrex measuring cup. Start heating the milk and cream in a saucepan. Meanwhile, place the ¼ cup sugar and water in a small, heavy saucepan and bring to a boil. Continue cooking until it becomes a light caramel syrup. (This will take 8 to 10 minutes, depending on the pan.) When the milk/cream mixture has started to steam, *very carefully and slowly* pour the sugar syrup into the milk/cream mixture stirring constantly. It will bubble and froth.

2. Remove from heat and let cool for 1 minute, then pour slowly into the egg mixture, whisking constantly. Place the hot prebaked pie shell on the middle rack in the preheated oven. With the rack pulled one third of the way out, pour the hot filling into the pie shell. Very gently push in rack and bake for about 25 minutes or until the center 2 inches of the pie is still wobbly. (The custard will continue to cook as it cools.) Turn pie around in oven after 12 minutes, so that it cooks evenly. Cool on a wire rack for 2 hours before serving.

Black and White Cream Pie

The inspiration for this recipe came from the 1951 edition of *The Time Reader's Book of Recipes*, although a similar recipe won a prize in the 1954 Pillsbury baking contest. This is a cream pie with a layer of chocolate, topped with baked meringue. (The grated chocolate floats on top of the custard mixture to create its own separate layer.) Unlike a custard pie, this has a very creamy, thick filling. I tried this recipe with a basic custard pie filling (one whole egg per cup of milk) and it didn't work since the filling was too light. It needed a thicker filling so I used mostly egg yolks instead of whole eggs and used a combination of heavy cream and milk. I also used a prebaked pie shell and heated filling so that the crust would be crisp. Having made it a few times, I find that most of the chocolate does rise to the top although a small amount may end up underneath the custard.

1   hot partially prebaked 8- or 9-inch pie shell (see page 302)

FOR THE CUSTARD FILLING
1   large egg
3   large egg yolks
½   cup sugar
½   teaspoon vanilla extract
⅛   teaspoon salt
1½   cups milk
¾   cup heavy cream
2   ounces semisweet chocolate, grated

FOR THE MERINGUE
3   large egg whites, room temperature
½   teaspoon cream of tartar
¼   cup sugar

1. Bake pie shell following instructions on page 302. Meanwhile, gently whisk the egg, yolks, sugar, vanilla, and salt in a 4-cup glass measuring cup. Heat the milk and heavy cream in a saucepan until the mixture starts to steam. Take off heat and let cool 2 minutes. Pour into a 4 cup glass measuring cup and let cool for 30 seconds. Slowly pour into egg mixture and whisk gently. Add grated chocolate to mixture and *do not stir.*

2. When pie shell is partially baked, place it on the middle oven rack. Pull rack about one third out and pour the custard mixture into the pie shell. (Most of the grated chocolate should end up on top of the custard.) Close oven door, leave at 375 degrees, and cook for 20 to 25 minutes or until the perimeter is set but the center 2 inches is still a bit wobbly. Cool on a wire rack for 2 hours.

3. Heat oven to 325 degrees. In a large bowl, beat whites on high speed until soft peaks form. (This can also be done by hand.) Add the cream of tartar and sugar and beat until stiff but still glossy. Pile on top of pie, being careful to spread meringue out to touch all of the edge of the pie shell without any spaces. Bake 5 to 10 minutes, until meringue browns nicely. Chill in the refrigerator before serving.

Master Recipe for Diner Cream Pie

Unlike the recipe above, this is what most Americans would refer to as a cream pie. It is thicker, since it uses cornstarch, and has a whipped cream topping. This is diner food similar to the great, thick slabs of pie that one finds in the refrigerator cases behind the counter. I tested different numbers of egg yolks and found that 8 yolks was best, producing a somewhat smoother filling than 7 yolks. It is very important to let the custard cook sufficiently in the saucepan, so that it thickens properly, to about the consistency of mayonnaise. Otherwise, it will never properly set up. Yes, the heavy cream is necessary. After all, this is a *cream* pie! Versions with a higher proportion of milk just didn't have the right texture. I also tried using evaporated milk, a traditional ingredient in this sort of recipe, which helped the pie to set up nicely, but I preferred the fresh milk version.

1	prebaked 9-inch Graham Cracker (page 311) or American (page 339) pie pastry shell
½	cup plus 2 tablespoons sugar
⅛	teaspoon salt
3	tablespoons cornstarch
8	egg yolks
2½	teaspoons vanilla extract
1½	cups milk
2	cups heavy cream (1 cup reserved for whipped cream topping)
2	tablespoons unsalted butter, room temperature
1	teaspoon brandy or rum

1. Make pie shell (see recipe below). In a medium saucepan, whisk together ½ cup of sugar (reserve 2 tablespoons), the salt, and the cornstarch. Add the yolks and 2 teaspoons of the vanilla, then slowly pour in the milk and 1 cup of the heavy cream, whisking constantly. Cook over medium heat, stirring frequently with a straight-edge wooden spoon, until mixture starts to steam, then stir constantly, scraping the bottom of the pan as you stir. When mixture thickens to the consistency of mayonnaise, remove from heat and whisk in butter and brandy. Place in a bowl, place plastic wrap directly on the surface, and refrigerate until cold. Place metal mixing bowl and beaters from an electric mixer (or a metal bowl and a whisk) in the refrigerator or freezer.
2. Put remaining 1 cup of heavy cream, reserved 2 tablespoons sugar, and remaining ½ teaspoon vanilla in a chilled bowl and beat on medium speed for 60 seconds. Increase speed to high and whip until peaks are firm and smooth. (If beat-

ing by hand, just whisk until peaks are firm and smooth.)

3. Spoon chilled custard into pie shell and top with whipped cream.

Graham Cracker Crust

The bottom of a drinking glass is effective for pressing the crumbs into the pie plate. Note that when this crust comes out of the oven after prebaking, it will appear a bit dry and loose. However, it will set nicely as it cools.

- 9 graham crackers
- 2 tablespoons packed brown sugar
- 4 tablespoons (½ stick) butter, melted

1. Heat oven to 350 degrees. Process graham crackers to fine crumbs in the bowl of a food processor. Add sugar and process a few seconds to mix. Add butter and process until well blended. To do this by hand, place crackers in a sturdy plastic bag and pound with a heavy saucepan. Add to a bowl, stir in the sugar and then the melted butter. Stir until well mixed.

2. Press mixture into a pie plate.

3. Chill in refrigerator for 20 minutes. Bake in preheated oven for about 15 minutes. Remove just before crust starts to brown. Allow to cool before filling.

MAKES ONE 8- OR 9-INCH PIE CRUST

COCONUT CREAM PIE VARIATION

Reduce vanilla extract to 1 teaspoon. Heat oven to 350 degrees. Place 2 cups shredded sweetened coconut in a single layer in a large baking pan. Toast 5 to 7 minutes, stirring frequently to promote even cooking. Remove when golden brown. Add 1½ cups toasted coconut to the filling in the saucepan once the milk has been whisked in. Sprinkle the remaining ½ cup coconut over the top of the whipped cream once the pie is assembled.

CHOCOLATE CREAM PIE VARIATION

The problem with chocolate cream pie is that the excessive amount of dairy in this recipe dulls the deep flavors of the chocolate, resulting in a very mild chocolate taste. However, I still don't find too many extra slices left over when I serve it.

Reduce vanilla extract for custard mixture to 1 teaspoon. Melt 4 ounces of semisweet chocolate in a microwave at 50 percent power for 2 minutes; stir, and heat another 1 to 2 minutes until melted or melt in a double boiler or use a metal bowl placed over a medium saucepan with simmering water. Add to the custard mixture along with butter. Stir until combined.

BANANA RUM CREAM PIE VARIATION

Substitute 2 tablespoons dark rum for the brandy. Slice 2 large ripe bananas into ³⁄₁₆-inch slices. Place half the filling in the pie shell, cover with bananas, and cover with remaining filling. Top pie with whipped cream.

Butterscotch Cream Pie Variation

Substitute ¾ cup packed dark brown sugar for the granulated sugar. Add only ⅔ cup heavy cream to the custard mixture. Melt brown sugar in a heavy-bottomed saucepan with 4 tablespoons butter over medium heat until mixture is fully melted and bubbly, then cook for 4 to 5 minutes. Remove from heat and, after 30 seconds, add the reserved ⅓ cup heavy cream. Stir to combine and then add to the custard mixture after it has thickened. Continue to cook custard following the directions in the master recipe.

Lemon Meringue Pie

This is one recipe that ranges from a brilliant pairing of tart, lemony filling offset by a luxurious, smooth topping cradled in a buttery, crisp crust to what most of us have come to expect from the local diner: a thin, rather tasteless filling topped with an airy, weeping foam served in a gummy, undercooked shell. Finding the perfect lemon meringue pie was a serious challenge.

The first issue was the filling. Most fillings are made from cornstarch, water or milk, sugar, egg yolks, salt, butter, and lemon zest and juice. Starting with a basic combination, I found the filling to be uninspired: starchy, dull, too sweet, and lacking in a bright lemony flavor. Reducing the sugar was a big help. I used a little over 1¼ cups instead of the 1½ to 1¾ cups called for in most recipes. I also brought back the amount of cornstarch from 6 tablespoons to 5 tablespoons and reduced the amount of water. The filling was now smoother and richer and much less gummy. Using dairy for some or all of the water simply tempers the acidity, thereby muting the lemon flavor of the filling while dulling the color to a pale yellow. I was using 3 egg yolks and found that when I increased the quantity to 5 yolks, the filling was richer and smoother. Six yolks was too much of a good thing. Now the filling was almost perfect, yet I felt it could be a just a bit tarter, so I reduced the sugar to 1¼ cups less 1 tablespoon and it was perfect.

The foamy meringue topping has always bothered me since it is too airy to pair successfully with the filling. My first thought was that an Italian meringue (made by whipping egg whites with a hot sugar syrup) would be a good choice since it is smooth and satiny rather than airy and insubstantial. I started with a meringue made with 3 egg whites, 6 tablespoons sugar, 2 tablespoons water, ¼ teaspoon cream of tartar, and ½ teaspoon vanilla. One tablespoon of cornstarch mixed with ⅓ cup water, cooked into a paste, was used to stabilize the topping. (The use of cornstarch to prevent a meringue topping from weeping was reported in *Cook's Illustrated* in an article by Pam Anderson.) The topping was a bit too stiff and not plentiful enough so I added 1 additional egg white without increasing the sugar with excellent results. I then tried to cut back on the cornstarch and found that 2 teaspoons worked fine although 1 teaspoon resulted in a meringue that wept and puddled.

Finally, I overcame the problem of a pasty, undercooked crust by using my master recipe and prebaking it, adding the filling when it was hot. I also found that, since the meringue needs to be browned, a moderate oven temperature is best. A hot oven will make the top of the meringue bead.

Lemon Meringue Pie

1   partially prebaked 9-inch pie crust (page 302)

FOR THE FILLING
1¼   cups less 1 tablespoon sugar
5   tablespoons cornstarch
¼   teaspoon salt
1¾   cups cold water
5   egg yolks
⅔   cup lemon juice
1   tablespoon lemon zest
2   tablespoons butter

FOR THE MERINGUE TOPPING
2   teaspoons cornstarch
4   tablespoons water
4   egg whites, room temperature
¼   teaspoon cream of tartar
6   tablespoons sugar
½   teaspoon vanilla extract

1. Prepare the pie crust and prebake according to instructions. (While it is baking, prepare the filling.) When the crust is done, remove it from the oven, leave the oven door open for 1 minute, and reduce the heat to 325 degrees. Adjust oven rack to the middle position.
2. *For the filling,* mix the first four ingredients (sugar through cold water) in a 2-quart nonreactive saucepan. Bring mixture to a simmer, stirring frequently. When it starts to turn translucent add the egg yolks one at a time, whisking after

each addition. If at any time the mixture starts to lump, remove it from the heat and whisk vigorously. Next, add the lemon juice and zest and bring the mixture to a simmer, whisking constantly. The filling will be very thick. Remove from heat, stir in the butter until it melts, and cover to keep warm.
2. *For the meringue topping,* place the cornstarch and 2 tablespoons water in a small saucepan over low heat and stir constantly. The mixture should turn into a translucent paste. Remove from heat.
3. In a large bowl and with an electric mixer, beat the egg whites until frothy. Add the cream of tartar and beat until soft peaks form.
4. In a small saucepan, combine the sugar with the remaining 2 tablespoons water. Bring to a boil and cook until the mixture reaches 238 degrees (a digital instant-read thermometer is helpful here) or when a small amount dropped into a glass of cold water will form a soft, gummy ball.
5. Start beating the whites again with the mixer. Add the hot sugar syrup in a thin stream. Add the cornstarch paste and vanilla. Beat until the meringue forms 2-inch peaks and is stiff but still smooth and moist.
6. Place pie filling back on the stove and reheat over low heat until hot. Immediately pour into the warm pie shell. Working quickly, begin to distribute the meringue over the top of the pie with a rubber spatula, being careful to attach the topping to the crust all the way around the edge. (This will prevent shrinking.) Use a spoon or fork to create small peaks on the surface of the meringue. Bake until the meringue is golden brown, about 15 minutes. Cool on a wire rack to room

temperature before serving. Serve at room temperature or chilled.

Master Recipe for Ice Cream

We use an old White Mountain ice cream freezer, an electric model, with its large wooden paddles and large metal canister that holds a double recipe. We make it on the back porch in the summer, pouring in ice and rock salt, listening to the change in the sound of the motor as the ice cream thickens. When it starts to labor hard, the kids show up, fighting over who gets to lick the paddles, that first cold, creamy taste of homemade peach ice cream or coffee or chocolate chip. That first lick always tastes better when the ice cream is still soft, halfway between a custard and a frozen dessert.

No matter how you freeze it, there are hundreds of recipes for ice cream, the basic ingredients being used in slightly different proportions. The objective is to create a creamy, not icy, dessert that is not so fatty that it loses the fresh, clean taste one associates with great ice cream. I started by trying all egg yolks versus a combination of whole eggs and yolks. I found that I slightly preferred 1 whole egg plus 2 yolks to just 4 yolks. I also tried different amounts of sugar and determined that ⅔ cup was optimum, a slightly lower amount than used in most recipes, but one that allows the flavor of the cream and vanilla to shine through. I also used a higher proportion of heavy cream to milk (2 cups cream to 1 cup milk), which made the ice cream richer. Finally, I cooked the custard base before adding the heavy cream (the cream is simply stirred in after cooking), which yields a fresher, creamier flavor. This also expedited the chilling process. Try to avoid ultrapasteurized heavy cream, since it has little flavor. If you can find organic heavy cream (it will probably be pasteurized), this has the sweetest, most complex flavor. Of course, if you can find real unpasteurized heavy cream from a local dairy, then you can experience the real thing; rich, sweet, and full of complex flavor.

1   (4-inch) piece of vanilla bean or
     1½ teaspoons vanilla extract
1   cup whole milk
⅔   cup sugar
1   whole egg plus 2 yolks
2   cups heavy cream

1. Split the vanilla bean in half lengthwise, scraping both sides with a paring knife. Reserve both the pod and the scrapings. Combine milk, ⅓ cup of the sugar, and the reserved vanilla pod and scrapings in a heavy saucepan over medium-high heat. (If using vanilla extract, do *not* add it now.) Bring mixture to 175 degrees, stirring occasionally.
2. Meanwhile, beat the whole egg and egg yolks with the remaining ⅓ cup sugar with an electric mixer or a whisk until pale yellow and thick, about 2 minutes with a mixer or 4 minutes by hand.
3. Remove ½ cup of the hot milk mixture from the saucepan and add slowly to the beaten egg yolks while whisking vigorously. Whisk this mixture back into the saucepan. Over low heat, cook mixture until it reaches 180 degrees on an instant-read thermometer, stirring constantly (about 5 minutes). Custard should be the thickness of heavy cream but should not

boil or bubble. If the mixture starts to give off a fair amount of steam, take off the heat for a few moments and stir vigorously. This is a sign that the milk/cream mixture is about to boil.

4. Pour custard through a fine-mesh strainer into a nonreactive bowl. Remove vanilla pod (if using) from strainer and add to mixture. If using vanilla extract, add it to the custard now. Place bowl into a larger bowl filled halfway with ice water to cool. When mixture reaches room temperature, cover bowl with plastic wrap and refrigerate. It is best to refrigerate custard overnight or for at least 6 hours. (The temperature is less critical if you are using an expensive electric ice cream machine or the old-fashioned models such as White Mountain that depend on ice and rock salt for cooling. However, newer machines with removable liners that are chilled in the freezer cannot successfully make ice cream with a warm custard base.)

5. When chilled, remove vanilla pod (if using), stir, and place in ice cream freezer. Follow manufacturer's directions. When done, place ice cream in the freezer to freeze solid. (The ice cream will still be soft after churning in the machine.)

MAKES ABOUT 1 QUART

CHOCOLATE CHIP VARIATION

Add 3 ounces chopped semisweet chocolate (or chocolate chips) 1 minute before churning is completed.

OREO COOKIE VARIATION

Add 1 cup coarsely crumbled Oreo cookies 1 minute before churning is completed.

CHOCOLATE ICE CREAM

Increase sugar to 1 cup, adding ¾ cup to the milk mixture and the balance to the eggs. Beat ⅓ cup unsweetened cocoa powder into the whipped egg mixture.

COFFEE ICE CREAM

Stir 3 tablespoons of instant coffee or espresso powder into the milk mixture before heating.

BURNT SUGAR ICE CREAM

The idea for the recipe comes from Kate Newton, a relation of Jean Eisenhart, who lives just across the valley from us. It is one of her family's favorite recipes and is now one of ours as well.

Increase sugar to 1 cup, using just ½ cup sugar to make the custard. When step 3 has been completed (the custard is cooked and still in the saucepan), combine ½ cup sugar with ¼ cup water in a small saucepan. Cook covered without stirring over medium high heat until sugar becomes dark and mahogany colored. Pour into the custard mixture and stir to combine. Proceed with master recipe.

Fresh Berry Ice Cream

I tested using the master recipe for ice cream as a base for fresh fruit ice cream, and the rich texture and flavor simply overwhelmed the delicate fruit. I therefore reduced the fat level to produce a fresher, livelier flavor by using less heavy cream and more milk. I also tried to reduce the number of eggs but found that when using only 2 whole eggs, the ice cream became very icy and airy and had little flavor. I found, after much experimentation, that 4 yolks was best, especially when paired with milk and only ¼ cup of heavy cream. Although this sort of ice cream is a bit icier than the smoother master recipe, I find it more refreshing and in keeping with the notion of fruit ice cream.

The biggest problem, however, was the fruit. Simply adding fresh strawberries to ice cream results in chunks of frozen, icy fruit with little flavor. At *Cooks Illustrated,* we tried briefly cooking the fruit, which does add a lot of flavor and also reduces the moisture content. In my opinion, though, the fruit loses some of its fresh taste. In further testing, I discovered that mixing the berries with sugar and lemon juice and then letting them sit overnight did the trick. The berries become infused with the sugar syrup, which is much less likely to become icy when chilled with the ice cream. In addition, 1 tablespoon of liqueur helps to reduce iciness. Although most of my testing was done with strawberries, I found that raspberries and blackberries also work nicely. To boost the fruit flavor of the ice cream, I also found that puréeing half the fruit and adding it to the ice cream base contributes a great deal of flavor; the rest of the fruit is then added near the end of the freezing process.

1	pint strawberries (washed, hulled, cut into quarters lengthwise and sliced into ¼-inch slices, about 3 cups) or 1 pint whole blackberries or raspberries
½	teaspoon lemon juice
1	cup sugar
1	tablespoon Grand Marnier or other liqueur
2	cups less 2 tablespoons whole milk
¼	cup heavy cream
4	large egg yolks
1	teaspoon vanilla extract

1. In a medium bowl, combine the prepared fruit, lemon juice, and ⅓ cup sugar. Let stand, stirring occasionally, until the sugar is dissolved and a syrupy liquid forms in the bowl. Add the liqueur and refrigerate for several hours or overnight, until the berries have absorbed the liquid and are soft and cold.

2. Position a fine sieve over a medium bowl which has been set in an ice water bath. Set aside. Heat milk, cream, and ⅓ cup of the sugar in a medium-size heavy saucepan over medium-high heat until steam appears, about 5 to 6 minutes. Turn off heat.

3. Meanwhile, whisk the egg yolks with the remaining ⅓ cup sugar in a medium bowl until just combined. Do not overmix, which creates excess foam. Stir half the warmed milk mixture into the beaten yolks until just blended. Return this milk/yolk mixture to the saucepan containing the reserved milk. Over medium-low heat, stir mixture constantly until it reaches 180 degrees on an instant-read thermometer. Steam should appear, the foam should subside, and the mixture should just begin to thicken. (Do not let the mixture boil or the egg yolks will curdle.) Remove from heat and immediately strain custard into the chilled bowl set in the water bath. Stir in the vanilla. Cool custard mixture to room temperature and then cover and refrigerate at least 4 hours or overnight. (The temperature is less critical if you are using an expensive electric ice cream machine or the old-fashioned models such as White Mountain that depend on ice and rock salt for cooling. However, newer machines with removable liners that are chilled in the freezer cannot successfully make ice cream with a warm custard base.)

4. Meanwhile, strain the liquid from the chilled berries; put half the berries in a blender or food processor and purée. Stir this mixture into the chilled custard and pour into an ice cream freezer. Follow manufacturer's directions. When the ice cream is the consistency of soft-serve ice cream, about 25 to 30 minutes, add the remaining berries and allow to mix 2 minutes longer. Transfer ice cream to an airtight, covered container. Freeze until firm, about 1 to 2 hours.

MAKES ABOUT 1 QUART

The Apple Orchard

I AM SITTING AT a neighbor's kitchen table in Vermont on a raw Sunday in early May. A good run of windows gives me a sweeping view of our farm across the way, the pale yellow farmhouse squatting in a former cornfield, a row of dancing white birches holding back the oaks, maples, and hickory, protecting our open upper fields from the encroaching forest. Just a few trees have sprouted leaves, a pale yellowish-lime color on the poplars, deep maroon buds and a hint of pink on the wild cherries. As I walk home, I stop in our apple orchard; the whips of Macoun and Northern Spy have matured now, the trunks the width of my forearm. A hint of wood smoke still lingers from an early morning fire, the wind is from the west, gusting through the valley. And then the sun breaks out between running clouds, a farmhouse down the road lights ups, pale greens and muddy browns surround a blaze of country white. And I know when October comes, and I sink my teeth into the flesh of a fresh-picked Macoun, I will be able to taste that raw day in May, the tart bite of wind, the fresh burst of color.

This essence of apple, the tart and the sweet, the crisp, upright texture, the tang of fruit flavor like a burst of sunlight on a cold day, is what must be honored and preserved in a good apple pie. These sensations are fleeting and lose

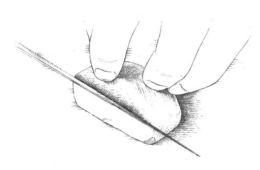

To core and slice an apple, cut it into quarters and then make a diagonal cut to remove the core. This is quicker and easier than using a corer. Now the cored quarter can be cut into thinner slices.

their balance quickly; a Macoun going soft in the late fall; a McIntosh losing its bite in storage. Those cooks who treat the apple like an above-ground potato, to be slathered with cinnamon and sour cream, too much sugar and a starchy thickener, do themselves and the apple disservice, like harnessing a good pacing horse to a mower or keeping a beagle chained to its house during rabbit season. Like children, each apple variety has its distinctive personality and should be let out of the shadows of murky fillings to stand on its own.

Real Vermonters are very much like old-fashioned cold-hardy apples. Unlike some of the more recent transplants, grafted onto dwarf rootstock for quick production and easy picking, the old farmers matured slowly, growing on their own family roots, slowly taking hold in the thin, clay soil. Some look as if they are in need of remedial pruning, a mustache gone awry or a wild, untended look in the bright, keen eyes come March, but the stock is hardy and resistant to change. Like some of the older apple varieties — Pound Sweet, Tolman Sweet, Lodi, and Crispin — the old-time Vermonter is also endangered, the one-room schoolhouse now closed, the small dairy farm an economic curiosity, and the hard-worked and much-loved team of horses now used for horse draws rather than cutting hay, plowing fields, or drawing stone sleds.

Today, as I sit at the kitchen table planning a second orchard, I am thinking about abandoning the new disease-resistant varieties, ignoring the semidwarf whips that come to bear fruit so quickly. I'll plant an orchard of full-growth old-fashioned varieties — Freedom, Winter Banana, Blue Pearmain, and Liberty — and bide my time. And long after the newer varieties have run their course, chainsawed and replanted, my full-growth trees will be in full production, with thick, sturdy trunks and ten bushels of apples each in October.

BACK LAST FALL, when apple varieties were fresh and plentiful, I started a series of blind tastings, to find out once and for all which varieties of apples are best suited to baking. I tried seventeen different varieties, including Jona Gold, Braeburn, Macoun, Fuji, McIntosh, Empire, Crispin, Golden Delicious, Granny Smith, Royal Gala, Spencer, Rome, Red Delicious, Cortland, Winesap, Rhode Island Greening, and Jonathan. I tossed them with sugar, spices, and lemon juice, baked them in ramekins, and found a few favorites, although I soon determined that this approach had drawbacks. The winners were Macoun, Royal Gala, Empire, Winesap, Rhode Island Greening, and Cortland. Northern Spy (once called "Northern Pie," because of its suitability as a baking apple) was not tested, due to lack of availability, but it is a personal favorite and I recommend it. I discovered a wide range of flavors, sweetness, acidity, shape, color, and texture and was curious how different varieties are developed.

A call to Eugene Kopferman, a horticulturist at Washington State University, revealed that many popular apples such as Braeburn, Golden Delicious, and Red Delicious are the result of "chance seedlings." Each seed within an apple contains slightly different genetic material, much like sisters and brothers from the same family. So, if one were to plant two separate trees using two different seeds from, say, a Golden Delicious, the resulting fruit and the size of the tree itself could be quite different. (Another reason for this difference is that in uncontrolled circumstances, the pollen carried by a bee could come from any variety of apple tree that happened to be nearby. It would be like children who share the same mother but have different fathers.) A variety, therefore, which is the result of a "chance seedling" is just that; a seed was planted and resulted in an unexpected new variety.

Most new varieties, up until the advent of genetic engineering, were created by cross-pollinating trees, taking the pollen from one tree and using it to pollinate the flowers of another. (For example, an Empire is a cross between a Red Delicious and a McIntosh.) Today, however, genetic engineering has taken over. Desirable

DNA characteristics are identified and then transferred to bits of leaves using an organism called agrobacterium. This mixture then takes root and generates a new tree. (A good analogy is the African violet. Pick off one of its leaves and stick it directly into a pot of soil. It will take root and grow a new plant.)

I was most interested, however, in finding out why so many terrific varieties, so popular in the early part of the century, are now hard to find. Jim Cranney at the U.S. Apple Association told me that since the advent of national distribution after the Second World War, production shifted from small to large growers and from the East to the West Coast, especially in the arid regions of Washington State where the combination of climate and irrigation increased production per tree. (In 1996 Washington State produced 133 million cartons, or 5½ *billion* pounds of apples; New York State produced only 1 billion pounds.) Smaller growers, those farmers who often produce better-tasting, older varieties, can't compete on price or marketing muscle, so your local supermarket is unlikely to stock a Northern Spy, a Macoun, or a Rhode Island Greening, although, in recent years, it is easier to find Golden Delicious, Rome, Fuji, and Gala. (The five top-selling apples in the United States, among 100 varieties that are grown commercially, are, in order of popularity, Red Delicious, Golden Delicious, Granny Smith, Rome, and Fuji. Rhode Island Greening and Northern Spy make the list, but only securing fourteenth and fifteenth place respectively.) Bucking the consolidation trend is the advent of specialty food stores and farmstands, both of which are supplied by smaller growers with local varieties. This may account for the 38 different varieties currently grown in New York State alone.

This tasting also revealed, however, that an apple variety is no guarantee of consistency. One week a Granny Smith apple pie was top-notch with plenty of juice and flavor; the next week it was bland and dry. Unlike store-bought pickles or canned tomatoes, a particular variety of apple can change radically in taste and cooking properties by virtue of the weather, the growing conditions at the orchard, the storage facilities, and the length of time spent in your local supermarket. (Apples are stored in a 31 degree, low oxygen — 2 to 3 percent — environment, which retards respiration and, in the words of an industry expert, "puts the apples to sleep." Because of sugar content, apples freeze between 28 and 29 degrees.) Perhaps my most useful word of advice, then, other than having recommended a few favorite varieties, is to bite into an apple before baking with it. It should be tart, crunchy, and juicy, with strong apple flavor.

Speaking of flavor, this is also a science. There are six basic characteristics: sweetness (this is referred to as brix or the amount of soluble solids), tartness (this comes mostly from the amount of malic acid in the apple), fruitiness, texture, color, and shape. (Apples are made up of soluble solids and water. The solids carry the sugars and a high percentage of solids to water indicates a sweet apple.) According to Dr. Susan Brown, a specialist in apple breeding at Cornell University, the ratio between sweetness and tartness, called the brix/acid ratio among apple breeders, is a key measure of desirability. A good-tasting apple should be well balanced in this regard. In addition, it is important to have enough sweetness and acidity present, regardless of the ratio. In storage, both sweetness and acidity will decrease, some varieties holding better than others. Braeburn keeps well, for example, but Jona Gold and Gala have short storage lifespans. Fruitiness or apple flavor is more complicated. Scientists have developed a technique

APPLE YIELDS BASED ON SIZE AND PREPARATION METHOD

I finely chopped, coarsely chopped, and sliced three different sizes of apples to determine how much each type would yield. I also measured how many apples it takes to make both an 8-inch and 9-inch pie. I like a thick slice of pie so I mound the sliced apples up above the rim of the pie plate. As a result, I use more apples than most standard recipes.

SIZE IN DIAMETER	SLICES	COARSE CHOP	FINE CHOP	9-INCH PIE	8-INCH PIE
Small, 2¼ inches	1 cup	1¼ cups	⅞ cup	8 apples	7 apples
Medium, 2¾ inches	1⅓ cups	1½ cups	1¼ cups	6 apples	5 apples
Large, 3¾ inches	1¾ cups	2 cups	1⅔ cups	5 apples	4 apples

called charm analysis using a combination of the human nose and a gas chromatograph. A trained researcher with a highly developed sense of smell can identify different flavors or characteristics, which are then measured by machine. This eventually leads to a blueprint, sort of a DNA profile, of the different volatiles or aspects of apple flavor. This can then be used to measure the potential desirability of a new breed of apple. Texture is also key. A Fuji, for example, holds well up to a week when sitting in a basket on a kitchen counter (always store apples in the refrigerator) whereas a Macoun would start to get soft. Unfortunately, color and shape are still the overriding factors. To make matters worse, according to the U.S. Apple Association, consumers and supermarket managers insist on bright, primary colors for apples. Ever wondered why a Granny Smith often tastes unripe? That's because they are usually picked too early, when they are bright green, a color that consumers and store managers prefer. The best Grannies are light green, indicating a riper, more mature apple. (In general, more muted colors indicate a riper specimen.) This insistence on bright colors is one reason apple production has moved west. In a desert climate, the light is more intense, which yields brighter-colored apples.

Finally I set out to test apple yields, since apples vary in size and the preparation method is not always the same.

Bavarian Apple Cake

I tried making this recipe both as an upside-down cake and also right side up and the latter won hands down. This is a crumbly, rich cake with a nicely browned topping. The juices and sugars caramelize with butter and the nuts are sweet, toasted, and crunchy. This recipe works both as a coffee cake and also as a rustic dessert.

3	large, firm, tart apples, peeled, cored, and thinly sliced
¾	cup granulated sugar
¼	cup packed brown sugar
1	teaspoon ground cinnamon
½	teaspoon freshly grated nutmeg
½	cup coarsely chopped pecans or walnuts
8	tablespoons (1 stick) unsalted butter, softened
2	eggs
2	tablespoons buttermilk
1	teaspoon vanilla extract
1	cup flour
	Pinch of salt
1	teaspoon baking powder

1. In a large bowl, combine the apple slices with ½ cup granulated sugar, the brown sugar, cinnamon, nutmeg, and nuts. Heat oven to 350 degrees. Butter and lightly flour a 9-inch springform pan. **2.** With an electric mixer, whip 4 tablespoons butter with the ¼ cup reserved sugar until light and fluffy, about 3 minutes. Add eggs one at a time and beat each one until incorporated, about 1 minute total. Add buttermilk and vanilla and beat another 30 seconds. Sift together the flour, salt, and baking powder onto wax paper. Fold the flour mixture into the butter/egg mixture with a rubber spatula until incorporated. Spread the batter, which will be very thick, evenly over the bottom of the pan with the spatula. The layer of batter will be very thin.

3. Heap the apple mixture evenly over batter. (Fussy bakers can arrange the apples in concentric circles.) Dot the top with the remaining 4 tablespoons of butter cut into small pieces.

4. Bake about 45 minutes or until a cake tester inserted deep in the center of the cake comes out dry. Remove from the oven and allow to cool on a wire rack for 20 to 30 minutes before removing the sides of the springform pan. Serve warm or at room temperature.

SERVES 8

Applesauce

Many applesauce recipes have all sorts of unnecessary ingredients including apricot jam, ginger, even butter, which I feel is best used when serving applesauce as an accompaniment to a savory dish such as roast pork. I did find that a hint of lemon zest and cinnamon was welcome, but otherwise this is a simple and straightforward recipe. To speed things up, I often coarsely chop the apples, throwing everything into the cooking pot, and then use a food mill after the applesauce is cooked to remove the skins, seeds, and fibrous core. For really large quantities, I chop the apples with my cider mill, which has a large hand-cranked grinder and can process 100 pounds of apples in just a few minutes. I suggest making the largest possible quantity as applesauce freezes well.

3	pounds apples (about 8 medium apples), peeled, cored, and quartered
2	tablespoons apple cider or water
	Juice of 1 lemon
¼–½	cup sugar or honey
1	1 x 3-inch piece of lemon zest
1	cinnamon stick, about 3 inches long
2	tablespoons unsalted butter (optional)

1. Place prepared apples in a nonreactive 3- to 4-quart saucepan and toss with apple cider or water, lemon juice, and ¼ cup sugar. Stir to coat. Add the lemon zest and cinnamon stick. Cover and cook over very low heat for about 30 minutes or until apples are tender. Stir frequently.

2. Taste for sweetness. If mixture is too tart, add up to another ¼ cup sugar. Raise heat slightly and cook uncovered for 10 to 15 minutes, beating frequently with a whisk. Remove from heat and whisk in the optional butter.

MAKES ABOUT 3½ CUPS

Apple Butter

Apple butter is nothing more than spiced, sweet applesauce which has been cooked down to a thick consistency. Marie Briggs put up dozens of 1-quart Ball jars of apple butter every fall. Most of the apples were small wild apples with spots and not a few worms, but these were trimmed off or cut out before cooking. The apples were collected in large empty grain sacks, which were strong enough to hold more than one bushel at a time. When the bags got too heavy, the kids would drag them across the ground all the way to the side porch. We used to slather Marie's apple butter on a thick slab of just-toasted anadama bread after a cold November afternoon spent grouse or deer hunting.

1   recipe applesauce (above) or 1 quart store-bought applesauce
¼   cup apple cider
½   cup granulated sugar
½   cup packed brown sugar
¼   teaspoon freshly grated nutmeg
¼   teaspoon allspice
¼   teaspoon cloves
½   teaspoon cinnamon

Stir first 4 ingredients together and place in a casserole dish. Bake in a 325 degree oven for 3 hours, stirring occasionally. Add remaining ingredients, stir, and return to the oven for 1 additional hour.

Raw Apple Muffins

I owe this recipe to Marion Cunningham, author of the revised *Fannie Farmer Cookbook* and of one of my favorite books, in which this recipe appears: *The Breakfast Book*. The first time I made these muffins for coffee hour at church, I got three requests for the recipe. They are rich, spicy, and fragrant and not difficult to make. I have cut back on the sugar, substituted melted butter for some of the vegetable oil for flavor, and reduced the amount of baking soda. I also have sprinkled a bit of granulated sugar on the top. Note that since these muffins are mostly raw apple held together by a bit of batter, they will rise only modestly.

4   cups cored and diced apple (peeling is optional)
¾   cup sugar, plus additional for sprinkling
2   eggs, lightly beaten
4   tablespoons (½ stick) butter, melted
¼   cup corn oil
2   teaspoons vanilla extract
2   cups all-purpose flour
1   teaspoon baking powder
½   teaspoon baking soda
1   teaspoon cinnamon
¼   teaspoon nutmeg
¼   teaspoon allspice
½   teaspoon salt
1   cup raisins (optional)
1   cup walnuts, cut into large pieces (optional)

1. Heat oven to 325 degrees. Grease two muffin tins with either soft butter or a vegetable spray or line them with paper liners.
2. Use 3 medium mixing bowls. In the first, mix the apples and sugar. In the second, stir together the next 4 ingredients (eggs through vanilla). In the third, whisk together the next 7 ingredients (flour through salt).
3. Stir the egg mixture into the apples and mix with a large rubber spatula. Sprinkle the flour mixture over the apples and mix with your hands or with the spatula. The batter will be very stiff. Sprinkle the optional raisins and walnuts over all and mix until blended. Using an ice cream scoop or large spoon, fill muffin cups until they are at least ¾ full.
4. Bake about 12 minutes, then turn tins around in oven. Bake an additional 12 minutes or until a straw inserted into the center of a muffin comes out clean. These are best served warm.

MAKES 16 TO 20 MUFFINS

Rich Nutmeg Cinnamon Apple Cake

I have tried this recipe with both all-purpose and cake flour and found that the latter is preferable, producing a more tender product. I also tried using buttermilk, but found that the cake was a bit coarser. I like to use lots of apples in an apple cake and have therefore increased the quantity to a full 5 cups, more than one finds in most recipes of this type. You might note that I do not call for lemon juice, but since the sliced apples are mixed with the sugar and spices, they will not discolor and the lemon juice is not necessary. This cake can be served as a coffee cake for breakfast or with tea in the afternoon or as a simple dessert.

5	cups peeled, cored, and sliced apples (about 4 large apples)
2	teaspoons lemon zest
2¼	cups sugar
½	teaspoon ground nutmeg
1	teaspoon ground cinnamon
½	teaspoon ground allspice
3	cups cake flour
1	teaspoon salt
1	tablespoon baking powder
½	teaspoon baking soda
2	sticks (½ pound) unsalted butter, softened but still firm
4	eggs
⅔	cup milk
2	teaspoons vanilla extract

1. Heat oven to 350 degrees. Grease and flour a 10-inch tube pan. Toss apples with lemon zest, ¼ cup sugar, nutmeg, cinnamon, and allspice.

2. Whisk together the flour, salt, baking powder, and baking soda. In a separate bowl, beat the butter until pale and fluffy, about 2 minutes. It is easiest to do this with an electric mixer, but it can be done by hand with a whisk. Gradually add the remaining 2 cups sugar and beat for an additional minute. In another bowl, beat the eggs until light colored, about 3 minutes. Add the milk and vanilla to the beaten eggs and beat to combine. Add both the flour and egg mixtures to the butter/sugar mixture in 3 batches, beginning and ending with flour. Beat on the lowest speed until just combined after each addition. Do not overmix.

3. Pour ⅓ of the batter into the bottom of the prepared pan and spread to cover. (The batter will be very thick.) Add ½ the apples in an even layer. Using a rubber spatula, add another ⅓ of the batter in globs over the apples and smooth a bit. Do not worry about making an even layer of batter — during baking the batter will melt and form a smooth layer. Next, add the rest of the apples and batter. Smooth the top a bit with the spatula (it won't be perfectly smooth) and place in the heated oven. Bake 50 to 60 minutes or until the top springs back when lightly pressed and when a cake tester comes out clean. Let stand in pan on a cooling rack for 10 minutes and then remove from pan. Let cool at least 30 minutes before serving.

Last-Minute Apple Pie

The idea for this recipe comes from Jacques Pépin, who included a similar recipe in *Jacques Pépin's Table*. I use a pastry dough with more butter and also prefer a tarter apple than Golden Delicious, but the results are similar. This recipe is incredibly quick and easy and is used in my household as the quintessential last-minute dessert when I have nothing else in the house except a few apples and pantry staples. The concept is simple. Place peeled, cored, and halved apples on pie dough, roll up the sides, sprinkle with a little sugar, and bake. Be sure to chill the pastry dough for at least 30 minutes before rolling out, since a relatively thin dough is required. If you do not have apricot jam, try using applesauce instead.

FOR THE PASTRY DOUGH

- ¾ cup all-purpose flour
- 2 teaspoons sugar
- ¼ teaspoon salt
- 5 tablespoons unsalted butter, frozen
- 2 tablespoons very cold water

FOR THE FILLING

- 2 large tart apples (Granny Smith, Empire, Braeburn, etc.), peeled, cut in half, and cored
  Juice of 1 lemon
- 2 tablespoons apricot jam or applesauce
- 1 tablespoon sugar
- ¼ teaspoon ground nutmeg

1. Place flour, sugar, and salt in a medium mixing bowl. Grate the frozen butter into the bowl containing the flour mixture. Toss the butter to coat with the flour and then press together the butter and flour with your thumb and fingers until the mixture is pale yellow and slightly coarse, 1 to 2 minutes. Add water and mix with a rubber spatula. Press together to form a ball. Wrap in plastic and chill for at least 30 minutes.
2. Heat oven to 400 degrees. Remove

dough from refrigerator and roll out on a well-floured surface to a 10-inch circle. (To make rolling easier, you can sandwich the dough between two layers of plastic wrap or wax paper.) Place rolled dough in the refrigerator on a baking sheet while you prepare the filling.
3. Toss apples with lemon juice, then hollow them out a bit with a 1-teaspoon metal measuring spoon or a small melon baller. Chop the trimmings. Place ½ tablespoon of jam into each the cavity of each halved apple and place apples, cut side down, in the center of the rolled-out dough. Sprinkle the chopped apple around the halves.
4. Fold the edge of the dough up over the apples to create a border and to hold in the juices while baking. (The dough will not cover the pie.) Mix together the sugar and nutmeg and sprinkle over the pie. Bake about 40 minutes or until apples are thoroughly cooked and the crust is nicely browned.

SERVES 4

FOOD PROCESSOR VARIATION

Do not freeze butter. Simply use cold, refrigerated butter and cut into ½-tablespoon pieces. Place flour, sugar, and salt in the bowl of a food processor. Pulse to combine. Add butter pieces, toss to coat, and then process for 5 seconds. Add water and process another 5 seconds. If dough does not come together, add a bit more water and pulse to combine. Press into a ball, wrap in plastic wrap or wax paper, and chill for at least 30 minutes. Heat oven to 400 degrees and proceed with the recipe above.

Free-Form Apple Pie

This is a very simple pie, since only one layer of crust is used and it is simply placed on a jelly roll pan and filled with apples. Be sure to use a baking pan with sides so that any juices that may leak out do not end up on the floor of your oven.

1	recipe for 9-inch single-crust pie (page 302)
3	firm, tart apples
1	tablespoon lemon juice
¼	cup plus 1 tablespoon sugar
	Generous pinch of cinnamon
	Generous pinch of nutmeg
	Vanilla ice cream for serving

1. Roll out pastry to an 11-inch circle and place on a jelly roll pan lined with parchment paper. Fold the edge of the pastry over about ¾ of an inch all the way around. Now fold the pastry over a second time to create a thick rim of crust. (The center of the pie should be about 9 inches in diameter.) Use your fingers to pinch the edging together to make it higher. Complete the edging by fluting it with your fingers. (Hold the thumb and forefinger of one hand about ½ inch apart on the outside of the edge and then push dough between them with the index finger of your other hand.) Chill in refrigerator for 30 minutes.

2. When the crust is almost chilled, heat oven to 400 degrees and adjust rack to middle position. Peel, core, and slice the apples into twelfths. (Quarter them and then cut each quarter into thirds.) In a medium bowl, toss them with the lemon juice, ¼ cup sugar, and the cinnamon and nutmeg. When the crust is ready, remove from the refrigerator and sprinkle with the remaining tablespoon of sugar. Next, place the prepared apples in the center of the crust. Spread them as evenly as possible over the surface of the tart.

3. Bake in the heated oven for 15 minutes, then lower the heat to 350 degrees. Bake for an additional 30 minutes or until the crust is browned and the apples are soft. Cool for at least 10 minutes. Serve with vanilla ice cream.

AMERICAN APPLE PIE

Earlier in this chapter, I discussed a tasting of 17 different apple varieties and listed my favorites. However, I discovered that many varieties are not available nationwide and many are only available during the fall. Therefore, I set out to devise an apple pie recipe that used only all-season, nationally distributed varieties. Of those apple varieties that are ubiquitous, I tested the top nine sellers and determined that Red Delicious, the number-one American apple, made terrible pies but that Granny Smith and McIntosh both had excellent qualities; the former was tart with good texture and the latter had excellent flavor. But each of them also had drawbacks: a pie made with just Grannies was too sour and a bit dull in flavor and the McIntosh pie was too soft, more like applesauce than apple pie. A pie made with both varieties, however, was outstanding. The Grannies held up well during cooking, while the Macs added flavor and the mushy texture was actually welcome. It provided a nice base for the harder Grannies and soaked up some of the juice. Finally I had a good year-round combination.

As for the other ingredients: I had always used butter in my pies, using up to 6 tablespoons in a deep-dish pie. Over the years I had cut this back to a more modest 2 tablespoons, but when I taste-tested pies with and without butter, the leaner pies won hands down. Butter simply dulls the fresh taste of apples. Lemon juice, though, is absolutely crucial to a good pie. By properly balancing the sweet with tart, a good apple pie tastes like a crisp October morning rather than a muggy August afternoon. In the end, I settled on 1½ tablespoons of juice with 1 teaspoon of zest. (However, one cannot take an overly sweet apple and balance it successfully with lemon juice. The acids in lemon juice — citric acids — have different flavor characteristics than the malic acids found in apples. It would be like substituting vinegar for lemon juice. It is equally difficult to balance the flavor of an overly tart apple using sugar, since white granulated sugar is entirely different from the sucrose found in an apple.)

Spices were another matter. In order to give the apples the upper hand, I used only small amounts, ¼ teaspoon or less, of cinnamon, nutmeg, and allspice, the latter adding unexpected balance to the lemon juice. Vanilla was voted down by my tasters as a meddlesome addition. The choice of sugar was clear-cut. Plain white sugar didn't overpower the fruit, whereas light or dark brown sugar obscured flavors.

Even a cursory review of apple pie recipes reveals a wide range of preferences for thickeners, the most common being flour, tapioca, and cornstarch. I did try flour and tapioca and found them unnecessary given our combination of apples, the Macs reducing nicely and creating their own thickener. (I tested our master recipe with individual varieties of apples as well and found that they were best without thickeners.) In addition, a bit of tart, thin juice gives an apple pie a breath of the orchard, whereas a thick, syrupy texture is dull by comparison.

Many cookbooks claim that letting apples sit in a bowl with the sugar, lemon juice, and spices, otherwise known as macerating, is a key step in developing flavors and juice. I found, however, that this simply caused the apples to dry out, making them rubbery and unpleasant. In addition, the apples themselves lose flavor, having exuded all fruitiness into the juice. So macerating, a frequent step in apple pie making, was clearly out.

I ran across this same texture issue once again when investigating the thickness of the apple slices. At first I thought that I could control texture by varying the thickness of slices. When tested, I found this not to be the case. A ½-inch slice cooked no more slowly than a ¼-inch slice. It turned out that baking time was the more crucial issue. I had been baking the pies for 20 minutes at 425 degrees and then 25 minutes at 375 and found that the apples were undercooked, often turning rubbery. By increasing baking time to 55 minutes (25 minutes at 425 and 30 minutes at 375), the juices bubbled, the crust turned a rich brown, and the apple slices were cooked through.

Although I had already done my

homework on the crust in *The Cook's Bible,* there were a few loose ends to tidy up. One of the *Cook's Illustrated* editors was concerned about pies in which the top crust sets up quickly, leaving an air space between it and the apples, which reduce in volume as they cook down. (She suggested precooking the apples to solve the problem. This, by the way, was a common method of making apple pies in the eighteenth century. The stewed and strained apples were turned into a crust, or paste as they called it, and then baked with the usual spices, although rose water was sometimes suggested as an ingredient as well. I have tested this method and find that the resulting pie loses the fresh, tart flavor of the apples.) With my crust recipe, however, this is not an issue. There is sufficient shortening cut into the flour so that the crust sinks down onto the apples as they cook. I did notice that this high ratio of shortening produces a very flaky crust, one that is not easily cut into perfect slices. In addition, there is still a fair amount of juice, which I find essential for good flavor, and the filling may spread slightly once the pie is cut into individual slices. Second, I wondered if we could solve the problem of the soggy bottom crust. Partial prebaking of the crust is the obvious solution but one that is not practical for a two-crust pie and, in my opinion, not worth the effort. I tried coating the bottom of the crust with egg white and, in a separate test, sprinkling a layer of bread crumbs on the crust, but neither helped. I tested four different types of pans — glass, ceramic, metal with holes, and metal without holes — and it didn't make much difference, although glass is cheap, cleans up easily, and does a slightly better job of browning the crust. I did find that overall cooking time was a factor; the longer, 55-minute baking period being substantially better. With longer baking times in a glass pie plate, I did have some success. The outside of the crust was crisp while the inside was still moist, and none of the tasters found this particularly objectionable.

I also wondered what sort of wash might be applied to the top of the pie to give it color. Whole eggs, with or without milk, turned the pie an unpleasant yellow. Egg yolks only yielded dark yellow splotches, and when paired with cream the top surface was shiny and reminiscent of store-bought apple pies sold at third-rate diners. I did like, however, a simple mixture of egg whites and sugar. The pies had a pretty, frosted appearance, maintaining a natural, lighter color. To finish up the testing, I tried baking a pie with no air vents and it turned out just fine. My pastry recipe is so flaky that steam found its own way through small cracks in the top crust. Vents are attractive, though, and probably make sense with tougher doughs that use less shortening.

Finally, I wanted to find out if a pie could be assembled, frozen, and then baked later. I tried this overnight, after two weeks, and then after a month. The overnight freezing was pretty good, the two-week method yielded flavor which was a bit muted and apples which were slightly on the spongy side, and the full month of freezing was a disaster. The apples were puffy, without much flavor, and the crust was oily and dense. If you wish to freeze an unbaked pie for up to two weeks, put it in the freezer for two to three hours, then cover it with a double layer of plastic wrap and return it to the freezer. To bake it, remove the pie from the freezer, unwrap it, brush it with egg white, sprinkle with sugar, and place directly into a preheated oven. After baking it for the usual 55 minutes, reduce the oven heat to 325 degrees, cover the pie with foil so as not to overcook the crust, and bake for an additional 20 to 25 minutes.

Please note that this filling is loose, not thick and firm, which means that the individual slices will not be picture perfect. However, through extensive testing I have found that this somewhat juicier pie is dramatically improved in flavor.

Apple Pie

FOR THE CRUST

2½	cups flour
1	teaspoon salt
2	tablespoons sugar
12	tablespoons (1½ sticks) chilled butter cut into ¼- to ⅜-inch cubes
½	cup chilled solid vegetable shortening
7–8	tablespoons ice water

FOR THE FILLING:

4	Granny Smith and 4 McIntosh apples (8 to 9 cups sliced)
1½	tablespoons lemon juice
1	teaspoon grated lemon zest
¼	teaspoon salt
¾	cup plus 1 tablespoon sugar
¼	teaspoon freshly grated nutmeg
¼	teaspoon ground cinnamon
⅛	teaspoon ground allspice
1	egg white, lightly beaten

1. For the crust, pulse flour, salt, and sugar in food processor fitted with steel blade. Scatter butter pieces over flour mixture, tossing to coat butter with a little of the flour. Pulse machine 5 times in 1-second bursts. Add shortening and continue pulsing until flour is pale yellow and resembles coarse cornmeal, with butter bits no larger than small peas, 4 to 6 more 1-second pulses. Turn mixture into medium bowl. (If you do not have a food processor, mix flour, salt, and sugar in a large bowl with a whisk for 30 seconds. Grate butter and shortening — both of which need to be placed in the freezer for 30 minutes before grating — into the bowl containing the flour mixture. Gently toss the grated butter and shortening with your fingers to coat with the flour. Do not overmix at this point or the butter will melt and the dough will become sticky and hard to handle.)

2. Sprinkle 6 tablespoons of ice water over mixture. With blade of rubber spatula, use folding motion to mix. Press down on dough with broad side of spatula until dough sticks together, gradually adding up to 2 more tablespoons of ice water if it will not come together. Shape into ball with hands; divide the dough into two balls, one slightly larger than the other. Dust lightly with flour, wrap separately in plastic, and refrigerate for at least 30 minutes.

3. Remove dough from refrigerator. The dough is ready to be rolled when it is still cool to the touch but you can push your finger halfway down through the center. If the dough has been chilled for more than 1 hour, it may have to sit on the counter for 10 to 20 minutes to soften. Heat oven to 425 degrees.

4. Roll larger dough disk on lightly floured surface into a 12-inch circle about ⅛ inch thick, the depth of a quarter. Transfer and fit dough into a 9-inch glass pie pan, leaving dough that over-hangs the lip in place without trimming. Refrigerate dough while preparing the fruit.

5. Roll smaller disk on a lightly floured surface into an 11-inch circle. Transfer to a baking sheet and refrigerate until ready to use.

6. Peel apples, quarter, and remove cores. Slice each quarter into thirds, about ½ inch thick. Toss with lemon juice, lemon zest, salt, ¾ cup sugar, and spices.

7. Turn fruit mixture, including any juices, into pie shell. Lay the top pastry over top. Trim top and bottom edges to ½ inch beyond pan lip. Tuck this rim of dough underneath itself so that folded edge is flush with pan lip. Flute dough in your own fashion, or press with fork tines to seal. Cut four slits at right angles on top of pie to allow steam to escape. Brush egg white on top of crust and sprinkle 1 tablespoon of sugar evenly over the top.

8. Place pie on bottom rack of oven. Bake until crust is lightly golden, 25 minutes. Reduce oven temperature to 375 degrees and continue to bake until juices bubble and crust is deep golden brown, 30 to 35 minutes.

9. Transfer pie to a wire rack. Let cool to almost room temperature, about 4 hours. Pie is best eaten after it has completely cooled, even the next day.

CRYSTALLIZED GINGER APPLE PIE

Add 3 tablespoons of chopped crystallized ginger to apple mixture.

DRIED RAISIN, CHERRY, OR CRANBERRY APPLE PIE

Combine 1 cup dried fruit (chopped coarse if large) with the lemon juice and 1 tablespoon applejack, brandy, or cognac. Let sit for 30 minutes. Toss with apple mixture.

FRESH CRANBERRY APPLE PIE

Add 1 cup fresh or frozen cranberries to apples, and increase sugar in filling to 1 cup.

Apple Snow

This is a classic American recipe made from egg whites and applesauce and does not sound promising, but is actually quite good. If you chill this mixture before serving and it starts to soften, it can be whipped a second time to make it stiff.

3	egg whites
¼	cup granulated sugar
1	cup applesauce

Beat the egg whites until they form soft peaks. Start adding the sugar in small amounts and continue beating. When stiff but still moist, add the applesauce and continue beating until the applesauce is thoroughly combined and the mixture holds stiff peaks. Pile into goblets and serve immediately, or chill and serve. If the mixture starts to soften in the refrigerator, just whip it again for a minute or two until stiff.

SERVES 4 TO 6

Apple Fritters

I have had plenty of trouble with fritter batters over the years. Most recipes turn out a very thick batter, some almost as dense as a bread dough. This version is about right, thick enough to coat the apple slices, but not gluelike. I also found that apples don't soak up flavors when marinating (in rum, for example) as other fruits such as pineapples do, so don't bother.

2	medium to large apples
2	eggs
⅔	cup milk
1	tablespoon butter, melted
1	cup flour
¼	teaspoon salt
2	teaspoons sugar, plus extra for dipping
	Vegetable oil for frying

1. Peel and core the apples. Cut them into 16 wedges each.
2. Separate eggs and reserve the whites. In a medium bowl or blender mix together the egg yolks, milk, and melted butter. In a small bowl, combine the flour, salt, and 2 teaspoons of sugar. Add to the egg yolk mixture and blend or whisk until smooth. (The batter can be made several hours ahead up to this point.) Beat the egg whites until stiff but not dry, and fold them gently into the batter.
3. Heat about 3 inches of oil in a deep skillet or Dutch oven to 350 degrees. Dry the fruit, dip each wedge into the batter, and drop it gently into the hot oil. Fry until golden brown, about 1 minute per side. Drain on paper towels or brown paper, then roll in granulated sugar. Serve warm.

SERVES 4 TO 6

Applesauce Cake

This recipe was given to me by a neighbor, Jean Eisenhart. It is a family recipe originally developed by Louise Mercy Ives Barrows Claghorn. It is simple to make, moist, and typical of a Vermont dessert: sturdy, dependable, and full flavored. It has two interesting features: mixing hot applesauce into creamed butter and mixing baking soda with hot water before adding to the recipe. I tried simply whisking the baking soda into the flour and the recipe turned out about the same, although I have left the original instructions intact for the sake of authenticity.

8	tablespoons (1 stick) unsalted butter, softened but still firm
1	cup sugar
1	cup unsweetened applesauce
½	teaspoon cloves
½	teaspoon cinnamon
½	teaspoon nutmeg
½	teaspoon allspice
½	teaspoon salt
1	teaspoon baking soda
2	tablespoons hot water
2	cups all-purpose flour
½	cup raisins

1. Heat oven to 350 degrees. Grease a standard 8- or 9-inch loaf pan with butter. Beat the butter and sugar with an electric mixer until light, creamy, and fluffy, about 1 minute on medium speed and then 3 minutes on high. Meanwhile, heat the applesauce in a small saucepan.
2. Add the spices and salt to the applesauce and stir to combine. Mix the

baking soda with the 2 tablespoons hot water and stir this mixture into the applesauce as well. Add the applesauce mixture to the creamed butter/sugar and stir to mix.

3. Whisk together the flour and raisins. Stir into the applesauce/butter mixture until well blended. Pour into greased loaf pan and bake for about 45 minutes. Start checking after 35 minutes. The top should spring back when pressed with the flat side of a fork. Remove from oven and place on a cooling rack for 5 minutes. Turn out of the pan and let sit for 30 minutes. This cake is best served warm, perhaps with a bit of whipped cream.

Pan-Caramelized Apples with Nutmeg and Cinnamon

Many of the older families in our town are Finnish and therefore there are a large number of saunas, most built near a stream or pond, so that the occupants can streak out through the snow in the dead of winter and cool off. (One of the saunas in town is across the road from a stream and rumor has it that the owner, a woman, has been caught more than once like a deer in headlights, running stark naked across the road.) Perhaps the most popular sauna used to be owned by the Skidmores, Jenny, Harry, and their two sons, Willy and Sonny. The Skidmores also had a dry sense of humor, as do most Vermonters, and back in the 1960s a new road was put in across from where Willy Skidmore lives today and the spot where the sauna still stands. Pretty soon, a new sign went up by the new road, declaring

that this was Tudor Road, named after another local family. That got some attention since Vermonters don't care much for showy behavior. After a few weeks, a sign went up across the road, in front of Willy's place. This sign read "Skidmore Boulevard."

We have just finished building our own sauna, which stands by the pond in our upper pasture. It has a small front room which is used for dressing, but it also has a table, where we often serve dessert or a light snack after the sauna when everyone has a good appetite. This is the dish I often serve there since it is good cold and is sweet but refreshing. It is also simple to make. Apples or pears are cooked in a large saucepan with sugar, lemon juice, salt, and cinnamon until most of the liquid has boiled off, the fruit is soft, and the juices have caramelized. When made with apples it is nothing more than a coarse applesauce, although when made from scratch and served with heavy cream and nutmeg, it is a real eye opener. Be sure to try the pear variation, which is even better.

6	large apples
1	tablespoon lemon juice
½	cup sugar
1	cup apple cider
1	teaspoon grated lemon zest
⅛	teaspoon salt
½	teaspoon ground cinnamon
¼	teaspoon ground allspice
	Grated nutmeg to taste
	Heavy cream for serving (optional but recommended)

1. Peel, core, and slice the apples into ¼-inch-thick rounds and toss with lemon juice in a 3-quart saucepan. Add the remaining ingredients except the nutmeg and bring liquid to a boil over medium-high heat. Adjust heat to maintain a slow boil, stirring occasionally.

2. Cook for about 20 minutes or until fruit is very soft and a few pieces still hold their shape. Most of the juices will have evaporated and the rest turned dark and syrupy and most of the apples will have cooked down to a coarse applesauce texture. Either serve warm or chill before serving. To serve, mound fruit in a circle on a dessert plate or bowl, top with a small amount of freshly grated nutmeg and pour a bit of optional heavy cream around the edges.

CARAMELIZED PEARS

This is even better than the apple recipe, since pears add an unexpected flavor to this dessert. Simply follow the recipe above, using pears, but omit the apple cider and increase sugar to ⅔ cup. Pears will exude more juices.

Summer Fruit

FOR YEARS WE HAVE BEEN traveling up to the Hicks Orchard in Granville, New York, to pick fruit for our pies and cobblers. Susan and Dan Knapp run the place, a big old farm with thousands of trees: sour cherries, apples, plums, and blueberry bushes. A small family graveyard sits just down from the house, the entrance framed by a beautiful curved apple tree, an old Lodi. Inside, there are a few stooped walnuts. The white-picketed side yard is planted in the summer with morning glories, hollyhock, and delphinium; in the fall there are black-eyed Susans and glorious red sedums. The dirt driveway runs up to one of the large red barns, the front used for a sales office where pick-it-yourself customers can borrow white plastic buckets to hold the blueberries or large waxed cardboard boxes for the cherries. Hicks's also sells two kinds of cherry pitters, jams and jellies, honey, cider, and picked fruit sold by the pint, plus books on growing your own orchard, small country cookbooks, and advice on pickling and canning.

Hicks's is New York State's oldest picking orchard, being in continuous operation since 1905, the year that the pickers got so drunk on payday that the family had to open up the farm to their friends and neighbors. The first day was a Sunday, and a great crowd arrived by horse and buggy, carrying chicken and potato salads for a picnic to be served once the work was done. The fruit (just cherries in 1905) all got picked and it was such a success that the farm remains a U-Pick operation to this day.

We take the kids every July for the sour cherries and then again in early August for the blueberries. My youngest, Charlie, walks through the blueberries in boots, a yellow shirt, and a diaper, picking off the small tart berries. Our two daughters fill a half-bucket each, the other half having made it no farther than their mouths. It's hot; the kids soon get bored and then sit down by the small irrigation pond covered now by a film of green scum, under a large willow tree, looking for frogs or throwing stones. When we get home, we freeze many of the blueberries as is, without washing. The sour cherries are combined with sugar and ascorbic acid to keep the color and then frozen in large plastic bags. (I use a commercial product, available in most supermarkets, called Fruit Fresh, which is no more than corn sugar, ascorbic acid, and silicon dioxide, which keeps the mixture from forming into clumps.) I also leave aside plenty of fresh fruit for pies and cobblers, which I make just about every night, the leftovers served for lunch.

I started my own orchard about five years ago, with some twenty-five trees, mostly apple, including Macoun and Northern Spy, plus a few newer varieties that are cold-hardy for zone 3 and disease resistant with good pruning characteristics. I also have two sour cherries, two plums, and two pears, and will be planting more trees next summer with more apples, a peach variety that does well in the cold, and a few sweet cherries. Unlike the annual vegetable garden, fruit trees are like children. They have good years and bad (some apple varieties such as Macoun tend to alternate fruit-bearing years), each requires very different pruning, some become infested with borers because the mulch was piled too close to the trunk of the tree, the bark of others just above the rootstock tends to crack from the fierce glare of the sun off the snow (that's why I have now painted the lower trunks of my trees white), and others just seem to take the soil better, flourishing where others may droop or have a heavy drop of fruit in June or not produce many flowering buds. I fertilize each of them, water them, shape the branch structures to bear heavy loads of fruit, and walk the orchard every day; first thing in the morning and then at sunset, counting fruit, planning my approach to the winter's pruning, checking the soil to see if it is either too wet or too dry. At first, an orchard is simply a place where young whips are planted, but over the years those whips mature and then the orchard becomes a place where on a winter's night I might hear the loud snort of a deer standing under one of my tall plums or see a flock of sheep grazing between rows of semidwarf apples. I love an orchard because it grows slowly over years, even decades, gradually revealing one's skill or lack of it as a gardener, one who plans carefully and tends to his chores. Mistakes are not easily forgotten, but when those small whips finally grow and bear fruit, it is a reminder that everything matters in the long run. I look out over my slowly maturing orchard and can see my inexperience, my impatience in the angled trunks or the weak, crossed canopies, but I can also see determination and patience in the red and yellow fruit hanging in the thinning September sun. Perhaps it is just that orchards are slow creatures, children who take constant care and attention, always with an unknowable result. It is this I love most about Vermont, about country life. Time is measured by a very different calendar, one that truly takes the measure of a life and a man.

OVER THE YEARS, I have eaten a wide variety of fruit desserts and have often been confused by the difference between crisps, crunches, crumbles, and Betties. Simply put, there are lots of old-fashioned desserts consisting of fruit baked with bread, cake crumbs, flour and butter, oats, crackers, and the like. In the days when home cooks were frugal, this was an easy way to use up stale leftovers while providing a bit of variety in terms of texture and flavor. All of these American home desserts are most likely based on older European recipes. One such European dish is called Veiled Maiden or "Country Lass with a Veil" and is pretty much a Betty, or a crunch, made with fruit and browned bread crumbs. It may also include a bit of jam. The earliest version of this recipe I have found comes from Denmark.

A crisp is fruit baked with a topping made from butter, sugar, and flour; however, many variations qualify as crisps, including those with ingredients such as nuts, cake or cracker crumbs, or corn flakes. A crunch, although it is often confused with a crisp by many authors, is, according to *The Joy of Cooking*, fruit sandwiched between two layers of buttered bread crumbs. A Betty, however, is fruit baked with buttered bread crumbs, not necessarily sandwiched in two layers, which makes it pretty close to a crunch. (I have seen recipes for Betties that do call for a top and bottom layer of bread crumbs.) A crumble, for which there seems to be some consensus, is a crisp that uses oats along with the flour. All of these definitions aside, common usage suggests that crisps have a top layer of streusel, crumbles are crisps using oats, and crunches and Betties are fruit layered with bread crumbs.

Despite the problem of nomenclature, I have found a few good rules for making baked fruit desserts. First, most recipes call for too much sugar, to the point that the fruit flavor is lost. In addition, the level of sugar must be paired to the fruit on hand, one pint of blueberries being very different from another in terms of sugar level. Second, Minute tapioca is the thickener of choice for baked fruit desserts. I have tested flour, cornstarch, and arrowroot and found that either the texture or flavor is wanting in all of them, the tapioca providing the cleanest, brightest flavor. Finally, I prefer to bake fruit desserts in relatively shallow dishes so the fruit cooks quickly and evenly.

Master Recipe for American Pie Dough

A combination of butter and lard (or in this case Crisco) is nothing new. I have found recipes that are 100 years old which suggest using this pairing. Having tested this extensively, I know that butter provides a great deal of flavor and the

Crisco yields a flaky pastry. I was interested to discover, however, that cookbooks often suggested making an American shortcut version of puff pastry, even when preparing a pie. The dough, or "paste" as it was often referred to, was prepared and then rolled out, cut, stacked, folded, and then this process was repeated. Today, of course, we simply combine the ingredients, chill the dough, roll it out, and then place it in the pie plate.

I have provided both a hand and food processor version of this recipe. A box grater works very well with the cold butter and shortening and isn't that much more work than using a food processor. If using the latter, cut the butter into small bits by halving the stick of butter lengthwise with a large knife, rotating the stick 90 degrees, and then cutting again. Then cut the stick crosswise into ¼-inch pieces. Leave butter in the refrigerator until you need it. Otherwise it will soften while sitting on the counter. Dough should be rolled about ⅛ inch thick (about the thickness of a quarter).

FOR A SINGLE-CRUST 8- OR 9-INCH PIE

1¼	cups all-purpose flour
½	teaspoon salt
1	tablespoon sugar
6	tablespoons unsalted butter, chilled in freezer for 30 minutes
4	tablespoons all-vegetable shortening (e.g., Crisco), chilled in freezer for 30 minutes
4–5	tablespoons cold water

1. Mix flour, salt, and sugar in a medium mixing bowl. Grate butter and shortening into the bowl. Toss flour and fat mixture about 8 to 10 times until all the butter and shortening are coated with flour and mixed evenly throughout the flour. Break up any clumps with your fingers as you toss the mixture.

2. Sprinkle 3 tablespoons of water over the mixture. With blade of a rubber spatula, use a folding motion to mix, then press down on dough with the broad side of the spatula until dough sticks together, adding up to 1 tablespoon more water if dough will not come together. Shape dough into a ball with your hands, then flatten into a 4-inch wide disk. Dust lightly with flour, wrap in plastic, and refrigerate for at least 30 minutes before rolling.

FOOD PROCESSOR VARIATION

Mix flour, salt, and sugar in a food processor fitted with the steel blade. Both the butter and the shortening should be chilled in the refrigerator but not frozen. Cut butter into ¼-inch pieces and scatter over the flour mixture, tossing to coat butter with a little of the flour. Cut butter into flour with five 1-second pulses. Add shortening and continue cutting in until flour is pale yellow and resembles coarse cornmeal with butter bits no larger than small peas, about four more 1-second pulses. Turn mixture into a medium bowl. Follow directions starting at step 2 of the master recipe.

10-Inch Regular and 9-Inch Deep-Dish Variation

These ingredients are for oversized single crust pies.

1½	cups all-purpose flour
½	teaspoon salt
1	tablespoon sugar
8	tablespoons unsalted butter, chilled in freezer for at least 30 minutes
4	tablespoons all-vegetable shortening, chilled in freezer for at least 30 minutes
5	tablespoons ice water

Double-Crust 8- or 9-Inch Variation

The dough should be divided into two balls, one slightly larger than the other. The former is used for the bottom crust, the latter for the top.

2¼	cups all-purpose flour
¾	teaspoon salt
2	tablespoons sugar
11	tablespoons unsalted butter, chilled in freezer for at least 30 minutes
7	tablespoons vegetable shortening, chilled in freezer for at least 30 minutes
6–7	tablespoons ice water

Double-Crust 10-Inch or 9-Inch Deep-Dish Variation

With these larger quantities, make sure that the butter and Crisco are sufficiently processed into the flour. Otherwise, the crust will be very tough and will shrink if prebaked.

2½	cups all-purpose flour
¾	teaspoon salt
2	tablespoons sugar
12	tablespoons unsalted butter, chilled in freezer for at least 30 minutes
8	tablespoons all-vegetable shortening, chilled in freezer for at least 30 minutes
7–8	tablespoons ice water

Master Recipe for Fruit Pie

Pies were not always made in pie plates. Among the many ingenious Yankee inventions was a pie iron, two skillet-shaped pieces of iron, hinged together. The pie dough was placed in one side, topped with fruit filling, then another layer of dough, and then the irons were closed. The pie iron was cooked on one side and turned over; the iron was opened, and then the pie was cooked until done. This was an easy way of baking a pie over a fire when no oven was available.

These days, of course, pie-making is a lot simpler. But there are some rules to follow. First, both the sugar and the tapioca are variable in this recipe, depending on the sweetness and juiciness of the fruit. Tart blueberries, for example, can take a full cup of sugar. Very sweet berries, however, can do with ¾ cup or even a bit less. The tapioca will also depend on the fruit and the cook's preference for juiciness in the sliced pie. If you want perfect individual pieces, with no juice running out onto the pie plate, go with the 4 to 5 tablespoons. Less juicy fruit will firm up nicely with 3 to 4 tablespoons.

1	master recipe for American Pie Dough, Double Crust Variation (page 341)
8	cups prepared fruit (sliced, cored, peeled)
1	teaspoon grated orange or lemon zest
2	teaspoons lemon juice
¾–1	cup sugar
3–5	tablespoons Minute tapioca
2	tablespoons butter (optional)

1. Make the pastry dough and refrigerate for at least 30 minutes (let warm up for 10 minutes at room temperature if refrigerated for more than an hour).
2. Heat oven to 400 degrees. Toss the fruit with the other ingredients and let sit for 15 minutes. (If you are making a lattice-top pie, toss the fruit with all ingredients except the tapioca. Separate one quarter of the fruit and toss the balance with the tapioca. When filling the pie shell, add the larger amount of fruit first and then top with the quarter without tapioca.)
3. Roll out half the chilled pastry dough so that it fits a 9-inch pie dish with a half-inch overlap. Push dough down onto edges of plate and then cut with scissors so it is even with the rim of the pie plate. Add fruit mixture and dot with optional butter. Place in freezer while working with top crust. Roll out remaining dough, place over pie, and trim edges,

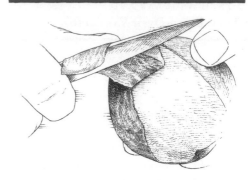

To peel a peach, place it in boiling water for 25 seconds, then quickly immerse it in ice water. The skin will peel off easily with a paring knife.

leaving a half-inch of overlap. Fold top layer under bottom layer and crimp with a fork or your fingers. Cut air vents. Or create a lattice top, using ½-inch-wide strips of dough. If pie dough is very soft, place in freezer for 10 minutes before baking.
4. Place on a baking sheet, place in oven, turn oven down to 350 degrees, and bake for one hour. Check and rotate, if pie is not browning evenly, after 35 minutes. Juices should bubble before pie is removed from oven.
5. Let pie sit and cool to room temperature before serving so that juices thicken (allow at least one hour).

STRAWBERRY-RHUBARB VARIATION

Use 3 cups of strawberries and 3 cups of rhubarb. Cut rhubarb stalks into one-inch pieces. Hull and slice strawberries. Use 1 tablespoon of orange zest (instead of 1 teaspoon of lemon). Add ¼ teaspoon of vanilla extract to the fruit mixture.

PEACH VARIATION

Add ½ cup brown sugar, reduce white sugar to ¼ cup, and add 1 tablespoon crystallized ginger diced into small pieces along with ¼ teaspoon nutmeg, ¼ teaspoon allspice, and ¼ teaspoon salt to the peach mixture.

BLUEBERRY VARIATION

Omit the orange zest. Add ¼ teaspoon of allspice and a pinch of nutmeg to blueberry mixture. Use ¾ cup sugar if blueberries are sweet. I do not recommend frozen blueberries — in a taste test against fresh, they were deemed virtually inedible.

CHERRY VARIATION

Use 4 cups of drained canned pitted sour cherries packed in water, 1 cup of sugar, ⅛ teaspoon allspice, ⅛ teaspoon cinnamon, ⅛ teaspoon almond extract, 1 tablespoon brandy, and ¼ cup quick-cooking tapioca. Eliminate the orange zest, but use the lemon juice. If cherries have been canned in a syrup, drain, then rinse with water and drain again. Use 3 tablespoons of tapioca instead of ¼ cup for cherries packed in syrup.

Apple Pandowdy

This is nothing more than fruit baked in a shallow dish, topped with a layer of pie dough. Halfway through baking, the fruit is removed from the oven and the crust is cut and pushed down into the fruit, a process referred to, according to Richard Sax in *Classic Home Desserts,* as "dowdying." (However, I have also seen recipes that simply call for inverting the dessert after it is baked, the crust being served on the bottom and not broken up and mixed with the filling.) When testing I saw no point in mixing the crust and fruit halfway through cooking. This method simply made the crust soggy. Instead, I prefer to mix crust and fruit after baking. Note that the pear version does require a thickener and less sugar, since pears are both more watery than apples and also sweeter.

1	Recipe American Pie Dough (one 8- or 9-inch pie version)
8	cups apples or pears
1½	tablespoons lemon juice
1	teaspoon grated lemon zest
¼	teaspoon salt
¾	cups granulated sugar
¼	teaspoon nutmeg, freshly grated preferred
¼	teaspoon cinnamon
⅛	teaspoon allspice
1	egg white, lightly beaten
1	tablespoon sugar for topping Heavy cream or ice cream for serving

1. Prepare the pie pastry and chill, wrapped in plastic wrap, for at least one hour. Heat oven to 425 degrees.
2. Peel, core, halve, and slice the apples about ½-inch thick and toss with lemon juice in a large bowl as you work. Add the lemon zest, salt, sugar, spices, and toss with your hands to combine.
3. Turn fruit mixture, including any juices, into a large (at least 9-inch) pie pan or shallow baking dish (a 9- x 12-inch or a 7-

x 13-inch pan is fine). Roll out the chilled pie pastry and place over the top of the fruit, trimming the sides to fit the baking dish. Don't worry about any tears or holes, since the crust will be cut into small pieces after baking. Cut three parallel slits in dough top to allow steam to escape. Brush egg white (in a pinch, you can use water) on top of crust and sprinkle 1 tablespoon of sugar evenly over the top.

4. Place baking dish on the bottom rack. Bake for 15 minutes at 425 degrees and then lower oven temperature to 375 degrees and bake for another 25 minutes or until top crust is well browned, the apples are cooked through, and the juices are bubbling. Remove from oven and place on a wire rack.

5. Using the thin front edge of a metal pancake turner, cut the pie pastry into 1-inch squares and use a spatula to press the pastry down into the filling. Serve warm (cool for 20 minutes to allow the juices to thicken a bit) and serve with heavy cream or ice cream.

SERVES 6 TO 8

Pear Pandowdy Variation

Substitute pears for apples. Add 4 teaspoons Minute tapioca along with the lemon zest, salt, sugar, and spices and reduce sugar to ⅔ cup.

Blueberry or Peach Grunt

This is similar to a cobbler except that the mixture is cooked on top of the stove in a covered Dutch oven so that the dumplings steam rather than bake. Although the tops of the dumplings are not particularly attractive since they are steamed, they are soft and fluffy. I find that this dish is best served after sitting for 15 or 20 minutes. A grunt should be warm, not hot, to let the full flavors of the fruit shine through. I prefer to make this recipe with either blueberries or peaches. I find that frozen blueberries are very sweet and need only ½ cup of sugar.

FRUIT MIXTURE

8	cups washed and well-drained fruit
	Juice of half a lemon
¼	teaspoon ground allspice (optional)
¼	teaspoon ground nutmeg
½–¾	cup sugar, depending on the sweetness of the fruit
1	tablespoon Minute tapioca

DUMPLING DOUGH

2	cups flour
¼	teaspoon salt
1½	teaspoons baking powder
½	teaspoon baking soda
2	tablespoons sugar
4	tablespoons (½ stick) butter, melted
1	cup buttermilk
	Heavy cream for serving

1. Toss fruit with lemon juice, allspice, nutmeg, sugar, and tapioca in a cast-iron Dutch oven.

2. In a mixing bowl, whisk together the first 4 ingredients (plus 1 tablespoon sugar) of the dough recipe. With a rubber spatula, stir in the melted butter and then add as much of the buttermilk as needed to produce a wet biscuit dough.

3. Cover the Dutch oven and bring the fruit to a simmer over medium-high heat. Lower the heat to maintain a steady sim-

mer, uncover, and spoon dumplings over the fruit using a soup spoon. Sprinkle with the remaining 1 tablespoon sugar.
4. Cover the Dutch oven with aluminum foil and then replace the top. Continue simmering for about 15 minutes or until the dumplings are cooked through.
5. Let stand for 15 to 20 minutes to cool. Spoon individual servings into bowls and serve with heavy cream.

SERVES 8

Country Fruit Cobbler

This is the recipe I bring to our Fourth of July picnic, which is held right after the parade. We start midmorning, harnessing the workhorses in their stalls, buckling on the collar, slinging the harness over, settling the hames down onto the collar and hooking it into place, and then pulling the britchen (the part of the harness that goes over the rear of the horse) into place over the rump. Hitching up a team to a wagon is more difficult. The pole straps usually need adjusting and the team has to be backed up into the whipple trees and hooked up in the right sequence. This is where experience counts. One wrong move and the horses can easily become tangled up or spooked. Once the big teams are hitched, however, there is no time to lose as the large workhorses are restless and anxious to move. I play in the band (banjo or keyboard), which is pulled in a wagon driven by Junior Bentley, and our repertoire is limited to our signature song, "Grand Old Flag," plus "The Caisson Song," "America the Beautiful," "Yankee Doodle Dandy," and "American Patrol." We also have a tuba, a flute, a clarinet

(played by the minister), a keyboard, sometimes a fiddle, and one drum. The parade starts at the yellow farmhouse and then runs up to the church and back, a motley crew of oxen, horse-drawn wagons, buggies, a hay elevator, tractors, and a few neighbors on horseback.

Having made this dessert for many years, I have discovered, through trial and error, a few good rules. First, the fruit has to be ripe. You can make a decent cobbler from second-rate fruit, but never a great one. I have also tested a variety of optional ingredients including ginger, lemon rind, and vanilla and find that simple fruit and sugar work best, with just a touch of lemon juice. Thickening is another matter. You do need some thickener, as a plain fruit mixture will be too loose and thin. I find that two tablespoons of Minute tapioca works best, having also tested flour, cornstarch, and arrowroot. Flour and cornstarch are too gluey, masking the taste of the fruit. Arrowroot works well, but is too expensive. By the way, use a full 8 cups of fruit, not the meager 6 called for in some recipes. It takes little extra time, fits a standard two-quart baking dish, and you are unlikely to have leftovers.

Cobbler can be topped with pie pastry dough, which is heavy on shortening, or a simple biscuit dough. Having tested both, I prefer the latter. The dough puffs up light and tender, the perfect foil for the syrupy juices. I prefer to use a mixture of butter and vegetable shortening, the former for flavor and the latter for lighter texture. Buttermilk is key. It delivers a whopping dose of lactic acid that reacts with the baking soda to create plenty of high-rise texture and tenderness. I use baking powder and baking soda, the former for lift during the fifteen-minute baking time and the latter for an immediate boost of leavening, which starts as soon as the dough is mixed.

The secret to this recipe, however, is how the dough is handled. Instead of rolling it out and cutting it into rounds or simply fitting it to the top of the baking dish, I simply pull off small clumps of dough and plop them onto the fruit. This minimal handling also ensures tender cobbler dough; too much rolling and cutting breeds a tougher end product. Since it takes the fruit a lot longer to cook, I place the untopped fruit into a moderate oven for 20 minutes. Only then do I add the cobbler topping, finishing in a hotter oven for the final 15 minutes.

If you are familiar with cobbler recipes, you will note that I use a whole lot of dough, about 50 percent more than most recipes. As a friend of mine pointed out, she doesn't like to get cheated on either the fruit or the dough, and she feels that most recipes leave you short in the biscuit department. If you only have an 8-inch square pan, use 6 cups of fruit; a 9 x 11-inch pan can take a full 8 cups.

Master Recipe for Cobbler

FRUIT MIXTURE

8	cups prepared fruit
	Juice of half a lemon
½	teaspoon lemon rind, minced (optional)
¾	cup sugar
2	tablespoons Minute tapioca

COBBLER DOUGH

3	cups flour
¾	teaspoon salt
1	tablespoon baking powder
¾	teaspoon baking soda
3	tablespoons sugar
5	tablespoons unsalted butter, chilled
3	tablespoons vegetable shortening, chilled
1	cup buttermilk, or as needed
2	tablespoons sugar for sprinkling

1. Preheat oven to 350 degrees. Prepare fruit (wash, peel, hull, core, slice, etc.) and cut into bite-size pieces if necessary. Make sure that fruit is well drained. Toss fruit with lemon juice, optional rind, sugar, and tapioca. Pour fruit into a 2 quart baking dish.
2. In the bowl of a food processor, combine the first five ingredients of the cobbler dough recipe (flour through sugar) and pulse for 2 seconds to mix. Then add the cold butter cut into small pieces. Process in five 1-second bursts. Add shortening and process in another 5 to 7 bursts until flour is slightly yellow in color and the texture of coarse meal. (This can also be done by hand in a large bowl. Whisk together the dry ingredients and then cut in shortening with a pastry blender or 2 knives.)
3. Transfer flour mixture to a large bowl and gradually add the buttermilk, mixing with a rubber spatula. Add only enough buttermilk so that the mixture just holds together. This may be as little as ¾ cup or slightly more than 1 cup. Now lightly press dough together into a rough ball.
4. Place dish with fruit mixture into oven. When fruit has cooked for 20 minutes, remove from oven. Pull off clumps of dough about the size of large golf balls and place

on top of fruit. The dough will be uneven and rustic looking. Sprinkle dough with sugar.

5. Raise oven heat to 425 degrees. Bake for an additional 15 minutes or until dough is browned and fruit is bubbly and tender. Allow to cool for 30 minutes before serving with heavy cream or vanilla ice cream.

SERVES 8

SWEET-MILK VARIATION

Substitute regular milk for buttermilk, add 3 teaspoons cream of tartar, and reduce baking powder to 1 teaspoon.

BLUEBERRY VARIATION

Add ¼ teaspoon of allspice to fruit mixture. Since blueberries range from very sweet to quite tart, the amount of sugar required will vary from a mere ½ cup for very sweet berries to a full cup for tarter fruit.

STRAWBERRY RHUBARB VARIATION

Use 4 cups rhubarb and 4 cups strawberries. Add 1 teaspoon of orange zest. Add ¼ teaspoon of vanilla extract to the fruit mixture. Use 1 cup sugar.

BLUEBERRY PEACH VARIATION

Use 4 cups of blueberries and 4 cups of peaches. Add ¼ teaspoon of allspice, ¼ teaspoon of freshly grated nutmeg, and ½ teaspoon of lemon juice.

PEACH RASPBERRY VARIATION

Use 5 cups peaches and 3 cups raspberries. Add ¼ teaspoon nutmeg, ¼ teaspoon allspice, and ¼ teaspoon salt. Increase tapioca to 3 tablespoons — raspberries give off a lot of juice during baking.

GINGER PEACH VARIATION

Replace sugar with ½ cup brown sugar and ¼ cup regular sugar. Add 1 tablespoon crystallized ginger diced into small pieces and ¼ teaspoon freshly grated nutmeg.

Apple Compote with Prunes and Apricots

You can make a variety of substitutions here, using pears instead of apples, using a combination of both, or using different dried fruits such as figs or peaches. For a cleaner flavor, use water instead of apple cider and add ½ cup of sugar to the mixture. Beware of organic Turkish apricots. I have purchased them at a local health food store and they are very dark, with little fruit flavor. I prefer dried apricots that have a bright orange color. The most important part of this recipe is getting the apples to cook through but still hold their shape. Since all apple varieties are a bit different, you will have to adjust the cooking times accordingly. This recipe is loosely based on a similar recipe from Marie Simmons.

2	cups apple cider
1	cup white wine
¼	cup sugar
1	bay leaf
4	whole cloves
1	3-inch strip orange rind
½	cinnamon stick
¼	teaspoon salt
½	cup dried apricots (if whole, cut in half)
½	cup prunes, pitted
4	tart, firm medium-size apples
1	tablespoon freshly squeezed lemon juice
¼	teaspoon vanilla extract
	Plain yogurt for serving (optional)

1. Combine the first 8 ingredients (apple cider through salt) in a wide saucepan and bring to a simmer. Add the apricots and prunes to the simmering liquid, cover, and cook for about 15 minutes. Meanwhile, peel, core, and then cut the apples into twelfths (quarter them, then cut each quarter into thirds), tossing them with lemon juice in a medium bowl as you work. Add the apples to the other fruit and continue cooking until tender, 5 to 7 minutes. (The time will vary a great deal depending on the type, size, and freshness of the apples.)

2. Pour fruit mixture into a large strainer set over a bowl. Pour the juices, along with cinnamon stick, orange rind, and bay leaf, back into the saucepan and place the fruit in the bowl. Over medium-high heat, boil the juices until you have 1½ cups of liquid, about 3 minutes. Let cool for 10 minutes off the heat, discard the peel, bay leaf, and cinnamon, add the vanilla, and then pour over the fruit. Let cool to room tempera-

ture for serving. Serve with plain yogurt, if you like.

PUTTING THE CRUNCH BACK IN CRISPS
Simply stated, there is nothing crisp about a crisp. This simple baked dessert, made from sweetened apples topped with a combination of sugar, butter, and flour, inevitably comes out of the oven with a soggy top crust. A few recipes go so far as to refer to this classic dish as a crunch, a term which has no bearing on the flat, dull, overly sweetened crumble that serves as a streusel. The task, therefore, was quite simple. I wanted to put the crunch back in the crisp.

To make sure that others shared my opinion, I asked the *Cook's Illustrated's* test kitchen to bake a crisp from the new *Joy of Cooking* and then a second recipe from *A Feast of Fruits* by Elizabeth Riely. The former produced a very light, sandy-colored topping which was not at all crisp, and the topping from the Riely book was almost runny in texture. Both used a simple combination of sugar, flour, and butter and neither was satisfactory. Additional testing revealed that this simple combination of ingredients, regardless of proportions, could not produce a crispy topping.

My first thought was to test oats. In the *Cook's Bible,* my master fruit recipe called for an oat/flour topping and, after much testing two years ago, I concluded that a one-to-one ratio of flour to oats was best although other recipes called for a wide range of ratios from a two-to-one ratio of oats to flour to a three-to-one ratio of flour to oats. Although I preferred my recipe, I was disappointed with the flour/oatmeal topping because it was chewy, a bit like soggy cardboard. In fact, I wondered if I wouldn't prefer baking apples without any topping at all.

Still in search of a crunchy topping, I moved on to test a variety of other ingredients, including corn flakes, cookie crumbs made from vanilla wafers, graham crackers, and Grape-Nuts. The corn flakes were crispy but made for an odd combination with the baked apple mixture; cookie crumbs were also crispy but too sweet; graham crackers were relatively crispy but the flavor was unwelcome on the fruit; and Grape-Nuts created the effect of chewing on tiny pebbles. I excluded cake crumbs because very few home cooks have extra slices of cake sitting around the house. I also left out bread crumbs, since this sort of baked dessert is usually referred to as a Betty or crumble, not a crisp. Having seemingly run out of options, I reviewed my crisp recipe from the *Bible* and found a variation using nuts instead of oatmeal. This turned out to be a winner. Nuts produced a crispy streusel and added a pleasant complementary flavor to the underlying fruit. I preferred pecans and almonds to walnuts, the latter having a slightly bitter aftertaste.

The next question was one of technique. It turned out that how one cuts the butter into the flour is crucial. This is one task ideally suited to the food processor, although a hand method can produce good results. The butter, a key ingredient, must be very cold, taken straight from the refrigerator. I found it best to use three 4-second pulses to combine the flour and butter and then five to six 1-second pulses once the nuts are added. With a pie pastry, one wants the

flour to resemble a coarse meal. With a crisp, the topping should be more thoroughly processed, until it has the consistency of wet sand (although over-processing will result in the mixture clumping together). If, however, one does not own a food processor, the mixture can be worked by hand. In this event, one wants the butter to be cool but slightly softened. (You can measure the temperature of the butter with an instant-read thermometer. The ideal temperature is 67 degrees.) Unlike pie pastry, the flour must be thoroughly coated with butter, otherwise the streusel will be floury and not at all crisp. On the other hand, if the butter is melted — and we tried this method — the topping turns to mud.

The next issue was the sugar. Some recipes use all granulated, some all brown sugar, and others use a mixture. The all-granulated version had little flavor, while the all–dark brown sugar version was too strong and the all–light brown sugar seemed a bit soggy. I found that half granulated and half light brown was best. It was crisp but also had a nice flavor. The ratio of flour to sugar was also crucial. Too much sugar and the topping was hard and too sweet. Too little and the topping was bland, floury tasting, and did not hold together. The best ratio turned out to be ½ cup sugar to ⅓ cup flour. I also wanted to test whether the nuts should be toasted first and found that this was unnecessary — they toasted during the baking time. I also discovered that ¾ cup of nuts was the proper amount.

How to sweeten and thicken the fruit was also problematic. Many recipes use no sweetener at all with the fruit, simply placing a layer of very sweet streusel on top and then baking. The problem with this method is that the fruit itself is lackluster, especially when preparing this dessert with tart apples. It is much like boiling pasta in unsalted water, expecting the sauce to carry the flavor. You simply end up with dull, unsalted pasta. On the other hand, I found that it is best to keep the fruit mixture on the tart side to provide a nice contrast with the sweeter topping. So for 8 cups of apples, ⅓ cup of sugar was deemed optimal; with 6 cups, use ¼ cup of sugar. With ripe peaches, which are sweeter, you can easily reduce the sugar to ¼ cup when using 8 cups of fruit. Although this recipe cries out for a juicy filling (the juices carrying a great deal of flavor), I decided to try using a thickener. Based on a prior series of tests with baked fruit desserts, the thickener of choice was Minute tapioca since it absorbed liquid nicely without a gummy texture or a starchy aftertaste. Two tablespoons was too much; there were almost no juices left in the pan after baking. One tablespoon was better, but no thickener at all was best, the juices resulting in a much brighter-tasting dessert.

In terms of flavorings, I opted for a fairly high concentration of lemon juice (the juice of half a lemon) plus ½ teaspoon of lemon rind. This is consistent with my recipe for apple pie, which appears in this book (page 328). Very small amounts, ¼ teaspoon each, of both cinnamon and nutmeg were a nice addition. Other recipes we found had a heavy hand with the spices (one recipe used a whopping 1½ teaspoons of cinnamon) which dulls the fresh, tart flavor of the apples.

A little freshly grated gingerroot can be added for a variation. For the apples themselves, I am fond of the McIntosh/Granny Smith combination I devised for my apple pie recipe since both varieties are available year round. The Macs have good flavor and the Grannies keep their shape. Of course, a good firm, tart seasonal apple is also recommended. A blind tasting conducted a year ago determined that Macoun, Royal Gala, Empire, Winesap, Rhode Island Greening, and Cortland and Northern Spy were preferred.

I have worked up two quantities for this recipe: one using 6 cups of apples and then a double recipe for bigger pans. The basic recipe can be baked in either a 9-inch pie plate or an 8 x 8 x 2-inch baking dish. Use a 13 x 9-inch dish for the double recipe. Baking temperatures were also tested, starting at 325 degrees and running up to 425 degrees in 25 degree increments. At 325 and 350 degrees, the filling was overcooked by the time the topping browned and crisped properly, although the lower temperature never actually browned the streusel satisfactorily. At the two higher temperatures, the fruit never cooked all the way through before the topping started to burn. The 375 degree oven was just right, delivering cooked fruit and a nicely browned topping. In a final refinement, I found that raising the oven temperature to 400 degrees for the last 10 minutes of baking did produce a slightly crisper streusel. Be sure to cook the apples thoroughly. The Macs should cook down into a sauce and the Granny Smiths should be soft but still hold their shape. Undercooking yields leathery fruit and too much liquid.

Master Recipe for Fruit Crisp with Nut Topping

A crisp is a casual cobbler. A simple streusel is tossed over a dish of fruit and baked. The problem with most crisps is that the topping often becomes sticky and soft and the oats, an ingredient used in many crisps, are tough and taste like cardboard. This recipe is best made with apples or peaches. I tested plums and nectarines and found them to be unsatisfactory. You can, however, add blueberries to the peaches or raspberries to the apples. If you have a food processor, use it for the topping.

FRUIT MIXTURE

6	cups apples, peeled, cored, and cut into 1-inch dice
	or
6	cups peaches, peeled, stones removed, cut into ½-inch wedges, then cut in half lengthwise
	Juice of ½ lemon
¼	cup sugar
½	teaspoon lemon rind, minced
½	teaspoon fresh gingerroot, peeled and grated (optional)

TOPPING

⅓	cup all-purpose flour
¼	cup light brown sugar
¼	cup granulated sugar
¼	teaspoon ground cinnamon
¼	teaspoon freshly grated nutmeg
¼	teaspoon salt
5	tablespoons unsalted butter, cool but slightly softened
¾	cup chopped pecans, walnuts, or almonds or a combination

1. Heat oven to 375 degrees. Toss prepared fruit with lemon juice, sugar, lemon rind, and optional ginger in a large bowl. Set aside.

2. In a medium bowl combine the first six ingredients of the topping recipe (flour through salt) and toss with your hands to combine. Add the butter and rub into the dry ingredients until the mixture looks crumbly and well mixed. Add the nuts and toss with your hands to incorporate. *Be sure not to overmix* or else the topping will become a sticky mass. (If this happens, simply place the topping in the refrigerator until it becomes firm and then break it into crumbs.)

3. Place the fruit in a 9-inch deep dish pie plate or square 8 x 8 x 2-inch baking pan. Sprinkle topping over fruit and bake 30 minutes. Increase oven temperature to 400 degrees and bake for an additional 10 minutes. (Fruit mixture should be bubbling and topping should be a deep golden brown.) Let cool for 15 minutes. Serve with heavy cream or vanilla ice cream.

SERVES 6 TO 8

DOUBLE RECIPE VARIATION

Double all of the ingredients but use a 13 x 9-inch baking dish.

FOOD PROCESSOR VARIATION

This is the simplest, most foolproof method for making a crisp. Follow step 1 of the master recipe. Next, use very cold butter, right from the refrigerator. It should be quite firm. Cut it into ½-inch pieces. In the bowl of a food processor pulse together flour, brown sugar, granulated sugar, cinnamon, nutmeg, and salt. Add the butter and pulse 10 times for 4 seconds each. The mixture will first appear like dry sand, with large lumps of butter, then like coarse cornmeal. Add nuts, then pulse again 4 or 5 times, 1-second pulses each. At this time, the topping should look like slightly clumpy wet sand. Be sure not to overmix, or it will become too wet and homogenous. Top fruit and bake as directed in the master recipe.

BLUEBERRY PEACH CRISP

Replace 1 cup of peaches with 1 cup of blueberries.

RASPBERRY OR BLACKBERRY APPLE CRISP

Replace 1 cup of apples with 1 cup of raspberries or blackberries.

Biscuit-Style Shortcake

In *The Cook's Bible*, I suggested using baking powder biscuits as the basis for a simple shortcake. I often use this recipe but I also like a variation on the theme by slightly increasing the amount of sugar and also adding an egg yolk. This gives the biscuits more tooth, which helps them stand up to the fruit. It is easiest to make this recipe in a food processor, but the hand method is also straightforward.

To zest a lemon, draw a zester (a small kitchen tool that has small holes instead of a blade) across the skin of a lemon or orange. This removes the "zest" or the peel without the bitter white pith underneath. For most recipes, the zest is then chopped.

FRUIT

4	cups fresh berries (blueberries, strawberries, blackberries, or raspberries)
¼–½	cup sugar
½	teaspoon lemon zest, minced (optional)

BISCUITS

2	cups flour
½	teaspoon salt
2	teaspoons baking powder
½	teaspoon baking soda
3	tablespoons sugar
½	teaspoon vanilla extract
5	tablespoons butter, chilled in the freezer for 30 minutes
2	tablespoons solid vegetable shortening, chilled in the freezer for 30 minutes
1	egg yolk
¾	cup buttermilk

WHIPPED CREAM

1½	cups heavy cream
2	tablespoons sugar
1	teaspoon vanilla extract

1. *For the fruit,* mix berries, sugar, and optional lemon zest and let stand at room temperature for 45 minutes. Chill. Place the bowl of an electric mixer or any metal bowl in the freezer or refrigerator along with a whisk or beaters from an electric mixer.

2. *For the biscuits,* heat oven to 425 degrees. In a medium bowl, whisk together the first 5 ingredients of the recipe (flour through sugar). Grate the cold butter and shortening onto the flour mixture. Using your fingertips, work the butter and shortening into the flour mixture until the flour is slightly yellow in color and the texture of coarse meal. This will take 2 to 3 minutes.

3. Whisk the egg yolk into the buttermilk with a fork. Gradually add the buttermilk to the flour mixture, mixing with a rubber spatula. When mixture starts to hold together, press the dough with the side of the spatula. Note that you may use a little more or less than the ¾ cup buttermilk called for in this recipe.

4. Turn onto a floured surface and roll out dough very gently to a thickness of ½ inch. Cut out rounds with a biscuit cutter (I use a 2½-inch cutter and serve 2 biscuits per person), place them on a cookie sheet, and bake in the preheated oven for about 10 minutes, turning sheet after 5 minutes in oven. Remove from oven.

6. *For the whipped cream,* whip cream with the sugar and vanilla using chilled bowl and beaters.

7. Serve the fruit with 2 biscuits per person and whipped cream. Traditionally, the biscuits are cut in half for serving but I prefer them whole, as they do not get as soggy from the fruit syrup.

SERVES 6

FOOD PROCESSOR VARIATION

Do not freeze but simply chill butter and shortening in the refrigerator. After preheating the oven in step 2, combine the first 5 ingredients in the bowl of a food processor. Process for 2 seconds to mix. Add the butter, cut into 1 tablespoon bits, and pulse seven times for 1 second each. Add shortening and pulse another six times or until mixture looks like coarse meal (the flour should take on a slightly yellowish hue from the butter). Turn mixture into a large bowl and proceed with step 3.

ALMOND VARIATION

Add ½ teaspoon of almond extract to the dough. Before baking, moisten tops of cut biscuits with milk and sprinkle with ½ cup of sliced almonds. Top with a sprinkling of sugar.

BLUEBERRY PEACH VARIATION

Use 2 cups each of blueberries and sliced peeled peaches. Assemble fruit mixture and let sit for 1 hour before proceeding with recipe.

Baked Peaches with Bourbon and Brown Sugar

Peaches were often baked or broiled and then served with game or as simple desserts, sometimes with a flavored custard sauce. As is often the case, too much sugar (and sometimes bourbon) was used

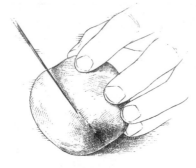

1. To stone a peach, cut around the peach along the natural crease in the skin.

2. Holding the peach in both hands, twist the two halves and then slowly pull apart. Unripe peaches will not separate easily.

in older recipes, detracting from the fresh flavors of the fruit. Here is a simple, lower-sugar recipe. Note that the juices from the peaches make a simple sauce with the brown sugar.

¼	cup packed light brown sugar
	Pinch nutmeg
3	peaches, peeled, halved, and pitted
1	tablespoon butter, cut into small pieces
1	tablespoon bourbon
	Vanilla ice cream for serving

1. Heat oven to 400 degrees. Butter a 2-quart baking dish and evenly coat with brown sugar, adding a pinch of nutmeg on top. Place peaches in the dish, cut side down. Scatter butter around the pan. Add bourbon. Cover with aluminum foil and bake for 15 minutes.
2. Remove from oven, remove foil, and check to see if the butter and sugar are forming a sauce at the bottom of the dish. Stir, if necessary, to combine. Cover and continue baking for 10 minutes or until peaches are just soft. The time will vary,

depending on the size and ripeness of the peaches. Remove from oven and cool for 5 minutes. Invert each peach half in a bowl and top with a scoop of vanilla ice cream. Spoon sauce over top and serve.

SERVES 6

Stewed Rhubarb

This is simple to make and a good way of using up a large rhubarb patch. Use the higher amount of sugar if the rhubarb is very sour. Many of our neighbors in Vermont eat rhubarb raw, sprinkled with a bit of salt, almost like celery. To determine sourness, therefore, just take a bite.

1	pound rhubarb (about 3½ cups), leaves removed, cleaned and cut into 1-inch pieces
½–¾	cup sugar
2	tablespoons honey
1	teaspoon lemon zest
2	tablespoons lemon juice
¼	cup water

Combine ingredients in a medium saucepan. Bring to a boil, cover, and simmer for 6 minutes. Uncover and simmer an additional 6 or 7 minutes or until thick. Stir gently, only once or twice, to preserve the texture of the rhubarb.

MAKES ABOUT 4 CUPS

Rhubarb Fool

In a traditional fool, the fruit and whipped cream were often not folded together but added to the goblets in separate layers. Make sure that the stewed rhubarb is cooled when you make this recipe.

1   cup heavy cream
2   tablespoons granulated sugar
½   teaspoon vanilla extract
1   recipe stewed rhubarb, chilled or at
    least cooled to room temperature

Chill beaters and bowl for best results. Place all ingredients (except rhubarb) in chilled bowl and beat with an electric mixer on medium speed for 1 minute. (Cream can also be beaten by hand with a whisk.) Increase to high speed and beat into stiff peaks. Fold rhubarb into whipped cream. Fill large goblets or wine glasses and chill before serving. (The whipped cream and rhubarb can also be served in alternating layers.)

MAKES 4 LARGE SERVINGS

Master Recipe for Fruit Pudding

There are all sorts of puddinglike desserts that are mixed with fruit. A clafouti, which I don't much care for, is one example; the texture is fleshy, like a very starchy, tough custard. Although the outside edges of this pudding are much like a clafouti, the inside should be soft and custardy. You can use this recipe with almost any fruit, although traditionally it was most often prepared with apples. (I have also tested it with blueberries and peaches and I find sweet, ripe peaches work best.) The fruit does end up on top of this pudding, which is just fine for a simple country pudding. By the way, this recipe should not be served more than an hour after baking. The texture of the custard is vastly better when it is warm, not at room temperature.

3   cups prepared fruit (peaches
    preferred) (washed, cored, seeded,
    and cut into bite-size pieces)
1   tablespoon lemon juice
2   teaspoons lemon zest
⅔   cup flour
¼   teaspoon salt
¼   teaspoon ground nutmeg
½   cup sugar
1   cup milk
½   cup heavy cream
4   large eggs
2   teaspoons vanilla extract

1. Heat oven to 350 degrees. Butter a shallow casserole or oval baking dish (the sides should be short and the pan should be wide — an 8 x 12-inch pan is about the right size). Toss the fruit with the lemon juice and zest and pour into the baking dish.

2. Whisk together the flour, salt, nutmeg, and sugar. In a separate bowl, whisk together the milk, heavy cream, eggs, and vanilla. Add the flour to the milk mixture and stir very gently with a whisk just until smooth. Do not overbeat. Pour over fruit. **3.** Bake 30 to 40 minutes or until custard sets. The center 2 inches should still be wet and custardy. It will finish baking out of the oven. Remove from oven and serve warm, not hot, but no longer than 1 hour after baking.

SERVES 6 TO 8

APPLE VARIATION

Soak ⅓ cup raisins in ⅓ cup bourbon for 1 hour and then drain. Use apples for the fruit, peeling, coring, and slicing them into wedges, about 8 wedges per apple. Toss raisins with apples.

On the Farm for the Holidays

IT IS MID-OCTOBER, when our family presses apple cider and makes applesauce, a day that marks for me the beginning of the holiday season. It is the last hurrah of summer's warm, busy days; the morning frost burns off by 7:30, when the sun strikes out over the hollow. There is still a hint of yellow from September's richer hues, but the light is thinner now and the air so clear that I can look out across our valley and make out individual leaves, five-pointed sugar maples, shagbark hickory, or the long, slender leaves of white ash. The sun breaks over the valley in random streaks, flaming the top of a peak and a row of maples just behind the old cemetery, and washes down the curve of a mountainside, the light spilling down onto the side of a white farmhouse across the way, the pale stripes of clapboards spotlighted against the deep shadows of the surrounding hay field. Now the great yellow and russet maples emerge from the morning twilight, framed by a stand of spruce. The mountains to the north are distant, the trees diminished in color and size to create a simple backdrop of autumn wallpaper, no individual colors or shapes standing out. As I peer out the bedroom window, I can see the valley to the west filled with light, the limes, golds, and yellows offset by the deep hues of an evergreen, the great, reaching fingers of bare branches, and the occasional splash of white from the curving, sinuous trunk of a birch.

The timothy in the lower field no longer pushes up strongly from the earth but sits listlessly, pale green, mottled with browns, waiting for winter. The hives have just a few bees around the narrow openings, not the frenzied activity of pollen-laden workers soaring in from great heights, then gliding, heavy, sometimes misjudging and landing short on the grass. The stand of corn is brown and withered, the heads of the giant sunflowers have turned dark, their necks broken.

In our gardens, the doe-colored stalks of daylilies lie windswept by the old stone wall, a few still standing straight, others a tangle of leaves and withered flowers. The dead hosta stand in swayed poses like ballet dancers, their stalks arched and lithe, leaves curving in great moplike tutus to the ground. A small bed of spiky bachelor buttons still has bursts of blues and salmon and cranberry and brilliant white. The zucchini and tomatoes are long gone now, a spray of deep orange cherry tomatoes lie on the black plastic ground cover, tasteless after the first frost. But the great stalks of brussels sprouts are weighted with their small cabbages, the lettuce, carrots, and radishes are still vibrant and upstanding as is a large bed of beets and turnips, their tops to be harvested for dinner. In the orchard, the semidwarf apple trees are heavy with bright red fruit, but the leaves have started to fall, making the trees appear frail and thin. I pick a ripe Macoun before breakfast, biting hard into the dense, crisp flesh.

After breakfast, the whole family pitches in to make cider. Hundreds of pounds of wild apples have been picked during the week, filling large plastic tubs and flimsy plastic shopping bags. I sort out the larger, healthier specimens and put them aside for applesauce. The others, stained with black rust or misshapen, twisted and gnarled, are washed in a huge horse trough and then put through the grinder on the Jaffrey cider press, the large red metal wheel easily turned by hand, grinding and crushing the apples into a juicy mash that falls into the pressing barrel below. It's quick work; even my two-year-old son pitches in, dropping apples into the hopper, and then watching their instant transformation. When the barrel is full, the thick wooden lid is placed on top and then screwed down with the long wooden handle of the press, squeezing out a stream of reddish-brown juice, which gushes out of a small hole into the large pot below. The sun is warm, the yellowjackets are circling the sweet mash and juice, and the white five-gallon bucket is half full of cider, floating a film of light froth, sweet and mahogany colored.

When the cider has been made, the pressed apple mash dumped onto the herb garden and rototilled into the soil, we freeze it in old half-gallon milk containers, the tops secured with plastic wrap and rubber bands. I then grind up the larger apples for applesauce, placing them in two huge stockpots sitting on the old stove along with a bit of the new cider, a cinnamon stick, lemon juice, and a good deal of honey from last year's crop, now partly crystallized. The skins soften, the mixture cooks down in the pot, and the applesauce slowly reddens and deepens in color. I pass it through an old food mill perched on top of a large stainless cooking pot, reversing the turn of the handle to scrape up the seeds and skins from the mesh filter and then starting back in a clockwise motion, slowly pushing more sauce into the pot, juicy and vibrant with the tart underpinnings of lemon and wild apple married to the deep, perfumed sweetness of clover honey.

In late afternoon, a cold breeze moves in from the northwest and the shadows deepen across the valley. The large maple which stands guard in front of our small farmhouse is furious with color, the last rays of the sun picking it out from the darkened field. The sounds of our children coming back home along the dirt road float up to the house, small packets of conversation carried by the wind, a stream of familiar voices flowing by the house and up into the deep, still shadows of the woods. The kitchen is warmed by the large cast iron stove as we start to prepare a dinner of pork chops, mashed potatoes, applesauce, roasted beets sautéed with their greens, and a dessert of apple crisp. Neighbors stop by and are invited to stay for supper, the adults gossiping in the kitchen as the kids play checkers and Parcheesi in front of a crackling fire in the living room. Night descends, the temperature drops quickly, and then dinner is served family-style, and we talk of rabbit hunting and poaching deer.

Our neighbors leave and I walk them out to their pickup. The night is cold and as I watch their taillights grow smaller, the headlights sweeping across our lower field, I glance upward at the night sky, the great expanse of which makes me stop for a deep, cold breath. Darkness has washed over our small yellow farmhouse, shadows have drifted down from the forest in the twilight, wrapping around the chimney, blanketing our small ship like a dense bank of fog. Through a dimly lit window, I see our three children, snug by the fireside, their faces glowing in the soft flickering light.

THE WINTER holidays in Vermont are about hunting, the only time Vermonters will take a walk in the woods. In September, the good hunters go out, looking for deer trails and apple trees, and "pens" or "corrals" where the deer press down the tall grass and make their beds. Deer stands are put up early, the experienced hunters going out just before dawn and then in late afternoon to check the local population. Black powder muskets are cleaned and tested at seventy-five yards; a coffee can is nailed to a tree, the large lead balls nicking at the sides until a good shot collapses the center and knocks it to the ground. Too much powder and the rifle kicks hard, the butt slamming against your shoulder if you forget to press it close. On a cold day, the small metal caps that provide the spark are hard to pick up. They misfire occasionally or they go off but don't ignite the powder. We practice with our hunting bows too, firing at small foam targets set out by the orchard. Missed shots are hard to find, the arrows slipping unseen into the side hill, or hiding just beneath the surface of the grass. But this is close-in work, most local bow hunters not willing to take a shot over thirty yards. A wounded deer has to be tracked and killed, and longer shots are unlikely to hit home.

But grouse hunting is my sport. I take long afternoon walks with my younger daughter, Caroline, along old logging trails, alert for the adrenaline rush of beating wings, move the safety off, take quick but careful aim, and then squeeze slowly and evenly. A woodcock shoots up like a rocket, winging straight to the treetops, and then moves off parallel to the ground. As we warm to the hunt, we walk up over an old town road, past abandoned tree stands, felled birches, their upper branches now on the ground providing cover for younger birds. The small hollow is gray, the sun already passing us by, but ahead, up past the next ridge, a stand of birch and poplar is ablaze with the late afternoon sunlight. Through woolen caps we can hear the drumming of woodpeckers and the creak of boughs in the light wind; the great frozen trunks reverberating with a hollow, empty sound. It is the Saturday after Christmas and we can smell wood smoke in the air, its slightly sweet scent a reminder of our small farmhouse, just the roof and smoking chimney visible as we emerge back into an open field from the darkening forest behind us. As we near the house, the yellow clapboards now in view, we walk past a field of evergreens, the smaller, more shapely specimens cut for our Christmas trees. It reminds me of the Lincoln place, just down the road, a run-down shack on the edge of a field filled with trees. (It used to be a large sap house, with an evaporator that ran a good twenty feet long.) For two weeks in December, the Lincolns offer cider and hot chocolate and people come from miles around to pick and cut their own tree. But not everyone in town buys their trees. One old-timer in particular, Rob Woodcock, had different ideas about harvesting Christmas trees. One

of our neighbors heard some commotion just across the road during a snowfall. Tires were spinning and an engine was being gunned. A few minutes later, the neighbor drove up the road and found a pickup. Then there was a shot, and there was Rob Woodcock, appearing out of the spruces, with a long dirty-gray beard and trailing a Christmas tree. The neighbor indicated that he hadn't heard a chain saw. Rob seemed puzzled. He said it was a lot easier to shoot the top off the tree with a shotgun than use a saw!

Slow-Roasted Thanksgiving Turkey with Gravy

As stated in *The Cook's Bible*, my favorite method of preparing turkey is to roast it at low oven temperatures. This produces succulent meat and also solves the problem of the breast meat overcooking by the time the dark meat is ready. However, I have altered this recipe a bit from the original, using a low temperature of 250 degrees rather than 200. Many home ovens are not properly calibrated and therefore some cooks may be trying to roast a bird at temperatures below 200 degrees. This will take a very long time and is also a bad idea for safety reasons. It is also important *not* to stuff the bird. At such low temperatures, the stuffing will take a long time to come up to temperature, thus providing an opportunity for bacteria, should there be any, to multiply. Also, do not truss the bird. The thighs and legs will cook faster if allowed to stick out, allowing better circulation of hot air around the joints. The recipe below is for a large bird. See the variation which follows for smaller birds.

1   18- to 20-pound turkey
3   tablespoons butter, melted
    Salt and freshly ground black pepper
1   tablespoon cornstarch

1. Remove giblets. Wash turkey with cold water inside and out and pat dry.
2. Heat oven to 350 degrees. Brush turkey breast with melted butter. Sprinkle generously with salt and pepper. Place the turkey, breast side down, on a roasting rack and put rack in roasting pan. Cover turkey and pan tightly with aluminum foil and place in oven.
3. Roast for 1 hour. Reduce heat to 250 degrees. Roast for 3 more hours. Turn bird breast side up, brush with melted butter, and sprinkle with salt and pepper. Cover again and roast an additional 3 hours. Check internal temperature of the thighs. If they have reached 170 degrees, remove bird from oven and heat oven to 500 degrees. (Continue to roast at 250 degrees if the internal temperature of the thighs is not up to 170 degrees.) When oven is up to temperature, remove foil and roast bird, breast side up, an additional 5 to 7 minutes, or until the skin is nicely browned.
4. Four hours before serving, place giblets, excluding liver (the liver is relatively large, smooth, and dark colored), in a 3-quart saucepan (you may also add a cut-up carrot, onion, celery stalk, and fresh herbs in cheesecloth if you like). Add about 2½ quarts of cold water and bring to a boil. Simmer uncovered for 3 hours, or until you have reduced the liquid by about two thirds. Strain broth

through a fine strainer or cheesecloth. Reserve.
5. When turkey is cooked, add 3 tablespoons of drippings from the roasting pan to a saucepan with the reserved broth. Boil rapidly for about 10 minutes or until the liquid is reduced by about one third. Mix cornstarch with 2 tablespoons of water and whisk into sauce. Simmer for 5 minutes. Add salt and pepper to taste.
6. Let bird rest for 20 minutes, carve, and serve with gravy.

Small Turkey Variation

Smaller birds need between 5 and 5½ hours of roasting at low temperature instead of the 7 hours required for a 20-pound bird. Be sure to check the internal temperature of the breast meat; it should register 170 degrees and the thigh meat should register 180 degrees when the bird is done (slow-cooked turkeys can be cooked to a higher internal temperature than birds roasted at higher oven temperatures without drying out).

1   12- to 14-pound turkey
3   tablespoons butter, melted
    Salt and freshly ground black pepper
1   tablespoon cornstarch

Follow master recipe, roasting bird for 1 hour at 350 degrees and then 2 hours at 250 degrees. Flip bird breast side up and brush with melted butter and sprinkle liberally with salt and pepper. Roast for an additional 2 hours 15 minutes. Check internal temperature of the thighs. If they have reached 180 degrees, remove bird from oven and heat oven to 500 degrees.

(Continue to roast at 250 degrees if the internal temperature of the thighs is not up to 180 degrees.) When oven is up to temperature, remove foil and roast bird, breast side up, an additional 5 to 7 minutes or until the skin is nicely browned.

Brown Sauce with Sage and Onion

On a farm, gravy was an everyday affair, used liberally to fix up leftovers. Marie Briggs was fond of "milk gravy," a form of the French béchamel sauce made with a roux (butter and flour) and milk. Although the cooking and dining at the farmhouse wasn't fancy, the gravy always made it a bit more special. This recipe is my version of a last-minute sauce that can be served with turkey. It is so good that I even suggest using the broth made while roasting the turkey as the base for the sauce. This is also a good sauce for leftovers and other occasions when making a homemade stock is not practical.

2	tablespoons butter
1	tablespoon olive oil
¼	cup minced onion
1	cup white wine
3	tablespoons brandy
1½	cups beef stock, homemade or canned
½	teaspoon dried sage or 2 teaspoons fresh, minced
2	tablespoons cornstarch
	Salt and freshly ground pepper to taste

Combine butter with the olive oil in a sauté pan over medium-high heat. When hot, add the onion and sauté for 5 min-

utes. Add the wine, brandy, stock, and sage and bring to a boil. Cook until liquid has been reduced by 50 percent. Add cornstarch to ⅓ cup water and stir until dissolved and smooth. Whisk cornstarch mixture into boiling liquid. Simmer until thickened. Season to taste with salt and freshly ground black pepper.

Poultry Stuffing with Variations

American stuffings were usually made from cheap, available ingredients such as stale bread, crackers, or potatoes. A basic country stuffing was often made from nothing more than stale bread, salt pork, an egg, hot water, sage, salt, and pepper. A cracker stuffing was simply crackers, melted butter, hot water, and seasonings. This recipe is a bit more elaborate, and I have designed it as a master recipe so that you can use any combination of grains, bread cubes, fruit, and nuts. Note that this recipe is designed to be baked separately from the bird (you should not stuff a turkey that is roasted at low oven temperatures) and therefore it has more liquid than regular recipes to prevent it from drying out in the oven. Since it only takes a half hour to bake, it can be put into the oven at the point the turkey is done, since the bird should rest for 20 minutes before carving. This recipe can easily be doubled or tripled for larger crowds.

4	cups cooked rice, barley, kasha, millet, bulgur, cornbread, or homemade bread cubes
3	tablespoons unsalted butter
1	tablespoon olive oil

1½   cups chopped onion

½   cup chopped celery

¼   cup chopped scallions or chives

¼   cup chopped parsley

½   cup canned chestnuts, apples, prunes, or raisins, chopped (optional)

½   cup walnuts, pecans, or almonds, toasted (optional)

½   pound sausage meat, crumbled and browned

2   tablespoons minced fresh sage, thyme, or oregano or 1½ teaspoons dried

¼   cup white wine

¾   cup chicken stock

¾   teaspoon salt

Freshly ground black pepper to taste

1. If using homemade bread, it should be chopped into ½-inch cubes and then spread out onto a baking sheet in one layer. The cubes should be baked in a 225 degree oven for 25 to 40 minutes, depending on the type of bread, until they are dry and hard. Or simply leave them out on the baking sheet for 2 to 3 days.

2. Heat the butter and olive oil in a skillet and sauté onions for 5 minutes over medium heat. Add celery and scallions and sauté for 2 minutes. Mix together all ingredients in a large bowl. Prunes and raisins must be soaked in hot water for 5 minutes before draining and chopping, or they may be soaked in a 50-50 mixture of sherry and water for 2 hours.

3. Heat oven to 375 degrees. Butter a 2-quart baking dish and add stuffing. Cover with aluminum foil and bake for 15 minutes. Remove aluminum foil and bake for an additional 15 minutes or until the stuffing is brown and crisp on top.

SERVES 6

PRUNE APPLE VARIATION

Add 2 apples which have been cored, peeled, and diced and 1 cup pitted prunes cut into ½-inch pieces to the onion mixture. Use 2 cups of bread cubes instead of 4 and eliminate the white wine, reduce the chicken stock to ¼ cup, and add ¼ cup apple juice.

MUSHROOM VARIATION

Add 2 cups of chopped fresh mushrooms (any type will do) to the onions while sautéing along with an additional 1 tablespoon of olive oil. Eliminate the fruit and nut additions.

SAGE APPLE VARIATION

Add 2 apples which have been cored, peeled, and diced to the onion mixture. Use 2 cups of bread cubes instead of 4 and substitute ¼ cup chicken stock and ¼ cup apple juice for the wine and chicken stock. Use sage for the fresh herb.

MASTER RECIPE FOR COUNTRY HAM

One Southern cook once commented that the making of a ham dinner, like the making of a gentleman, starts a long time before the event. This is quite true, especially when dealing with a country ham. A dry-cured ham, also called a country ham, is packed in salt, which draws out water and slows the growth of bacteria. Other ingredients in cured hams include sugar, which improves texture and offsets saltiness, spices such as pepper, and saltpeter, which not only helps reduce bacteria but contributes to the color of the final cured product. Whether wet- or dry-cured, many hams are then smoked to add flavor and to help preserve the meat. Some hams are smoked for up to two weeks, and a "fully cooked" ham has been smoked to an internal temperature of at least 155 degrees. Hams are often aged as well. A country ham, for example, is started in the very late fall, cured, smoked, and then hung for about six months through the winter, spring, and summer.

For a ham that is advertised as "ready to eat," simply preheat the oven to 325 degrees and cook until the internal temperature reaches 140 degrees. However, country hams, such as Smithfield, usually require soaking and scrubbing before cooking. (A Smithfield ham is, technically speaking, a ham that has been produced within a few miles of Smithfield, Virginia, although the term "Smithfield-style" is used by many producers.) Some cooks serve country hams without cooking, as one might serve the Italian prosciutto; thinly sliced and in small portions.

In general, a country ham will be salty and strongly flavored. The dry-cure method concentrates flavors and also makes a coarser meat. (A country ham must lose at least 18 percent of its weight during curing and aging.) Country hams are a bit like single-malt Scotches — they vary tremendously in flavor and quality and are hard to judge as a group. Although country hams are available in supermarkets, liquor stores, and delicatessens throughout the South, they are mostly mail order items in the rest of the country. Be careful when purchas-ing a ham labeled as a "portion." The best cuts may have been removed. A country ham will keep a very long time, but don't freeze it, because its flavor will deteriorate quickly.

One of the benefits of this recipe is that the ham can be left in the hot water for a long time after cooking without any adverse effects, which makes it perfect for entertaining. I remove the hock, because otherwise it is difficult to fit the ham into a pot. Use a hacksaw for this step. The recipe below is based on a similar recipe by Sarah Fritschner published in the November/December 1996 issue of *Cook's Illustrated*.

Country Ham

1	country ham, 12 to 15 pounds, hock removed
4	carrots, cut into large pieces
4	ribs celery, cut into large pieces
3	medium onions, cut into large pieces
2	tablespoons whole cloves
1	tablespoon whole black peppercorns

1. If the outside of the ham is moldy, scrub with a wire brush under running water.
2. In a large tub or lobster pot, soak ham for at least 24 hours, changing the water every 8 hours. Hams that are aged less than 6 months do not need to be soaked.
3. Drain ham and place it in a cooking pot with remaining ingredients. Cover with water. Bring water to a boil and then reduce to a bare simmer. Cook until in-side of ham reaches 140 degrees on an

instant-read thermometer, 3 to 4 hours. Turn off heat and leave ham in cooking liquid. When ready to serve (ham can be left in cooking liquid for hours), remove ham to a cutting board and carve. Serve thin slices, since country hams are full-flavored and salty.

SERVES A LARGE CROWD

Roast Goose with Gravy

Steaming or boiling a fatty bird is a wonderful technique for rendering much of the fat before roasting. I use this method for both duck and goose. I also find that the skin is improved, rendering it crispier. By the way, the goose is best if simmered one or two days before roasting. However, this is optional and the whole recipe may be made the day you are serving. Do not stuff the goose during roasting. Instead, prepare the stuffing separately. I suggest using the Prune Apple variation of the master stuffing recipe, page 365. For a simpler gravy, use the Brown Sauce with Sage and Onion, page 364.

1   goose, 10 to 12 pounds
3   tablespoons butter, melted
1   tablespoon cornstarch
    Salt and freshly ground black pepper
    to taste

1. Remove the neck, giblets, and the wing tips and reserve for the gravy . Also take out any leftover quills with a small pair of needlenose pliers. Rinse the goose inside and out in plenty of cold water. Prick the skin all over with a fork.
2. Fill a very large pot two thirds full of water and bring to a boil. Add the

prepared goose and simmer gently for 45 minutes. If you have time, refrigerate uncovered overnight or up to 48 hours. If not, proceed with step 3.
3. Heat oven to 325 degrees with a large roasting pan on a rack set toward the bottom of the oven. Place the goose breast side up on a large roasting rack. Brush breast, legs, and thighs with melted butter and sprinkle with a generous amount of salt and freshly ground black pepper. Turn goose so one side is facing up. Remove roasting pan and place on top of stove. Place rack with goose in pan and replace pan in oven. Roast for 30 minutes. Remove pan from oven, turn bird to other side, and put back into oven. After an additional 30 minutes, turn bird breast side up. Continue roasting for 30 minutes or until breast meat registers 150 degrees on an instant-read thermometer. Increase oven to 425 degrees and roast until the inside of the thigh registers 165 to 170 degrees. Remove from oven and let sit uncovered for 20 minutes before carving.
4. Four hours before serving, place giblets, excluding liver, in a 3-quart saucepan (you may also add a cut-up carrot, onion, celery stalk, and fresh herbs in cheesecloth if you like). Add about 2½ quarts of cold water and bring to a boil. Simmer uncovered for 3 hours, or until you have reduced the liquid by about two-thirds. Strain broth through a fine strainer or cheesecloth. Reserve.
5. When goose is cooked, add 3 tablespoons of drippings from the roasting pan to a saucepan with the reserved broth. Boil rapidly for about 10 minutes or until the liquid is reduced by about one third. Mix 1 tablespoon of cornstarch with 2 tablespoons of water and whisk into

sauce. Simmer for 5 minutes. Add salt and pepper to taste.

6. Carve goose and serve with gravy.

SERVES 8

Cranberry Chutney

I am not a big fan of uncooked relishes or chutneys for the holidays. Some recipes call for throwing everything into a food processor, including whole oranges, pulsing, and that's it. Cooking blends the flavors and also dissolves the sugar. I also have browned the onion in this recipe, although I use as little oil and butter as possible to maintain a light, fresh taste to the chutney.

2	teaspoons vegetable oil
1	teaspoon unsalted butter
1	medium onion, diced (about 1 cup)
4	cups cranberries, rinsed and picked over
1¼	cups sugar
½	cup orange juice
3	tablespoons cider vinegar
⅛	teaspoon ground cloves
⅛	teaspoon ground allspice
½	teaspoon salt
	Freshly ground black pepper to taste
½	cup chopped toasted pecans or walnuts (optional)

1. Heat a 3-quart nonreactive saucepan over medium heat. Add the butter and the oil and, when the foam subsides, add the onion. Cook for 6 to 8 minutes or until the onion is golden brown.

2. Add all of the remaining ingredients except the optional nuts and cook cov-

ered on medium for 7 minutes. Uncover the pan, stir, and lower heat to medium-low. Simmer uncovered for another 8 minutes, stirring occasionally. Add the optional nuts and cook for an additional 2 minutes or until all of the berries have popped and the mixture is a uniform color.

MAKES ABOUT 1 PINT

Ginger Rhubarb Sauce

This recipe comes from Eva Katz, the former test kitchen director at *Cook's Illustrated*. It is a simple sweet-and-sour sauce to make and goes well with goose as well as fish or chicken.

2	tablespoons white wine vinegar
½	cup sugar
2	tablespoons water
4	cups cut-up rhubarb, leaves removed, washed and cut into ½-inch pieces
1	tablespoon fresh gingerroot, peeled and finely chopped
⅛	teaspoon salt
	Freshly ground black pepper to taste
1	tablespoon lime juice

In a large saucepan, heat vinegar and sugar over medium heat until sugar dissolves and caramelizes, turning a light brown color. Add water — stand back to avoid being spattered — rhubarb, and ginger. Stir to coat rhubarb with sugar mixture. Reduce heat to medium-low and cook for 10 minutes. Stir once or twice. Add salt, pepper, and lime juice. Stir and taste. Adjust seasonings. Serve with chicken or fish.

Spiced Cashews

During the week between Christmas and New Year's, it is usually cold enough to freeze the pond, and we clear the snow one afternoon, everyone pitching in with shovels. That evening, we invite a few neighbors over after dinner, make a bonfire next to the old picnic table just by the edge of the pond, and then I set out an old railroad lantern in the middle of the ice for light. The kids play hockey with a big plastic puck, often losing sight of it in a snowbank, and all of us take at least a few turns around the lantern. But for the adults, the real attraction is standing by the great fire, telling stories and exchanging gossip. We drink hot cocoa and also bring a few light snacks, perhaps a few marshmallows for the kids and some of these spiced nuts for the adults. And on a clear night, we look out over the small valley, and watch the sparks from the hot fire rise up into the cold, dark air.

1	egg white
1	tablespoon water
1	pound salted cashews
⅓	cup sugar
2	teaspoons cumin
2	teaspoons coarse or kosher salt
1	teaspoon cayenne pepper

Heat oven to 250 degrees. Whisk egg white with one tablespoon water until foamy. Add cashews and toss to coat. Transfer to a strainer. Shake and drain for 2 minutes. Meanwhile, wipe out bowl and add remaining ingredients. Add nuts and toss to coat. Place nuts on a baking sheet and spread out in one layer. Bake for 40 minutes. Stir, making sure that the nuts are still spread out in one layer, and bake 20 to 30 minutes more until they feel dry. Loosen with a spatula and cool.

Popovers

These are quite simple to make, but remember to grease the pans thoroughly. You will require a popover pan for this recipe.

1	cup flour
¼	teaspoon salt
2	eggs
1	cup milk
4	tablespoons (½ stick) butter, melted

1. In a large bowl, combine the flour and salt and stir to mix. Add the eggs and the milk and whisk to combine completely. Let stand for 30 minutes in a cool place.
2. Heat oven to 450 degrees. Adjust rack to the middle position. Using a pastry brush, grease the popover pan very generously with the melted butter. A small amount of butter should puddle in the bottom of each cup.
3. After batter has rested for 30 minutes, pour it into the prepared pan and bake for 15 minutes. Lower the oven to 350 degrees and bake for an additional 15 to 20 minutes or until they are browned and crisp. Serve at once.

MAKES 8 TO 12 POPOVERS

Pumpkin, Butternut Squash, or Sweet Potato Pie

This is a basic custard pie that uses pumpkin, squash, or sweet potato purée in place of the milk. If the crust starts to overcook during baking, cover it with aluminum foil, leaving the filling still exposed. If you like a smooth pie, pumpkin purée is best. If you prefer a bit more texture, use the squash or sweet potato filling. I have also tried other varieties of winter squash with less success. Their texture was either too wet, too "slippery," or they did not have sufficient flavor. Note that it is important to add the hot filling to a hot pie shell to produce a crisp crust.

| 1 | hot partially prebaked 9-inch pie shell (page 302) |

FILLING

2	cups canned pumpkin, butternut squash, or sweet potato purée (one 15-ounce can is approximately 2 cups)
¾	cup packed brown sugar
3	tablespoons molasses
½	teaspoon salt
¼	teaspoon nutmeg
¼	teaspoon powdered ginger
½	teaspoon cinnamon
⅛	teaspoon cloves
1	cup heavy cream
3	tablespoons bourbon
3	eggs

1. To prepare the sweet potatoes, bake them according to the directions on page 67. When cool, remove the skins and mash. To prepare butternut squash, cut the squash in half and remove the seeds. Lightly oil a baking sheet and place squash cut side down onto sheet. Bake in a 375 degree oven for 1 hour or until the squash is very soft. Scoop out the flesh and mash.

2. Heat oven to 425 degrees. Whisk together all ingredients except the eggs in a medium saucepan. Place over low heat and cook, stirring occasionally, until bubbling. Remove saucepan from heat and whisk in eggs one at a time. Pour filling into still hot prebaked pie shell and place on a baking sheet in the oven.

3. Bake for 10 minutes, then lower heat to 350 degrees. Turn pie around so that filling bakes evenly. If the crust starts to become too brown, cover it with strips of aluminum foil. (Or you can purchase metal pie crust covers in specialty cookware stores.) Bake 13 to 15 minutes longer, but start checking the pie after 8 minutes and every minute thereafter. A custard pie will set up quickly. Check by jiggling pie slightly. Mixture should be puffed up and set around the perimeter but still wobbly in the center (about a 2½-inch-diameter circle in the middle of the pie should not be set — it will continue to cook and firm up after the pie is removed from the oven). Note that the sweet potato and squash versions of the pie will set up a bit more quickly. Check the crust on these versions after 7 minutes instead of 10.

4. Remove from oven and let cool on a rack for at least 1 hour before serving. Serve with sweetened whipped cream or vanilla ice cream.

Farmhouse Trifle

The problem with most trifle recipes is that they have tarted up a rather simple recipe, one that is not that different from Italian tiramisù, which has suffered the same indignities. Trifle is nothing more than leftover bread or cake with some custard, whipped cream, and jam. However, some older American recipes call for a much more elaborate dessert, one that is a dish filled with finely broken biscuits, sweet yeast bread (which was called a "rusk"), and spice cake, soaked with wine, covered with boiled custard, topped with a syllabub (made in the old days from whipped egg whites, white wine, grated lemon zest, and cream), and then garnished with jelly and flowers. Even back then, it was a showstopper.

For a modern kitchen, I find that chiffon cake makes an excellent base, brushed with a bit of amaretto; then I add a good deal of custard (most trifles are wanting in this regard) folded into whipped cream. I do not use raspberries, which are insanely expensive out of season, or the jam, which makes it too sweet, or the small almond cookies, which simply complicate matters and, in my opinion, detract from the dessert. Finally, I sift a bit of cocoa, which adds both color and a nice contrast in flavor, onto each layer and then on top of the dessert. The recipe still takes an investment in time, although it can be prepared early in the day and refrigerated. In fact, this dessert tastes better the next day, as the custard has time to work its magic on the cake, and since there is no fresh fruit, there is no bleeding of colors, which makes this sort of dish look a bit shopworn after sitting too long.

1	recipe Chiffon Cake (page 274), cut into 2 layers and then cut into ¾-inch slices
1	recipe Pastry Cream (see below)
⅓	cup amaretto or Grand Marnier or other liqueur
1	recipe Whipped Cream (recipe below)
½	cup unsweetened cocoa powder

FOR THE PASTRY CREAM

4	cups milk, half-and-half, or light cream
12	egg yolks
1	cup sugar
½	teaspoon salt
5	tablespoons cornstarch, sifted
2	teaspoons vanilla extract
¼	cup rum
4	tablespoons unsalted butter (optional)

FOR THE WHIPPED CREAM

1	cup heavy cream, very cold
¼	cup sugar

1. Bake the chiffon cake, cool, and slice.
2. *For the pastry cream,* heat the milk in a small saucepan almost to a simmer — the milk will start to form small bubbles around the edge of the pan. In a 3-quart saucepan, whisk the yolks with the sugar and salt until the mixture is thick and lemon-colored, 3 to 4 minutes. Add the cornstarch and whisk to combine. Add the heated milk very slowly and mix to blend.
3. Over medium-low heat, whisk the custard for 30 seconds. Continue cooking, being careful not to let it boil, for 7 to 8 minutes, stirring constantly with a wooden spoon. (If the mixture starts to steam heavily, it is almost at a boil. Take it off the heat and whisk vigorously to reduce the temperature.) Be sure to scrape the bottom and sides of the pan as you stir. When

done, the custard should be the consistency of a thick sauce, although it may contain a few lumps. Remove from heat, stir for an additional 30 seconds, and add the vanilla, rum, and the optional butter. Strain through a sieve into a bowl to remove any lumps. Press a piece of plastic wrap or wax paper onto the surface of the custard. Refrigerate until cold. You can make the pastry cream a day ahead of time. Just before using, whisk until smooth.

4. *For the whipped cream,* chill a large bowl and whisk or the beaters from an electric mixer. Add the cream and sugar to the bowl and beat on low speed (if using an electric mixer), gradually increasing the speed over the next minute until the mixer is on high. Beat until the cream is thick and can easily hold a 2-inch peak. Fold the chilled pastry cream into the whipped cream.

5. *To assemble the trifle,* select a clear glass bowl with tall, straight sides. (Trifle can also be made in any large bowl if you do not care about presentation.) The bowl should hold about 16 cups. Arrange cake slices in a fallen domino pattern around the perimeter of the bottom of the bowl. (The slices may have to be trimmed to fit properly in the bowl.) Fill in the center with additional slices. (You should have used about ⅓ of the cake slices at this point.) Brush cake slices with ⅓ of the amaretto. Spread ⅓ of the pastry cream mixture over the top of the slices. Sift ⅓ of the cocoa over the pastry cream. Repeat the steps above twice until you have used up all of the cake and the pastry cream.

6. Place trifle in refrigerator for at least 2 hours (or it can be made a day ahead) before serving. If you like, serve with a few chocolate shavings on top.

SERVES 8 TO 10

Master Recipe for Steamed Pudding

This recipe makes a lot of pudding, but since it is so time consuming I prefer to make a large quantity. However, the recipe is easily halved. Most pudding molds seem to come in two sizes. The larger one is big enough for this recipe; use the smaller mold if you halve the ingredients. If you do not have a mold, you can use a bowl. To keep out the steam while cooking, simply place a piece of parchment paper over the top of the bowl and tie it with twine; then place a piece of aluminum foil tightly over the top. I also found that although some recipes call for larger cubes, the pudding tasted best when made with smaller bread crumbs; the texture is more even. To determine when the pudding is cooked, stick a knife deep into the center (it should come out clean), and press the top with your fingers (it should be firm and springy). This may sound obvious, but you should also check that the bowl or pudding mold will easily fit into the pot or steamer. Be sure that it can be removed easily, because a scorching-hot metal mold is quite tricky to work with if there is little clearance in the pot. By the way, you don't have to use a steamer. Any large pot will do. Simply place the mold or bowl on a trivet or cooling rack placed in the bottom of the pan. Note that some pudding molds have a tube in the center. This speeds up cooking, so check the pudding after about ⅔ of the cooking time stated below. Finally, I found that these puddings are easier to unmold and serve if they are cooled for a full hour after cooking.

6	cups fresh bread crumbs
8	tablespoons (1 stick) unsalted butter, melted
2½	cups milk
1	cup heavy cream
4	large eggs, separated
1¼	cups sugar
2	tablespoons bourbon, brandy, or rum
2	teaspoons vanilla extract
½	teaspoon salt
1	Flavoring variation recipe (see below)

1. Set a rack in the bottom of a wide pot. (A large Dutch oven works well — make sure that the pudding mold or bowl fits easily into the pot.) Add water to come up even with the bottom of the rack. Bring water to a simmer while preparing the ingredients.

2. Butter a deep, ovenproof bowl (or use a pudding mold). In a large bowl, toss bread crumbs with melted butter. Add milk and cream and set aside. In another bowl, whip the egg yolks for 2 minutes with a hand-mixer or with a whisk. Add 1 cup of the sugar and beat an additional 2 minutes on high speed or whisk vigorously. Add the liquor, vanilla, and salt. Fold into the bread crumb mixture. Fold the flavoring ingredients into the bread crumb mixture.

3. Whip egg whites until billowy. Add the remaining ¼ cup sugar and beat until the whites hold a 2-inch peak. Fold into pudding mixture.

4. Pour batter into prepared bowl or mold. Cover bowl with a piece of parchment paper and tie tightly with string. Cover parchment tightly with a large piece of aluminum foil, or cover mold with wax paper and then cover tightly with lid. Make sure that water is up to a simmer, place mold or bowl on rack, and cover pot.

Steam for about 2¼ hours or until a knife inserted into the center comes out clean. If making 2 smaller puddings, check after 1 hour. If using molds with a tube in the center, check after ⅔ of the cooking time, 40 minutes for a small mold and 1½ hours for a large one. Remove from pot and let cool on a rack for 1 hour before serving. Cut into wedges and serve warm with whipped cream or ice cream.

CHOCOLATE VARIATION

Melt 8 ounces of semisweet chocolate with 2 tablespoons instant espresso in the top of a double boiler or in a microwave. (Zap for 2 minutes uncovered on 50 percent power, stir, zap again for 1 additional minute, stir, and then heat again for another 30 to 60 seconds to finish.) Toss 1 cup of raisins with ¼ cup bourbon or rum and eliminate the bourbon in the master recipe. Omit the vanilla in the master recipe. Add 1 teaspoon cinnamon, 1 teaspoon nutmeg, and ¼ teaspoon ground cloves to the egg mixture in the master recipe. Fold all of the above into the bread crumb mixture before folding in the egg whites.

CRANBERRY NUT VARIATION

Add the zest and juice from 1 orange to the egg yolk mixture, which is then folded into the bread crumb mixture. Fold 1 cup toasted chopped pecans or walnuts and 1 cup of dried cranberries into the bread crumb mixture before folding in the egg whites.

Rum-Soaked Fruitcake with Dried Apricots, Dates, and Bourbon

Last year, we gave a covered dish supper just after New Year's and invited about 50 of our neighbors. We borrowed tables and chairs from the church and set them up in the living room, covered with paper tablecloths. The food was good, one guest bringing a Vermont vichyssoise made from potatoes and wild leeks; others brought casseroles, a potato gratin, salads, and of course the fluffy pink gelatin dessert that shows up at virtually every country potluck supper. (Like some sort of overdressed tart, this is the offering that grabs the attention of the farmers, who gaze with a fixed eye at the pink fluff long before it is time for dessert.) Adrienne and I provided a country ham and a smoked turkey, and we made this fruitcake along with butterscotch brownies and baked custard for dessert.

The problem with most fruitcakes, of course, is that they are dense, very sweet, and full of citron and candied cherries. This sort of confection would store nicely in the barn for at least a year without refrigeration. Like most folks, I don't find this kind of cake enjoyable. I do, however, like a fruitcake made with dried fruits and with a whole lot less sugar. This is such a cake, albeit much lighter and more "caky" than the traditional heavy fruitcake. You also don't have to let it sit for a month or two. It can be eaten immediately.

1	cup dark raisins
½	cup golden raisins
1½	cups chopped dried apricots
1	cup chopped dried dates
⅔	cup bourbon or rum
1½	cups flour
½	teaspoon nutmeg
½	teaspoon allspice
½	teaspoon salt
2	sticks (½ pound) unsalted butter, softened but still firm
½	cup sugar
3	eggs
1	cup molasses
1	teaspoon vanilla extract
1	cup toasted and chopped pecans

1. Heat oven to 300 degrees and adjust rack to the middle position. Grease and flour two 9 x 5-inch loaf pans.

2. Soak the raisins, apricots, and dates in the bourbon for at least 1 hour. Sift together the flour, spices, and salt onto a piece of wax paper.

3. In a large bowl, beat the butter until light, about 2 minutes with an electric mixer. Add the sugar and beat an additional 2 minutes. Add the eggs, one at a time, and beat for 20 seconds after each addition. Add the molasses and vanilla and beat about 30 seconds more or until thoroughly combined. Add the dry ingredients and beat by hand or on the lowest speed of the mixer until combined. Add the fruit (and the bourbon) and nuts and fold with a rubber spatula until combined. Pour the batter into prepared pans and smooth tops with the spatula.

4. Bake for about 1 hour 30 minutes or until cake feels firm to the touch and starts to pull back from the sides of the pans. Cool for 5 minutes in the pans, remove them, and let them cool completely on a wire rack before serving.

MAKES 2 LOAVES

Moravian Wafers

Our family makes these wafer-thin cookies every Christmas and they are my personal favorites. They are a bit spicy since the batter contains finely ground black pepper. It is easiest to roll the dough into a log, chill it thoroughly, and then slice it into thin wafers rather than rolling it out. There is a small Moravian cemetery just down the road from us, so we know that our part of New England was settled by Moravians as early as the mid-1700s.

2	cups flour
½	teaspoon salt
1	teaspoon baking powder
½	teaspoon baking soda
1½	teaspoons cinnamon
1	teaspoon ground ginger
½	teaspoon ground cloves
½	teaspoon finely ground pepper (optional, especially for kids)
8	tablespoons (1 stick) unsalted butter, softened but still firm
¾	cup sugar
½	cup molasses
1	egg yolk

1. Sift together the first 8 ingredients (flour through pepper).

2. In a large bowl, beat the butter with an electric mixer until light colored, about 2 minutes. Gradually add the sugar and beat for 1 minute. Add the molasses and egg yolk and beat until combined. At the lowest speed, beat in the dry ingredients until combined.

3. Lay a piece of plastic wrap about 20 inches long on a flat surface. Using a rubber spatula, scoop the dough in a long row down the middle. Form the dough into a log and wrap the plastic around it to completely cover the dough. Using your hands, continue to shape the dough into a smooth log (roll and press it), wrap thoroughly, and then refrigerate for several hours or overnight.

4. Heat oven to 350 degrees. Grease 1 or 2 cookie sheets or line them with parchment paper. Unwrap the dough and cut with a very sharp, thin knife into ⅛-inch-thick slices. Arrange slices on the cookie sheets and bake for about 8 minutes or until they are light-colored. Cool on a rack and store in an airtight container.

MAKES ABOUT 90 WAFERS

Preserving

EW OF US ARE LUCKY to have a sense of history, not of our country's heritage necessarily, but something more personal, a finger pointed out the window to signal where old Crofut's car ran off the road, or the cellar hole where once stood the west side Congregational church, at a time when our town had at least three places of worship and two dance halls. In the nineteenth century, our town also boasted seven schools, two stores, two sawmills, a stagecoach tavern, and an assortment of factories making clothespins, oyster barrels, brush backs, and cheese, plus a gristmill, a flaxmill, and two blacksmith shops. Art Mears used to run a general store out of his house just across from the church, selling flour, sugar, oatmeal, kerosene, ammunition, beef, tobacco, and the like. In those days, everything was sold out of barrels, even gingersnaps, and no fresh goods were available. Dandelion, milkweed, and mustard greens were all picked on the farm, vegetables were grown, milk was turned into cheese and butter, meat was had from wild game and hogs (which were salted down for preserving), and berries were picked during the season. Since the growing season was so short, most everything was preserved — from beef tongue which was pickled, to fruits made into jam and fruit butters, to corn which was turned into succotash, and root vegetables which were kept down in the cellar. (Evan Jones notes in *American Food* that succotash was originally a dish made from dried beans and corn, the recipe coming from American Indians who named it *msickquatash*. Summer succotash was made from fresh corn, cream, and shell beans, the latter first having been cooked slowly with bacon and onion.)

There was another store run by Minor Herd up in Beartown when there was a full-time logging operation run by the Wilcox family. The mill was run by steam power and they sawed squares for chair stock, which was pulled by teams fifteen miles to the next town down the main road, past the church, the store, and the town hall (which burned down twenty years ago and was rebuilt). That part of town even had a boardinghouse and dance hall for the workers. Today, none of these buildings is still standing except the Methodist church (we outlasted the Congregationalists) and the number-two schoolhouse, which is no longer in use. The population has dropped from 1,187 in 1810 to about 250 full-time residents today. But in the old days families were bigger. Ten kids, all delivered without a doctor, were common, and that's why such a small number of families could support seven school districts. The last school, the number-two schoolhouse, was finally closed in 1952, because the state demanded indoor plumbing.

It is worth remembering that the pace of life was quite different then. Everything moved by horsepower, up and down the main road. When it snowed, things would come to a stop for two or three days. Mail was delivered by horse and buggy and the mailman was known to be predictable, showing up in pretty much any weather. (Even back in the 1960s, the mailman was known to check the woodstove at Harry Skidmore's place during his morning rounds when nobody was home.) Dowsers were hired to locate a good spot to dig a well. They would cut off a forked branch from an apple tree and hold it in front of them with arms crossed. The branch would pull downward when water was near. (Fraiser Mears did the dowsing in our town, talking to his rod as if it were alive. He'd say, "Tell me, Mr. Stick, how far is it?" or, "Tell me, Mr. Stick, is it deep?") And some of our neighbors still remember when they saw their first car; Russell Baines didn't see one until he was eleven years old. They weren't good for much in those days, Russell points out, "If you could drive ten miles and back without a flat, you bragged about it." One farmer figured he could solve the problem by putting rope in the tires so they would have something to run on after they went flat. It worked fine until the rope heated up from friction and burst into flames. But farmers love their horses, and animals do have a practical side. Junior Bentley once told me about the difference between tractors and horses: "On a cold morning, I always know that a horse is going to start up."

Like a good jam or jelly, our town has preserved much of the past, perhaps more so than other places. As a kid, I used to do a lot of hunting, walking along the ridges which were crisscrossed with old stone walls. I found pieces of pottery, rusted pieces of metal, sap buckets, old blue and green glass bottles, and the occasional knife and fork. The past is still with us in the relics, the cellarholes, and the old sap houses. And once in a while we'll still hook up a team and an old seeder and plant a meadow, or rig up the old binder to a pair of mules and cut corn. But the dance halls, kitchen hops, and Saturday nights down at the Grange are gone as are most of the old-timers who stopped by the old yellow farm-house. If you ask an old-timer about the past he is likely to shrug it off at first, saying something about hard work and long winters. But if you are patient and sit awhile, he'll remember sitting in a wagon with his girlfriend, bundled up against the cold, taking the team over to a square dance, or the time that he walked into the yellow farmhouse and Marie sat him down to tea, offering a fresh-baked nutmeg doughnut or a big slab of warm country white slathered with homemade butter. He won't admit it but he knows that the past is constantly replaced with something of lesser stature, the original slowly fading but worth preserving before it is lost and forgotten, captured only in books, not in the hearts of men.

VERY FEW cooks today have memories of putting food by, which was the only way we could enjoy summer foods in winter. Modern transportation has changed all of that; one can get even the most seasonal produce such as raspberries in the dead of winter. But I am a great fan of eating seasonally. I look forward to an abundance of corn in late August, but not an ear to be had the rest of the year. This contrast makes the time of year important. For a real farmer a hundred years ago, that first taste of spring greens must have been divine, as was the taste of summer jelly in the dead of winter.

But in our small town, there are still many folks who can tomatoes and green beans, who make jams and jellies, freeze apple cider, and who put by a bit of venison whenever the opportunity arises. This is not a question of preserving because it is fashionable. It is how they get through the winter. In the summer, abundance is cheap and that's the best time to stock your larder. In the old days, of course, preserving foods was a necessary art. Fruits were cooked and preserved in a sugar syrup, cucumbers and melons were pickled, as were the rinds of watermelons, marmalades were made from quinces and other fruits, codfish was dried and salted, many vegetables were brined, and of course fruits and herbs were dried. Even fresh peas were preserved in bottles by storing them in mutton fat!

But this chapter is not a practical guide to saving money through canning and preserving. This is about those foods that are enhanced by the preserving process or, at the very least, made into something special, something worth experiencing in its own right. Pickled beets and crab-apples, blackberry preserves, rhubarb chutney, and brown-sugar peach jam are all worth eating any time of year. I also have included some simple preservation methods for foods that are truly difficult to find most times of year or are so expensive during winter months that a bit of advance planning makes a lot of sense.

Do You Need to Use Pectin for Fruit Jams, Preserves, and Jellies?

First of all, I don't like pectin. It produces a gummy, hard-set jelly with an underlying bitter aftertaste. The problem is that natural pectin levels vary by both type and ripeness of fruit. Each batch is different, so it is hard to gauge whether one needs any pectin at all at the outset of a recipe. Very high-pectin fruits, which include tart apples, crabapples, black currants, red currants, cranberries, gooseberries, lemons, grapefruit, tart plums, quinces, loganberries, and grapes, don't need any pectin. Medium fruits such as apricots, blackberries, plums, raspberries, and sweet apples usually don't require pectin either, if you don't mind a less firm end product. However, peaches, cherries, fresh figs, pears, strawberries, and blueberries are low in pectin and may need some help. Slightly underripe fruit has more pectin than very ripe fruit. To increase the pectin level of a jam naturally, simply use three parts ripe fruit to one part underripe. All of the recipes in this chapter use no pectin at all, except for peach jam, which I find does need some help in setting up.

After much testing, I determined that adding the pectin at the end of cooking, if at all, was the best method. In Rodale's *Preserving Summer's Bounty,* there is a simple metal bowl test, which can be used to determine the pectin level. When the preserve mixture reaches 220 degrees it is at the correct temperature, but that does not mean that the mixture has enough pectin to set up on its own. To establish whether or not the mixture will set, Rodale suggests the following test (which I repeat almost verbatim): Float a light metal mixing bowl in a larger bowl or basin filled with ice water. Drop a teaspoon of the preserve mixture in the bottom of the floating bowl. Because metal conducts heat well, the mixture will cool quickly. Once it's cool, run your finger through the mixture. It is ready if it doesn't run back together. If this attempt fails, cook the mixture four or five minutes longer and try again. If it fails again, it is now time to add pectin to the preserves. (One package per four cups of fruit is stirred into the mixture off the heat and then put back on the burner and boiled for two minutes.) I found that adding pectin at the beginning of cooking speeds up the cooking time, which is a benefit, but I found that I preferred the texture of the fruit when the pectin was added after cooking.

Too Much Sugar

Most older recipes call for an overwhelming amount of sugar, sometimes more sugar by volume than fruit. I have found that one cup of sugar to four cups of prepared fruit is about right. Note that the term "prepared fruit" is important because most recipes call for four cups of fruit, yet once strawberries, for example, have been hulled and sliced, the volume has been reduced substantially. Therefore, it is always best to measure fruit for preserving after preparation. If you prefer sweeter preserves, start with the 1 cup called for in the master recipe, cook the fruit until it stops foaming, and then add additional sugar in ¼ cup increments.

How to Sterilize a Jar

Immerse the jar in boiling water for 10 minutes if you live at sea level. Boil an extra minute for each 1,000 feet above sea level. Do not boil the lids. After the jars have been sterilized, place them face down on a clean cooling rack to drain. Place the lids in a medium bowl and pour over enough of the hot water to cover. Allow the lids to sit in the hot water until needed.

Choosing the Right Pan

I am a big fan of a wide — at least 12-inch diameter — nonreactive skillet for making preserves. The fruit cooks quickly, which helps to preserve its fresh taste. So don't use a high, narrow saucepan. Bring the fruit mixture up to temperature as fast as possible and you'll preserve what is important — the fresh taste of just-picked fruit. I have also found that it is best to cook fruits in small batches; they cook faster and their flavors are therefore better preserved.

About an Instant-Read Thermometer

Many recipes for jam and the like call for bringing the fruit mixture up to a specific temperature, usually 8 degrees above the boiling point of water. This would be 220 degrees at sea level. If you live at an altitude greater than 1,000 feet, bring some water to a boil and measure it with an instant-read thermometer. Now add 8 degrees to this temperature and this is the jelling point for your altitude.

Most preserving books have all sorts of methods for determining when a jam or jelly is cooked, including the cold-spoon test and the cold-sauce test. Having made my fair share of jellies over the years, I find both of these methods inadequate and I now use the Rodale method (see above), a good thermometer, and a practiced eye. Forget the inexpensive candy thermometers. They are hard to read, since the dial covers such a wide range of temperatures (up to 400 degrees). It is almost impossible to tell the difference between 215 and 220 degrees, a crucial distinction for the home canner.

Therefore, I strongly suggest that you purchase an expensive digital instant-read thermometer. This will quickly register the temperature (in 5 seconds or less) as opposed to the more traditional candy thermometers, which can take a minute or more to come up to speed. You will also get a perfectly accurate reading, which is essential. Although these devices (the King Arthur Flour Baker's Catalogue has an excellent model) are very expensive (over $40), they can be used for bread baking, roasting, and plenty of other kitchen tasks. This is one tool that is worth every penny.

Although a thermometer is helpful, I find that depending entirely on temperature yields inconsistent results. In fact, once you are experienced, you will no longer require a thermometer. After some experience, you will notice that fruit cooks down in three stages. First, the fruit releases its liquid. Next, the mixture starts to foam. Finally, it begins to thicken. The best way to determine if the jam is done is to draw a wooden spoon across the bottom of the skillet during the last phase. When it leaves a trail and the mixture has thickened substantially, it is done. Of course, the thermometer is a good guide until you have a feel for the proper texture.

When Do You Need a Water Bath for Canning?

All jams, jellies, conserves, and preserves can be cooked on top of the stove and then simply stored in the refrigerator for up to three weeks. (I have stored jams much longer than three weeks without water bath canning, but to be safe, it is worth the extra trouble.) Those that are made from acidic foods combined with plenty of sugar hold longest. If you intend on making a very small amount of jam, for example, there is no point in going through the bother of canning.

Water Bath Canning

Most sweet or acidic foods are canned by placing the food in hot, sterilized jars, attaching the sterilized lids, and immersing the jars in rapidly boiling water for 10 to 12 minutes. Directions come with boxes of canning jars. It is important to purchase a jar lifter; otherwise you will find it quite difficult to get the hot, small glass jars out of the water. Once the contents cool, the metal lid should become concave, creating a tight seal. Any jars without tight seals need to be put through the process a second time or simply stored in the refrigerator and consumed quickly.

Rhubarb Apricot Chutney

Rhubarb is full of water and needs to be cooked down to the point when the mixture starts to thicken and loses its watery consistency. Although this chutney can be made with raisins or currants, I prefer the flavor of dried apricots paired with rhubarb. This makes only three 8-ounce jars but since this is not an everyday condiment, that should see you through the year. If you want to make this as a gift, double or triple the recipe. The caramelized onion is an optional ingredient since it complicates the recipe but it adds a soft, sweet counterpart to the rhubarb.

2	cups brown sugar, firmly packed
1	cup cider vinegar
2	teaspoons lemon zest, chopped
4	cups rhubarb, leaves cut off, washed, and cut into ½-inch pieces
½	teaspoon ground cinnamon
1	tablespoon minced fresh gingerroot
1	tablespoon rum
1	cup dried apricots, chopped
¼	teaspoon salt
1	cup walnuts or pecans, coarsely chopped
1	large onion, caramelized in 1 tablespoon butter, ¼ teaspoon salt, and ½ teaspoon sugar until a dark mahogany color (see Roasted Onion Relish on page 384 for directions) (optional)

1. Place the first three ingredients in a wide nonreactive saucepan and cook over low heat, stirring frequently, for 2 minutes or until sugar dissolves and mixture is boiling. Add the next 3 ingredients (rhubarb through ginger) and raise heat to medium. Cook, gently stirring 2 or 3 times, for about 20 to 25 minutes or until rhubarb is cooked down, thickens a bit, and loses its watery appearance. Add remaining ingredients, except the onion, and cook an additional 2 minutes. Mixture should be thick at this point and the rhubarb will be very soft. Add the optional caramelized onion at this point.

2. Spoon rhubarb mixture into hot steril-ized jars. Follow directions for water bath canning or cover with scalded lids and refrigerate for up to 3 weeks

MAKES THREE 8-OUNCE JARS

Bourbon Cherries

I vastly prefer using sour cherries for this recipe, and since brandy is not truly American, I prefer to use bourbon, al-though brandy, since it has a simpler, less complex flavor, lets the taste of the cher-ries shine through. (Until recently, I thought that the best bourbon was Maker's Mark. The gold-topped bottles are slightly superior to the more common red-topped variety. However, I was just given a bottle of Knob Creek, which is slightly smoky, similar to a single-malt Scotch. But this is topnotch sippin' bour-bon and too good for this recipe.) Bour-bon cherries make a terrific gift, especially if you choose an attractive glass container. I serve these cherries with a simple dish of vanilla ice cream.

4	pounds ripe sour cherries, washed and dried
1	cup sugar
¼	cup water
¼	teaspoon almond extract
4	cups bourbon or brandy

1. Stem and pit one quarter of the cher-ries using a cherry pitter (see page 27). Tie the pits in a small piece of cheese-cloth. Place the pitted cherries and the pits in a large nonreactive saucepan. Add the sugar and water and bring to a boil over medium heat. Reduce the heat and simmer for about 15 minutes, or until the juices thicken and a syrup forms. Remove from heat and discard pits.

2. Sterilize a large container, about one half gallon, and place the whole cherries inside. Stir together the cherry syrup, the almond extract, and the bourbon or brandy and pour mixture over cherries. Cover with a lid. Store in a cool, dark place. Let sit for at least 6 weeks before using to allow the flavors to develop.

MAKES ONE HALF GALLON

Preserved Watermelon Rind

The first time I tasted preserved water-melon rind, I was sitting at a wood table covered with a hand-stitched plain white tablecloth in a simple white farmhouse, looking out across a field of rich green alfalfa. The chunks of watermelon were served in a small cut-glass bowl with a tiny serving spoon. I'll never forget that first taste; a heady perfume of cinnamon and cloves, like a breath of the Far East in a small Vermont town. I think I'd pre-fer to eat the preserved rind of water-melon any day over the bright red flesh.

1½	pounds watermelon rind, peeled, pink flesh removed, and cut into ½-inch cubes (about 4 cups or ¼ of a small watermelon)
5½	quarts water
½	cup coarse salt
3	cups sugar
	Zest and juice from 1 lemon
	Zest and juice from 1 lime
1	(4-inch) piece cinnamon stick
2	teaspoons whole cloves

1. Soak rind overnight in a large bowl in 4 quarts of the water into which the salt has been stirred.

2. Drain rind and place in a large non-reactive saucepan or Dutch oven with 3 cups of fresh water. Bring to a boil and reduce heat to a simmer. Cook for 45 minutes or until rind is tender. Drain and reserve.

3. Rinse saucepan and put in all remaining ingredients, except the rind, along with 3 cups of fresh water. Bring to a boil, stirring to dissolve the sugar. Boil for about 5 minutes or until sugar dissolves and a syrup forms. Add rind and cook until it becomes transparent, about 40 minutes.

4. With a slotted spoon, place rind in sterilized, dry jars. Ladle in syrup to within ½-inch of rims. Process in a water bath. Store for up to 1 year in a dark, cool place.

MAKES 2 PINTS

Roasted Onion Relish

Many recipes suggest roasting the onions in an oven, but in testing, I found that the stovetop method was simpler. They browned better and it was easier to keep an eye on them as they cooked. This relish goes nicely with any sort of meat, especially pork and chicken.

4	tablespoons (½ stick) butter, softened
3	tablespoons extra-virgin olive oil
4	pounds white onions, peeled and thinly sliced pole to pole
1½	teaspoons salt
1	tablespoon sugar
4	teaspoons fresh thyme, chopped
¼	cup balsamic vinegar (optional)

Heat a large — at least 12 inches — skillet over medium heat. Add the butter and oil. When the foam subsides, add the remaining ingredients. Lower the heat and cook, stirring occasionally, until the onions are nut brown. This will take 45 minutes to 1 hour. The onions will become very sweet and reduce to about 2 cups. Let cool to room temperature, pack into sterilized jars, and store in the refrigerator. The onions will keep at least 2 weeks.

MAKES 2 CUPS

Master Recipe for Freezer Jam

Perhaps the easiest and best method for storing jam is to freeze it! Although I use the freezer for many things, I had never thought of making a jam that is not cooked and then putting it into the freezer for storage. The idea for this recipe comes from *Jams, Jellies, and Preserves* by Linda Ferrari (Prima Publishing, 1996) although I have significantly lowered the amount of sugar — most jam recipes are much too sweet for my taste — and removed the corn syrup. I found that the best way to crush the fruit was in a large bowl with a potato masher. I also found, however, that freezer jams tend to be a bit loose in texture compared to regular jams. Do not try this recipe with peaches, since they are low in pectin and will not set up properly.

4	cups prepared fruit (blueberries, strawberries, raspberries, blackberries, or sour cherries); strawberries preferred
2	cups sugar
2	tablespoons lemon juice
1	package powdered pectin
½	cup cold water

1. Wash and dry the fruit. Pit if necessary. Chop and then crush in a large bowl using a potato masher.

2. Add the next 2 ingredients and stir to combine. (If you use sour cherries, increase sugar to 3 cups.) Let fruit mixture stand for 30 minutes. Stir pectin into the cold water in a small saucepan. Bring to a full boil and cook for 1 minute. Pour into the fruit mixture and stir for 3 minutes until well combined and cooled.

3. Ladle jam into hot, sterilized jars. Wipe rims and seal with lids. Let stand at room temperature for 24 hours, then place in freezer for up to 1 year. Defrost and store in the refrigerator.

MAKES FIVE 8-OUNCE JARS

Peach Jam with Bourbon and Brown Sugar

I don't bother peeling the peaches, since this takes quite a lot of extra effort. If, however, you prefer them peeled, they must be dipped in boiling water for 25 seconds, instantly removed to a bowl of cold water, and then peeled. The long cooking time in this recipe ensures that the skin will be tender. Besides, the jam looks less refined, more like a country jam.

6	cups peaches, washed, pitted, and coarsely chopped
1¾	cups packed light brown sugar
6	tablespoons lemon juice
½	cup bourbon
1½	cups granulated sugar
1	package powdered pectin

1. Combine prepared peaches with the brown sugar and lemon juice and ¼ cup

of the bourbon and let sit on the counter overnight, covered.

2. Transfer peach mixture to a wide non-reactive pan with a lid. Add remaining bourbon. Bring to a boil. Cover, reduce heat, and simmer for 15 minutes, stirring occasionally. The peach chunks will be translucent. Remove lid, add granulated sugar, and cook rapidly, constantly stirring, until it reaches a temperature of 220 degrees (use a digital instant-read thermometer). Remove pan from heat, stir in pectin, and boil for 2 minutes more. Ladle into jars and process in a water bath.

MAKES FIVE 8-OUNCE JARS

Master Recipe for Simple Fruit Jam

This recipe is a simple workhorse recipe for any type of fruit. Sweet blueberries, strawberries, and plums require only 1 cup of sugar but tart blackberries and raspberries may require 1¼ cups. If you are not sure, start with 1 cup, cook the mixture for a few minutes, and then add additional sugar if necessary. I prefer not to peel peaches, since the jam is much more beautiful with the skins. If you want to make a seedless raspberry or blackberry jam, start with 6 cups of berries and purée them in a food processor or mash them with the back of a large spoon. Press them, using a large rubber spatula, through a fine sieve to remove the seeds.

4	cups prepared fruit (measure after washing, pitting, and slicing into small pieces if necessary), such as peaches, strawberries, blueberries, raspberries, blackberries, or plums

1 cup sugar, approximately
¼ cup fresh-squeezed and strained lemon juice (about 1 large lemon)
1 package powdered pectin, if necessary

1. In a large nonreactive skillet (do not use a saucepan), combine prepared fruit with the sugar and lemon juice and let sit for 2 hours.
2. Bring the mixture to a boil over medium heat, and cook until the sugar is dissolved. Raise heat to medium-high and cook, stirring frequently, until the mixture becomes foamy. At this point, you may skim the surface if the foam is excessive. Continue cooking until the mixture starts to thicken and the liquid becomes syrupy. Be sure to stir constantly once the thickening process begins. After a couple of minutes, the mixture will become substantially thicker and a wooden spoon will leave a trail on the surface of the skillet. Do not overcook. Mixture will thicken as it cooks. Use the Rodale metal bowl test (see page 381) to check for doneness. Add pectin to mixture if necessary and cook another minute, stirring constantly, until dissolved. (Most fruit will not need the pectin.)
3. When ready, ladle into sterilized canning jars, leaving ¼ inch of head space. Either let cool to room temperature and freeze or refrigerate for up to three weeks.

MAKES 1½ TO 2 CUPS OF PRESERVES

LONG-TERM-STORAGE VARIATION

If you want to store your fruit preserves for more than a few weeks without refrigeration, you will need to increase the sugar to 1¾ cups to create an environment hostile to bacterial growth. Follow the directions in the recipe above, using the larger amount of sugar, and then can the fruit according to the directions at the beginning of this chapter.

Rhubarb Ginger Jam

This is another good way to use up extra rhubarb. I find that vanilla bean tastes much better than extract in this recipe.

2 pounds rhubarb (about 8 cups)
2 cups sugar
⅓ cup minced or grated fresh gingerroot
½ vanilla bean, split, with seeds scraped into pan

Wash and trim the rhubarb and slice into ½-inch pieces. Place all ingredients in a large nonreactive saucepan. Bring to a simmer. Cook, stirring occasionally, for 20 to 25 minutes on medium heat until the mixture reaches 218 to 220 degrees on an instant-read thermometer. Skim any foam from the top and remove vanilla bean. Let sit for 5 minutes. Jam can at this point be stored in sterilized canning jars or water-bath canned per the instructions at the beginning of this chapter.

MAKES 6 CUPS

Strawberry Rhubarb Jam

This is just like having strawberry-rhubarb pie filling in a jar.

1 pound rhubarb, washed and sliced into ½-inch pieces (about 4 cups)

1½ cups water
4   cups strawberries, washed and
    hulled
2   tablespoons lemon juice
2   teaspoons orange zest
    Generous pinch (about ¼ teaspoon)
    of nutmeg, allspice, and cinnamon
4   cups sugar
1   tablespoon butter

1. Combine the first two ingredients in a nonreactive medium saucepan and cook until rhubarb is tender, about 8 to 10 minutes. Drain.

2. Combine cooked rhubarb with remaining ingredients in a large (12-inch) nonreactive skillet and bring to a boil. Reduce heat until mixture bubbles steadily and cook until the temperature reaches 218 to 220 degrees on an instant-read thermometer. Stir frequently. Remove from heat and skim off any foam. Let sit for 5 minutes, then ladle into sterilized jars. Cool and freeze, or follow canning instructions at the beginning of this chapter.

MAKES 6 CUPS

Bread and Butter Pickles

Some recipes call for pickling lime, which renders the cucumbers crunchy. Since most home cooks don't have this ingredient on hand, I prefer to make my bread and butter pickles without it. They aren't quite so crunchy, but a big forkful of semitransparent sweet pickles with half-moon arcs of onions is just the thing to accompany a cold supper on a hot evening in July.

1   pound nonwaxed pickling
    cucumbers

3   tablespoons coarse salt
¾   pound onions, peeled, cut in half pole
    to pole, and sliced ¼ inch thick
4   cups cider vinegar or white wine
    vinegar
1   cup granulated sugar
¾   cup lightly packed light brown sugar
1   teaspoon ground turmeric
1   tablespoon celery seed
1   tablespoon mustard seed
1   tablespoon dill seed

1. Scrub cucumbers, cut off ends, and then slice ¼ inch thick. Place the slices in a large bowl; cover with the salt and one tray of ice cubes. Add cold water to cover. Let stand on the counter for half a day or overnight. Transfer cucumbers to a colander, rinse, and drain well. Rinse out the original bowl and transfer the cucumbers back to it. Add cold water to cover and stir to rinse cucumbers of salt. Drain. Repeat twice. Taste one slice. If too salty, repeat rinsing and draining until saltiness is diminished. Drain well. Place equal amounts of cucumbers and onions into hot, sterilized jars. (The easiest method to distribute the vegetables evenly is to place them in a large clean plastic bag and shake.)

2. Place remaining ingredients in a large, nonreactive saucepan and bring to a boil. Continue cooking at a boil for 5 minutes. Pour this vinegar mixture into the filled jars. Poke cucumber and onions with a skewer to make sure that there are no air pockets. Leave ¼ inch of headroom. Seal with 2-piece lids and process for 10 minutes according to directions at the beginning of this chapter. Let processed pickles sit for a month and then chill before serving.

MAKES 2 QUARTS

Crab Apple Jelly

The dirt road that runs by our farm is lined with a good number of crab apple trees, which produce huge quantities of fruit every other year. Last spring was cool and the blossoms stayed on the trees for a good two weeks, small and paperwhite along the tawny fields. The crop was a record-breaker, so we had to find something to do with all of the apples. We bagged bushels of them in old feed bags and fed them to the deer up in the back pasture. But we also made pint after pint of this spicy crab apple jelly. By the way, I don't bother cutting out any blemished or rotten sections of the apples. It's not worth the effort. Simply don't use any specimens that are in bad shape. Otherwise, this step could take more time than it takes to make the jelly.

4	quarts crab apples, washed, stemmed, and quartered
3–4	tablespoons fresh squeezed lemon juice, strained
	About 2¼ cups sugar

1. Place apples in a wide nonreactive skillet or saucepan. Add cold water to cover. Bring to a boil, reduce heat to a simmer, and cook until apples are very soft, up to 1 hour. Mash occasionally with the back of a large wooden spoon.
2. Line a large colander with 4 thicknesses of cheesecloth cut long enough so that the ends can be tied into a bag later. Let the cloth hang well over the sides. Place the colander over a large deep bowl. Ladle the fruit with a slotted spoon into the colander and let drain for 2 hours. Gather up the ends of the cheesecloth and tie together. Now suspend the bag directly over the bowl, removing the colander. (The cheesecloth can be tied to a wooden spoon which straddles the mouth of the pot or bowl.) Let drain either overnight or until dripping stops, another 1 to 2 hours.
3. Discard apples and add 2 tablespoons lemon juice to the apple juice. Taste. Add up to 2 tablespoons more until the apple juice is tart but not overly acidic. Measure the amount of juice, then pour it into a large nonreactive saucepan or skillet. Add ¾ cup of sugar per cup of juice and stir to dissolve. Place pan over high heat and bring juice to a boil.
4. Boil rapidly until the temperature reaches 218 to 220 degrees. Remove from heat, skim off any foam, and pour hot liquid into sterilized canning jars, leaving ⅛ inch of headspace. Seal with sterilized 2-piece canning lids. Cool and store.

MAKES 4 CUPS

SPICY CRAB APPLE JELLY

I can't reasonably claim that this is an old Vermont recipe, but since I have so many crab apples I have to find a variety of uses for them. This makes a beautiful gift, since one whole chile pepper is suspended in each jar. Follow the recipe above but add 4 chopped fresh red chilies to the apples before they are cooked. After the boiled jelly has reached the proper temperature, pour it into the canning jars, leaving ¼ inch of headspace. When the jelly has semi-set, insert one washed and dried red chile that has been slit in half lengthwise and the stem removed. Pierce any air pockets with a skewer. Seal with sterilized 2-piece tops.

Index